Miners, Milkers & Merchants

Miners, Milkers & Merchants

From the Swiss-Italian Alps

to the

Golden Hills of

Australia and California

MARILYN L. GEARY

Foreword by Giorgio Cheda

Published in the United States by Life Circle Press.

Letters written by Luigi, Francesco, Alessandro, Virgilio Rotanzi and
Carlo Patocchi appear in various works by Giorgio Cheda and were
translated into English by the author.

Library of Congress Control Number: 2020911492

Geary, Marilyn L.
*Miners, Milkers & Merchants : from the Swiss-Italian Alps to the
    Golden Hills of California and Australia*

ISBN 978-0-9825378-0-0 (print)
ISBN 978-0-9825378-4-8 (ebook)

Cover Photograph
Ex-voto in the Church of Madonna del Sasso, Orselina, Ticino,
oil painting by Giovanni Antonio Vanoni.
Inscription: G.R. (Graces Received), Ticinesi going to Australia in 1856,
with the image of the Madonna del Sasso hung on the ship's mast.

Life Circle Press
Post Office Box 382
Woodacre, CA 94973
(415) 488-1211

To my immigrant ancestors who left their
villages in Bohemia and the Apennines
to seek a better life.

ROTANZI FAMILY TREE

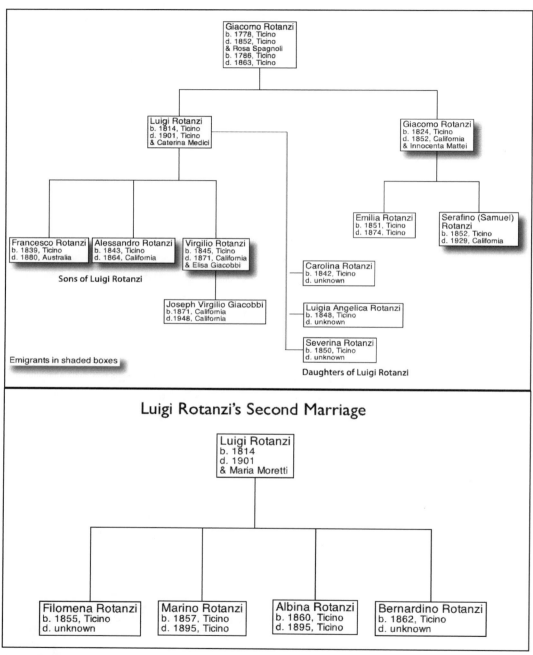

Based on Rotanzi Family Tree from the Patriziato di Peccia

EPIGRAPH

Come rapidi gli anni sen vanno!
Uno e morto un'altro arrivo
O mia terra un buon capo dell'anno
Doltre mare col cuore ti do.

Son lontano, mia patria, lontano
Son lontano lontano da te!
Ma se tanto remota e la mano,
Oh! Il mio cuore il mio cuore non è.

How fast the years pass!
One dies and another arrives.
O my land— from overseas with all my heart
I wish you a good New Year.

I am far, my homeland, far
I am far, far from you!
But even if my hand is distant,
Oh! my heart, my heart is not.

Excerpt of a poem written by Antonio Pedranti, a villager from Broglio. Pedranti included his poem in a letter he wrote to his family and friends on November 18, 1881 from Valley Ford, Sonoma County, California.

Ex-voto in the Church of S. Maria delle Grazie, Maggia, painting
by Giovanni Antonio Vanoni listing some of the ship passengers to
Australia, 1868 who gave thanks for their safe arrival.

CONTENTS

FOREWORD

The history of the world is a history of emigration. Humans are the only animals that have been able to adapt to the most diverse ecological environments: from the desert to polar ice, from the rainforest to the slopes of the Himalayas. Limiting ourselves to Western civilization after the geographical discoveries, Europeans not only immigrated to all continents, but also brought millions of African slaves to the Americas. Knowing the conditions in which human movements have shifted in the past offers a better awareness of the convulsions of those who encounter each other in a world shaken by globalization and dangerously divided between North and South, between democratic and non-democratic systems.

From the beginning of the nineteenth century to the First World War, the European population increased from 188 to 458 million inhabitants. Peasants, who had represented three quarters of the labor force, were reduced to one quarter, providing the considerably larger contingent of emigrants both within the European continent and overseas. The opening of the great American spaces attracted fifty million Europeans in a century, especially when steamships managed to cross the Atlantic in a few days and trains could transfer them to the Far West. Among these, four hundred thousand Swiss settled in the eastern part of the United States, while almost all the Ticinesi preferred California.

More than fifty years have passed since I began to tenaciously search for the letters of the peasants who sailed for Melbourne. They had little luck digging in the golden sands around Ballarat, Hepburn and Bendigo. The recovery of over 350 letters made it possible to accurately reconstruct this exceptional migratory phenomenon that marked the history of the Locarno valleys in the mid-nineteenth century. In them, one senses pulsating, almost to the breaking point, the many pains and scant joys experienced by their authors on the endless course across the world's oceans and among the hills of Victoria, so different from their Alps.

One thousand of the twenty-seven thousand Ticinesi immigrants to California between the late nineteenth and early twentieth centuries became owners of approximately eighteen hundred square kilometers of land, their main settlements along the coastal chains and in the Sierras. This area corresponded to the four districts of origin of most of the ranchers: Vallemaggia, Locarno, Leventina and Bellinzona, comprising two-thirds the area of Ticino canton. These courageous ranchers, who soon became American citizens, experienced a radical change in social status. The secret of their success lies in the opportunities offered by the Golden State, but above all in their assumption of responsibility and loyalty to the spirit of tradition. The ambition to succeed, using one's own powers to carry out challenging goals, as well as frugality, enabled their essential, albeit risky, investments to result in many enterprises, not only commercial, in their many prosperous communities. Their efforts were energized by a network of patriotic and related organizations and nurtured, for half a century, by the newspaper *La Colonia Svizzera* published in San Francisco.

From the ranches that the pioneers managed to buy and operate, substantial capital arrived in Ticino for generations to improve the standard of living of those who stayed at home. Although a lack of savings investment in the regions most needing economic development negatively impacted the future of some alpine valleys, and many savings of the "American uncles" faded with the bankruptcy of the Ticino banks in 1914, the investment of work and of money in California paid off.

With this research Ms. Geary scrupulously analyzes the migrations to explain their history in an original way. Following the vicissitudes of the Rotanzi family from Peccia described in letters sent from Australia and California, we gain a glimpse of the demographic history woven between the continents. She has understood that letters of ordinary people bring back to life witnesses to a past which the present must not erase. They allow us to get to know a society from the inside through the beliefs and representations, continuities and transformations of the peasant and artisan worlds. These must be interpreted in the same way as the masks, myths and totems of the anthropologist Claude Lévi-Strauss: essential tools for getting to know the people, the environment and the culture on which they were nourished.

These correspondences, inlaid with flourishes of popular testimonies, are custodians of the past, ethnological caskets with multiple keys from which many stimuli can be extracted to revive the lives and authentic feelings of men and women who have entered into a specific economic and social reality.

An example: Virgilio Rotanzi described in detail his promotion from milker to merchant, from Marin County to San Francisco.

> The business works like this: we receive products from the country, principally butter, cheese, eggs, chickens, veal, leather, tallow, etc., that is, products that can be consigned for which there is a market. They are sold for the producer's account or for whomever sent it, deducting the cost of transport and we receive 5% of the amount as payment for the effort and service of selling it. . . . My work starts at 7 am and ends at 6 pm. It's my duty to receive and register the merchandise that comes in, sell and buy merchandise to send to the ranchers when orders are received, and deliver them the accounts and explanations of transactions made for them.

The letter, dated May 30, 1869, documents one of the many opportunities offered to newcomers by an expanding economy; the traditional market was quickly replaced by a new, American-type company, specializing in marketing. Rotanzi's business partner was Charles Martin, owner of eighteen square kilometers of land around Petaluma: four more than the entire surface of Cevio, where he remained registered under the name of Carlo Martinoia, a successful pioneer who helped many new arrivals settle in their adopted homeland. His villa in Cevio, the "Ticino capital of California," has been designated an historical monument.

In the finely-grained pages that Ms. Geary offers to her readers, one discovers people of flesh, bones and spirit who communicate in a simple way, using a lexicon crisp as freshly baked rye bread and an phraseology steeped in Americanisms. By comparing the language used to name the implements related to mountain goats and mountaineers with the English needed to fit into an increasingly demanding economy, the causes and consequences of overseas emigration are better understood. The differing relationship with the land, animals and, above all, the market, allows us to reconstruct the changes that also occurred in ways of thinking. Reading the letters, consulting the notarial deeds, calculating the acreage of the ranches and learning from the interviews granted by their owners, one discovers a fresh face of emigration. California offered emancipation, triggered by the mirage of gold to meet economic needs, but orchestrated and set to music with the development of the land that guaranteed its continuity and success.

Ms. Geary hasn't simply plumbed the depths of the letters. Exacting research in the Ticino archives and in Marin County, as well as the examination of the press and local newspaper publications—witnessed by the rich bibliography—has allowed her to highlight the original socio-economic framework in which the integration took place in a rapidly evolving society, fostered by the discovery of gold, the transcontinental railroad and the mechanization that marked the evolution of American democracy.

A big thank you to those who created this compelling history, woven between Switzerland, Australia's gold country and California's large ranches: two coveted destinations that made peasants dream of emigrating from the mountains of Ticino.

—Giorgio Cheda
(translated by Marilyn L. Geary)

PREFACE

This is an immigrant story, one many of us share with forebears who, pushed out by harsh conditions, left home lured by promises of a better life elsewhere. Luigi Rotanzi and his three sons, whose letters form the backbone of this book, took part in a mid-nineteenth century migration from Ticino, the Italian-speaking canton in Switzerland. That exodus forever changed them, their alpine homeland and the places they settled. The Rotanzi brothers, like most Swiss Italians who left at that time, had not intended to immigrate. They thought of themselves as sojourners, heading off to make their fortune, then coming home as soon as possible. Many of their compatriots did return, some with wealth, others burdened with debt. Yet many stayed abroad, making a lasting impact on their new lands.

Shipping Agent Notice, *Gazzetta Ticino*, January 17, 1855

I am a grandchild of immigrants. My Italian grandfather, in broken English, sold fruit from his orchard to send his four children to college. My Bohemian grandparents ran a small-town grocery store, never forgetting their Czech origins. My childhood, suffused with my grandparents' foreign languages and cultural differences—wiener schnitzel and dumplings on Saturdays, ravioli and funghi on Sundays—drew me to explore the struggles and achievements of the uprooted.

I came across the Rotanzi letters as I thumbed through Giorgio Cheda's book *L'emigrazione ticinese in California*, which I found on a library shelf at the Marin County Free Library. The book contains letters of Swiss-Italian immigrants to California, providing first-hand accounts of the immigrant experience. Amidst the Italian text, mostly incomprehensible to me, the word "Ghirardelli" popped out from a page.

Curious about the connection between the letter writer and the famous chocolate maker, I translated the letter Virgilio Rotanzi had written to his father and learned that Domingo Ghirardelli had given Virgilio his first job in California. Intrigued, I translated another letter, then another. I discovered a second brother, Alessandro, then a third, Francesco. As I uncovered more pieces of their story, I became intent on finding out all I could about what compelled these young men to leave home, how they got along in their new lands, and how they dealt with successes and failures.

Francesco, the eldest Rotanzi brother, journeyed from his small village of Peccia to the Australian gold fields in 1855, part of the first wave of emigration from Ticino in the mid-nineteenth century. His letters speak of daily life in the Daylesford and Hepburn Springs gold mining community, an area in the Australian state of Victoria where many Italian speakers sought fortunes in the mines. Francesco's brother Virgilio departed for California in 1861, and Alessandro headed for California two years later. By the time these two emigrated, California appeared to promise better opportunities than Australia, yet both Virgilio and Alessandro struggled to survive, peddling fruits, vegetables and cheeses from the dairy lands and orchards surrounding San Francisco Bay.

Letters the three brothers exchanged with their father Luigi back home in Peccia form the main source for their story. In these letters, the young men spoke of their thrills at launching new ventures, wonder at seeing throngs of ships in LeHavre's port, excitement at buying a promising dairy ranch, and frustrations with mining in dank, dangerous tunnels for elusive gold. Throughout, they sustained hope that the next gold mine or next venture would bring fortune, while their worried father urged them to return to their alpine village.

The Rotanzi brothers did not become famous or wealthy, yet their stories and letters are remarkable, not only for their glimpses into daily life in the mid-nineteenth century, but also for the window they open onto the emotional lives of those far removed from family and home. Luigi Rotanzi, ever concerned for his sons' well-being, closes a letter to Francesco with the urgings of an anxious parent unable to control an offspring's destiny: "Dear Cecchino! I recommend you to God. Take care of yourself, try to stay healthy, watch out for dangers, deceptions, bad company and come home as soon as you can. That's what all of us want. All of us pray for you."

The letters also speak to the experiences of today's many migrants, from Hondurans and Guatemalans braving dangerous desert border crossings in the U.S. Southwest to Africans and Syrians clinging to overloaded boats off the Sicilian island of Lampedusa. They risk everything familiar to reach strange, new lands of greater opportunity. These modern immigrants share with the Rotanzi brothers an immense hope and profound yearning for a home they may have lost forever.

This work is deeply indebted to Professor Giorgio Cheda, whose studies of Ticinese emigration and collections of letters form the basis of this book. Professor Cheda grasped the importance of preserving these letters as an homage to the spirit of Swiss-Italian emigrants and as a record of their struggles and accomplishments. Poverty drove them to search for a living elsewhere, but their hearts remained with their home in the Alps. Cheda's collection of letters in *L'emigrazione ticinese in Australia* and *L'emigrazione ticinese in California* are a treasure trove of stories that reflect not only on the history and experiences of a small group of alpine emigrants but on all those who leave home for foreign lands.

Ticino Districts

Vallemaggia Towns and Districts

Radegonda Calanchini from Cevio, c. 1888
Caption: Our porter during the alp inspection on Alp d. Sascola

AUTHOR'S NOTE

Parts of this story must remain in mystery. Only a portion of the letters written by the Rotanzi brothers and their father have been found and published, leaving gaps in the chronology. Additionally, the 1906 San Francisco fire and earthquake destroyed many relevant documents. Rather than invent a fictional story, I have adhered to available facts, gleaned where possible from primary source documents.

In a common practice, the letter writers often only used surnames when referencing friends and acquaintances, making accurate identification of individuals, in some cases, impossible. In this work of nonfiction, I have not changed names, invented characters or created events. Where I suggest possibilities as to what may have occurred or how individuals may have felt, I clearly indicate them as conjectures. In cases where birth years are known, but exact birthdates are not available, I have estimated ages, which may be off by a year. Although I have made every effort to ensure that the information in this book is correct, errors inevitably slip in when reconstructing events more than one hundred years past.

The Rotanzi correspondence covers a period of about twenty-five years, from Francesco's departure in 1855 to his death in 1881. Each chapter, based on one or two letters, quotes from the authors, at times extensively. Rather than summarize and interpret meaning, I have kept as close as possible to the text, letting the Rotanzis voice their dreams and dilemmas in ways that only they can.

Translating the letters proved challenging. Although the Rotanzis were well-educated, they wrote in an archaic Italian with a sprinkling of dialect, sometimes omitting punctuation. I have aimed to stay true to their voice and to the formality of their language, adding punctuation and paragraph breaks when necessary for readability. Brackets [..] indicate added explanations within the text.

In the early years of migration to Australia and California, Italy had not yet become a unified country. Swiss Italians, particularly in Australia, built strong bonds with northern Italians, many of whom had fled their homeland for political reasons. I have referred to this group of immigrants to Australia as Italian speakers, as they shared common cultural, linguistic and immigrant experiences.

Those who come from the canton of Ticino call themselves "Ticinesi." I have chosen instead to use the noun "Swiss Italian" and the hyphenated adjective "Swiss-Italian," as the terms are more commonly used in English. Because Swiss Italians speak Italian and have Italian surnames, they are often thought to be Italians. They share a language and many aspects of culture with northern Italians, particularly those from Lombardy and Piedmont. However, since the Battle of Marignano in 1515, in which the Old Swiss Confederacy lost control of Milan and large parts of Lombardy, the border has remained stable. Switzerland and Italy have significantly different social and political structures. Swiss Italians identify as Swiss nationals. They are not Italian.

The Rotanzis are just one of the many Swiss-Italian families torn apart by emigration in the second half of the nineteenth and the early twentieth centuries. Their experiences are both unique and universal. Tracing their paths in detail also reveals the lives of their compatriots, their friends and associates with whom they wove a network of relationships that crossed distant continents and bound them to home.

PROLOGUE

When Francesco Rotanzi left for Australia in 1855, railroads and tunnels had yet to be carved through the Alps. The mammoth mountain range stood as a formidable barrier, cutting Ticino off from the rest of Switzerland and northern Europe. With the massive Alps blocking access to the German and French cantons in the north, Ticino remained isolated from many advances of the Industrial Revolution.

Starved for arable land, lacking resources to sustain their families, many Swiss Italians followed a traditional pattern of seasonal migration. They naturally gravitated for work and trade across the southern Swiss border into Lombardy. There they found people who spoke the same language and practiced many of the same customs.[1] Each autumn and winter, as they had for centuries, men and boys from Ticino's alpine valleys migrated down into Lombardy and Piedmont to work as stonemasons, chimney sweeps, carpenters, bakers, and similar tradesmen. Seasonal migration provided much needed earnings in the winter. In the spring, the workers headed north again into Switzerland, to their wives and children, their crops and animals. Some skilled craftsmen, such as stonemasons and sculptors, fresco painters and stucco specialists, found their talents in great demand and brought their families with them for longer sojourns.

Beginning in 1848, a series of political and economic events made these migrations difficult and then impossible. Nationalist revolutions raged throughout Europe, flaming the fervor of northern Italians who chafed under rule of the Austrian Habsburg monarchy in Veneto and Lombardy. Resentment of foreign occupation grew, as Giuseppe Mazzini and other Italian revolutionary leaders directed a nationalist movement called the Risorgimento to unite an independent Italy free of the Habsburgs.

Aided by Swiss Italians sympathetic to their cause, thousands of Italians fighting to overthrow Austria and unify Italy took refuge in Ticino, particularly around the major towns of Bellinzona, Lugano and Locarno. Some Swiss Italians volunteered to fight with Giuseppe Garibaldi, the military commander leading campaigns to unify Italy. Others provided asylum and helped rebels gather arms and print propaganda.

In retaliation for this aid, the Austrians set up a series of economic blockades. After a riotous but failed insurrection in Milan in early 1853, Governor Field Marshal Joseph Radetzky, the Viceroy of Lombardy-Venetia, expelled all Swiss Italians from Lombardy and Veneto and sealed off the border. This blockade forced an estimated six thousand Swiss-Italian laborers back into Ticino.

Swiss Italians could no longer buy grain to make bread. They couldn't sell their cheese, livestock, and other products in Lombardy. Bread prices almost doubled between 1853 and 1854.[2] The blockades, along with bad weather, poor harvests, a potato blight, and an epidemic of foot-and-mouth disease that ravaged livestock, brought Ticino to a state of near starvation.[3] Without corn, barley, or chestnuts, families like the Rotanzis scraped by on whatever they could find. Villagers likened food shortages to the famine of 1815 when they made polenta from hay and straw and scavenged for walnuts, carloni (an indigenous wild nut), beech tree bark and vine tendrils.[4]

One reporter described the blockade and expulsion as "executed with a rigor which would have delighted the heart of an Attila or Nero. Men, women, children of all ages, the old, the sick, the convalescent, all have been expelled; women heavy with child have been able to obtain a few days of grace from the Austrians. Those who were to be expelled were driven together at Milan like a flock of sheep..."[5]

Cut off from making a living in Lombardy, the displaced Swiss workers desperately searched for ways to survive. Seasonal migration had always been a way of life. Swiss Italians had traditionally migrated to England, France, the Netherlands and other European countries for work that lasted more than a season. Now they began to look beyond England and the European continent.

Two stonemasons, GianBattista Giovannini and Giovanni Antonio Palla, presumably searching for work as laborers, were among the first to head for Australia from the Vallemaggia, an alpine valley in Ticino. They left separately in early 1851, a few months before news of Australia's gold discovery raced around the world. They soon ended up in the gold fields. After Palla returned with riches in 1854, news of his good fortune spread throughout the region.[6]

Shipping agents were quick to capitalize on news of the gold rush. Eager for profits, they spread the word through numerous postings in the *Gazzetta Ticinese* touting fortunes to be made in the Australian gold fields. These ads formed part of a massive propaganda campaign encouraging voyages that enriched ship owners and their agents while plunging emigrants into a mire of debt.

To promote emigration, German companies opened agent offices in Locarno and other major cities in Ticino and the northern Italian regions. They set up stalls at local markets around Lake Maggiore, touting the treasure to be had across the seas. Companies offered to lend passengers their fare in exchange for a portion of future earnings. The massive campaign enticed many Swiss Italians to undertake the voyage, which took four months under the best conditions. From March 1854 to the end of June 1855, during the time Francesco Rotanzi began his journey, some two thousand Swiss Italians left Ticino for Australia.[7]

Local village councils, eager to reduce a population that could not be supported by scarce local resources, offered loans to villagers willing to put up their homes and possessions as collateral in exchange for funds to make the speculative voyage. To raise money, local councils cleared forests belonging to their villages and sold timber to speculators from other Swiss cantons. With groups of villagers co-signing communal loan contracts, emigrants relied on one another to repay onerous financial obligations. Heavy chains of debt bound them to each other and to their villages back home. All suffered financially when one of the group became sick or died.

The cost of travel from Locarno to Melbourne was about 560 francs. An average loan, secured with a mortgage, amounted to about one thousand francs, which paid for transport, a passport and a little extra for food and lodging on arrival. Five percent interest, on top of the loan amount, burdened the emigrants with enormous debt before they even started. One thousand francs amounted to about the price of six cows, thirty-seven goats or two year's wages for a teacher—a fortune to poor subsistence farmers who often bartered for what they couldn't produce themselves.[8] In mid-1855, the Swiss Federal Government imposed restrictions on lending for purposes of emigration. Yet the wave of migration persisted. Populations continued to decline as villagers took off to find work elsewhere.

From the 1850s through the early 1900s, some twenty-nine thousand Swiss Italians emigrated from Switzerland for Australia and California.[9] That figure hardly registers next to the nearly two million Irish that came to the United States between 1820 and 1860, yet one in five inhabitants, twenty per cent of the population, left Ticino in an exodus that drained the region.[10] Many of them came from the Vallemaggia, a small valley just thirty miles long that lost nearly forty percent of its population to Australia and California between 1850 and 1930.[11]

Like the Rotanzis, most immigrants believed they would not be gone long. Work on a far-off continent would quickly bring income, and they would return to their families and alpine villages in Ticino in no time. Many did repatriate. It's estimated that about one-third of those who had traveled to Australia returned home between 1855 and 1870.[12] By 1900, about half of those who had gone to California had permanently returned home. [13]

In 1930, California was home to 6,800 residents born in Ticino and about ten thousand born in California to Swiss-Italian parents.[14] Some men, after establishing themselves, returned to their villages to bring back a bride. Many of their children also married Swiss Italians, creating communities mirroring relations in villages back home. Connections to Ticino in these first generations remained strong, bolstered by a tight network of close familial and communal links that bound the immigrants together with their alpine origins.

These settlers were the fortunate ones. Others, unable to survive the hazards of immigrant life, died in foreign lands far from home and family. These oft-forgotten souls, their ill-fated lives cut short before they had a chance to fulfill their dreams of finding fortune, are also part of the story.

ONE

"I would not wish this trip on anyone."
November 2, 1855 - Letter from Francesco in Melbourne to Luigi in Peccia

* * *

Peccia, home to the Rotanzi family, is a small village nestled nearly three thousand feet up the Lavizzara Valley, one of three valleys branching off the Vallemaggia in the Swiss canton of Ticino. Jagged mountain peaks loom over the cluster of houses. Fusio, the town up the road from Peccia, is reached by a series of dizzying hair-pin turns. Beyond Fusio, at a certain point, only mule tracks and footpaths criss-cross the Alps.

Rivers and mountains shape the contours of Ticino, a roughly triangular region about fifty miles long from north to south, roughly half the size of the state of Maine. Mount Ceneri divides the canton into two parts: the sottoceneri to the south, a relatively flat area around Lake Lugano; and the sopraceneri, the northern mountainous area home to the Vallemaggia and the Rotanzis' village.

In the mid-nineteenth century, a single road, poorly maintained, and a chain of mountain trails connected villages in the Vallemaggia. Life in an isolated alpine village like Peccia could be brutal. A visitor in 1864 described Peccia as "an extremely poor village, with a wretched inn." As for the main road to the village, "between neglect and accidents it is now scarcely passable."[1]

Sheltered in simple houses built of stone chiseled from the surrounding mountainsides, villagers barely scraped together a living from rocky soil they shaped into terraced fields. Raising a few sheep, cows and goats for meat and cheese, villagers shared much of the work and resources, including mountainside grottos where they stored oil, cheese and wine. Women washed laundry at communal sites along the river. In the spring, groups of villagers herded their animals up to the *Monti*, the lower pastures about three to five thousand feet above sea level. There they stayed in small shelters, making butter and cheese, cutting hay, then bringing it down to the village for storage.

In the summer, men and boys known as *Alpigiani* herded the cows and goats of several families higher into the Alps, driving them up perilous mountain trails to pastures just below the snow line. While in the alpine meadows, they found shelter in communal huts where they made cheese, which they brought down to the village and divided among the families.

Such work demanded strong, healthy men, as noted by writer Samuel Butler, who, on his travels to the area in the 1880s, observed men carrying hay down from meadow to village:

> An average load is four hundredweight [almost four hundred
> pounds]. The man is hardly visible beneath his burdens. He will
> go down rough places almost at a run and never miss his footing.
> The men generally carry the hay down in threes and fours together
> for company . . . then back up again . . . Two such journeys are
> reckoned enough for one day. This is how the people get their *corpo
> di legno e gamba di ferro* . . . their bodies of wood and legs of iron.[2]

In the soil surrounding their homes, the villagers grew potatoes, rye, barley and corn, gathered chestnuts from the forest and grew grapes on small mountain terraces. Without irrigation and knowledge of crop rotation, families barely harvested enough produce for themselves. Few had a surplus to sell at the fortnightly market in Locarno, the nearest commercial town, located at the base of the Vallemaggia on Lake Maggiore.

Some sold cooking pots made from local soapstone called *laveggio* or *sass da lavegg* in dialect. This soft, malleable stone, known for its heat conducting properties, gave Val Lavizzara its name. For centuries, workers had been forming this stone into a *pigna,* a stove centrally located in a home's main room to radiate warmth throughout.[3]

Francesco Rotanzi had grown up knowing the shapes of surrounding mountain peaks: Pixxo della Vena Nuova, Pixxo Ruscada, Monte dell'Ovi, Pixxo Mascarpino and many others. He also knew most, if not all, of Peccia's three hundred or so residents, many of them his relatives—first and second cousins, uncles and aunts.[4] With them, he had herded goats, sheep and cows

The Vallemaggia, view to the north-northwest, Pizzo delle Pecore

up steep trails to alpine meadows above Peccia and climbed through beech and linden forests on footpaths leading to nearby hamlets. At the local church, he had witnessed their baptisms, confirmations, weddings and funerals. With them, he had celebrated saints' days and the turning of the seasons. Together they shared ancient tales of witches, gnomes and spirits who flew with the howling wind on the blackest of nights.

Francesco had shown his brothers—ten-year-old Alessandro and eight-year-old Virgilio—how to tend their family's few stock animals. He had watched his three younger sisters grow old enough to help their stepmother, Maria, with household chores, washing and mending clothes, making a polenta of ground chestnuts or corn boiled in milk over the kitchen fire. Carolina was just coming into her teen years, and Luigia Angelica was about seven. Even Severina, who was only five, could help gather herbs and vegetables from the garden.

Francesco's mother, Caterina Medici, had died in 1850, probably in childbirth with Severina. Two years later the children's father, Luigi, had married Maria Moretti. He had needed a woman to help care for his brood of five, including toddler Severina. Now Maria was pregnant with Luigi's baby. Francesco would not be home to greet his new half brother or half sister. He was leaving just as the family gained a new mouth to feed.

From birth, Francesco had breathed crisp, fresh air and tasted clear, crystalline water. He had grown accustomed to vistas of stunning natural beauty, snow-laden mountain peaks and cascading waterfalls. He had roamed in meadows blanketed with vibrant blue alpine Columbine and delicate pink mountain clover. As a young boy, he could splash in mountain pools and climb on massive granite boulders in the Maggia River, whose flow ribbons its way past Peccia, then courses twenty-five miles through the Vallemaggia into Lake Maggiore at Locarno.

Typical stone construction in the Vallemaggia

Francesco had his father to thank for lending him the seven hundred francs needed for his voyage to Australia. This loan represented an amount close to three years' salary as a teacher.[5] The Rotanzi family was by no means wealthy, but its members descended from merchants who had prospered in Bern's Kramgasse (Grocers Alley) during the eighteenth century. Although their wealth had declined, their middle-class status gave them options.

Luigi's position as an educator and judge for the Vallemaggia district enabled his family to live better than many neighbors. With the loan, Luigi also gave Francesco the moral support to risk the long and arduous trip across the waters.

Luigi belonged to Peccia's patriziato, an informal governing body composed of men from the village's oldest families. In a tradition reaching back to the beginnings of the Swiss Confederacy, the patriziato of

Road near Peccia

each community managed its common areas: the huts, meadows, and forests owned and shared by the village.[6] This joint responsibility strengthened close ties between villagers.

Francesco's training as an educator gave him more options than many compatriots who had no other choice than to emigrate to survive. Yet, despite years of study, he had decided to toss aside his future as a schoolteacher and follow his dreams of the wealth to be mined in Australia. The lure of gold in far-off Australia outshone his dull prospects as a schoolteacher in Ticino. For a youth from a remote mountain village, taking these first strides towards a foreign land on the far side of the world was both exhilarating and frightening. What wonders would he find ahead?

On May 20, 1855, after gazing one last time at his childhood home and its neighboring clusters of drystone dwellings, sixteen-year-old Francesco Rotanzi turned onto a rocky path that would lead him to the remote gold fields of Australia. With each step, he moved farther away from known comforts of his home, his family, their plain meals of polenta or potatoes, the stone stove that had kept him warm on icy winter nights, the animals he had raised from birth.

To reach Hamburg, Germany, port of embarkation for Melbourne, he had to cross the Alps, an arduous climb over the 6,909-foot San Gottardo Pass. It would be nearly three decades before travelers could take a train through a nine-mile-long railway tunnel carved into the Alps. In 1855, emigrants crossed the San Gottardo Pass on foot, by mule, or in a coach with at least four horses.

Francesco did not make this journey across the Alps alone. Over one hundred Swiss Italians traveled with Francesco on the same ship, the *Agen und Heinrich*, a result of German shipping agents heavily promoting their voyages departing from Hamburg. Passengers included one other villager from Peccia, one from neighboring Fusio and forty-six from Cevio, where Francesco's father served as district judge.[7] Francesco undoubtedly made the trip overland to Hamburg with one or more of them. Together they would navigate the large European cities where foreign languages and customs could be confounding.

Hospice San Gottardo, 1860–1890

The dangerous ascent over the Alps required extreme caution. Battista Strozzi, an emigrant who had made the journey just two months before Francesco, wrote home from Dover that two of his companions had fallen ill:

> These two find themselves a little sick in the city of Dover, and the reason was the ascent of San Gottardo which they climbed too quickly and sweated a bit. And as a consequence they burst a lung. We have left them still in bed but it seemed to me that they were beginning to recover.[8]

Travelers also risked avalanches such as the one described by a foreign newspaper a few years after Francesco's crossing. The article warned of the San Gottardo pass in winter, reporting that a massive avalanche had raged down onto the road, burying all in its path––the several vehicles, the many passengers, the horses and drivers.[9]

On his journey, Francesco passed the hospice at San Gottardo, where, since the thirteenth century, poor and sick travelers had found respite. In medieval times, it had offered shelter and food to pilgrims making their way to and from Rome and Jerusalem. In the course of 1868 and 1869, the hospice distributed 19,175 free rations, along with clothing, to 8,620 needy travelers; thirty-eight had been found in near-frozen conditions.[10] Navigating the San Gottardo Pass safely required stamina, courage and a lot of luck.

Francesco must have sighed with relief once he had made his way through San Gottardo and reached Andermatt. Yet he still faced another obstacle. He had yet to pass over the steep Schöllenen Gorge, a chasm over three miles long. As he crossed the ravine between its sheer granite walls, the rushing Reuss River roared below. This gorge had been impassable for centuries until a footbridge was built in the thirteenth century.

For many Swiss, the gorge evokes the legend, deeply embedded in cultural memory, of how the bridge got its name—the Devil's Bridge. The men who built rocky mule paths and bridges through the Alps in the thirteenth century had stopped short at this gorge. The perilous site, scene of many drownings, confounded their engineering skills. Legend says that they asked the devil to build the bridge for them. He agreed, but only if he would own the first soul to cross over.

With the devil's work done, the locals thought they would trick him by pushing a goat out across the bridge. Outraged at this deceit, the devil trounced off to find a massive stone to smash what he had created. While hauling a gigantic boulder back to destroy the bridge, the devil met an old woman carrying a cross. Shocked and alarmed, he dropped the enormous stone and raced off to safety.[11] Such tales were common when Francesco was a child, along with reminders to offer prayers

Devil's Bridge (1860-1890)

and give thanks for a safe journey at the tiny chapels found along paths through the mountains.

Having reached the shores of Lake Lucerne, Francesco took a boat across the lake, then a coach to Mannheim where he boarded a train to Hamburg. In Mannheim, Francesco chanced upon two relatives, Battista and Tranquillo Rotanzi, the latter a cousin of Francesco's father, Luigi. Along with many others leaving the Vallemaggia, this pair had their sights set on California, betting that it offered greater opportunity than Australia.

California or Australia? Francesco knew next to nothing about either place. Still, he had made his choice. He had signed a contract. Never mind California. He continued on to Hamburg, the start of his sea voyage. For better or worse, he was heading for Australia and the fortune he hoped to find there.

At the busy dock on Hamburg's Elbe River, Francesco boarded the steamer that brought him to the *Agen und Heinrich*, the 260-ton German merchant barque that would take him across the seas. As the steamer approached the ship, Francesco had his first look at the sailing vessel that would be his home for the next few months. He took in its length, its breadth, its towering three masts that carried twenty-four sails.

Was it sea-worthy? Was it sturdy enough and manned well enough to sail through the vicious winds and thunderous waves that would batter its sides in raging storms? And who was the captain? Was he an expert navigator? How would he manage the sailors' quarrels, the passengers' grievances, the precious supplies of food and water? Francesco had never seen an ocean, let alone a sailing ship. He could only try to imagine what it would be like to be surrounded for months on end by vast stretches of water with no land in sight.

Francesco watched as sailors loaded barrels of pickled pork, dried peas, flour and sugar meant to last the long journey. Excited passengers from scattered villages in the Vallemaggia greeted one another and chattered in groups. German police inspected their documents. Francesco listened with the other emigrants as the Swiss Consul told them about their rights and rules of the voyage.

Preparations complete, on May 31, 1855, the *Agen und Heinrich* set sail. It would travel down the coast of Africa, across the Equator, around the Cape of Good Hope, and over the icy Southern Ocean past Victoria's Shipwreck Coast to Melbourne. Travel time depended on the winds and could take up to six months.

Many of the voyagers traveled in cramped steerage quarters, an area between decks originally intended for cargo, but which shipowners had converted to temporary passenger berths. Once the ship reached its destination, the crew removed the minimal furnishings in steerage and converted it back to a cargo hold for transporting wool, gold and other goods back to Europe.

Both passengers and crew members risked catching cholera, typhoid fever and other infectious diseases that spread easily throughout the ship's crowded living spaces. Steerage fostered the growth of lice, bedbugs and bad feelings. Leonardo Pozzi, a thirty-five-year-old villager from Giumaglio who would join his two brothers in Australia, described steerage accommodations on the *Agen und Heinrich* in a letter home: "Below decks, the ship could best be compared to a stable, though a stable at least has light. But it was hell for the poor devils accommodated there, even to be seated. Many of them had to eat in their beds . . ."[12]

Emigrants particularly dreaded the steerage area, below the water line, during storms, when sailors sealed off the hatches to prevent water from entering, but which also blocked light and ventilation. In complete darkness, the ship reeling in raging waters, trembling passengers prayed for their lives and for violent tempests to pass so they might breathe ocean air and see light once again.

Francesco likely fared better up above in second class with Leonardo Pozzi. There, in something like an overcrowded room, the more fortunate travelers slept four to each hard, flat bed, which Pozzi described as being "like one of those tables used for rearing silkworms."[13]

Francesco's count of 118 passengers from the Vallemaggia included only one female, a woman from Cevio. Although this woman probably accompanied her husband, she undoubtedly suffered from deplorable accommodations and lack of privacy. Those sailors holding the traditional belief that women on board brought bad luck could not have been considerate.

In his first letter home, Francesco reported that "The captain was not bad, but the sailors were barbarous and cruel, like Turks or worse…I would not wish this trip on anyone." Pozzi calculated that there were "13 sailors including the captain, two pigs (which makes 15) and two dogs (which makes 17)."[14]

Francesco wrote that the food "was awful, awful and scarce… We had rice soup, or orzo, beans, peas or sauerkraut without any condiments – food worse than pig slop. The meat was very salty, and several times all spoiled… The water was bad, but we treated it like gold. We had one mug of it for two of us." Francesco may have craved water, but after months at sea, it could grow polluted with algae and contaminated by bodies of drowned rats and mice that had fallen into the open barrels.

Some voyagers became sick from cholera, which caused severe diarrhea. It became nearly impossible for them to stay clean. If newspapers were not available, they would have used vinegar-soaked rags, shared by all using the toilet. These filthy rags also encouraged the spread of typhoid and dysentery. Both passengers and crew could be thankful that the toilet, known as the head, sat at the front in the bow to allow winds that propelled the ship forward to blow the vile stench away from them.

Three men from the Vallemaggia died at sea during the *Agen und Heinrich's* long voyage. Passengers witnessed burials of their fellow emigrants, whose corpses, wrapped in canvas or laid in a simple coffin, then weighed down with pig iron or lead, were tossed over the side. They silently bowed their heads during the Committal Prayer, a page from the Catholic Liturgy read at sea burials to "commit the body of our brother to the deep."[15] They would have known themselves lucky to be alive.

Later, Francesco, Leonardo Pozzi and many others sent word home warning fellow villagers to consider carefully before signing contracts with shipping agents. Pozzi railed against the devious agent, "The most esteemed, reverend and swindling Mr Müller . . . a real trader in human flesh," who "had the gall to enlist passengers with the lying promise that he had a ship equipped especially for passenger transport, and that it was possible to buy everything in case of need."

Despite their complaints, Francesco and other passengers on the *Agen und Heinrich* suffered little compared to those on the *H. Ludwina*, which had left Antwerp two weeks before Francesco's departure.[16] Its passengers, 176 emigrants from Ticino and northern Italy, arrived in Sydney weeks after Francesco's ship had reached Melbourne.

On arrival, the emigrants looked so miserable and thin that friends who had come to meet them were brought to tears.[17] The passengers had endured 149 days of near starvation. Abuse had begun even before the ship left Antwerp. The captain had kept passengers on board with nothing to eat for twenty-two hours. When they requested food from the Chief Mate, a fight broke out, resulting in two passengers bleeding from knife wounds and the mate and another seaman locked up in the Antwerp jail.

During the voyage, the captain charged outrageous prices for moldy bread and other rotten food. Their funds exhausted, passengers exchanged their clothing for some small bits to eat. The captain made the sick pay for broth, and during the final part of the voyage, he withheld fuel for cooking, forcing passengers to eat "uncooked Indian corn and water."

To make matters worse, the *H. Ludwina* disembarked in Sydney instead of Melbourne as the passengers had expected. The voyagers discovered on arrival that they had landed more than five hundred miles from the gold fields in Victoria. Already weighed down with debt, rather than pay for another steamer ticket, many made the trip on foot.[18]

Francesco and his fellow passengers on the *Agen und Heinrich* luckily escaped such extreme abuses. They sailed through three storms, but mostly calm waters. Day after interminable day, they put up with bad food, filthy living conditions and hours of tedium. To pass the time, about forty men formed a singing group. Pozzi recalled the youthful enthusiasm of his compatriots: "We did sing I can tell you all the way, all young and happy full of hope of making a fortune in Australia, and then go back home again."[19]

Most ships headed for Australia in the 1850s followed the prevailing winds, which took them through a variety of climatic conditions and extreme temperatures from balmy seas to intolerable heat at the Equator, where the doldrums might keep them drifting for weeks. Then south past the Tropic of Cancer, they encountered icy chills and the threat of icebergs. Many immigrants could not dispel fearful memories of this trip, and rather than endure another such horrific voyage back home, made do with their lives in Australia.[20]

Francesco and his fellow passengers reached Australia's Hobsons Bay on September 21, 1855.[21] The trip had lasted nearly four months. Francesco passed the Equator on the Eve of St. John the Baptist (June 23) in heat he had never felt before, then rounded the Cape of Good Hope on about August 20.

Pozzi recalled, "We were so glad to land that all the way in the Yarra [River] up to the Melbourne wharf we were singing like nightingales." The passengers celebrated too soon, however, as the captain refused to let them disembark. He wanted the passengers to sign a document certifying his good conduct, so he held them back. When it became clear that none would comply, he finally released them after forty-eight hours.

Francesco arrived in Australia weak with fever, his sixteen-year-old body drained of strength. He had grown ill on a poor diet of "bad, unhealthy soup and two ounces of bread or lard in the middle of the day." Following a medical exam, health inspectors sent him and six other passengers to the Port Phillip Hospital. Two died shortly after arrival. Francesco was detained until his fever subsided.

Once recovered, he itched to be off to the mines. But his voyage and illness had given him a glimpse of how fragile life could be. In his first letter home dated November 2, 1855, Francesco let his family know that he "would not wish this trip on anyone." He told them of those travelers from Ticino who had died and of those who were staying in Melbourne "to regain their strength at a hotel operated by Italians." As a district judge, Francesco's father knew many people throughout the Vallemaggia and would want to know how Francesco's companions had fared on their arduous sea voyage to Australia.

Ending his letter announcing his safe arrival, Francesco asked his family to "Stay healthy and happy, oh my dear ones, and pray a little for me so that I may see you again soon." With luck, he would find his way safely along tracks winding through nearly seventy miles of bush to the gold fields northwest of Melbourne, discover gold in his diggings and return home to his family in no time.

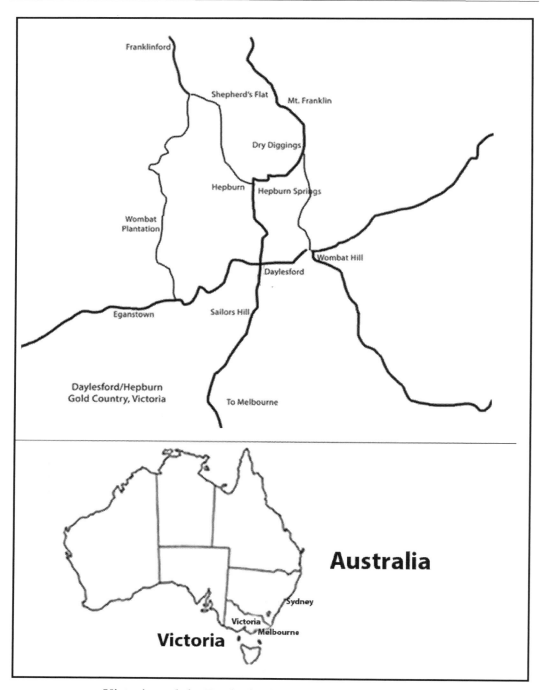

Victoria and the Daylesford-Hepburn Gold Country

TWO

"Mining is exhausting and scarcely profitable..."
November 15, 1856—Letter from Francesco in Jim Crow to Luigi in Peccia

On the way to Melbourne's city center, Francesco passed nearly three hundred sailing ships, most of them empty, anchored in Hobsons Bay, their tall masts poking the sky. Crews and even some captains had deserted ship for the diggings in the frenzy to find gold. Some of the few ships showing signs of life had been made into prisons to hold Melbourne's thieves, murderers and pimps. At the start of the gold craze in Victoria, nearly all of Melbourne's policemen had also taken off for the gold fields.

From the deck of the boat that took him from Port Phillip to Melbourne, Francesco could see a vast sea of tents covering the Yarra River's southern bank. Thousands of gold seekers, many from Great Britain, but others from places as far-off as Chile and Hungary, had built this massive tent city for shelter while gathering axes, shovels, blankets, pans and other supplies needed to dig in the gold fields. Francesco took in row after row, large tents for three or four persons, others not big enough for a person to stand up inside. These canvas or sailcloth sheets, some held up by just a few sticks, served as homes for thousands of immigrants. Francesco wondered, "Might he have to make such a flimsy tent his home? "

Street signs stood at row crossings to help newcomers find their way. Crude signboards advertised bakers, blacksmiths and tailors. Slabs of fly-specked lamb and bacon dangled in front of butcher tents. Barbers trimmed beards grown scraggly from months of neglect in the bush. Blacksmiths forged hatchets, rakes and scoops. Women washed laundry outside their tents in tubs filled with Yarra River water tainted with human and animal waste. Unlicensed sly-grog shops sold rotgut under the guise of lemonade. Aiming to buy picks, pans and shovels for the diggings, new arrivals crowded the tents of general stores.

When Francesco arrived, this Canvas Town south of the Yarra River was already home to over seven thousand people.[1] With few options, Melbourne's government had legalized this and many smaller settlements that had sprung up on empty plots throughout the burgeoning metropolis, charging each tent five shillings a week. The camps quickly turned into filthy slums. Makeshift shelters leaked and collapsed in strong winds and storms. Flooding washed out rows of tents. Heat brought flies, and with the swamp came mosquitoes. The camps lacked running water, toilets and showers. Dysentery and other diseases spread.

Men racing off to the gold fields left women and children abandoned and destitute. Unlucky miners without the funds to return home had no choice but to remain trapped in their tents. Canvas Town quickly became haunted by thieves and murderers, prostitutes and pimps. It was unsafe to walk through, even during daylight hours.[2] Newcomers like Francesco left Melbourne for the gold fields as quickly as possible, complaining of the city's high costs, dangerous streets and crude living conditions.[3]

Just a few years earlier, Melbourne had been a small, colonial settlement. When gold was discovered in California, the town's population shrank as Australians dropped everything to sail off for San Francisco in search of riches. Francesco did not know particulars of the gold discoveries in California and Australia. He only knew that he and hundreds of his fellow

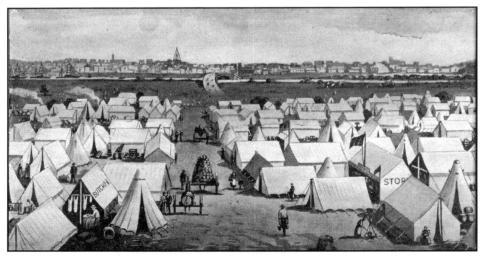

Canvas Town in the 1850s

Swiss Italians had taken off for one or the other of those places to dig for gold or find work. He knew that some villagers had returned with wealth. That was enough for him to give it a try.

Gold-seekers from around the world had sailed to Australia in droves because of one Australian forty-niner, Edward Hammond Hargraves, who had prospected in the California Gold Rush. He had not found gold in California, but he had recognized a similarity between California's foothills and those of the Blue Mountains near his Sydney home in New South Wales. Might gold be found there too? His perceptions and intuition proved true. In the spring of 1851, he announced to the Colonial Secretary in Sydney that he had discovered grains of gold in Lewis Pond Creek in the Blue Mountains. Hargraves later recalled turning to his guide and exclaiming, "This is a memorable day in the history of New South Wales. I shall be a baronet, you will be knighted and my old horse will be stuffed and put into a glass case and sent to the British Museum."[4]

As reward for his discovery, Hargraves received a position as commissioner of the Crown Lands for the gold districts, a reward of ten thousand pounds and a pension for life. Visiting England in lavish style, he met the Queen and lectured as a gold expert, but his self-aggrandizing narrative fell apart in 1890 when a Legislative Assembly committee found that it was not Hargraves, but his guides, who first discovered gold in Australia. Hargraves had simply taken all the credit.[5]

Australian gold diggers stopped racing across the oceans to California and began searching for gold in their native Blue Mountains. Alarmed by the massive population drain from Melbourne to the gold fields in New South Wales, the Victoria government offered a reward of two hundred pounds for any gold found within two hundred miles of Melbourne. Six months after Hargraves' announcement, gold was discovered in Victoria at Ballarat, and the frenzy began. Victoria's population increased nearly ten-fold over the next ten years.[6] Francesco and his fellow emigrants from Ticino added to the influx of English, Irish, Welsh, Germans, Chileans, Chinese and others eager to strike it rich.

Not all of Francesco's fellow immigrants intended to mine for gold.

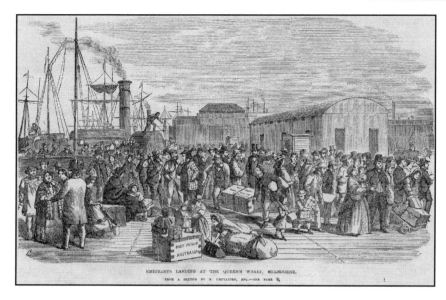

Emigrants Landing, Melbourne, 1863

Some expected to profit from the gold rush boom by working in their trades. What did they know, after all, about gold mining? They knew how to use stone to make buildings, how to cut wood to construct houses, how to raise sheep and cows and make cheese from their milk. They knew how to grow flax, grapes and silkworms. Led to believe that high-paying jobs would be plentiful in Australia, on arrival they discovered that the shipping agents had lied. One emigrant warned those back home: "Don't listen any more to those hateful schemers, who promise 25 to 30 francs a day to any type of laborer: don't believe this, because we left trusting that we would work in our trade, but instead we have to adopt the hoe and mattock and work in the mines."[7] Large companies hired laborers to do the heavy, dirty drudgery of mining, drilling through rock in deep, dank tunnels, hauling up ore for crushing. Many skilled jobs in Melbourne required knowledge of English.

An observer wrote to a local Sydney newspaper lamenting the arrival of nearly two hundred able-bodied immigrants from Ticino on the *H. Ludwina*, most of whom could not speak the language in Australia. Why weren't these emigrants taught some words of English during the long months of their journey?[8] Francesco and the others on the *Heinrich und Agen* had relied on

18

Leonardo Pozzi, who knew a few words and interpreted for them when necessary, receiving extra rations in return.

Unfamiliar with the customs and city life, Francesco stayed close to his companions. Some of the immigrants hospitalized with him on arrival transferred to the Melbourne City Hospital to continue recuperating from their voyage. Others entered a convalescent home for more rest. Still others found lodging at an Italian-run hotel. Francesco, eager to get started on making his fortune, set off with a companion for the gold fields.

To many Swiss Italians, the gold fields meant the Jim Crow Diggings, around which grew towns called Daylesford, Hepburn and Hepburn Springs. These three settlements about seventy miles northwest of Melbourne supported surrounding mining camps—Wombat Flat, Sailor's Creek, Doctor's Gully and Jim Crow Diggings, among others.[9] About four miles north of Daylesford, the two adjoining settlements of Hepburn and Hepburn Springs (at the time called Spring Creek) bustled with men mining for shallow alluvial deposits.

Italian speakers had been settling in this area since gold had been discovered in the early 1850s. By the time Francesco reached the gold country, about one hundred people, ten percent of Spring Creek's population, spoke Italian.[10] Many of Francesco's fellow passengers on the *Heinrich und Agen* had already arrived in this area, including Leonardo Pozzi, who had joined his twin brother, Alessandro, and his younger brother, Stefano.

Stefano Pozzi, arriving about a year earlier in 1854 on the ship *Carpentaria*, had managed at first to work in Melbourne as a watchmaker. Dissatisfied with his wages, he decided to join his brother Alessandro. He described his four-day trek to the Jim Crow Diggings in a letter home to loved ones:

> You leave from Melbourne with two woolen blankets, a billy [a
> pail or pot with lid] for making the tea, a steel frying pan for the
> steak, an axe to cut wood, the tin mug, a stock of tea and bread for
> one meal or another, and nothing else, not pants nor shirts more
> than a change. You leave from Melbourne early in the morning,
> and you travel all day through great plains and small hills without
> forest and in the evening you arrive at a thick forest, and you stop

and light the fire for dinner and then you pull up a blanket and use it as a tent and then it serves as a room and the ground for the bed. This is the life of all those who come to the mines.[11]

Stefano and his companions got lost on the way to the gold fields. Vast expanses of Australian back country land remained trackless. Carts and wagons had cut through fields, leaving ruts that crisscrossed this way and that over rough, unmarked trails that ran up and down gullies, between thick bushes and through muddy swamps.[12] After rains, the main roads became rivers, the paths turned into knee-deep mud. Several men had drowned attempting to swim the creeks on their way to the gold fields.[13] Some fortunate gold-seekers encountered aborigines who directed them through the wilderness to provisions, water and safe shelter.[14]

For three days, Pozzi and his fellow trekkers slogged through dense forests and creeks, without food, unsure of their whereabouts, until they finally stumbled on an aborigine settlement, the Loddon Aboriginal Protectorate Station. It had been built in 1841 by Edward Stone Parker, the Assistant Protector of Aborigines, to provide shelter and rations to the

Indigenous farmers at Parker's Protectorate, Mount Franklin, c.1858

native Dja Dja Wurrung people. As a protector, Parker was charged with learning the language and culture of the indigenous people and serving as a mediator in conflicts with the settlers. But when Pozzi and his group asked for food, Parker refused, claiming he was out of provisions. The men trudged on, their muscles aching, their stomachs empty, but now, at least, they knew the way to the Jim Crow Diggings.[15]

Making the same journey a year later, Francesco looked for signposts left by those who had gone before. He and his companion followed tracks through forests of stringy bark eucalyptus trees, avoiding ruts and rocks on the paths as best they could. They kept ever alert for bushrangers, escaped convicts who hid out in the bush to avoid capture, and ticket-of-leave men, convicts paroled from prison who combed the countryside hunting for victims to rob of their gold, money and supplies. At night in the dark of the forest, Francesco heard piercing screams of flying foxes, eerie howls of dingos and the chitters and grunts of wombats. Large herds of kangaroos shook the ground bounding down gullies to drink from the creeks.[16] Dare he close his eyes? Would he survive the night?

In Jim Crow and Spring Creek, Francesco once again found tents and shanties. Gold seekers pitched their canvas tents by the creeks. On word of a new gold discovery, they pulled up their temporary shelters and raced off to another site that might have better prospects. An early settler described the miner's accommodations: "The main track was bordered with tents and bark roof huts of rough-hewn sides or sheets of bark. Some were little better than a black's mia-mia [a make-shift shelter of branches, leaves, bark and grass] for the builder was frequently unskilled in bush carpentry, or too eager to begin his search for gold, or well aware that he might be leaving for another field."[17]

Francesco found a polluted, ravaged countryside, its creeks clogged with filthy water, a shocking contrast to the snowy peaks, crisp air and rushing waterfalls of his alpine home. Piles of gravel and debris covered the ground. Tunnels had been hollowed into barren hills stripped of greenery. He noted large mine shafts and men working strange equipment he had never seen before.

Swiss Tunnel at Jim Crow Diggings, 1858

As he became more familiar with mining life, Francesco would learn about the horse-powered whims and the whips that hoisted ore from deep shafts, the puddlers that separated gold from tons of clay, the massive quartz crushers, and the poppet heads that hauled ore buckets from below.[18] But now he looked with wonder at the odd devices in the scrappy mining camps. What were those odd contraptions? How could he make a living here?

In the boomtown of Spring Creek, Francesco came across a few hotels and stores among the tents and shacks lining each side of the road. Here he could find food and supplies at Dr. Francesco Rossetti's store, which drew Italian-speaking miners hankering for wine, cheese, salami and sausage. After Rossetti emigrated from Biasco in Ticino, he set aside his medical practice to sell food, tools and other necessities to miners.

Although miners at the Jim Crow diggings came from all over the world, the Chinese stood out with their long, braided queues, unfamiliar tonal language and non-Western customs. They engaged in fossicking, reworking the creeks abandoned by European miners, meticulously screening the sands for gold left behind. By law, they were forced to camp in specific areas.

In Hepburn, they settled by the Old Racecourse where they grew produce in large truck gardens and built a small commercial center.[19] They lived in a similar settlement in Daylesford near Wombat Flat.

Spring Creek diggings had become well known for rich gold findings. "Any man willing to work could win from one to three ounces a day," one digger noted in the early 1850s.[20] Along with miners came looters, gamblers and liquor-driven revelry. The diggings gained a mining commissioner and a police force. The government hired an escort, an officer and several armed men to safely transport gold from the diggings back to Melbourne.

Francesco must have been relieved to catch up with his friends from the ship. What had they discovered in the few weeks since arrival? Had they found gold? How could he get started? Francesco had a lot to learn. He set up his tent where he could amongst the others.

Francesco was fortunate for the company of his fellow Swiss Italians. Miners without companions could find the diggings a lonely place. One miner described the gold fields as "a chaos of strangers from all nations, rushing frantically from every quarter of the earth to enrich themselves . . . Who is likely to care for anyone but himself?" He saw men die alone without "the slightest clue to whom they were, or whence they came."[21] The tight-knit connections between Italian-speaking friends and relatives provided Francesco and his fellow gold-seekers needed support and protection.

Writing of his arrival in Melbourne a few weeks earlier, Leonardo Pozzi had posed a question shared by Francesco and his many compatriots: "Oh, how long a tail gold has! Through patience we have at last got hold of the end of it. But who knows how long it will take to get possession of the beast itself."[22] Leonardo had allowed himself three years to gain his fortune. He began working in the mines, back-breaking labor, for his brother Alessandro. He pushed a wheelbarrow through dark, narrow tunnels, often banging his head on rock ceilings despite crouching down low. Had the rewards been large enough, he would have continued, but he soon questioned whether he could make enough wealth to return home within three years. "The quantity of gold obtained by the gold miners round about, it gave me a very poor hope of the predicted or intended fortune."[23]

Francesco, writing home after one year in the diggings, entrusted his letter to two returning countrymen who could give his family first-hand reports of how things were going for him and his mates in Australia. Francesco told his family, "I have no established residence, but I settle here and there, wherever it is most convenient… For now I am here. Mining is exhausting and scarcely profitable for most of the miners. Some find gold. Others don't. It's a game of fortune. As soon as you get a lot of money, you have to spend a lot of it."

The easiest and least costly way to gather gold involved panning in the creeks and streams, sifting among the alluvial sand, clay and gravel for glittering specks of the metal. Many miners used the panning method so they could work independently with very simple tools, a pan or a cradle, to separate the heavy gold from gravel. However, by the time Francesco and Leonardo arrived, most of the alluvial gold to be found by panning had already been taken.

Jim Crow, a poor man's diggings, attracted individual miners who lacked the capital for large mining equipment. The immigrants pooled resources and formed small partnerships of four to five men. A four-man claim might form a square eight yards by eight yards. Fierce competition drove some miners to encroach deep underground on adjacent claims. To capture gold more quickly, miners might join together to build a puddling machine and buy a horse. Then they would strip the hills and gullies of dirt down to the bedrock, and use their horse-powered puddling machine, capable of treating tons of earth per day, to separate out the precious gold from the clay.

Mining quartz reefs was widely practiced in the region. Once miners found thick veins of gold-laden quartz, they would dig a shaft to follow the seam, hoist up the rock, and crush it to extract the gold. Still others sank shafts, sixty to one hundred feet deep, through the basalt lava flow, tunneling to the ancient river beds where gold lay trapped in the rock.

Accidents in the gold fields occurred frequently. Miners defied danger digging deep shafts and tunnels. Sharp and heavy mining equipment could rip flesh and shatter bones. In 1859, Vincenzo Perini wrote home to his family, "As long as we work in this trade, we are all subject to the risk of death."[24] That same year he wrote to Ticino informing his friend Giacomo Rusconi of the death of Battista Rusconi: "While we five partners were working in the tunnel on June 27, 1859 at 10:00 a.m., a large mass of earth of about three cubic yards fell, and the unfortunate man passed to a better life. He died in a few minutes. He couldn't even say a prayer."[25]

Pietro Lucini's miner's right

Francesco soon realized that he could not search for gold alone. He mined for a while with Fabrizio Crippa, an Italian from Monza who owned a hotel and butcher shop in Spring Creek. The back-breaking work of digging for gold offered no guarantees. Some Swiss Italians found work doing other kinds of labor, as woodcutters, carters or charcoal burners providing the mines with needed supplies. A few earned their living as bakers or butchers. Others opened pubs, restaurants and hotels. Many ended up working long hours for mining companies in low-end, risky jobs.

Francesco supplemented his income with other work, delivering bread and salami, macaroni and olive oil, tea and tobacco to the mining camps. He worked for Pietro Lucini, who had emigrated from Intra, an Italian town on Lake Maggiore very near the Ticino border. Unlike those who left Ticino for economic reasons, Pietro was a political exile fleeing persecution. The Lucini family, wealthy textile merchants, had taken up the cause for a united Italy.

Pietro had fought for independence from the Habsburgs, then fled political persecution by taking refuge in Australia. He arrived in Melbourne in 1854, where he opened a pasta factory, the first in Australia.

Hoping for more business in a larger community of Italian speakers, Pietro soon moved from Melbourne to Spring Creek. There he started a bakery and store where Francesco found work. Pietro's brother Giacomo joined him in the store. The Italian-speaking miners often needed credit for food and other essentials. The Lucinis bartered and provided such miners with weekly food rations in exchange for one-third of the gold these customers found.[26]

After one year, with high hopes for the future, Francesco still found life in Australia new and promising. He had discovered that he could make enough to support himself with a little left over for savings. Although he had the funds, he postponed paying off the loan from his father. "I would be able to pay it off now, but I want to wait a little while to get a bit of savings. Up to now, I am here willingly in this country. It is always about being able to make something better for ourselves. If luck plays out, I will be able to make good money. If things go badly, I will come home soon, and I will not need, thank God, to borrow to come home."

Francesco's half-sister Isolina was born during his absence. Suggesting that he might stay in Australia several more years, Francesco speculated that he would see Isolina "when she is almost grown." He explained "...as for having come to Australia, I don't find myself unhappy here. I don't know it very well yet."

He wanted to give Australia a chance. Despite his family's urgings and fear for his safety, Francesco was not ready to leave: "Tell Grandma that I thank her with all my heart but for now it's not time for me to come home. I take her into my heart until I can see her again." Francesco had landed on his feet. Eighteen years old, strong and able, he saw a promising future. "I am still young, and I have the time to risk making a fortune, if God agrees, and lets me come home to find you, dear father, with all the family, in prosperous health."

THREE

"All of us pray for you"
January 15, 1857—Letter from Luigi in Peccia to Francesco in Australia

Almost two years after Francesco's departure, Luigi's fears were growing as he sensed that his son would stay away much longer than expected. He wrote to Francesco:

> Our deepest anxiety is thinking of you, each hour fearing for
> your health, thinking of your hardships, of your long distance.
> Who knows how much suffering, how many risks, how many
> dangerous incidents have happened to you, or may happen to you,
> all things that bring me great sorrow. And so I would like you to
> come home.

News from Australia took about four months to reach Luigi, whether it came in letters or with repatriating villagers who could relay accounts of how Francesco was doing. At times, both Luigi and Francesco waited to receive a reply before sending another letter. At that rate, with the four-month transit time, if they wrote right away, they would each send and receive about two letters a year. During the long intervals, Luigi became ever more frantic with worry: "Your letters come so rarely. Receiving a letter from you, my dear son, is the most consoling thing in the world."

Luigi was facing dangers himself. Despite his forty years, he was obliged to take part in Switzerland's battles, in a skirmish against loyalists to the King of Prussia who wanted to bring Neuchâtel, a canton about two hundred miles northwest of Ticino on the other side of the Alps, back under Prussia's control. Called up to fight against the rioters, Luigi crossed the formidable San Gottardo Pass with his battalion on foot in deep snow. With fellow soldiers, he climbed from Airolo, an alpine village in the southern

Miners, Milkers & Merchants

foothills of the San Gottardo, to the top of the ridge on the southern flank of the pass. The soldiers lost sight of the Tremola Road that snaked up over three thousand feet in thirty-seven sharp hairpin turns. Its cobblestones lay buried deep beneath them. Luigi nearly froze as he waited in a long line of shivering soldiers for men in the vanguard to dig pathways through the shoulder-deep snow. Luigi described the experience to Francesco as "more frightening than combat." He felt fortunate to be sent home due to poor health. Ultimately, the Swiss Confederation subdued the Prussian loyalists, but meanwhile, political tensions made for an anxious, unstable peace.

Ticino Battalion on the San Gottardo Pass, January 1857

Luigi also lived with the constant threat of floods, landslides and avalanches. In his youth, Luigi had survived three massive deluges.[1] He had seen villagers lose their lives in raging waters. He had witnessed Peccia's church and more than twenty homes shattered by massive boulders and fierce torrents. The year after Luigi trudged across the Alps to fight against Prussian loyalists, a colossal landslide destroyed houses and several barns

28

in the village of Campo. Sensing that Francesco might worry about a recent downpour, Luigi reassured his son "Thank heavens the flood did not bring serious damage to the Canton. Peccia is intact, as it was."

A landslide in Someo, 1920s

Luigi still had sons Alessandro and Virgilio at home. They tended the family's two milk cows and helped Luigi raise two or three more calves to start a stable. Meat, dairy products and animals were bringing high prices in the market, and with more animals, Luigi's income would increase. Yet as an educator, Luigi valued formal learning above all. He sent his two sons away from home for high school. His two young daughters, nine-year-old Angelina and seven-year-old Severina, attended elementary school in Peccia. With three sons gone from home and Luigi occupied with judicial duties, Maria and her two step-daughters remained to tend to the animals and household chores. Maria spent much time caring for the toddler, Isolina. The young girls were charged, among other tasks, with the endless job of finding and hauling firewood for cooking and heating the house in winter.

Compared to many of their friends, Luigi's daughters were fortunate.

Although at times Luigi stayed in Cevio when performing his judicial duties, he still remained in Ticino. Many fathers and brothers had left for Australia or California. This massive exodus of men meant that the tough work of raising crops and livestock fell mostly to women and children. They cleared fields, repaired rakes and scythes, and hauled cheese and butter from high alpine meadows to Locarno's market. Lacking horses and oxen, they worked as draft animals, carrying on their backs heavy stones, manure, bundles of wood and bales of hay to feed livestock in winter. They often balanced these enormous loads while navigating precarious, narrow trails that wound high up sheer cliffs.[2]

Maggia River Overflow, 1920s

With little productive farming land, Maria and the girls cultivated every available patch of fertile soil, including tiny plots on mountainous inclines. On the steepest slopes, they needed to tie themselves with ropes to trees to avoid slipping. Such physically demanding labor took a toll on many women's health, resulting in horrible accidents and bone deformities. A local journalist lamented: ". . . we see our woman, not in clogs, but with bare legs and feet, degraded by carrying loads like beasts of burden, loads way beyond their strength, their health ruined so now they are unfit to raise a family and provide young children with the care they need."[3]

Due to migration, women outnumbered men by two to one in some villages. Women of marriageable age found few eligible bachelors. Some women, both young and old, pined for loved ones who had left them behind and found solace in the few men remaining at home. The count of babies born out of wedlock grew.[4]

Village Chapel in the Vallemaggia

While working high in the mountains, Maria might pause a moment before a little chapel to pray for her safety and for those in her family, especially for Francesco and others who had gone abroad to California or Australia. She knew their lives were in God's hands, and as she stood or knelt before images of the Madonna and saints, painted in muted colors on the tiny chapel walls, she could find comfort in prayer to Our Lady Mary, Mother of God.

Villagers who had narrowly escaped disaster gave thanks to the Madonna by commissioning a painting from local artist Giovanni Antonio Vanoni. They had the painting, an ex-voto offering, hung on the walls of the church to show how, by Mary's grace, they had been saved from a perilous accident. These paintings served to remind Luigi's fellow villagers that faith can bring miracles. They show women in peril: spilling head over heels down steep inclines burdened with heavy bundles on their backs and sliding down slopes as rocks pound their bodies from mountains above.

In each painting, the Virgin Mary hovers over the scene shining light and blessings on those she has saved from death. Immigrants to Australia also commissioned paintings depicting their voyage: a sailing ship full of men huddled together on deck, praying for protection while towering waves hurl the ship through a violent tempest. Above, the Madonna, a bright, glowing vision in the stormy sky, leads their ship away from the storm to safety.[5]

For centuries, the Catholic Church had dominated life in Ticino. Villagers marked time according to the seasons and the calendar of Holy Days. Peasants felt themselves part of the natural cycle in which divine will, the hand of God, controlled nature, causing good harvests, but also floods, avalanches, fires and disease. Faith pervaded daily life; in 1846, the patrician council of Cevio resolved to have a parish priest celebrate a Triduum, three days of prayer, to obtain good weather.[6]

Priests had kept records in Latin of village births, confirmations, marriages and deaths for generations. They had controlled the schools, teaching children to read, write, and do simple arithmetic, along with indoctrinating them in the catechism. Children were taught

Ex-voto, Giovanni Antonio Vanoni

that they had inherited the original sin of Adam and the tendency to be sinful, that they must confess their sins and attend mass often, particularly on Holy Days of Obligation. Priests taught the villagers that they as clerics represented Christ himself.

As a liberal educator, Luigi abhorred priestly power and religious indoctrination in the classroom. In his memoire, immigrant Giuseppe Strozzi described education in Ticino and some of the reasons why Luigi might object to schooling provided by the church:

> Until 1840 the schools in our country were very few and very bad.
> They were under the direction of the priests . . . The books were in
> Latin, so nothing was understandable. It was just a waste of time.
> It was not only in our village, but throughout the Canton. The
> worthy Franscini Stefano was the one who promoted education in
> our Canton. Finally little by little we saw many very good schools,
> very well-educated young men.[7]

Stefano Franscini has been called the "father of Ticino popular
education." His books influenced the development of a liberal constitution
for Ticino. As a political figure elected to the first Federal Council in 1848,
Franscini pushed for reforms and organized the first federal census.[8] His
progressive policies greatly influenced Luigi and his fellow educators.

Luigi also opposed the Conservative Party, a strong political force
and supporter of the Catholic Church. The Conservatives maintained that
church and state were one and that the Church should control education.
They supported the Habsburgs who ruled Lombardy and Veneto against
the will of the northern Italians.

In 1848, a wave of revolutions against traditional feudalist political
structures spread throughout Europe. People wanted democracy, freedom of
the press and an end to absolute monarchy. Aligned with these democratic
views, Luigi, as a Liberal Party member, favored a secular society, free from
Catholic domination. He joined *La Società degli amici dell'educazione del popolo*
(Society of Friends of the People's Education), an association of educators
advocating for liberal educational reforms, state control of religious and
educational institutions, and removal of priests and Catholic doctrine from
classrooms. Along with many Swiss Italians, Luigi supported General
Giuseppe Garibaldi and the revolutionaries in Piedmont and Lombardy
who fought against the pro-Catholic Hapsburg dynasty to create a united,
democratic Italy.

The deep rift between Conservatives and Liberals in Ticino resulted
in several violent attempts at control of the canton. Over the past decades,
power had shifted back and forth between the two parties. The current

political climate favored Luigi and his fellow Liberals. During Francesco's absence, Luigi had been appointed to a highly prestigious position, President of the Tribunale, the district court. His appointment could only have happened with the Liberals in power. Luigi informed Francesco of recent political events: "The Government was not changed and the Grand Council is composed almost totally of liberals. You don't hear talk of the *Orecchioni*." (*Orecchioni* is a derogatory term for the pro-Catholic conservatives.)

As a trusted judge in the district, Luigi often served as an informal mediator in family squabbles. He had heard rumors that one of the immigrants to Australia had cut off ties with his family. Luigi asked Francesco to find out what he could to help assuage worries of the young man's parents. He wrote to Francesco:

> I am fortunate because I know you would never do something like Giacomini from Brontallo––(God spare me from it. It would be my death.) He wrote a revolting letter to his father telling him to write no more to him, saying that he no longer wanted to come home. The poor father! I don't know what the world is coming to any longer! What world are we in? And what an unhappy mother! She is out of her mind!

Perhaps Luigi sensed that he, too, might lose a son. He wanted Francesco home. "If you don't have money for the voyage, borrow it, and I will repay it here." Luigi ended his letter with a series of anxious urgings, using his nickname for Francesco:

> Dear Cecchino! I recommend you to God. Take care of yourself, try to stay healthy, watch out for dangers, deceptions, bad company and come home as soon as you can. That's what all of us want. All of us pray for you. Write often so I won't lose track of you. I want detailed accounts of your life and your past encounters. Receive our greetings. We all send you them from the heart.

Despite his anxieties, Luigi could not stop his sons from leaving Peccia.

Map of California

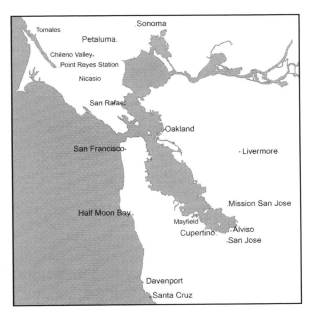

**San Francisco Bay Area
and Surroundings**

FOUR

"So far the trip has been a pleasure for me . . ."

February 19, 1861—Letter from Virgilio in LeHavre to Luigi in Peccia
April 6, 1861—Letter from Virgilio in New York City to Luigi in Peccia
May 19, 1861—Letter from Virgilio in Contra Costa to Luigi in Peccia

Six years after Francesco had taken off for the promise of gold in Australia, Francesco's younger brother Virgilio decided to emigrate too. Recognizing Virgilio's need to make a living, Luigi, despite his worries, lent him the funds for the journey.

In Francesco's absence, three children had been added to Luigi's family: Isolina, born the year Francesco left; Marino, another son, about four years old, and little Albina, still an infant. Virgilio had grown to an eager youth in his mid-teens, old enough to start making a living on his own. What could he do in Peccia? Mow and haul hay in the alpine meadows? Herd the family's few livestock from pasture to pasture? Log timber in the forests or haul stones from mountainside quarries? Virgilio had greater ambitions.

He had read Francesco's letters and had seen how his brother was faring in Australia. Francesco had not failed, but he had not made a fortune. Virgilio had heard promising reports about those who had immigrated to San Francisco and its surroundings. This city, bursting with wealth, first from California's Gold Rush and then the discovery of silver in Nevada, needed supplies and services for its growing population. Some Swiss Italians had started restaurants and stores. Others worked as milkers, ran dairies on leased land, or even owned their own ranches that shipped butter and cheese to San Francisco. So instead of joining Francesco, where he would have had the benefit of his older brother's years of experience, Virgilio chose to try his luck in California. He was joining hundreds of Swiss-Italian emigrants who had taken off for this state, admitted to the Union just a decade earlier. Virgilio knew he would find many familiar faces in California. How would he make his fortune? Would he open a store? Become a dairy rancher? Or maybe he would make a good living doing something he had never imagined.

Virgilio left Peccia on February 13, 1861 and met up with three young men from the nearby village of Brontallo. They trudged on foot down the valley, following the Maggia River to Locarno on Lake Maggiore. On the way, they heard the rumblings of waterfalls that cascaded through beech and chestnut woodlands. Tiny chapels high up the cliffs peered down on their passage.

Walking past clusters of small homes, each built of thick stones stacked together without mortar, Virgilio came across the same familiar landmarks his brother Francesco had passed six years earlier. As he entered Cevio's town square, he saw the town hall where Luigi held court and glanced at its facade covered with circles and rectangles. These crests represent German-speaking bailiffs who had ruled the Vallemaggia since the fifteenth century, when the Swiss Confederacy had annexed this southernmost, poorest region of Switzerland. Shields, banners, laurels, and crosses memorialized the bailiffs, absentee overseers who had done little to improve life in Ticino.

Ossuary, Coglio

A little off the main road, Virgilio could see Coglio's eighteenth-century ossuary, filled with bones of villagers long gone, trumpeting to all that death is ever near. Skulls, cross bones and skeletons dance over its surface. One brash skeleton, waving a scythe, warns passersby that "On the road I am waiting to kill you . . . " Down the road, the tiny Church of Santa Maria delle Grazie sat perched atop a knoll on the outskirts of Maggia.

Nearing Locarno, the young men reached the convoluted granite rock formations of Ponte Brolla and gazed down into its deep, narrow gorge. Ponte Brolla's Roman bridge marks an entrance to the Vallemaggia. Virgilio said goodbye to this small valley, his birthplace, its beauty and its poverty. He did not expect to find any place like it in California.

At Locarno, the young men boarded a coach for Airolo. Despite traveling in February, Virgilio found fine weather under a clear blue sky on the sled ride through the Alps to Andermatt. Blinding sun rays bounced off snow-clad mountain peaks, warming Virgilio's back. He wrote to his father and brothers, "I was happy as I passed S. Gottardo, as it was one of the most beautiful days to make this branch of the trip." At Andermatt, he and his companions took a steamboat across Lake Lucerne, arriving in Lucerne at two in the morning. There they stayed the night.

In three letters, one from LeHavre, another from New York City, the last from California, Virgilio outlined in detail the timings, transactions and costs of his trip. He only occasionally mentioned his three companions, as if he were making the journey alone.

> The following morning I left Lucerne at 10 am on the railroad train for Basel. I arrived in Basel at around 2:30 in the afternoon, and right away I found a French clerk who told me to go to the Vice Consul to get my passport authenticated. I went and had to pay 5 francs. These were useless expenses because afterwards I was directed to the shipping office of Mr. A. Zwilchenbart in Basel where I made a contract for transportation to New York.
> My passport was just as valid even without the authentication.

Virgilio had signed a travel contract with Andrea Zwilchenbart, an agent well-known for providing emigrant transport packages. The contract included train tickets from Basel to Paris and LeHavre, lodging, Atlantic ship passage, money exchange and customs services. Virgilio had to prepare his own meals with ingredients he had purchased, items like flour, butter, ham, salt, potatoes and vinegar. Virgilio soon discovered he had overpaid. "As soon as I completed the contract, I went to the hotel. In this hotel there were 11 Germans (Swiss) who had made a contract for transportation to New York with the same person for 10 francs less than us, 4 francs each."

Despite paying more than other travelers, Virgilio did well to sign a contract with Zwilchenbart, who had earned, over thirty years, a solid reputation for reliable services amongst emigrants throughout Switzerland. With pre-paid arrangements, this contract gave Virgilio protection from the throngs of swindlers who swarmed port cities preying on naive newcomers.[1] From his needless passport charges and contract overpayment, Virgilio learned that he must keep a sharp watch on finances.

From Basel, Virgilio and his travel partners took the train to Paris, disembarked at Gare de L'Est station, and lodged at a hotel that had been reserved for them by Zwilchenbart. From the station, Virgilio stepped out onto a long, broad thoroughfare, one of many that Napoleon III had commissioned Baron Haussmann to design in a massive reconstruction project to replace Paris' cramped, narrow medieval quarters.

Paris so amazed Virgilio that it left him at a loss for words. "After breakfast, it was time to go examine this great city a little. I can't describe the beauty and rarity of this city because I don't know where to start and I don't know whether I could end." If walking the Paris streets grew tiring, for a few centimes Virgilio could hop on a double decker omnibus for a ride through wide, straight boulevards to see Paris' new park, the Bois de Boulogne, and the city's modern, cream-colored limestone buildings, many six stories high.[2]

From Paris, Virgilio took the train to LeHavre, the port city on the north coast of France where he would board ship to cross the Atlantic. "After breakfast I went to inspect the ship on which I will leave for New York . . . It is large, beautiful, and luxurious because it is new, and it has three masts; its name is *Bavaria-New York*." A 908-ton packet sailing ship, the *Bavaria* made regularly scheduled voyages across the Atlantic carrying freight and passengers.[3] To Virgilio's inexperienced eyes, the *Bavaria* seemed large and new, but she was actually relatively small and had launched fifteen years earlier in 1846.

Virgilio had some time to explore LeHavre before leaving. "The rest of this day I walked the grand canals crossing all parts of this city—they are full of ships. I don't know if I could count up the buildings in Paris, but there are much fewer of them in this city than there are ships." Ships often docked in wait for suitable wind and weather conditions to depart. The many sailing ships and packet steamers blocked Virgilio's views of the docks, recently expanded to accommodate the growing trade in cotton from New Orleans.[4]

Prior to boarding the *Bavaria*, Virgilio posted his first letter to his father and brothers. "So far the trip has been a pleasure for me, and I hope that the rest of it will be as good. I will write you from New York if it is convenient and if time allows. I now live with the hope of having made a good contract with the gentleman in Basel [Zwilchenbart] and of arriving at my destination safe and healthy."

Leaving the port of LeHavre, Virgilio could see crowds of spectators along the northern pier, a gathering place for those who came to view ships leaving or entering port. As the *Bavaria* sailed out into the channel, Virgilio passed warships guarding the coastline. He could see LeHavre's industrial district, its munitions factories, and its shipbuilding yards recede to a line on the horizon, then vanish.

Timing of Atlantic crossings varied according to the wind and weather. Fortune favored Virgilio with smooth sailing, an easy crossing lasting thirty-seven days. Of the one hundred eighty or so passengers on the *Bavaria*, Virgilio and his friends found they were the only Swiss Italians among passengers from Bavaria, France and the German cantons of Switzerland.

Steamships would soon be the common mode of trans-Atlantic travel. They were much faster and safer than sailing ships. One out of every hundred steerage passengers died crossing the Atlantic on sailing ships in the years prior to the U.S. Civil War, while just one out of a thousand perished on steam voyages. By 1861, nearly one in three immigrants came to American on a steamship, yet Virgilio, like his brother Francesco, crossed the oceans by sail.[5] During the voyage, Virgilio saw the passenger count rise with the birth of a baby, but, unlike Francesco, he was spared having to witness burials at sea.

On March 31, about six weeks after leaving home, a happy and excited Virgilio arrived in New York City. On April 6, he wrote to his family:

Chapter Four

I have been well the whole time, and I hope and wish the same for
you and all those at home. I had a good trip with no rough waves
or any great disturbance except for one evening; we were given
good and abundant provisions, but we had great difficulty eating
them since we only had 12 stoves for around the 250 people on
the ship. After the first 15 days, coal became scarce. I then paid 5
francs to the cook for me and for my other three companions, and
he cooked for us twice a day.

Good weather and youthful enthusiasm shielded Virgilio from the
worst of steerage travel. Eager and adaptable, Virgilio had few complaints.
He had enjoyed the voyage. His youthful enthusiasm may have blinded him
to the wretched conditions in steerage and to a momentous event that took
place during his voyage. On March 17, 1861, while Virgilio was crossing the
Atlantic, King Victor Emanuel II became the first king of a united Italy. The
long battle against the Habsburg Empire, which had caused many Swiss-
Italian workers to lose their livelihoods, had ended in a victory for the
Risorgimento movement.

On arrival, Virgilio and his companions registered at Castle Garden,
an Emigrant Landing Center Depot operated by New York State prior to
the opening of an immigration station on Ellis Island.[6] There at Castle
Garden, at Manhattan Island's southern tip, emigration officials inspected
the *Bavaria*, and the ship's master recorded Virgilio and his companions'
names.[7] Although he was just seventeen, Virgilio gave his age as nineteen,
and his occupation as a farmer from Italy. His companions, Natale and
Antonio Giacomini, and Battista Fiori, villagers from Brontallo in their late
teens, were also listed as Italian farmers.

The Emigrant Landing Center aimed to outmaneuver scammers
who preyed on confused newcomers by offering bogus money exchange,
transport, lodging and employment advice. Virgilio and his companions
had reliable contacts for both lodging and passage to California, thus
avoiding the boarding house runners, baggage swindlers, money changers
and confidence men who took advantage of poor immigrants. With these
contacts, passed on by fellow Swiss Italians who had found them reliable
on earlier trips, Virgilio didn't need the services of the Swiss Benevolent

Society or the other ethnic-based associations that helped immigrants find their way around New York City and on to their ultimate destinations. He and his companions headed for 13 Crosby Street, a hotel run by the Italian-speaking Bartolomeo Benvenuto.[8]

Pacific Mail Steamship Company's Steamer *Sonora*

Benvenuto's hotel was located about a mile and a half up Broadway from Castle Garden. As Virgilio and his friends approached Crosby Street from Manhattan's lower tip, they passed block after block filled with theaters, music halls, hotels and restaurants. Broadway had become New York City's entertainment hub, a major commercial and tourist center. Delmonico's, New York's most popular restaurant, stood across from City Hall. Founded in the 1820s by immigrants from Ticino, the restaurant's fancy fare lay far beyond Virgilio's means.

It took just about half an hour for Virgilio and his friends to arrive at Benvenuto's hotel, located in the heart of a red-light district. Side streets around Broadway teemed with places serving "fast gentlemen" looking for "everything that makes time pass agreeably," readers could learn from *The Gentleman's Directory.*[9] Another little black book, the *Directory to the*

Seraglios in New York, Philadelphia, Boston, and all the Principal Cities in the Union, published by Free Loveyer in 1859, noted that Crosby Street, in its few short blocks, lay claim to eight houses of ill repute. Mrs. Wilson's at 19 Crosby Street stood just a few doors down from Virgilio's lodging.[10] On the other side of Broadway, Mercer Street was home to at least 19 bordellos. The Directory advised that a lonely traveler had any number of choices: Mrs. Hathaway's "fair Quakeresses;" Mrs. Everett whose "beautiful senoritas are quite accomplished;" Miss Lizzie Wright and her "French belles;" Madame Louisa Kanth's, which she ran "on the German order;" or Miss Virginia Henriques, where "its lady, its boarders, its fixins and fashions" were "of the Creole order."

How did Virgilio and his companions react to such salacious surroundings? Virgilio wrote home only of costs he incurred for steamship passage, lodging and money exchange.

> I must pay 25 francs for food and lodging, and I have given 500 francs for the steamship that leaves for California to Giosue Gianini who went today to reserve the tickets at the steamship office; this Mr. Gianini[11] is a most trustworthy man who has negotiated for hundreds and hundreds of men going to California. Since I didn't have American money, I probably lost around a franc for each pound sterling, and my companions lost about a franc for each Marengo.[12]

Impatient to reach his destination, a frustrated Virgilio found that he had missed the Pacific Mail Steamship Company steamer to Panama by only two hours. With timing of transatlantic crossings dependent on winds and weather, New York arrivals could not be matched with the steamships to Panama that departed three days each month.[13] Virgilio and his companions had no choice but to wait ten days in New York City for the next steamer.

With a ticket to Panama reserved, Virgilio remained positive and confident, but he had ten days to wait before departure. What could he and his friends do during those ten days? In Paris and LeHavre, Virgilio had written a sentence or two of his impressions of those cities, but he wrote not a word about his ten days in New York City. Virgilio found himself staying in the pleasure center of a massive metropolis of over eight hundred thousand people. How could he not be astonished by this bustling neighborhood with its fancy hotels, expensive shops and tawdry concert saloons offering cheap theater, liquor, and waiter girls hustling drinks and much more? Far from the distant village priest who had warned against the mortal sin of kissing a girl without committing to marriage, Virgilio and his three young friends had landed in what must have seemed like another world.

New York City had enough low-cost, morally upright attractions with appeal for young men just arrived from a remote alpine village as well. A few streets away from Benvenuto's, the Metropolitan Hotel, designed to resemble a Roman palazzo, took up an entire city block at Broadway and Prince Streets. That single hotel, on one block in Manhattan, could accommodate every villager in Peccia plus many more villagers from the Vallemaggia. A few streets away stood the five-story E. V. Haughwout Building with its innovative cast iron exterior. It housed the fashionable china and silverware emporium from which Mary Todd Lincoln had purchased the new, official White House china. Wealthy visitors who entered its luxurious interior, off-

View in Central Park, New York, 1861

limits to Virgilio, could ride the first passenger elevator in the world.

Virgilio was free to amble through Central Park, New York's new 840-acre public gardens in the heart of the city. A city manual boasted of the new park's offerings: "Pedestrians may roam at pleasure over miles of walks, some fashionable and much frequented, others retired and quiet, or over hundreds of acres of lawn, woodland, and meadow."[14] The young men from Ticino, accustomed to walking long distances on steep alpine paths, would find the mile and a half from Benvenuto's guest house to Central Park an easy jaunt up Broadway.

For a twenty-five-cent ticket, over fifteen thousand curiosity seekers came each day to the American Museum to gawk at showman P. T. Barnum's millions of curiosities. There they could gaze at displays of wonder ranging from mermaids to midgets, beluga whales to beavers, trained bears to butterflies. In the Cosmoramic Room, dioramas took visitors from the Rock of Gibraltar to Bonaparte's residence on the Island of St. Helena, from Jerusalem's Mount of Olives to the Turkish Sultan's Bath Room in Constantinople.[15] For

Ad for the Pacific Mail Steamship Company

Virgilio and his friends, surrounded by a new language, strange customs, and the brashness of big city life, wandering around the bustling streets of New York City might seem marvelous enough.

Yet Virgilio had arrived in a country that had started to rip itself apart. After President Abraham Lincoln's election in November, seven Southern states had seceded from the Union. The day after Virgilio left New York City for Panama, Confederates fired at Fort Sumter, and the American Civil War began. Eight days later, Union Square in New York City would swarm with over two hundred thousand supporters rallying for the Union cause. For the next four years, Virgilio's new home would be torn in two by a gruesome war. On arriving in San Francisco, he would find a city provoked by distant conflict, with pro-Union and pro-Confederate voices vying to control California's allegiance in the war.

On April 11, Virgilio made his way to Pier 42 at the foot of Canal Street to board the steamer *Northern Light*. A wooden side-wheel steamer with three decks, the *Northern Light* was headed for Aspinwall, a seaport on the Caribbean coast of Panama named for the man who built the railway across the isthmus.[16] The steamer could accommodate 250 first-class, 150 second-class, and four to five hundred passengers in steerage, where Virgilio and his friends berthed.[17]

More than a decade after the discovery of gold, masses of travelers still flocked to California from the East Coast. Virgilio joined adventurers, male and female, ranchers, physicians, merchants and military men, along with laborers, loafers, thieves and pickpockets, some of whom went to work before arriving in California.[18] One passenger remarked on conditions:

> The educated gentleman and the civilized savage occupy the
> same saloon, and pace the deck together when it suits their taste or
> convenience. In them everybody is at home; men of all countries,
> states, and conditions mingle and move about without restraint.
> Music lends its charm to keep the limbs of the passengers in
> pleasant exercise, and gambling-tables enable the "smart"
> men to skin such members of the green family as may fall into
> their hand . . . [19]

Virgilio missed by just six years a grueling, four-day trek across the isthmus from Aspinwall to Panama City. Instead of paddling rivers in dugout canoes and slogging through jungles rife with aggressive monkeys, poisonous snakes, and mosquitoes spreading yellow fever, he and his companions needed only a day to cross the isthmus on a forty-seven-mile train ride, with Atlantic and Pacific steamship and train schedules coordinated to make the trip even easier.

In Panama City, on April 21, Virgilio boarded the wooden side-wheel steamer *Sonora*, one of many Pacific Mail Steamship Company vessels that carried mail, cargo and passengers up the Pacific Coast, bringing back gold and silver from California's mines to finance the Union's Civil War efforts.[20] Virgilio spent fifteen days on this steamer, along with 750 passengers and a variety of pigs, cattle, turkey, geese, sheep, ducks, chickens and turkeys, slaughtered for meals as needed.[21]

Virgilio described this voyage to his family: "For the first 10 days on the Pacific Ocean, the trip went very happily. Then the sea became rougher and in the two last days there was a squall that disturbed me a little." The squall off the Santa Barbara coast lasted about 48 hours. "In general though, I had a happy trip, but it was very long, taking 83 days. The trip could have been done in 40 to 45 days, and I consumed nearly all my provisions." Virgilio had been overly optimistic, underestimating the time required for his entire journey. His Atlantic crossing alone took 37 days and would have taken longer had the weather been bad.[22]

On May 6, 1861, at around 7:30 in the evening, Virgilio arrived in San Francisco. As the sun set behind the *Sonora* making its way into the Bay, Virgilio could see in the far distance ahead the Contra Costa, San Francisco Bay's east shore, its barren, low-lying hills glinting gold from the sun's rays. To his right, at the narrowest point of entry through the Golden Gate Strait, the massive fortification known as Fort Point stood on its promontory protecting San Francisco from possible Confederate attacks. Mount Tamalpais loomed high above the headlands to his left.

As the steamship turned toward the wharf, Virgilio passed the small island on which stood the imposing Fort Alcatraz. The ship drew closer to the waterfront with its ragged shoreline of piers protruding into the Bay, revealing to Virgilio a grid of streets and buildings curving up and over the city's hills. He had finally reached the land of his dreams. What would he find here? Where would he begin?

When the *Sonora* entered the Golden Gate, the beacon on Telegraph Hill signaled to San Franciscans the ship's approach. It seemed that all of San Francisco's nearly fifty-seven thousand residents came rushing out to meet a Pacific Mail Steamship carrying mail from the East Coast. Newsboys began hawking newspapers the minute the steamer docked.[23]

The *Sonora* berthed at the Pacific Mail Steamship Company wharf at the foot of Folsom Street. Despite the evening hours, the wharf teemed with wagons, horses and drays, along with merchants meeting cargo, and residents greeting new arrivals.[24] Virgilio and his companions found familiar faces. Virgilio's "good friend" Giovanni Giacomini, a laborer on a Brannan Street dairy ranch, met the young men at the wharf. Possibly a relative of Virgilio's traveling companions, Giacomini returned to Switzerland a few days later, bringing first-hand news to Luigi of Virgilio's safe arrival.

Broadway Wharf in San Francisco, California, 1865

Virgilio wasted no time. Disembarking in San Francisco the evening of May 6, he began working at Domingo Ghirardelli's soda factory on May 8. Unable to speak much English, Virgilio found this job by asking a Swiss-Italian milk vendor where he might find employment. He had to travel one hour by steamship across the Bay to find Ghirardelli's Oakland factory. The job was not conveniently located, but it was work. Virgilio accepted a low salary of fifteen dollars per month, hoping that he would make more soon so he could pay off a good part of his debt.

Expecting to be employed at Ghirardelli's for at least several months, Virgilio asked his family to address their mail to "D. Ghirardelli. Branch San Francisco Oakland." Ending the letter to his father and brothers, Virgilio reassured them of his well-being. "I am in good health and always wish the same for you all. Time passes quickly, and I have food, drink and work, so I lack nothing." He had arrived happily enough, ready to begin working and saving his earnings.

D. GHIRARDELLI'S BRANCH,

Corner Broadway and Third street, Oakland,

Importers, Wholesale and Retail Dealers
in the
Finest And Best Assorted Stock of

GROCERIES,

Foreign Cognacs, Wines and Liquors, Native
Wines, English, French, China, Japan
and East India Goods,
Selected expressly for our trade.

SODA FACTORY.

Having furnished our patrons for a long period with the
best SODA ever manufactured in the State, we are proud
to make known that we have just received from Paris

A NEW APPARATUS,

with which we manufacture a superior article put up in

LAYE DECANTERS ON THE PNEUMATIC SYSTEM.

We call the attention of the Families, Restaurants, Bar-
keepers to the economy afforded by this new process.

Oakland Directory, 1869.

FIVE

"The sun's hot rays don't burn my face."

August 25, 1861—Letter from Virgilio in Oakland to Luigi in Peccia

About three months after arriving in California, Virgilio, in fine spirits, wrote to Luigi that his factory job was easier than tending cows and hauling hay in Peccia.

> Now I am here with a good boss. The work isn't hard, but with one thing or another I am always busy. Still with all that, the sun's hot rays don't burn my face. I work with a Frenchman who is talented and kind, and it isn't difficult to work with him. The man from Leventina [Carlo Petar] is hardly ever here because he goes out to take the merchandise and the soda to the surrounding towns.[1]

Virgilio's "good boss," Domingo Ghirardelli, was one of the wealthiest men in California. Ten years earlier, just two years after arriving in California in 1849, Ghirardelli had been named one of San Francisco's "Moneyed Men," worth twenty-five thousand dollars.[2] Born Domenico Ghirardelli in the Apennine mountains of Liguria, he learned to make sweets while apprenticed to a Genovese confectioner.[3] In his early twenties, he moved to Uruguay, then later to Lima, Peru, where he opened a confectioner's shop. James Lick, Ghirardelli's friend and fellow merchant in Lima, urged him to come to California after, as legend has it, the six hundred pounds of Ghirardelli's chocolate Lick brought with him to San Francisco promptly sold out to miners craving rare sweets.[4]

Ghirardelli, his first name changed from Domenico to Domingo from years spent in South America, took Lick's suggestion and sailed to California. He ran a tent store in Stockton, a general store in Hornitos in the gold region and then, in 1852, opened a chocolate shop on Portsmouth Square, site of San Francisco's central plaza during Mexican days when the town was

50

called Yerba Buena. By the time Virgilio began working for him, Ghirardelli also owned a store at 415 Jackson Street, located in San Francisco's busy commercial center. Nearby stood the four-storied Montgomery Block, then the largest building west of the Mississippi. Attorney and developer Henry Halleck built the massive structure, mocked as "Halleck's Folly" during construction, on a foundation of redwood logs held together with iron and planks from abandoned ships left in the harbor when their crews raced off to the goldmines. The completed building attracted well-known attorneys, engineers and other professionals who vied to pay astronomical rents for offices in the prestigious structure.[5]

San Francisco, 1864

Across from Ghirardelli's shop on Jackson Street, Nicola Larco, a fellow Genovese immigrant, ran a lucrative import-export business in a brick building that also housed offices of the Italian weekly newspaper *La Parola*, the Spanish and French consulates, and Chilean consulate for which Larco briefly served as consul. Ghirardelli and Larco, two of the Italian community's *prominenti*, acted as informal representatives of the Italian-speaking community. In 1869, Larco established San Francisco's first

Columbus Day celebration. Strong supporters of Italian unification, Larco and Ghirardelli contributed funds to Garibaldi's efforts to unify Italy and partnered to found *La Società Italiana di Mutua Beneficenza* to provide medical care and burial services for destitute Italian immigrants stranded far from home in San Francisco.

Over time Ghirardelli acquired many properties, building a successful company producing chocolates, syrups, liquors, and cordials, advertised in 1864 as the only chocolate factory in California. Prior to the Civil War, Ghirardelli's chocolate factory was one of only two in the entire country.[6]

Virgilio worked in the soda factory on Third and Broadway in Oakland, just a few blocks from Ghirardelli's home. This enormous estate, recalling Italian villas and gardens gracing Lake Como's shores, covered one entire block bounded by Clay, Jefferson, Second and Third Streets.[7] On weekends, Virgilio could find respite in Ghirardelli's gardens, open to the public on Saturdays and Sundays. There visitors enjoyed the scent of roses and honeysuckle, figs and magnolia blossoms. Water bubbled in a marble fountain filled with gold fish. Enormous urns, life-sized statues of Italian heroes such as Columbus and Count Cavour, and classical figures representing Mercury and Agriculture made guests feel as if they were strolling through the elegant grounds of a northern Italian villa.

In 1861, about fifteen hundred residents lived in the small town of Oakland.[8] San Francisco could be reached by hopping on one of the steam ferries that departed nearly every hour. On weekends, ferries arrived from San Francisco bringing picnickers looking for pleasure under the oaks. Oakland drew hundreds of people escaping the bustling city for diversion in, as one observer noted, "one of the loveliest and most beautiful places along the entire bay."[9]

Virgilio had little time for recreation. He described to Luigi his daily routine at his job:

> I start work in the morning at 5 or 5:30. First I take care of 3 horses
> that are in a barn. I also do that in the evening. Then I make 45
> dozen bottles of soda, refreshing drinks that are drunk like beer.
> The soda is of a clear color, sweet and strong, and at the same time
> tastes a little like lemon.

In 1784, Jacob Schweppe of Geneva invented the first industrial process to carbonate and bottle soda water. Decades later, Schweppes soda water became the official drink of the 1851 Great Exhibition in London where one million bottles were sold to six million visitors from around the world in the Crystal Palace in Hyde Park, a building constructed specifically for Schweppes and covering more than eighteen acres.[10] Despite its popularity, apparently Schweppes and other carbonated soda waters had not yet reached the Vallemaggia, as Virgilio described the drink in detail to Luigi.

> To make the soda, a steam machine puts a great force of water and gas in the bottle. It attaches the cork on each bottle so that the force of the gas doesn't push it out. And when you open the bottle you just have to cut the tie and the cork makes a pop around the cap.

> I finish working the soda machine and package 50 or 60 pounds of coffee; and in the days when we don't make soda then we make liquor and syrups.

Throughout his long work day, Virgilio breathed in pungent scents of sweet syrups and liquors, from absinthe, vermouth, curaçao and champagne to haut sauterne, french brandies and peppermint bitters. The rich, burnt aroma of roasted coffee beans suffused his nostrils as he packaged beans that Ghirardelli had imported, roasted and ground.

> It's a big warehouse where all kinds of liquors are made and sold; in the end it becomes 10 or 11 o'clock in the evening, and I go away to rest. I only hope to God that a bottle of soda doesn't break in my eyes or someplace else since the force of the gas very often breaks the bottles.

Volatile bottles could explode in an instant, as happened in a South Bay bottling firm. The *San Francisco Chronicle* described the tragedy: "While Fortunato Vilar, of the San Jose French Soda Works, was filling a bottle with soda this morning, the bottle burst, a portion striking his neck and cutting the carotid artery. He was attended by several physicians, but expired in half an hour. He leaves a mother and brother."[11]

Knowing that a work injury could ruin him, Virgilio told Luigi that he had decided to give up one precious dollar a month from his fifteen-dollar salary to pay for health insurance:

> Not long ago I took a subscription to an Italian hospital, the doctor
> of which is a certain Rotanzi from Leventina, a good man and a
> competent doctor. This subscription is the best bet for being well
> treated in case of illness. If you are not subscribed, you must pay
> 2 dollars per day for the cure of an illness, and if you don't have
> money, you are not well cared for.

Virgilio had faith in Dr. Antonio Rottanzi, a Swiss Italian from Faido and a
prominent physician in San Francisco's multi-ethnic immigrant community.
Dr. Rottanzi had come to California in 1855 with his brothers, Leopold and
Giosue. He served as physician for both the Italian Mutual Benefit Society
and the Swiss Benevolent Society, formed in 1849 with a mission to support

sick countrymen and those in financial distress.

Virgilio could not help but notice Rottanzi's
large front-page ads for health insurance in *L'Unione
Nazionale*, a local Italian language newspaper. To
purchase the insurance, he visited an office on the
corner of Third and Folsom Streets in San Francisco,
where Rottanzi and his brother Giosue also operated
a pharmacy. Unsure of what risks lay ahead, Virgilio
took a gamble on Rottanzi's insurance. With diseases
such as smallpox, typhoid, cholera and tuberculosis
commonplace, it could serve him well.

Virgilio's job exposed him to certain dangers,
but his travel partners, Battista Fiori (name later
changed to James B. Bloom) and Natale Giacomini,
faced far different threats. They had both settled into
ranch jobs near Tomales in western Marin County.
Just six months after arriving in California, the pair
found themselves with their necks in nooses about to
be lynched.

A man named Frank McGinnis had accused
them of stealing some fifteen or twenty dollars.

To make them confess and give back his money, McGinnis, with several helpers, put ropes around their necks to hang them. The *Sacramento Daily Union* reported that the "Italians [Swiss Italians often were assumed to be from Italy] had lately arrived in the country and could not speak a word of our language . . ." The men "hung two of them till life was almost extinct."[12] The *Marin Journal*, also conflating Giacomini and Fiori with Italians, reported on the aftermath: "After applying restoratives and rubbing the victims until consciousness was restored, they procured an interpreter and explained matters to the Italians, when it was discovered that they were innocent of the crime charged." After the real thief was found, he was "treated with a coat of tar and feathers and turned loose."[13]

Giacomini and Fiori must have been terrified by the assault, yet they had the wherewithal to ask for justice. They filed a complaint and at least one of the offenders was sentenced to six months in jail for the attempted hanging. Authorities took the case seriously and pursued two other offenders, whose cases, after a jury deliberated, were dismissed.[14]

Newcomers, especially without English language skills, could encounter intense hostility. The Chinese suffered the most discrimination. After just a few months in California, Virgilio, like so many other workers, complained to Luigi that the huge influx of Chinese workers was ruining the economy.[15]

> Expenses in California are still a little better but not by much
> and now it's getting worse due to the masses of people who are
> constantly arriving, principally the Chinese. They reduce rates,
> working for almost nothing. They don't spend money. Consequently,
> the people who would spend money don't have work.

Anti-Chinese sentiment among European workingmen ran high. Like so many other Westerners for whom the Chinese way of life seemed alien and threatening, a German author traveling in California wrote, "Thanks to their numbers, they encroached at once upon the rights of the white workingmen, worked in swarms in the mines, sent their gold out of the land and penetrated everywhere. Wherever they lived in great hordes in the cities, filth, sickness and fires were the inevitable results."[16] Such intense anti-Chinese fervor led to the Chinese Exclusion Act of 1882, a federal law restricting immigration of Chinese laborers.

Along with the turmoil of starting life anew in a foreign country, Virgilio faced a country torn asunder, writing that "the war of the United States also brings confusion." With the Civil War starting during Virgilio's travels from New York to Aspinwall on the *Northern Light*, he arrived in a San Francsico disrupted by the conflict. Just five days after Virgilio's arrival in San Francisco, nearly twenty thousand people gathered at Montgomery, Market and Post Streets for an enthusiastic pro-Union meeting. The *Daily Alta California* reported that the massive demonstration was needed "to show the Central Government at Washington that we are not indifferent spectators of the great events now transporting in the Atlantic States, and that the heart of California beats responsive to the efforts of the Government to put down treason..." Bands and military companies marched through the streets under "thousands of flags, and banners, and streamers, which floated in gorgeous array from housetops, steeples, liberty poles, windows, at doorways, and high in the air across the streets."[17] Banks closed for the event, as did some businesses.

Working eighteen hours a day, Virgilio had little time to think about the war or even explore his surroundings. Once when he did get a day off, he took the ferry, likely the *Contra Costa*, across San Francisco Bay to see a bull and bear fight. He had heard about the raucous animal brawls brought to California by Mexican vaqueros. He wanted to see one for himself. Such fights thrilled large crowds of miners and other early residents, giving them a chance to gamble over a bloody fight for survival. Would the colossal grizzly, hind foot bound to the Spanish bull's forefoot to make up for its massive strength, rip its opponent apart? Or would the hulk of a bull, blood seeping into its mouth from a nose slashed by fight promoters to increase its rage, gore the grizzly to death with its deadly horns? The crowd's wild cheers punctuated the grunts and growls of the crazed animals.

A few years earlier, an observer had described such an brutal event held at the Mission Dolores:

During this scuffle, the bull shattered the lower jaw of the bear, and we could see the shivered bones dangling from their bloody recesses!… neither the bull nor bear could stand any longer— their limbs refused to support their bodies; they had worried and lacerated each other so much that their strength had completely failed, and they dropped upon the earth, gasping as if in the last agony. While in this helpless condition the chain was removed from their feet, horses were hitched to them, and they were dragged without the arena, there to end their miseries in death.[18]

BULL AND BEAR FIGHT.

Century Illustrated Monthly Magazine, **Dec. 1890**.

The spectacle, unlike anything Virgilio had seen before, had aroused his curiosity, but he was not prepared for the brutal fight. "I was very sad when the bull fell to the ground and the bear choked sucking its own blood. People laughed and shouted, but I felt a lot of pain." By the time Virgilio observed this slaughter, such violent contests were on the wane.

As San Francisco grew tamer and the grizzlies became nearly extinct, bull and bear fights became illegal.[19]

Virgilio was paying a price to work at a steady job in a familiar setting where he understood the language. A group of farmers calling for seasonal laborers announced in a local paper that farmworkers in Santa Clara Valley could make "two dollars per day quick."[20] At fifteen dollars per month, Virgilio's wages were even lower than those of a female domestic,[21] yet he expected his starting salary to grow, and he could do worse.[22] Union Army privates earned thirteen dollars per month for putting their lives in danger.[23]

After just three months in this foreign land, new to its language and customs, Virgilio was well satisfied with his situation and assured his family, "I salute you with all my heart and suggest you don't worry about me because I am well and happy here." For now, Virgilio could settle in and grow familiar with new surroundings. Before long, he would need to move on if he wanted a faster way to fortune.

The Oakland Ferry and the Steamer Washoe, San Francisco, 1866

SIX

"The only thing is to be able to return home …"

July 23, 1861—Letter from Francesco in Hepburn to Luigi in Peccia

By 1861, more than six years had passed since Francesco had followed the river down the valley from Peccia to arrive in the gold fields of Victoria. He had left his grubby tent for a more solid shelter in the town of Hepburn, which in 1857 had only thirteen permanent structures: three cottages, a hotel, and nine stores.[1] He joined fortune seekers from around the world, many from England, Wales, France and Germany, in the small settlement and nearby camps next to a goldfield called the "Old Racecourse."[2]

Delivering bread, cheese and other goods for shop owner Pietro Lucini and working in the mines for Fabrizio Crippa did not satisfy Francesco's ambitions. He looked for other employment. Better suited to using his head than his hands, Francesco found a job keeping accounts for Crippa and Crippa's partner Battista Borsa, two businessmen in the Daylesford and Hepburn Springs region. His education served him well.

Italian speakers clustered together in the tough mining towns. The Pozzi brothers, Alessandro, Stefano and Leonardo, had opened a small store in Hepburn selling baked goods, groceries and liquor. When the store burned down in 1856, the Pozzis paid the Traversi brothers, immigrants from Cevio, to rebuild it, adding a drinking room where Francesco met with his countrymen to relax, exchange news and talk of home.

Leonardo Pozzi described the new establishment as "Something more than a place to drink."[3] There each August 15, Francesco could join fellow Italian speakers celebrating the Festa della Madonna––the Feast of the Assumption. With good company, hearty food and plenty of wine, accompanied by singing and dancing to familiar tunes played by the Traversi brothers, Francesco might well recall festival days with friends and family back in Peccia.

Carlo Traversi had taken his viola with him from Cevio over the Alps to Liverpool, playing it on the sailing ship *Miles Barton* across several oceans, then carrying it on the long trudge from Melbourne to Daylesford. As he had played for gatherings in Cevio, now he brought singing and dancing to the Swiss and Italian immigrants in Victoria. He eventually opened Carlo Traversi's Dancing Rooms at Old Racecourse in Hepburn where he put on Grand Dress Balls, advertising "Tickets to admit Lady and Gentleman 21 shillings. Dancing to commence at 8."[4] Such establishments brought Italian speakers together with other European immigrants over bottles of red wine and plates of pasta, known as "macaroni" in Australia.

Over the past six years since his arrival, Francesco had seen the makeshift tents and shacks of the early days give way to sturdier structures. Place names changed as transient mining camps developed into towns: Jim Crow and Wombat Flat grew into Daylesford; Old Racecourse turned into Hepburn, and Spring Creek became Hepburn Springs. Over time, Francesco saw businesses crop up that recalled his alpine home: Lafranchi's Swiss Mountain Hotel, Nazarro Sartori's Locarno, The William Tell Hotel, Lucia Brignoli's Helvetia, and Bedolla's Savoia Hotel, named in honor of Italy's royal family.

Bedolla's Spring Creek Hotel, c.1870

Several miles away at Franklinford, a few indigenous people of the Dja Dja Wuurung tribe still lived in bark huts at the Loddon Aboriginal Protectorate Station, a reserve founded by Edward Stone Parker, a Methodist preacher and Assistant Protector of Aboriginals. The British House of Commons had mandated the establishment of Protectorates to watch over the rights of indigenous people and to ease tensions between them and European settlers. Parker built a stone school where indigenous people could learn to read and write. He taught them how to farm on land offered to them in exchange for work, and he preached to them the Christian faith.

Early settlers had battled with indigenous Australian peoples over cultural differences and rights to land. Parker tried to mediate. He was thwarted in an attempt to bring several European men to trial for murder because the courts would not allow testimony from indigenous people. Considered savages, the indigenous Australian people could not swear on the Bible, so the courts would not admit their evidence.[5]

Miners stripped forests, rerouted rivers, killed wildlife and habitat, and tunneled deep into the earth, ravaging indigenous Australian peoples' sacred sites. Despite the havoc, some indigenous people actively participated in the rush for gold, acting as guides to the gold fields and sometimes mining themselves. They traded food and goods, particularly possum skin rugs, highly valued by miners for their warmth on cold winter nights. With manpower short in the early days after gold's discovery, indigenous men served as gold escorts on pack-horse convoys to safely transport gold from the fields to Melbourne and as Native Police Troopers to keep law and order in the camps.[6]

At one point, nearly two hundred indigenous Australian people lived on the Loddon protectorate, but when the colonial government closed it in 1850 to save on expenditures, just twenty or thirty remained. By the time Stefano Pozzi and his companions stumbled upon the Protectorate while searching for Jim Crow Diggings in 1854, only a few indigenous people were left on the site.[7]

An early Hepburn resident recalled that indigenous people frequently roamed from mine to mine, asking miners for food and tobacco.[8] "Victoria is now entirely occupied by a superior race," reported a legislative committee in 1858, "and there is scarcely a spot, excepting in the most remote mountain ranges, or dense scrubs, on which the Aborigine can rest his weary feet." The last survivor left the Loddon preserve in 1864.[9] In the ensuing years, the government of Victoria increasingly restricted rights of the remaining indigenous people, regulating where they could live and work and whom they could marry.

Not long after Francesco arrived in the Daylesford region, he saw easy pickings vanish. He no longer witnessed many new compatriots arriving in the area. In fact, many of his fellow countrymen had gone back home. Only a few brought riches back to Ticino. Others, having mortgaged their homes for empty promises of fortune, returned laden with debt. Some yearned for home but stayed in Australia rather than hazard another perilous ocean voyage. "The mines are becoming exhausted, the work scarce, and the income extremely limited," a government official in Ticino reported in 1859. "This mass migration mania will succeed in damaging and producing unhappiness and the poverty of so many peasants who would have had enough to survive on in their own country."[10]

Francesco often spent time in the neighboring village of Spring Creek, where buildings running along a ridge framed by alluvial gullies lined Spring Creek Road. There many of Francesco's friends and business associates lived and worked in a close community of Italian speakers who gathered at Miner's Hall for political debates, musical concerts and dances.

Some immigrants farmed on lands that spread across the sloping hills and valleys surrounding the villages. The Victorian Parliament had authorized a series of land sales to promote agriculture on vast acreage originally claimed by the Crown. Purchasers had to meet certain criteria, including British citizenship. The land sales prompted many Italian speakers to seek naturalization, including Fabrizio Crippa, Carlo Traversi and Alessandro Pozzi, who applied together with a group of nine other Italian speakers. Francesco did not apply for naturalization to purchase land. At one pound per acre, with only half of the sale amount required up front, the terms seemed attractive, but improvements had to be made to the land over time in order to obtain title to the property.[11] Francesco was no farmer.

Those who chose to farm grew oats, rye, corn, barley, potatoes, carrots, peas, cabbages and herbs, raising a much greater variety of produce on much larger plots than they had cultivated in the Alps. Sending to Ticino and Italy for seeds, they created gardens with flowering plants like camellias and wisterias, and orchards of mulberry, chestnut and olive trees. They made wine, cheese, sausages and pasta as they had in their homeland.

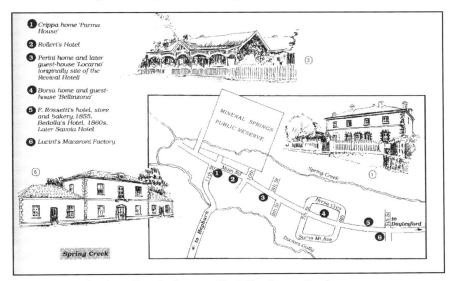

1 *Crippa home 'Parma House'*

2 *Rolleri's Hotel*

3 *Pertini home and later guest-house 'Locarno' (originally site of the Revival Hotel)*

4 *Borsa home and guest-house 'Bellinzona'*

5 *F. Rossetti's hotel, store and bakery, 1855. Bedolla's Hotel, 1860s. Later Savoia Hotel*

6 *Lucini's Macaroni Factory*

Spring Creek, later called Hepburn Springs

Francesco's employer, Fabrizio Crippa, purchased property at a Hepburn public lands sale and built an estate on Spring Creek Road, set on land that had once been marred by mining operations.[12] Crippa called his home Villa Parma and modeled it on the villas of his Northern Italy. With help from the Lucini brothers, Crippa constructed a two-story bluestone and brick building with dark stone trim, an underground cellar for wine storage and a grand entrance hall. In 1864, the local press celebrated Crippa's estate as "quite an ornament to the road."[13]

Surrounding Villa Parma, Crippa laid out extensive vegetable and flower gardens and an orchard of mulberry, pear and chestnut trees. He also created one of Victoria's earliest vineyards, planting fifteen thousand vines on about seven acres producing a twenty-ton grape harvest. Crippa's

Parma House was built to last.[14] Other structures in the area, farmhouses and drystone walls built by Italian speakers in the style of the old country, display masonry skills honed in the mountains of Italy and Switzerland. The sturdy farmhouses of bluestone or sandstone stand in sharp contrast to the wooden clapboard cottages built by immigrants from England, Ireland and Wales.

Along with mining ventures, vineyards and hotel operations, Crippa owned a butcher shop in Hepburn with his partner Battista Borsa for which Francesco kept the accounts. Among other meats, they sold what came to be known by English speakers as Bull Boar Sausages. They made this traditional sausage, known as *Luganica* in Ticino, from beef and pork enhanced with wine, garlic, sugar and spices such as pepper, cinnamon, cloves and nutmeg.[15] In these tasty sausages, Francesco and his friends found familiar flavors of home.

Lucini Macaroni Factory, 2016

Battista Borsa also lived on Spring Creek Road, a short distance from Crippa's Villa Parma. He eventually opened the Bellinzona Guest House on that road, named for his birthplace in Ticino. Along with his butcher shop, he operated a brewery with his brother Antonio in Daylesford, for which Francesco may have also kept accounts.

In 1859, Pietro and Giacomo Lucini built a home and opened the Roma Hotel along Spring Creek Road near their mine, which came to be called the Swiss Mountain Quartz Mining Company.[16] A few years later, they opened a macaroni factory in a building addition. Like many of the Italian speakers in the region, the Lucini brothers supported Italian republican leaders Giuseppe Mazzini and Giuseppe Garibaldi in the struggle for a free and united Italy. Giacomo Lucini proudly displayed his family's patriotic leanings in frescoes he painted on the walls and ceilings of the building—scenes of Intra, his tiny village nestled in forested mountains on the rim of Lake Maggiore, flags of Switzerland, France, Britain (Victoria) and Italy, and scenes from Verdi's opera, *Il Trovatore*.[17]

Giacomo Lucini's patriotic painted ceiling, 2016

If Francesco needed supplies or services not found in the villages, he could head for Daylesford, about two and a half miles from Hepburn. In 1864, Daylesford, the largest town in the area, had forty-five hotels and boarding houses, five breweries, eight churches and 265 dwellings occupied by miners.[18] Commerce centered on Vincent Street, where Alessandro Pozzi ran a bakery and his brother Stefano owned a wine shop and hotel.

Mining defined Daylesford's layout. Although most alluvial gold had already been gathered, riches still lay deep within the earth. Extinct volcanoes surrounding Daylesford made conditions ideal for tunnel mining. Thousand-year-old lava flows from the Wombat volcano had covered creeks containing rich gold deposits. Now by boring along underground creek beds, miners dug out the gold that had been buried for centuries. In 1864, a local news article described this change: "Its former name was Jim Crow, long known as a poor man's diggings . . . The first step to render it a large permanent field was made by a party of Italians, who drove tunnels into the hillside . . . tunneling soon became the feature of the place. Many of the hills are now completely honeycombed with mole-like passages."[19] This site, dubbed Italian Hill, became a maze of tunnels, some as long as two thousand feet. To bore through the hard rock, Swiss and Italian miners used stone working skills mastered in the Alps.

Daylesford, c.1873-1882

Cornish miners also brought their expertise to the area when the alluvial gold had all but disappeared and hard rock mining required heavy equipment. The Cornish Gold Mine Company worked Cornish Hill overlooking Wombat Flat. Like the Italian speakers, the Cornish miners found support with their compatriots.

Mines ran nearly around the clock. In 1864, the local newspaper noted that Daylesford was "literally studded, for nearly the whole of its circumference, with steam engines, engaged in drawing up to the surface the stores of precious stuff dug out hundreds of feet below....There are about a score such engines at this work day and night."[20] Miners found relief from their grueling labor by frequenting Daylesford's hotels and wine bars, which offered lively diversions— bands, dancing girls, wrestling matches and billiard competitions.[21] Attracted to the thrill of risky ventures, miners also bet on horses at a new racecourse south of town.

With thieves in the gold fields, sentries armed with shotguns, opium in the camps and rousing entertainment in the dance halls, the Daylesford-Hepburn region was anything but peaceful and calm. Immigrants from around the world mingled in the diggings and in town. A former resident recalled those bustling times: "Daylesford in the sixties was in the zenith of its fame. Gold was got freely. Back of Bedolla's Spring Creek Hotel diggers were making £100 per week...Saturday night was the late shopping time. The footpaths were so crowded that pedestrians walked on the roadway."[22]

Daylesford's main entertainment venue, the Royal Hotel and Music Hall, put on Penny Concerts and a band to delight dancers with polkas and quicksteps. The hotels competed for customers, offering counter lunches for one shilling with beer from Daylesford's breweries at three pence per pint. Some featured wrestling matches between Cornish miners, others ran billiard contests.[23]

After long hours of back-breaking labor deep in the earth scraping the soil for gold metal, miners craved entertainment in places like Traversi's Dancing Rooms. Antonio Ghidossi opined in a letter home that:

> Nearly all of the very many Swiss Italians who are now broke in
> Australia could have returned and made their little homes flourish.

In the early times they were all finding plenty of gold and, thinking it would never end, they used to pay a pound to get into a dance on Saturday nights and then they paid another ten or twenty to have a dancer for company for that evening, not including other expenses for drinks which were very costly at the time."[24]

Chinese miners, who scoured the adjacent alluvial fields, had been forced into separate settlements from the Europeans. They lived in a tent camp near Old Racecourse served by a jumble of provision stores, gold exchanges, restaurants, barber shops, opium shops, a hotel and at least one Chinese herbalist.[25] The settlement also included a Joss House, a place of worship whose English name derives from the Portuguese word "Deus," meaning God.

Chinese miners in the way to the diggings, c.1860-1871

The Chinese created garden plots near streams, growing vegetables to hawk at mining camps and nearby hamlets. Europeans flocked to the Chinese camp for diversion. Occasionally a traveling Chinese circus troop visited Hepburn to entertain miners with acrobatics and other amusements. An early Hepburn resident described the Chinese camp, recalling that "the younger miners were particularly fond of spending Sunday afternoons there. From all directions the Chinese journeyed to it to do their Sunday

68

shopping and to indulge their passion for gambling."[26]

Hatred of the Chinese ran high, with racial conflicts disrupting mining camps. In 1855, to reduce the influx of Chinese gold seekers, the Victorian Parliament passed the Chinese Immigration Act which levied a poll tax of £10 on each Chinese person arriving at a port in Victoria and limited the number of Chinese passengers on vessels to one for every ten tons. The tax was intended to pay for salaries of Protectors assigned to organize segregated Chinese camps and to keep those settlements clean, orderly and nonviolent. Ships carrying Chinese bypassed Victoria to avoid the law and landed instead at the port of Robe in South Australia, over two hundred miles from the gold fields. From there the Chinese had to tramp overland for several weeks, sometimes led astray by local guides who took their money, then abandoned them to lose their way.[27]

By 1859, about eight hundred of the nearly 3,400 diggers in the Daylesford region were Chinese.[28] A group of them camped in the Wombat Flat area where they engaged in fossicking, gleaning gold that others left behind. With fewer resources but greater patience, they often worked diggings that other miners had abandoned for easier pickings. These resourceful "Celestials," an 1862 *Mining Record* reported, with "thrifty almond eyes," would pick up discarded sluice boxes through which water had passed to separate gold from sand. Together they would spend days picking over the gold flakes left in the cracks. "It is remarkable how ready they are to turn the slightest waste

Chinese fossicker

of the precious metal to account. They seem to delight in infinitessimals. Europeans might with advantage take a few lessons from the Chinese, in thrift and perseverance."[29] Instead of constructing square or rectangular mining shafts, the Chinese built sturdier round shafts, perhaps in the belief that demons lurk in corners. Similarly, Joss House roofs curved up at the corners to deflect harmful spirits.

Finding the Chinese ways strange and distasteful, the Europeans feared that Chinese miners spread diseases. Reporting an outbreak of cholera and leprosy in the gold fields, a local newspaper denounced the Chinese for abandoning their sick companions, "flying away in hundreds, leaving their hapless doomed comrades to their fate."[30] These fearful reports were later debunked. The "cholera" turned out to be scurvy.

Tensions between the Chinese and Europeans over mining claims ran high. Chinese miners were frequently run off claims. In 1857, a newspaper reported on a riot in Golden Point, about thirty miles from Daylesford. A mob, crying "Down with the Chinese! Expel them from the gold fields!" chased away a group of Chinese miners after destroying their mining equipment. The Chinese raced for their camp, long pigtails dangling down their backs. The mob forced up to three hundred Chinese to leave the area.[31]

Francesco had many male friends, but he found few single Italian-speaking women for company. Only three Swiss-Italian women came to

Mining Scene Daylesford, c.1873-1882

Daylesford-Hepburn around the time Francesco arrived. In 1861, Daylesford had about three men for every woman,[32] but most of these women would not be considered suitable marriage partners for Francesco. In close-knit Vallemaggia, most marriages took place between couples born in the same village.[33] Some of Francesco's friends, like Stefano Pozzi, made a trip back to marry a girl from home. Others married Irish girls who at least shared their Catholic religion. Francesco remained single.

He had not sent a letter home for a long while. On July 23, 1861, Francesco finally wrote a brief note to Luigi.

> Most beloved father! To my great chagrin, imagining you would
> be anxiously waiting for my response, I have had to wait until now
> to answer your three letters of September 27th, November 25th,
> 1860 and March 26th, 1861. Not that the delay comes from some
> misfortune. Thank heavens I am still healthy and able, and my
> fervent desire is that you and all at home have stayed in
> good health.

Despite expressing concern that he had caused Luigi distress by not writing, Francesco put forward no excuses.

> Don't fear anything for us, dear father. With the help of heaven,
> hard work and goodwill, we will be able to return safe and sound to
> embrace you. One can overcome dangers with a good temperament,
> and misfortunes can happen anywhere and to anyone. The only
> thing is to be able to return home and to see you happy.

Although Francesco had not written, he had sent Luigi some money. He belittled this gesture with great deference to his father.

> It is not worth mentioning the little sum that I have sent you and
> you fill me with undeserved praise, because it is only what anyone
> would do, it is only the most basic duty. I am truly sorry that I
> could not send it before, and that I wasn't able to do more, and I
> long only for the moment that I can do better. I hope to God I never
> have to ask for help to come home, and when I can send you some
> money, it's entirely at your disposal for your well-being. Do not
> call it a good deed. It's my duty, but I regret not being able to do as
> much as I want.

Surprised to learn that Virgilio had left for California, Francesco expressed concern that Luigi would be left alone without support. Alessandro, about two years older than Virgilio, had completed training for elementary school teaching, but he too, wanted to emigrate.

> I am very content that Alessandro has succeeded well at the Scuola di Metodica, and I hope that he will be always interested in doing himself honor. When it is advisable for him to come here, to my way of thinking, I will not fail to give notice, but still it does not seem to be good to me that all the sons abandon their father when he most needs help and assistance.

Francesco could not let go of the dreams that brought him to Australia. He still hoped to strike it rich. He assured Luigi:

> I always work and always hope, but up to now I have not had very much luck. But I don't lack necessities, and the work is comfortable enough . . . Meanwhile, with the money I earn, I try the luck of the mines and I pray heaven that it will favor me so in some way I can prove to you my gratitude and my good wishes and fulfill however I can the duties of a son toward the dearest and best father.

Some miners did make quick fortunes in the mines. In 1858, a local newspaper announced that a Norwegian had arrived in the area alone and penniless. He befriended a fellow digger who gave him a share of his tunneling claim. "In the course of a few months a fortune of some three thousand pounds, sterling, has been realized. Home is now the object, and Norway will reap advantages from toil pursued in the gold fields of Australia."[34] Other miners took longer to gain fortunes. In 1862, the newspaper reported that an Italian named Le Franchi had mined gold worth twenty thousand pounds after "five years steady working at Daylesford."[35]

Reports of such finds gave Francesco reason to hope. Hadn't Fabrizio Crippa and the Lucini brothers found riches in the mines? Despite claiming to Luigi that he longed to return home, Francesco also yearned to win big. How much longer would he continue to gamble his earnings?

SEVEN

"I advise you to leave…"

October 18, 1861—Letter from Luigi in Peccia to Virgilio in California

Life for Luigi in Peccia waxed and waned to familiar rural rhythms and the ringing of church bells. According to seasonal demands, fields had to be worked, hay cut, chestnuts gathered and animals brought to market. Virgilio's last letter had arrived in Peccia while Luigi was away from home, occupied with bringing his cows from their winter grazing grounds to the bustling regional market in Locarno.

On October 18, 1861, Luigi sent Virgilio news of home and loved ones, but his letter was fraught with warnings.

> My worries continue for your dangers and pains. I am stressed as much as on the first day [you left]. It can't be otherwise because I am your father.
>
> My anxiety grows and it worries me that danger is so close when you are corking soda bottles; and if such danger can't be avoided nor prevented, this isn't the job for you. An accident can happen to you at any moment, and you would become a martyr, become blind or otherwise hurt yourself. So I advise you to leave. When harm is avoidable, take care not to fall into bad fortune.

Luigi had been ill for about a month with fever and dysentery, but now his health was back. At the age of forty-eight, he had begun adding children to his family with his second wife, Maria, whom he had married in 1852. He sent Virgilio accounts of the little ones, four-year-old Marino and toddler Albina: "Albina has been walking by herself for a month; Marino doesn't do anything but talk of you." He reported that eighteen-year-old Alessandro, eager to emigrate, patiently awaited news from Virgilio on costs and other conditions in California.

Luigi also described to Virgilio the harvest results, a report of each of his cows by name, including those he had sold at the market.

The harvest year was moderately abundant with the hay coming principally from the woods, from which we have taken 60 cartloads; potatoes and chestnuts (these we are harvesting now) but wheat is very expensive. In winter we let go Bullo, Stellino, Pometta, Raspino and Fratino as the cost of getting through the winter has never been this high. At home we have Becher, born late, Varozzino, born early in the season, and a little heifer born from Pometta on July 3rd. Bluscio fell on the Bolla Alp, so he was skinned at the end of August.

Locarno Market, unknown date

Agonizing doubts, entreaties, and anxieties sliced through Luigi's accounts of everyday life. How could he stay calm when two of his sons lived so far away and Alessandro planned to leave home as soon as one of his brothers gave the word? He concluded his letter with both encouragements and advice:

Dear son! I beg you keep in mind my suggestions. They are: if you regret being in that country, if health doesn't favor you, if you can't easily avoid dangers, or for any other reasons, if you don't like it, if you would rather not dwell on costs, [or if you feel obliged to] send me money when you can't afford to, write me at any time and I will take care of it; I would sell all that I possess rather than leave my dear sons to suffer far from me.

Luigi's reassuring words to bolster his own and Virgilio's spirits read like an incantation to ward off danger. He ended his letter with the admonitions: "Know how to pick friends, guard against any evil, and write to me often."

Cascade and Chapel, Vallemaggia

EIGHT

"Costs are high, but pay is very low…"

April 2, 1862—Letter from Alessandro and Angelo Mattei in New York to Peccia
May 11, 1862—Letter from Alessandro in San Francisco to Luigi in Peccia

Six months later, leaving Luigi to manage without his help, nineteen-year-old Alessandro emigrated from Peccia. From his brothers' letters, Alessandro saw that Virgilio's hopes still shone brightly, while Francesco, already seven years in Australia, had seen his dreams of quick riches and a speedy return to Peccia fade. He chose to follow Virgilio to California.

A villager named Angelo Mattei and another named Padovani kept Alessandro company from Ticino to New York, on through the Isthmus of Panama and up the Pacific Coast to San Francisco. Alessandro and Mattei wrote a joint letter to their families when they arrived in New York.

> Dear loved ones at home!!!
> We have arrived in New York. We have experienced an ocean voyage, and now we know the difference between traveling by land and by sea, and here is all of it: March 17th was the date we were scheduled to leave Havre. In fact, we left around one hour before midnight. We were taken to S. Antonio[1] in England, where we arrived the 18th, and from which we left the 19th. After leaving the seaport we immediately felt a squall shake us like a puppet. With some days rougher, others a little less, it continued for 5 or 6 days, after which we had some calm; at last then a little luck.

Alessandro described in detail the meals on the ship, such as they were.

> As for eating, we couldn't say we were really hungry, but we also did not eat very well. In the morning we had a cup of bitter coffee, salted butter, and a piece of hard and heavy black bread. We couldn't tell what it was made from. It was so tasty that the

bread from the first day still remained in the ship when we left it; The only good things were at mid-day: potatoes and meat. The portions were small, but we made sly in order to get another portion, or two or three more, according to what we could manage. In the early evening there was another cup of coffee and later tea that we didn't want to drink. Later on, we had small little white loaves of bread of a better quality, salted, uncooked fish, and vinegar of the worst quality.

These were our meals; but this isn't the worst, because I, Alessandro, was sick for 5 or 6 days. But the sickness wasn't severe, principally vomiting, and I couldn't take anything other than water. I felt very bad, and I couldn't stand on my feet from the rolling waves of the ship. Now that we are all very well, it is shameful to complain about it.

After suffering from seasickness for several days, Alessandro didn't want to grouse, but conditions in steerage, particularly over rough seas, caused more outspoken voyagers on similar journeys to complain: "At the entrance was a great barrel, and we wondered for what? We soon found out when everyone got seasick––they emptied the buckets into this barrel; near every bed was a bucket."[2] A practice on many voyages caused a different stench: "there, close to the hatchway, which of course was the entry into the steerage, stood three barrels, each of them half filled with kitchen refuse. These were standing directly under the rays of the sun…And there the foul stuff remained during the whole of our voyage…"[3]

Arriving in New York City the evening of March 30, Alessandro and his companions disembarked the next day to accompany fellow travelers from Genoa to a hotel run by Italians. Exhausted, Alessandro planned to rest a single night, then take off for Panama the following day, but even with steamships leaving New York City three times a month for Aspinwall, passenger demand far exceeded availability. The letter continued:

Ma che? Instead of being able to travel to California with the steamship that left yesterday, since the ship was already totally full, we had to stay until the 11th. As today was the first day that tickets for the 11th departure were being sold, we went to the shipping office; there was a huge crowd. With help from the hotel owner we were able to find the place where they distributed the tickets. If we had arrived only 5 minutes later, we would not have tickets now. There were enough people who couldn't get tickets left to fill up another ship, and these people have to remain here until the next departure on the 21st.

Registering Immigrants, Castle Garden, New York City, 1866

Like Virgilio, Alessandro was forced to wait ten days in New York City for the next departure for Panama. Because the Civil War still raged on, transport of Union soldiers took priority on steamships. What did Alessandro, who had only known life in a small village, think of the big metropolis? Like his brother, he did not write home of his experiences during his sojourn there, perhaps because they did not contribute to his goal of reaching San Francisco.

Finally Alessandro took off on Pacific Mail Steamship Company's wooden paddle steamer, the *Golden Age*.[4] First class passengers could enjoy a rich and varied fare: pearl barley soup, salt cod with egg sauce, mutton and capers, corned beef, corned pork, ham, beef ala mode, ox heart ala Jardiniere,

Golden Age **Bill of Fare,**
July 26, 1863

pig's head Milanese, baked mutton pies, mutton harricot, curried rice, roast beef, roast pork or roast mutton, a variety of vegetables, and for desserts, custard pudding, fruit pies, oranges, almonds, figs, crackers and cheese, coffee and teas.[5] Alessandro and his companions lived on the few provisions they had gathered together in New York.

Alessandro arrived in San Francisco on May 5, 1962, making the journey from Panama to San Francisco in fourteen days and six hours.[6] He had enjoyed much smoother waters than on his Atlantic voyage, but he had been cramped on the *Golden Age*.[7]

From New York, Alessandro had written to Virgilio that he was coming. Virgilio was too busy working to greet Alessandro as he debarked on steamer day, but Alessandro took the Contra Costa ferry across the Bay to Oakland. He found Virgilio "healthy and well-disposed and nearly bigger than me." Two years younger than Alessandro, Virgilio had grown taller since leaving Peccia.

Virgilio helped his brother find a job with Ghirardelli's company, not in Oakland, but in San Francisco. Alessandro started the very next morning. He wrote to Luigi on May 11, 1862, only a week after he arrived.

> My work is to make sacks of paper for coffee. Making the packages is easy work, but it keeps going continuously and it's necessary to do it fast and well. Pay is 15 dollars a month. Costs are high, but pay is very low, so I must have patience for a while.

Alessandro worked with a crew of thirteen, including four men from Ticino, two Frenchmen, a Spaniard, and the rest from Genoa. Coincidentally, one of the Swiss Italians had gone to school with Francesco back in Ticino. Alessandro wrote, "The Spaniard is the only one who knows how to make the chocolate, the other two do the work that I do, one brews the coffee, others make liquor, the others go with carts to sell and transport the merchandise and similar work."

Pacific Mail Steamship Company's Line, c.1865

Describing to Luigi the relative costs in California, Alessandro marveled at the low cost of clothing: "Here a dollar is valued at less than one of our francs. New shoes and clothes can be bought in three weeks or almost a month, but I wish to spend as little as I can. I want to hold costs down in order to pay off my debts quickly." Alessandro also wrote that Virgilio planned to resolve his debt to Luigi within the next six months.

Alessandro closed his letter with an apology. "[I] had to write very hurriedly because I didn't have time. Some books that I bought in New York are very expensive, but surely they will serve me well." If Alessandro's hours at Ghirardelli's were anything like Virgilio's, he would have little time to read his costly new books or even to explore the area. Young and healthy, he had to work as much as he could to pay back the money he borrowed for his trip to California.

NINE

"I was born on a mad planet…"

September 10, 1862—Letter from Carlo Patocchi in Placerville to Luigi in Peccia

In mid-September 1862, Luigi received a letter from his cousin Carlo Patocchi, who had been in California since the early 1850s, working as a butcher in the Sierra foothills about 125 miles from San Francisco.[1] Patocchi wrote to Luigi from Placerville, a town originally called Old Dry Diggings, then Hangtown, in the heart of California's Mother Lode region. Prompted to write to Luigi after receiving a letter from Alessandro, Patocchi expressed surprise to Luigi that Virgilio and Alessandro had arrived in the state.

Luigi could find some comfort knowing that Alessandro had made contact with a family member, but Patocchi's litany of struggles, which he compared to Napoleon's devastating defeat in the winter of 1812, must have given Luigi pause. Patocchi's relentless description of his losses, one atop another, could easily provoke Luigi's anxieties that Virgilio and Alessandro might also confront such difficulties.

> By April 1855, I had made about $4400 dollars. Then I lost five
> months to an illness that cost me $2000 dollars. Then the Bank of
> Adam Express failed and I was left without a penny.[2] California
> 1856: a fire cost me a loss of $600. On June 17, 1857, I lost my
> house complete with all the furniture and provisions in a fire.
> $2000. It's California. On January 3, 1860, I lost out on a loan to
> an American friend. I lost the sum of $1500. California! After I
> sold the slaughterhouse I went to the other shop that I still had in
> Marysville. I was like Napoleon in Russia. $1100. California! Then
> this past spring I had an illness for three months. I lost about $600.
> California! And then I couldn't count on the brother who owes me
> money. This is also California.

Patocchi's long string of bad fortune was topped by California's 1855 bank crash.[3] California banking was scarcely regulated at the time. Express companies offering freight services between New York and California branched into banking-related activities, including buying and selling gold dust, bullion and coin. When the banking firm of Page, Bacon & Company collapsed in St. Louis, a run on its San Francisco branch spread to other banks, causing the crash.

William Tecumseh Sherman, who ran the San Francisco branch of Page, Bacon & Company, watched the panic begin when a mail steamer pulled up to the Long Wharf in North Beach on February 17, 1855.[4] A passenger couldn't wait to disembark before shouting the news that Page & Bacon had failed.[5] Every bank in San Francisco closed its doors as investors raced to withdraw funds. Out of the fiasco, only Wells Fargo survived to cover its deposits. Carlo Patocchi, among thousands of miners who had invested in "certificates of deposit," lost everything.

Adding to his woes, Patocchi broke both his legs when his horse kicked him in the thighs. Unable to work for three months, his hopes vanished. Then with a turn of fortune, his spirit revived, and he began to make money again. Along with itemizing his struggles, Patocchi made sure Luigi knew that he was aware of the need to pay off his loan from the village council. Blaming his dead parents, he asserted that his reputation had not been tarnished despite still owing the money.

> That is California. Still California is good for me. I have another
> store. With the five languages I speak, Spanish, German, English,
> a little Chinese, I don't have to worry. A good reputation, better
> than that of my parents who have left me, even though I owe the
> Commune two or three hundred dollars, this is my parents' fault.
> I did not send them the funds, but I haven't lost my reputation…

In Marysville, gateway to the gold fields, Patocchi's butcher shop stood to prosper. Riverboats from San Francisco and Sacramento stopped at Marysville's port to let out prospectors making their way to the mines. As the supply hub for northern Sierra Nevada mining camps, Marysville had grown to over ten thousand people, becoming one of the largest cities in the state. Over ten million dollars in gold was shipped from Marysville during the height of the California Gold Rush.[6] Despite ups and downs, Patocchi had taken risks that were paying off.

Panorama View of Marysville, 1856

Patocchi learned from Alessandro that his mother had died. As he could not oversee his inheritance from half-way around the world, particularly given the unreliable postal service, he gave Luigi the job of overseeing the estate. Judge Luigi was particularly suited for the task, but Patocchi did not ask Luigi, he ordered.

> You will be the agent of my affairs regarding my house. Conduct these affairs as if I were there. I give them my half of the house. See how the rest of it goes and see if there is something that remains for me. If there is any dispute, I would let it go for the moment and let me know how to proceed. I no longer have any intention of coming back there.

Anticipating family squabbles, Patocchi provided Luigi with detailed instructions. He seemed confident that Luigi would follow them to the letter.

> Keep an eye on things. First the inventory, the will that my father made. Did he leave everything to my mother when he died? I didn't know anything about it. What about all this cheating and

entanglements? One side has always cheated the other. Who knows how it's been managed!

Go see how it is for me and then send me a summary of all debits and credits, how much of the wealth remains. There ought not to remain any household stuff such as furnishings. The silver spoons with the name Tortoni are mine. I give you them to hold for me until you have finished the inventory of all the various silver objects. See if things remain or if they have gone to hell with the rest of the business. I was born on a mad planet.

Patocchi had received no news from home for years, then suddenly he received five letters that arrived all at once, including one Virgilio had brought with him from Ticino and the one recently sent by Alessandro. A couple of the letters were two years old when they arrived. At the time, with mail delivery slow and unreliable, it took from about forty to sixty days for a letter to travel between Ticino and California.[7]

Path of letter from San Francisco to Maggia.

Sent in September 1861 from San Francisco overland by Pony Express via St. Joseph to New York to Queenston by Cunard to Locarno , October 31, 1861.

From 1860 on, the U.S. Postmaster directed all transcontinental mail to be sent overland, but the Civil War and skirmishes with Native Americans at times disrupted delivery. In a letter from San Francisco, a young man who had headed West in the California Gold Rush wrote to his mother that he understood why he hadn't received mail from her in a very long time. Thousands of letters had been delayed en route because the Overland Mail Company claimed that Indians had stolen their horses.[8]

Unable to depend on mail delivery, immigrants relied on word of mouth and hand-delivered reports for news of home. Travelers to and from Ticino often carried letters and also passed on rumors, inadvertently or purposefully, as family members grasped for clues and hints about how their loved ones were faring. Despite a decade abroad with no intentions of returning to Peccia, Patocchi still valued his reputation among villagers back home. He was pleased that Virgilio and Alessandro had come to California so they could witness and report back on his situation.

Path of letter from Cevio-Locarno to the Jim Crow gold fields.

Sent in February 1860 from Locarno via Southampton to Alexandria, overland by caravan route to Suez, by Peninsular & Oriental Line via Port Louis, Mauritius to King George's Sound-Adelaide-Melbourne; Stamped Melbourne, April 13 and by stagecoach Cobb & Co. from Melbourne to Jim Crow gold fields.

Patocchi took comfort knowing that his shop in Placerville, a town of about twenty-five hundred people, was worth more than his ancestral home in Ticino. His fellow immigrants also brought him business. "With all the friends and associates living in California, although I have had losses, I always have hope of making a comeback."Five months after writing to Luigi, Patocchi, at age thirty-eight, put down even deeper roots in California. He married Elisa Orrilli, a Frenchwoman of his same age, in El Dorado. For better or worse, another of Luigi's family members was staking out his future in the state of California.

View of D Street, Marysville, *Hutchings Illustrated Magazine,* **February 1859**

TEN

"I came here with all good intentions to do well…"

May 13, 1863—Letter from Alessandro in San Jose to Luigi in Peccia

Just a few months after arriving in California, Alessandro had become severely ill with a "great internal inflammation" that weakened him so much he couldn't work. Luigi, apprised of Alessandro's illness, had sent a letter aiming to bolster his son's spirits. From San Jose, a town about fifty miles south of San Francisco, Alessandro sent Luigi an update on his slow recovery, urging him not to worry:

> Dearest father, when I read your words on the paper, it seemed
> that I heard them from your own mouth. Along with courage, they
> seemed to give me strength and energy: they left me with one
> sure emotion. Seeing the worries and troubles I am causing you, I
> couldn't hold back the tears.
>
> Father, I console you that I am better, that God has listened to your
> prayers; since January 18th, God has already helped me with his
> grace; on this day the Yocco Brothers from Ossola, who have a
> well-known shop, let me enter their house, and offered me what
> they owned with an open heart and for nothing.

Fortune had favored Alessandro when he found the Yocco brothers, emigrants from Domo d'Ossola, an Italian town very close to the Ticino border. Gioachino Yocco had come to the California mines in 1849, partnering with Frenchman Louis Pellier. Finding little gold, the two men moved to San Jose, purchased property near Market Street and opened a nursery called City Gardens where they raised apricot, pear and peach trees for the expanding agricultural community.

In 1855, Yocco split with Pellier to open a grocery store with his brother Clementi.[1] Pellier continued City Gardens Nursery, planting prune trees brought by his brother Pierre from their homeland in southwestern France.[2] These trees produced the Prune d'Ente, a sweet, juicy plum known as the "Black Gold of the Aquitaine."[3] The fruit could be coated in lye, dried in the sun, then shipped to distant markets. Popularity of Pellier's imported prune trees boosted the enormous growth of Santa Clara Valley's fruit industry.[4] The valley became renowned as the Valley of Heart's Delight.

Prune Orchard and Vineyard, c.1890-1910

The Yocco brothers could afford to take in Alessandro without charge. Their well-situated grocery store in San Jose's downtown commercial district did a good business. Yet despite finding a safe place to rest and recover, Alessandro could not afford a doctor. With medical training scarce, only a few physicians practiced in San Jose. Medications typically prescribed by doctors included laudanum and morphine, lead acetate, calomel tablets or mercurous chloride, and blue mass pills, which also contained mercury. These toxic pills were used to treat a wide range of illnesses from tuberculosis to constipation, parasites to labor pains, syphilis to depression.[5]

At the time, Louis Pasteur was conducting experiments that led to his germ theory, but most physicians believed that disease was caused by agitation in nervous or vascular systems. Bloodletting, purgatives, emetics and

Chapter Ten

Ad for Popular Remedy

poultices were thought to relieve the body of agitation and bring it to a restful state.[6] Alternatively, homeopathic physicians thought that symptoms were the body's attempt to cure itself. These doctors prescribed small doses of substances that resembled the disease in question.

Lacking money for any of these treatments, Alessandro came under the informal care of an Italian woman, a well-known healer. Virgilio assured Luigi that this woman had been practicing medicine for a long time. She treated Alessandro with herbal folk remedies, including sarsaparilla, a South American woody vine plant whose roots have been used for centuries to reduce inflammation and detoxify the blood. Sarsaparilla also flavored a popular nineteenth-century carbonated drink similar to root beer. Without regulation, quack patent medicines thought to contain sarsaparilla were sometimes concocted from straw.[7] Alessandro had been taking extract of sarsaparilla several times a day for five months. His bleeding had stopped, but he still was not well.

Alessandro's debt worries only prolonged his illness. He yearned to recover quickly so he could pay back the money he owed his father.

> My main regret has always been that I have not been able to send anything, not at first, not now, not even the interest on my debts. And I have also prevented Virgilio from being able to send you the rest of his debt. I don't know how much you need! You haven't mentioned it, dearest father, since I see that you are afraid to cause me displeasure; but I can imagine it. I came here with all good intentions to do well, fortune was not favorable, have patience; I endure all in peace, only it is not right to have others suffer because of me.
>
> If things proceed as they would seem to be going now, in three or four months Virgilio will be able to send a little money; he is well, and more capable than I am. He knows English, French and Spanish. I know almost nothing of them, since I have been almost always shut up in the house.

Too weak to get around, Alessandro had to postpone his dreams of fortune. He had travelled far but now could do little. Recovery had to be his first priority. Without good health, he could not begin to earn the money he needed to pay off the debts he incurred for his journey to California.

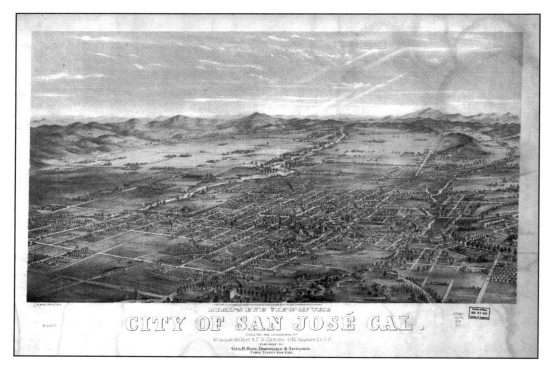

View of San Jose, 1869

ELEVEN

"I have to tell you only of misery…"

October 15, 1863—Letter from Virgilio in San Jose to Luigi in Peccia
November 22, 1864—Letter from Virgilio in San Jose to Luigi in Peccia

By mid-October 1863, Virgilio hadn't heard from Luigi for about six months. He had been worried about brother Alessandro's health. Tired of waiting for a letter, Virgilio finally broke down and wrote to Luigi, updating him on Alessandro's illness.

> Up to now Alessandro isn't completely recovered yet but he is in a
> light convalescence. When I wrote you the last time he was here in
> San Jose in a house of Italians. Now it's been around 15 days since
> he has gone to where our countrymen Bagnovini and Delponte
> live, where he is staying until he recovers.[1]

Alessandro's anxiety over covering his expenses and paying back his debt caused him to work when he should have been resting.

> I believe that he could have recovered much earlier, but when he
> was under the cure of some Italian woman, he always had some
> little thing to do. Once he worked for around two months and
> eventually sold beans in the city for two and a half months; the
> work wasn't hard and he didn't do it badly, but nevertheless it took
> him away from his recovery. We were certain that he became a
> little better the times he stayed resting. When he was nearly cured,
> he tried to stay away from all work so that he could be rid of
> the illness.

Virgilio had been working as a drayer, picking up goods that had come from San Francisco by steamer to the port of Alviso, then transporting them by horse and cart about ten miles to San Jose. Alviso, on the south-eastern shore of San Francisco Bay, served the Santa Clara Valley as a busy harbor and transportation hub. It took Virgilio about two hours to drive his cart from San Jose to Alviso on the Turnpike Road. The toll reduced his profits, as he was charged a dollar for a loaded wagon drawn by two horses and fifty cents for an empty cart. On the long drive, Virgilio had plenty of time to gaze over the vast stretches of open space, cultivated fields, rows of orchards and fertile gardens that blanketed the Santa Clara Valley.

A growing metropolis, San Jose had about three thousand residents in 1860.[2] A local historian extolled the San Jose of 1862 with inflated admiration:

> "its streets are wide, its fountains of pure water refreshing, and its orchards, gardens and vineyards render it fit to be the residence of gods . . . The streets presented a brisk business appearance; produce of every kind came pouring in from the valley, the teams conveying it blocking up the main thoroughfares by their number."[3]

SAN JOSÉ,
SANTA CLARA COUNTY, CALIFORNIA.
December 1859 *Hutchings' Illustrated California Magazine*

Virgilio joined throngs of drayers transporting the valley's bounty to San Jose's commercial center. But progress was changing the economy quickly, and Virgilio had to stay alert to survive. A train route from San Francisco had crossed the Santa Clara County line and soon would reach San Jose. Prior to the railroad, travelers from San Francisco to San Jose took a stagecoach or steamer from San Francisco to Alviso, then a coach to San Jose.[4] When the San Francisco & San Jose Railroad reached San Jose in 1864, steamship traffic to Alviso dwindled, along with the need for Virgilio and other drayers to haul products from Alviso's port. Virgilio informed Luigi of rapid changes:

> A railroad track goes from here to San Francisco; two months ago, the trains started to run the route, which takes them an hour. Here in California there are 5 or 6 railroad tracks finished or almost finished. The work advances rapidly so that within the space of 4 or 5 years, the railroads will connect with New York.

The transcontinental railroad under construction promised to link East Coast to West, upending current modes of transport. To keep up with changing times, Virgilio had started a truck garden on a small plot of land, peddling his vegetables from place to place from his cart. Congress had just passed the Internal Revenue Act in 1862 to help defray the costs of the Civil War, so Virgilio had to pay for licenses and taxes.[5] Virgilio's small venture had little success. Although he was making almost twice what his salary had been at Ghirardelli's soda factory, he did not find it profitable enough.

He had bigger dreams. He wanted to open a shop, although rapid changes made planning difficult. He wrote to Luigi that "Business is good, but the expenses are huge and the taxes of the city government are out of proportion; and since these are new, developing areas, prospects for a shop change quickly. Accordingly, there are those who make great fortunes and others who lose them."

Amidst these economic ups and downs, Virgilio suffered a profound and irreparable loss. Alessandro was only just twenty years old when he died, sometime in 1864. His stay in California lasted a little over two years. The cause of his death is unknown. He likely died and was buried in San Francisco, where Virgilio traveled to make funeral arrangements, although the location of his gravesite is also unknown.

Virgilio carried on without his brother as best he could. He had been selling vegetables for little profit, so he worked for a while at day jobs, then began working for a German, again in a soda factory. He was planning to quit and return to work for Ghirardelli's company when he also became sick. He described his illness to Luigi as "a strong fever, Malignant or Cerebral."

Fevers, a common cause of death in the nineteenth century, confounded medical experts. A cerebral fever was thought to be a brain inflammation, such as meningitis or encephalitis, whereas a malignant fever referred to typhus.[6] It's not surprising that Virgilio attributed his illness to two such diverse conditions when so few guidelines existed for distinguishing between fevers.

Prominent physician Dr. Alfred Hudson maintained that fevers were caused by poisons in the blood, each type of fever resulting from a different poison. Physicians treated fever patients like Virgilio with a toxic regimen of mercury pills and bloodletting, performed by placing glass leech cups on the skin to draw blood by suction, as Dr. Hudson described in one day's observations of a fever patient:

> Ninth day. The cupping gave immediate relief; cough and
> headache are much less severe, but he was wakeful and restless
> during the night; his face is flushed and hot; tongue dry and
> furred; pulse 98, with more power; three copious evacuations from
> the bowels. Ordered to have the head shaved and to be cupped
> to four ounces from the temples; to have two grains and a half
> of mercury with chalk thrice a day, and a saline draught with
> camphor mixture every six hours.[7]

It's a wonder that any fever patients survived the treatments.

Poor immigrants like Virgilio and Alessandro often became ill from unhealthy working and living conditions. The year of Alessandro's death and Virgilio's illness, the Italian Consul in San Francisco wrote to the Italian Ministry of Foreign Affairs describing the toll illness took on immigrants.

> Once here, far from finding the promised land, they had to take
> on arduous, poorly paid, and unsteady work; but, being too late
> to back out, they of necessity resigned themselves to their fate...A
> few for whom fortune had been less grim prepared to return to
> Italy to enjoy the fruits of their labors, only to contract diseases
> which robbed them of their savings and their health, medical care-
> being very poor in these inhospitable places.[8]

In 1849, San Francisco's Swiss immigrants formed *La Società Svizzera di Mutua Beneficienza* (the Swiss Benevolent Society of California) to help find employment, to offer assistance during illness and to provide burials for deceased members.[9] Of the organization's five hundred members in 1869, 315 came from Ticino.[10]

Such organizations provided essential services. In 1862, the Swiss Benevolent Society opened the small Italian and Swiss Hospital at the corner of Folsom and Third Street. Dr. Antonio Rottanzi became the physician in charge. Virgilio's early investment in Dr. Rottanzi's health insurance paid off. Whatever the treatment—leech cups, mercury pills, sarsaparilla or the natural tincture of time—Virgilio recovered from his illness. Thanks to health insurance purchased soon after he arrived, Virgilio had the benefit of a physician's care, and better yet, a physician from Ticino whom he trusted. Virgilio assured Luigi, "I was treated well enough at the hospital, and Dr. Rottanzi's good regimen has made all go all right, I promise you."

After passing on news of fellow immigrants and sending their good wishes, Virgilio apprised Luigi of his work and finances:

> Here in general everyone helps one another . . . but just like
> everywhere else, there's no lack of slackers. Once again, as at first,
> I have my cart from which I sell vegetables. I bought it, and as for
> loans, I owe still about 70 dollars to Bagnovini and 45 to Mattei. I
> invested the money to buy the wagon and the trappings, etc.

Due to his illness, Virgilio had worked only nine months in the past year. Concerned about his debt to Luigi, he mentioned that he had sent some money about a year ago and reaffirmed his commitment to pay off the complete amount. Virgilio would never get back the money he had lent to Alessandro, nor expenses for Alessandro's funeral. Virgilio hoped that Luigi did not need him to repay the loan now, but promised to be "untiring with my little help" should Luigi or Francesco need it.

Virgilio knew that selling vegetables would not make him wealthy. Impatient to get ahead, despite just recently going into debt for a vegetable cart, trappings, and horses, Virgilio bought into in a dairy with a fellow immigrant from Peccia. He wrote to Luigi, "I have agreed to partner with

Bagnovini to put together a dairy to sell milk. The business looks good and seems to me one of the best ways to get rich so I can return to embrace you…This dairy is the same that Bagnovini has had with the locksmith from Bignasco [Delponte] but I don't know if he is still in the company …"

Virgilio had made a casual partnership with Bagnovini, common among newly arrived immigrants lacking the knowledge and funds to formalize transactions. On the surface, the investment seemed safe enough. Virgilio and Bagnovini knew each other from home. Shared origins, common friends and distant familial relations had led Virgilio to make a deal without knowing all the details. Although he speculated that Bagnovini had partnered with Delponte in this dairy, Virgilio did not bother to identify all the partners prior to making the agreement. Both Bagnovini and Delponte had proven helpful with Alessandro, taking him in when he was ill and could not work. Virgilio had no reason to distrust them.

With this dairy, Virgilio hoped he had found the path to success. He was a hard worker. An onerous schedule requiring him to start in the early hours before sunrise did not discourage him. "My work every morning will be to come from about four hours away from here at two hours after midnight to sell the milk in this city." This dairy, a four-hour journey from San Jose, was not well-situated to sell milk. Raw milk must be kept cool or it goes bad quickly. With refrigeration unavailable, dairies producing milk operated near cities and towns. Located far from San Jose, Virgilio's dairy was better suited to produce cheese and butter. Its distance from the city made it unsuitable for selling milk.

Virgilio had suffered a series of heavy setbacks: Alessandro's death, a severe illness and worrisome debts. He reported to Luigi, "Unfortunately today at the end of the day I have only to tell you of misery." Yet he threw himself into his new venture, optimistic that the dairy could bring him fortune. "As God wishes! I haven't lost courage and hope."

TWELVE

"How many years have passed…?"

December 22, 1866—Letter from Francesco in Hepburn to Luigi in Peccia

Near the end of 1866, after more than a decade in Australia, Francesco seemed lonely and deflated, feelings made worse by holiday festivities. He wrote a very brief letter to Luigi in the days just before Christmas.

> Writing at this moment, in the last days of a poor year, the thought comes to mind: how are you, dear father and all those you love? And another: how many years have passed since we have been separated? . . . I yearn to break through the long block of time that has separated us.

Although he expressed a strong desire to reunite with Luigi, Francesco claimed that he could not return home yet due to "endless negotiations that have gone nowhere" with Borsa and Crippa concerning the dissolution of their partnership in the butcher shop. As the partners' accountant, Francesco had a handle on the company's business, which reached far beyond the Daylesford-Hepburn region.

From tiny Spring Creek, Francesco's clients championed their products to the wider world. The butchers presented their Italian sausages at the 1866-67 Intercolonial Exhibition held in the heart of Melbourne. This enormous exhibition displayed products from colonies throughout Australasia, including Tasmania and New Zealand, as well as French New Caledonia and Dutch Batavia. The exhibits displayed every imaginable regional product, from thick ewe's fleece to furry opossum rugs, from manure made from night soil to sturdy coconut husk doormats woven by prisoners at the Pentridge Penal Establishment.[1]

The Borsa and Crippa entry of twelve Italian sausages won honorable mention in the category of Meat, Fish and Fowl. Borsa went on to enter his sausages, along with Zampone di Milano (stuffed pig's feet), in the 1875 Victorian Intercolonial Exhibition.[2] Parma Red, the wine Crippa produced in his cellar, later received global acclaim, winning a bronze medal at the London International Exhibition of 1873 and an award at the 1876 Centennial Exhibition in Philadelphia, the first official world's fair.[3]

It took nearly a year after Francesco's letter to Luigi for the butcher shop partnership to come to a close. Francesco assumed responsibility for managing the dissolution. He placed a notice in the 1867 *Victoria Gazette* announcing that the Borsa and Crippa partnership had dissolved, and "all debts due to the said late firm will be received by Francis Rotanzi, who has the authority to give receipts accordingly."[4] Soon this butcher shop business would no longer provide Francesco with an excuse for staying in Australia.

Francesco's education suited him well as a secretary, an accountant and a leader in his community. Many of his fellow immigrants had been small-scale farmers and laborers in Ticino. They knew how to chisel stone, milk cows and grow crops like grapes and barley. Government and parish schools provided education, but many peasants needed to take their children from school to help with farm work.[5] In Australia, these illiterate peasants relied on their educated compatriots like Francesco to read to them letters from loved ones back home and to decipher the mysteries of this foreign land.

Francesco took a leading role in several community organizations, volunteering as secretary for the Swiss and Italian Association. This group sponsored the Hepburn Springs Italian Library, located at Bedolla's Spring Creek Hotel, later named the Savoia Hotel for the royal family of a unified Italy. Michele Bedolla, hotel owner and storekeeper, offered up space for this reading room so that fellow Italian-speaking immigrants might borrow and read books and newspapers sent from Switzerland and Italy.

In the library, Francesco and other educated and literate members of the community could find more than two hundred books and newspapers, in both French and Italian, from Rome, Ticino, Geneva and other far-off places.[6] Francesco's friends included Dr. Severino Guscetti, a former member of the Swiss Parliament and a liberal reformer, who had helped develop a compulsory education system. He was author of a history of Switzerland

and a book of grammar that was adopted in schools. He had also been president of *La Società degli amici dell'educazione del popolo*, the organization of educators to which Luigi belonged. Political tensions between liberals and conservative Catholics, including disputes over aid to refugees from the Italian unification struggle, had forced Dr. Guscetti to quit his position in government and emigrate with his family to Australia.[7]

Members Swiss and Italian Association

Reading materials from abroad brought much longed-for news. In the library, Francesco and his neighbors pored over the *Gazzetta Ticinese* for reports of happenings at home. They followed Giuseppe Garibaldi's every step, his trip to London, his victory with Italian forces against Austria, his march on Rome. They learned that the flag of Ticino's parliament would be draped in mourning for the death of U.S. President Abraham Lincoln.[8] They searched for news of California that might impact their many friends and relatives who had immigrated there. In 1874, they would read that a revision to the Swiss Constitution attempted to resolve the struggle between church and state. Births, deaths and marriages would be recorded by the state, not the church. The Jesuit order, which had fought for control of education and meddled in affairs of state in the name of papal infallibility, was banned from Switzerland.[9]

In 1865, a Melbourne news article remarked that the Swiss and Italian Association in Daylesford, with the largest Italian population in the gold-fields, "evidences the intelligence of the countrymen of the illustrious Garibaldi who have permanently settled at Hepburn."[10] Several of Francesco's friends had served with Garibaldi, including one of the Borsa brothers who had fought with the general in South America. Some veteran miners proudly wore their Garibaldi red shirts in the mines.[11] Hoping that their hero's brilliance would shine on their prospects, Swiss and Italian miners named the Garibaldi Gold Mining Company in honor of their hero.

Republican fervor and liberal ideas roused by the Italian unification movement continued to influence Daylesford-Hepburn's Italian-speaking community as its members pursued democratic social causes. In 1866, a committee in Melbourne collected funds for war-wounded soldiers who had fought for Italy's independence. Francesco contributed, along with many other Swiss Italians. He joined Dr. Guscetti, the Lucini brothers and other like-minded liberals to put into practice in their community the democratic values they embraced for a united Italy.

Mining operations were destroying many of the numerous springs in the Daylesford and Hepburn Springs area, clogging creeks and streams, stripping hills of vegetation, drilling tunnels into hillsides and leaving debris to mar the land.[12] Once the easy alluvial gold had run out, miners had taken up sluicing, flowing streams of water over soil to find and extract the gleaming metal. This type of mining required massive amounts of water to wash gold from the earth, along with powering steam engines and other mining equipment. As Victoria lacked sufficient surface water, miners devised ways to catch and store rainwater, building dams from which they formed channels called "water races" that ran sideways down hillsides, bringing water to their claims by gravity.

Winter rains helped provide water, but dry summers could force miners to stop until a change in climate made more water available. The Melbourne *Age* complained in June 1865:

> The want of water still continues to be felt on many of the gold-
> fields, and fears are beginning to be entertained that the winter
> will pass without the want being supplied. We learn that at
> Daylesford, out of twenty-seven races, each of them above three
> miles in length, only one or two are supplying as much as a sluice-
> head of water.[13]

Yet construction continued, and by 1868, a network of water races nearly 2,500 miles long traversed the hills of Victoria.[14]

In a process called puddling, miners broke up clay to find the gold within. Horses, and later steam engines, drove sharp metal disks called harrows through a mixture of clay and gravel in a circular trench to loosen the soil, which was then panned or put through a cradle. Miners removed dirt down to bedrock, stripping tons of earth away from the hillsides and devastating the landscape. The resulting sludge blanketed the ground and clogged rivers and streams. Writer and digger William Howitt decried the environmental effects of mining:

> We have begun to destroy the beauty of this creek. It will no longer run clear between its banks, covered with wattles and tea-trees, and amongst its shallow parts overgrown with foreign-looking shrubs, flags, and cypress-grass. A little while, and its whole course will exhibit nothing but nakedness, and heaps of gravel and mud. We diggers are horribly destructive of the picturesque.[15]

Deserted Diggings at Spring Creek, 1859

Thanks to the area's extinct volcanoes, over seventy springs in the area provided waters containing health-giving minerals absorbed from the volcanic rock. Francesco and other Italian-speaking residents, familiar with the healing properties of Europe's renowned spas and mineral springs, saw that mining was destroying the waters. Meeting in the reading room at Bedolla's hotel in 1864, the group gathered together to see about preserving the area's remaining springs.

There Francesco recorded the first meeting minutes of the Committee Established for the Mineral Springs of Hepburn, organized to petition the government to assess the waters' properties in order to create a mineral springs reserve. The Committee consisted of nine members, including Fabrizio Crippa, one of the Lucini brothers, Michele Bedolla, Vincenzo Perini and Francesco's good friend Severino Guscetti.[16]

Francesco served as honorary secretary. He devoted much of his time and energy to saving the springs. After eleven years in Australia, he had mastered English well enough to write letters and petitions to the colonial government requesting that the waters be assessed by chemists, doctors and other experts. The efforts paid off. Tests found that the spring waters had great medicinal value. The *Daylesford Advocate* reported, "If the waters of the Hepburn Mineral Spring possess anything like the healing virtues for which the different speakers give them credit . . . it was no vain boast which said Daylesford might yet become the most celebrated town in the colony."

In 1865, the committee's continued efforts finally brought about the first mineral springs reserve in Victoria. A little over an acre for the mineral springs was protected, which increased in the early 1900s to an area of thirty hectares, about seventy-four acres.[17] By 1869, use of the springs had grown popular. The *Daylesford Mercury* exuded enthusiasm:

> We are almost afraid to say how much of the invigorating and
> sparkling nectar from the bosom of mother earth inveterate spring
> water drinkers will imbibe at a single visit, but twelve tumblers
> is not an unknown quantity. The spring is now highly charged
> with carbonic acid, and issues freely from the pipe inserted by the
> committee last year.[18]

Today, thanks to Francesco and his fellow committee members, the Daylesford and Hepburn Springs region is known as Spa Country, drawing thousands of visitors from nearby Melbourne and beyond who come to enjoy the mineral springs' curative properties.

Francesco also joined civic and social organizations that extended beyond his Italian-speaking community. With his friends Stefano Pozzi and Albino Paganetti, Francesco became a member of the Freemasons and the Odd Fellows. Both organizations had Italian-speaking members, but many more members came from the broader Anglo community. Francesco did more than join. He served as financial secretary for the Hepburn Odd Fellows Lodge and became Worshipful Master, the highest office, in the Mt. Franklin Freemasons Lodge of Hiram.[19] In this top leadership role, he directed the lodge activities, kept order, led the rituals and decided which charities the lodge would support. With the mining district's unique needs in mind, Francesco's lodge scheduled meetings on the first Thursday of the month on or before a full moon. Moonlight enabled lodge members to better navigate the muddy tracks and streets in town, preventing deaths and injuries that commonly occurred at night from falls into abandoned mine shafts.[20]

The Masons focus on three principles: brotherly love, relief and truth. With the stone mason as metaphor, instead of building stone structures, members work to build character. The Freemasonry organization is highly structured and ritualized, replete with allegory and symbols. To become a Worshipful Master, Francesco would have spent an enormous amount of time and energy attending meetings and learning rituals. Given the heavy commitment required, Freemasonry guides its members to put family first, then work, then Freemasonry.[21] Francesco apparently overlooked those priorities, as he focused on his organizational duties while neglecting to write to Luigi and family back in Ticino.

Many Italian speakers supporting Italy's unification joined Freemason lodges around the world. Garibaldi, the Italian unification movement's hero, promoted Freemasonry as a way to unite progressive thinkers across the globe in the struggle to establish democratic governments. Other Italian unification movement leaders, including politician Giuseppe Mazzini and statesman Camillo Benso joined the Freemasons.[22] With its goal to "make good men better," Freemasonry attracted forward-looking, revolutionary thinkers. Lodges offered asylum to political refugees from autocratic regimes.

The Pope and Catholic clerics staunchly condemned Freemasonry as incompatible with Church tenets, first prohibiting membership in the organization in 1738. Catholics who joined the Freemasons or publicly supported them were automatically excommunicated, dying an enemy to God and his Church.[23] The Catholic Church also forbade membership in the Odd Fellows and similar societies. By joining these groups, Francesco rejected the tenets of the faith in which he had been raised. He fraternized with like-minded liberals aiming to improve themselves, their community and the greater society. Luigi would support Francesco from afar in these affiliations, as he also sided with progressives against the Catholic conservatives in Ticino.

Francesco didn't put all his energies into volunteer and social activities. In 1865, still hoping to find gold, he had applied for a quartz claim at White Hills, Spring Creek. Gold mining in Victoria had evolved from the early days of individual miners panning and cradling in creeks and rivers. With the need to bore ever deeper into the earth, mining technology grew more complex, requiring greater amounts of capital and labor. Men formed cooperatives and public companies, turning once independent miners into employees. Francesco's quartz claim required a significant capital investment and possibly a cooperative to share costs, labor and rewards.

Many of Francesco's associates had substantial stakes in gold mining concerns. Fabrizio Crippa had partnered with Pietro Lucini in a mine and crushing machine at Doctors' Gully in Spring Creek. Michele Bedolla had invented a crushing machine that he set up opposite his Spring Creek store. In 1866, a tongue-in-cheek article appeared in a local newspaper reporting that Bedolla's crushing machine could be seen in operation "whenever there is any wind." Two men, a miner and a "broken down Daylesford sharebroker" supposedly managed the sails.[24] A target of good-natured humor, Michele Bedolla had earned respect in the greater Hepburn/Daylesford community.

He held his elected position as councilman on the local shire council for forty years.

Francesco had purchased two shares in the Garibaldi Gold Mine, but his involvement in mining went beyond stock and claim investments. Using his accounting and administrative skills, he became employed as a mining company manager, assuming significant responsibilities for company assets. His job included posting notices of mining company meetings in local newspapers. In mid-1866, six months before his year-end letter to Luigi, Francesco had placed a notice in the newspaper for the Lady Darling Quartz Mining Company, announcing that a meeting would be held at Pozzi's Store at Old Racecourse "to empower the manager to sell and dispose of the claim, plant, machinery and assets of the company."

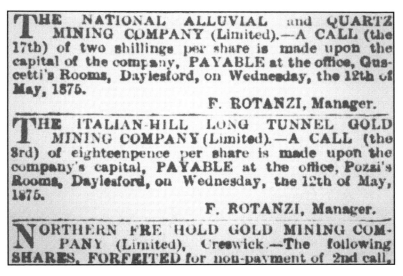

The National Alluvial and Quartz Mining Company (Limited).—A Call (the 17th) of two shillings per share is made upon the capital of the company, PAYABLE at the office, Guscetti's Rooms, Daylesford, on Wednesday, the 12th of May, 1875.

F. ROTANZI, Manager.

The Italian-Hill Long Tunnel Gold Mining Company (Limited).—A Call (the 3rd) of eighteenpence per share is made upon the company's capital, PAYABLE at the office, Pozzi's Rooms, Daylesford, on Wednesday, the 12th of May, 1875.

F. ROTANZI, Manager.

Northern Free Hold Gold Mining Company (Limited), Creswick.—The following SHARES, FORFEITED for non-payment of 2nd call,

The Age (Melbourne), May 7, 1875

Moreover, just three weeks after writing his letter to Luigi, Francesco placed a notice of assets and liabilities for the Swiss Mountain Quartz Mining Company located near Doctor's Gully. This mining company, originally called Lucini's Reef Gold Mine, had been formed by Pietro Lucini. As part of the statement, Francesco listed under liabilities his manager's salary and wages of about one hundred pounds per year. By managing the accounts of more than one mining company, Francesco was making a good living.[25]

Despite his solid employment, mine investments, and many social connections, Francesco still speculated in his letter to Luigi whether California might bring better fortune. Virgilio, who hoped Francesco would join him for moral and financial support, painted a promising picture of the two brothers working together. Positive reports from friends and relatives in California had reached the Italian-speaking community in Victoria, causing some Swiss Italians to migrate once more to yet another foreign land.

Francesco was no longer the young boy of sixteen who had left home with dreams. He was now twenty-eight years old. He no longer believed, as he had written to Luigi in 1855, that he had the time to risk making a fortune. With average life expectancy at about forty-five years, Francesco had passed mid-point.[26] He described to Luigi the difficulties of moving to yet another foreign country at his age.

> They write me of excellent news from America, and those that
> can judge the two places speak of America as more favorable than
> this country. I hope that I could do well, as I know the English
> language, and I could learn French and Spanish, which I hope
> would be helpful and might guarantee a prosperous occupation.
> With all this, it's hard to accept that after so many long years
> in Australia, I would have to immigrate now to another distant
> region instead of the land that is dearest to us. On the one
> hand, I would like to flatter myself that by dint of perseverance,
> my constancy would be rewarded. On the other hand, it's
> discouraging to have experimented so long without success. The
> good prospect of a better opportunity in California and at the
> same time the idea of being with my brother makes me rather
> favor California for that reason.

What would cause Francesco, so deeply invested in his community, to leave the life he had created in Victoria to start anew in California? Why did he complain to Luigi that he had not had success? For more than a decade, he had built strong relationships and a solid reputation. His associates trusted him with significant responsibilities and steady work. His peers had elected him to leadership positions. Francesco may have wanted to gain wealth from his quartz claim and mining investments, but more likely he used his lack of success in mining speculation as an excuse to stay in Australia.

By now, Francesco was signing his name Francis. He had assimilated. Despite Virgilio's pleas, Francesco would not come to his brother's rescue. He could not bear to tell Luigi and Virgilio that he would stay in Australia. In the end, expressing ambivalence about leaving, Francesco said he wanted to see what would develop. He would remain in Australia "for several months, at least until there's a definite solution to the affairs with my partners." Unwilling to disappoint Luigi, Francesco reassured him that "the most beautiful moment of my life will be to find myself securely at your side."

Vincent Street, Daylesford, 1862

THIRTEEN

"It's not death that I fear…"

June 4, 1867—Letter from Virgilio in Mission San Jose to Luigi in Peccia
August 2, 1867—Letter from Luigi in Peccia to Virgilio in California
August 16, 1867—Letter from Luigi in Peccia to Francesco in Australia

Alone and vulnerable, Virgilio yearned for Francesco to join him in California. It seems that the dairy ranch he had purchased in late 1864 had not done well for him. Now in mid-1867, he made yet another speculative investment. Bagnovini had enticed Virgilio into buying a dairy ranch burdened with liabilities, then had returned to Ticino after closing the deal, leaving Virgilio to run the ranch on his own. Heavily in debt, Virgilio tried to make the best of it, as he described in a letter to Luigi written from Mission San Jose in early June 1867.

> I think I made a good deal, especially if my brother comes from Australia, but I have incurred many debts, which concern me.
>
> There is much wood on the land. I think its value greatly exceeds what the property cost. The location is excellent for raising animals so that if my brother came, he could start a butcher shop for which I could furnish almost all the animals needed. I would be most content if he came, not having seen him for so much time. I think of the good company that we would have and the needed help that he could give me.

Desperate, Virgilio had no choice but to ask for Francesco's help. His hopes for the ranch weren't necessarily unrealistic. The growing population in San Francisco and surroundings needed fuel and charcoal for both industrial uses in blacksmithing and smelting, and for residential cooking and heating. Several of Virgilio's acquaintances from Ticino had offered to purchase his trees to produce charcoal.

Italian speakers had been making charcoal from oak and willow trees in the area since the early 1850s.[1] Groups of Italian-speaking immigrants traveled from ranch to ranch, contracting with landowners to clear trees in exchange for wood to make into charcoal in a lengthy and labor-intensive process.[2] Virgilio's ranch seemed to have potential, not only for charcoal and beef, but also for dairy production.

Virgilio craved the company and help of his older brother. He was in a tight spot. Yet, if Francesco did not come to California, Virgilio had to swallow his pride and ask for his financial support.

> If he does not come, I would be obliged to ask him for
> his help because of some money I owe. I pay a very high
> interest: 18 per cent a year and on the rest 12 per cent. I
> received a letter from Bagnovini in the past few days which
> states that the loan must be paid very shortly.

Some of Virgilio's fellow immigrants from Ticino had found fortunes in ranching. One of them, Virgilio's travel mate Natale Giacomini had been by Virgilio's side every step of the way from the Vallemaggia through New York to San Francisco. Giacomini had thrived in California. In the six years since arrival, Giacomini had purchased a ranch in Marin County's Chileno Valley. By 1870, he owned real estate worth twelve thousand dollars and personal assets amounting to five thousand dollars.[3] In 1866, James Bloom (Battista Fiori), another of Virgilio's travel partners, had also purchased a ranch in that area. While Virgilio's travel companions had been building solid fortunes, Virgilio had been amassing mountains of debt.

Giacomini and Bloom were just two of the many Swiss Italians who, with hard work and mutual support, prospered in the booming dairy industry of Marin and Sonoma Counties.[4] Newcomers first worked as milkers and laborers. In several years, they could save enough to rent dairy land. With frugality, perseverance, and loans from fellow countrymen, they could eventually buy land of their own.[5]

The Swiss weren't the only immigrant group that looked in large numbers to dairy ranching as a way to become established in California. Portuguese ranchers from the Azore Islands operated dairies located primarily in Marin's southern and eastern ranch lands. Their path to success mirrored that of the Swiss Italians, but both groups initially faced similar hostility and discrimination.

In 1870, the *Marin Journal* reported complaints of unemployed ranch workers: "This county has reached a pretty pitch when a white man can't get a day's work—what white men ought to be getting forty dollars a month for, greasy Swiss and Portugees do for fifteen in Summer and for grub in Winter." Another railed against "them d—d Chinese and them other Coolies, the Portugees and Swiss."[6] Later that year, the same newspaper reported on complaints that "Swiss, Portuguese and Italians are ruining the dairy business by renting cows at a price per head which 'white men' who have to expend something for christian food, cannot afford to pay."[7]

In December 1881, the *Sonoma County Democrat* reported that Switzerland "bundles up her rogues and crippled paupers and exports them to New York" and sends its criminals to California. An outraged group of Swiss Italians protested against the slanderous article, maintaining that their countrymen had "as much honesty, industry, and good citizenship as any other people either native or foreign-born."[8]

Over time, much of the animosity faded. As the immigrant ranchers grew more prosperous, they were held up as model community members. In 1883, the same *Marin Journal* praised the Swiss, who owned some of the county's best ranches, as "the most successful of all American citizens." They came as "penniless boys" and now own ranches "bought at figures as high as $50,000 to $75,000." The article attributed their success to "good health, industrious habits and the frugality that is born in the Old World…They have no extravagant habits, no wild associates, no fast proclivities." They start in the humblest capacity, then "they learn their business thoroughly, and before you know it they are capable of managing a large dairy themselves, and have money enough to lease or buy a ranch."[9]

On the sale of yet another ranch to a Swiss buyer, a letter to the editor of the *Marin Journal* in 1883 suggested that the Swiss "are gaining possession of a large part of Marin county." But rather than complain of the loss, the writer maintained that it offered "a lesson of purpose, industry, and economy." The

Americans must live as the Swiss live: "Work early and late; work every day except Sunday; dress plainly, and live simply. Earn something and save all of it." And if the Swiss live on bread and cheese, it is worth the sacrifice with a goal in mind. "They are taking the land but they earn all they take."[10]

Virgilio saw the path many others had taken to success. Yet unlike those Swiss Italians whose virtuous qualities like frugality and restraint helped bring them success, Virgilio lacked patience. He giddily skipped over many hard years of working as a milker and manager of a rented dairy. Despite limited experience, he jumped directly into purchasing a ranch. In his rush to acquire a fortune, he leapt in over his head.

> One of the peculiarities of those people is their disposition to assist each other. This disposition takes the form of a practical mutual aid system. A poor boy comes to the country and begins by working in one of the dairies by the month; if he proves himself industrious, honest and saving of his wages, in the course of two or three years, he can command sufficient capital to rent and carry on the largest dairies in the county. His countrymen, who are able, take a practical interest in him, and by small loans for a long time, and at small interest, he is soon in possession of funds to make the first payment of fifty per cent, of the rent money of a good dairy of cows. The second and third payments he is able to meet from the business itself, and the poor boy is, in a very short time, one of the stable men of his neighborhood and is known among the bankers of the town by his stated and increasing deposits. Soon, instead of money he deposits his title papers and is the owner in fee simple of a section or two of Uncle Sam's domain and a citizen of his adopted country.
>
> —*Pacific Rural Press*, July 6, 1872

Luigi found Virgilio's letter on returning home from Cevio, where he had spent several days performing his judicial duties. He replied to Virgilio immediately on August 2, 1867. Without acknowledging Virgilio's dilemma, Luigi sought to assuage Virgilio's anxiety: "I expressed in a letter to Bagnovini what you have told me. He has nothing to complain about." It seems than Virgilio could rely on Luigi's help to manage his indebtedness to Bagnovini. Luigi also made it clear to Virgilio that Francesco was not likely to leave Australia for California. In his last letter to Luigi, Francesco had "said nothing regarding us nor regarding you." Virgilio should not plan on older brother Francesco coming to his rescue.

Luigi shared a bit about family life in Ticino. "My dear Virgilio! We are all well, and we are about to make the hay, except for me, for when I am not in Cevio, I do things around the house. Isolina and Marino tend the animals we have at home, and Albina and Bernardino (he will be 5 years old on September 24th) come a little bit with one and a little bit with another, skipping along!"

Although three sons had gone abroad, Luigi still had a household full of children from his second wife Maria: Isolina, also called Filomena, age twelve; Marino, ten; Albina, seven; and Bernardino, five. These half-siblings were near strangers to Francesco and Virgilio. Virgilio had never seen little Bernardino, and Francesco had never known any of his step-siblings. Of their sisters, Carolina had married, whereas Luigia, also called Angelica, and Severina, in their late teens, still remained at home.

With two sons scattered across the globe, Luigi reached out in his letters to guide them as best he could. He did not admonish Virgilio for making poor choices or even mention the debts, but two weeks later, on August 16, 1867, unable to keep thoughts of Virgilio's dilemma to himself, he wrote to Francesco lamenting Virgilio's "fearless ambitions."

Luigi's only consolation was that Virgilio was healthy. He knew Francesco would be familiar with Virgilio's driven nature, commenting, "How well you will recognize those aspirations." He made no attempt to persuade Francesco either to join Virgilio in California or to stay in Australia Forlorn and full of doubts, but without comment, he paraphrased the letter for Francesco in Virgilio's voice.

> Bagnovini rented a ranch with animals in partnership with
> Sartori. But due to a disagreement with the owner and pressured
> by his creditors, I had to buy all of it. They love that I am in their

debt. I think I've made a good business deal, especially if my brother comes from Australia. I have incurred many debts, and they occupy most of my thoughts. The area I purchased has a lot of wood, which I think will pay the land costs. The land is excellent for raising animals, so if my brother came, he would be able to start a butcher shop.

Almost all the animals needed are there, I wouldn't need to look for others. I would be very happy if he came since we haven't seen each other for so long. He would make good company, and he would be able to help me when I need it. And even if he does not come, I will be forced to ask him for his help for some money. I have to pay interest of 18% per year. The lowest rate here is 12%. I owe Bagnovini $730, which leaves me $600, enough for rent.

The work I do is the most interesting that I have had up to now, requiring greater effort and activity than all the other jobs that I have had in California. I direct the interests of a dairy. I am not pressured by anyone, and I often go outside the dairy to sell cheese in a cart.

There it is, dear Cecchino, what your dear brother Virgilio has to say. I don't know how to comment, nor how to make suggestions. I remain like a statue, and it's all a maze to me. I am hopeful, I am fearful, but I remain warm and cordial.

Luigi was clearly upset, yet the full impact of Virgilio's financial troubles withered in the face of a cholera epidemic raging in Italy and southern Ticino. Cholera also struck Zurich at this time, with 428 deaths from August to October 1867.[11] Recognizing the danger, Luigi wrote to Francesco, "A little more, a little less, debts can be repaid, but the only priceless thing is health."

In the nineteenth century, cholera pandemics swept the globe, killing thousands of people. Spread by ingestion of bacteria (Vibrio cholerae) in food and water, cholera caused diarrhea, fever and vomiting in victims who died after just a few hours. In the mid-1800s, the source of cholera was still a mystery. Some physicians attributed the disease to miasma, the fumes from fetid waste materials such as decaying plant and animal matter. In 1862, one physician reported that "the cholera was something outlandish, unknown, monstrous… and seemed to recall the memory of the great epidemics of the middle ages."[12]

With threat of death from cholera at his door, Luigi turned to his faith. He acknowledged to Francesco that the epidemic was beyond his control. His fate was in God's hands.

> We must resign ourselves that it will advance. But worst case,
> I do not dread it. It's not death that I fear, but fear itself and its
> consequences. In any case, you are my support, you and Virgilio,
> both the most dear. I trust your brothers and sisters and the
> entire family to God's will without tears and regret.

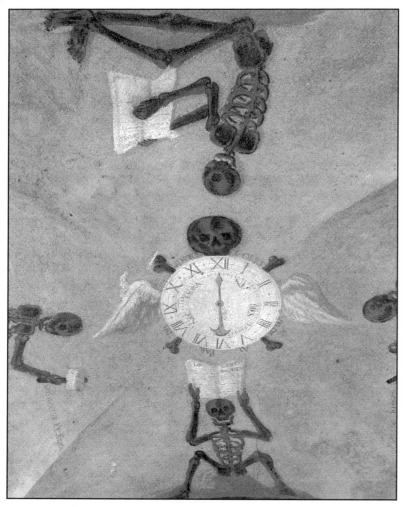

Ceiling, Church of S. Maria Assunta and S. Giovanni and Ossuary, Cevio

FOURTEEN

"Now many have just arrived here from Australia"

December 31, 1867—Letter from Virgilio in Petaluma to Luigi in Peccia

By October 1867, the cholera epidemic in Ticino had subsided.[1] The Vallemaggia had been spared. On the last day of the year, Virgilio wrote to Luigi from Petaluma about another new business venture. Somehow he had managed to break free from his ill-conceived ranch purchase. Although his other debts remained, at the start of a new year, once again Virgilio had fresh hopes.

> After having a fine finish to the bad business of the ranch and ending the quarrel with Sartori (He still regrets that he couldn't cheat me one more time before I got out of it), I have come here to open a shop with Orazio [Franzoni].
>
> It's winter now, and it's rained almost continuously this month, so business isn't going well, but we are rather satisfied all the same. It's the best thing that I was able to undertake given concern for the interest of the various debts that I have. In the store we carry all the items necessary for family use except hardware and trinkets, cloth or clothing; in this area where we are there are around two hundred Swiss of which over half are served by us. We have little recognition yet but in the spring we may put out a cart to serve the families in order to get more activity. With help from good weather, we appear to have a good future.

Among his many debts, Virgilio still owed money to his father for the journey to California. Luigi had offered Virgilio an "Act of Emancipation," which Virgilio was reluctant to accept because he claimed that he didn't fully understand it. An Act of Emancipation is a legal declaration that frees a minor from a father's authority and protection and gives the minor the right to administer his own possessions.[2] It also frees the father from responsibility for the son's debts and obligations. At twenty-two, Virgilio was no longer a child. Luigi, well-versed in the law, perhaps saw this act as a way to remind Virgilio that his financial obligations could affect his family at home. Virgilio claimed to not understand what this declaration meant. Apparently confused by its implications, he hesitated to accept it unless he had reassurances that it would not harm the family. That Luigi suggested cutting financial ties through this Act of Emancipation may have bruised Virgilio's pride. Had he failed so badly that his father wished to protect himself from his actions?

Petaluma, 1871

Virgilio located his new store in Petaluma, Sonoma County's boom town, which was thriving as the industrial and mercantile transport center of the North Bay. The chicken ranches and egg processing plants that were to bring Petaluma renown as the "egg capital of the world" had yet to come, but plenty of other products shipped from Petaluma's wharves. Many West Marin ranchers considered Petaluma their commercial center, despite its location in Sonoma County.

116

San Francisco, only about forty miles away, could not be easily reached by land. Bridges across the Bay had yet to be built. The Petaluma River provided access to San Francisco Bay. Despite the shallow river's twists and turns, merchants and farmers shipped goods by its waters, a far less costly transport than the circuitous land route around the Bay. Warehouses and wharves lined the river. Hay and grain for San Francisco's horses filled the McNear warehouse, the largest fire-proofed warehouse in California.[3] Scow schooners and steamers carried wool, hay, grain, potatoes, dried fruit, vinegar, fish, hides, hogs, sheep, horses and cattle to market. The many dairies in the region transported shiploads of butter, cream and cheese to the ports of San Francisco and Oakland.

Petaluma exploded with commercial activity. By 1870, it would have seven hotels, seven livery stables, two flour mills, a glove factory, three tanneries, a marble works, a pottery, eleven blacksmith and wagon making shops, six carpenter shops, three tin shops, four tailor shops, four cabinet-makers, one candy factory, one cooper shop, one agricultural implement manufacturer, ten insurance agencies, three lumber yards, eight lawyers and ten doctors. It had eighteen schoolteachers, two banks, two breweries, along with numerous drug stores, furniture stores, variety stores, cigar stores, butcher shops, bakeries, grocery stores, dry goods stores, laundries and twenty-seven saloons.[4] Virgilio and his partner could expect to see their business, if managed well, grow prosperous along with the town.

As the North Bay's shipping and commercial center, Petaluma drew many cultural attractions. Should he wish to spend for frivolities, Virgilio could attend presentations by renowned entertainers. In 1866, crowds heard Mark Twain lecture on the Sandwich Islands, soon rechristened the Hawaiian Islands. The local paper panned his performance as "reprehensible," claiming that "as a lecturer he falls below mediocrity."[5] In 1869, General Tom Thumb with his wife Lavinia Warren, members of P.T. Barnum's Circus, enthralled large audiences. The popular, diminutive performer gave his impressions of Napoleon Bonaparte, just as he had earlier entertained President Lincoln at the White House.

Enthusiastic about his prospects, Virgilio wrote to Luigi about developments in the region, including the move for an eight-hour workday. In 1867, more than two thousand workers marched up San Francisco's Market Street to Union Square. Plasterers, bricklayers, hod carriers,[6] stonecutters, lathers, riggers, carpenters and painters protested to limit the workday to eight hours.[7] To Virgilio, who had toiled eighteen hours a day in Ghirardelli's soda factory, the movement to limit workers' hours must have appealed.

Sonoma County's population included several hundred Chinese, typically paid one dollar for an eleven-hour work day.[8] With completion of the Transcontinental Railroad in 1869, many Chinese laborers who had built the railroad became available for other work, competing with Irish and other European immigrant laborers for jobs. Anti-Chinese protests grew.

Expecting that economic developments in the area would interest Luigi, Virgilio described them in some detail:

> Agriculture makes great progress and large quantities of products are exported. Many factories have been already established here: paper, powder, glass, cloth, sugar, leather shops, etc., etc. There are already several railroads. The land is already nearly all occupied and valued at high prices. In general, foodstuffs are less expensive than in Europe. The taxes, imposed by the district and city governments are exorbitant. Liquor is taxed at 600 per cent above the cost to produce it. In certain parts of California they produce a variety of wines in very large quantities.

> Wool forms a great branch of commerce. Work in the country is done with machines moved with the force of horse or steam. They plow, plant and cultivate the soil at the same time with instruments of horse or steam, size it, transport and beat the grain with a machine moved by the same force, and the grain is transported with wagons to the granary already bagged.

Perhaps Virgilio thought these signs of progress would help convince Luigi that opening a shop in Petaluma showed sound judgment. He expected Luigi would be curious about the mechanization in agriculture. In the Vallemaggia, peasant farmers used sickles and scythes to cut hay from alpine meadows to carry down steep trails in enormous bundles on their backs or on the backs of mules. In California, steam-driven agricultural tools dramatically increased yields and reduced labor. Instead of tilling the soil by hand, future farmers would be chief engineers or factory owners, with workers serving as mechanics and drivers.[9]

Despite such progress, law and order lagged behind. Stagecoach robberies occurred frequently. During 1871, thieves held up stagecoaches on the Healdsburg-to-Cloverdale route north of Petaluma eight times in six months.[10] The robbers included Black Bart, the legendary thief and poet who, on a few of his stage robberies, left behind rhymes scratched on the list of goods and passengers carried.

Co-owner of a small enterprise, Virgilio took pleasure in managing his own hours and working conditions. He delighted as old acquaintances arrived from Australia bringing news of Francesco. If they reported truthfully, Virgilio would know that Francesco was doing well, both financially and socially. Despite the newspapers Virgilio sent to Australia containing reports of burgeoning economic growth in the San Francisco region, Francesco had little reason to uproot himself to join his brother. He had woven himself into a tight group of associates who shared business ventures, cultural origins and community interests.

Immigrants continued to arrive in California from Ticino and Australia, gaining support from friends and relatives who had come earlier during the rush for gold. The Swiss Italians drew strength from their large community. With over two hundred fellow countrymen in the Petaluma area, Virgilio had good reason to believe that his store would be a success.

Letter from Luigi to Francesco, June 5, 1868

FIFTEEN

"A disgraceful and fatal blow…"

June 5, 1868—Letter from Luigi in Peccia to Francesco in Australia

Six months after learning about Virgilio's latest business venture, Luigi remained anxious. Despite Virgilio's optimistic hopes for his new store in Petaluma, he had not divulged how much money he owed from the "bad business of the ranch," and this question plagued Luigi. Without details, he tended to think the worst. Almost a year had passed since Luigi had first outlined Virgilio's plight to Francesco. Beside himself with anxiety, in June 1868, Luigi once again wrote to his son in Australia, spilling out his fears for Virgilio's welfare.

> No one is kinder and more virtuous than dear Virgilio, your worthy brother. But so unlucky. He had various starts that gave hints of hope and good fortune; but all goes badly for him; and his latest enterprise, the dairy, gave him a disgraceful and fatal blow. He was deceived and tricked in the purchase. He had little practical experience and too much passion for putting himself in such a speculation; he fell into the hands of Bagnovini, who is profiting from Virgilio's credulity, good faith, and loyalty. And good Virgilio, he went around and roused himself to make the purchase from a certain Foscalina, a former associate with Bagnovini in various dishonest activities (our poor Virgilio found out about them afterwards) who assured him that he would receive 4700 gallons of milk, etc.…1000 francs for the pigs, and slowly, slowly other similar gains!? Lies!!

That Virgilio's poor investment enabled Bagnovini to return home particularly embittered Luigi. With Virgilio floundering in a distant land, Luigi could only express his despair and frustration to Francesco, even farther away on a remote continent.

> Good Virgilio believed everything and has assumed several of
> Bagnovini's vendor debts. Without this fraud, Bagnovini would
> never have been able to repatriate. Infamy!! The milk was just 470
> gallons; he lost more than 1000 francs on the pigs and many other
> expenses. This lasted nine months, and then desperate, he cut it
> off. It looks like a mess in the future. Poor Virgilio, I don't dare say
> what . . . fear . . . illness . . . despair . . . who knows?
>
> I don't know how much he has lost, as he hasn't said what sums he
> has assumed to pay, but the fact is he has had a dreadful outcome.

In his obsessive quest for success, Virgilio flitted here and there, ever
drawn to what he hoped would be greater opportunity. His indebtedness
and erratic changes in pursuits drove Luigi mad with dread. With mail
taking months to reach Ticino, Luigi could barely keep up with his son's
volatile moves. He wrote Francesco of the latest developments:

> Soon after, in the autumn of 1867, with the support of good
> friends, he proceeded to Petaluma, where he set up a shop with
> Orazio. Now, since March 18th, while continuing the association
> with Orazio, he has been in San Francisco attending to a shipment
> of butter and other products, requested by Carlo Martinoja,[1]
> husband of Caterina Traversi, our neighbor in Cevio; he doesn't
> know yet if it will be a partnership or an actual salary . . . God
> bless him, poor Virgilio . . .

Virgilio had connected with a successful businessman, Carlo Martinoia,
a wealthy, well-respected dairy owner and commission merchant who
hailed from Cevio, the Vallemaggia's administrative center. Luigi's position
as district judge in Cevio may have influenced Martinoia's offer to Virgilio,
but Martinoia, a power broker who knew nearly everyone in California's
Swiss-Italian community, often helped fellow immigrants get a start. Many
began as workers on his ranch lands.

Arriving during the California Gold Rush, Martinoia had made a
fortune through hard work, smart investments and a great measure of good
luck. Born in 1829 to a poor family in Cevio, he began laboring at the age
of fifteen as a mason's helper, first in France, then in Africa. He reached

122

California via the Isthmus of Panama on June 15, 1852, arriving in San Francisco at age twenty-two with little money and no knowledge of English.

He did have two friends, Carlo Scalmanini and Battista Frapolli, who had arrived in San Francisco in 1849. Martinoia had worked by their sides as a stone mason in Algiers.[2] Scalmanini and Frapolli had struck gold in California's mines. With their gains, they returned to San Francisco to open the Swiss Republic Restaurant on the Long Wharf.[3] Their establishment, located in the heart of the city's busy commercial shipping district, offered both food and lodging to merchant seamen whose ships anchored along the wharf. Before long, Scalmanini and Frapolli owned a grocery store on Commercial Street. The two Swiss Italians formed part of Martinoia's extensive business network in San Francisco's Italian-speaking community, which included owners of bars, restaurants and boarding houses such as the Swiss Exchange and the Swiss Union Hotel.

Like Scalmanini and Frapolli, Martinoia had also found fortune in the mines, possibly east of Sacramento in Amador County. He spent some time in the Santa Cruz area, then in about 1857, he purchased a dairy ranch in Chileno Valley near San Antonio Township in West Marin.[4] By 1860, Martinoia owned real estate valued at thirty-six hundred dollars and a personal estate worth three thousand dollars.[5] He employed three Swiss laborers, one of whom, Giuliano Moretti, a fellow immigrant from Cevio, would become his partner in several future business ventures.

In August 1862, Martinoia added to his holdings by purchasing more land in Chileno Valley, this time from Henry W. Halleck, whom President Lincoln had appointed General-in-Chief of the Union Armies. The deed was recorded to a Charles Martin, since by 1862, Carlo

Charles Martin, c.1870

Martinoia had anglicized his name.[6] About a month after the purchase from Halleck, Martin married Caterina Traversi, a woman from his hometown of Cevio. He and Caterina began a family, eventually raising seven children, three boys and four girls.

Over the next few years, Martin expanded his holdings by purchasing more land in Chileno Valley, sometimes partnering with Giuliano Moretti. Ultimately, he owned 5,029 acres of dairy land in western Marin County. His vast ranch lands, about ten to fifteen miles west of Petaluma, spread over golden-green meadows and rolling hills speckled with cattle grazing on grasses. He and Caterina lived with their children in the original ranch cottage until 1883, when Martin renovated the building, converting it to an

The Martin Home in Chileno Valley

expansive Italianate Victorian home to accommodate his large family.

One of the first Swiss Italians to ranch in Marin County, Martin drew others from the Vallemaggia to the region. By sponsoring fellow countrymen, over time he helped remake the complexion of the region's dairy community. In 1860, Martin's dairy ranching neighbors had Anglo surnames like Ward, Wilson, Archibald and Jones. Ten years later in 1870, Martin's neighbors included DeMartini, DeMartin, Garzoli, Tognazzini, Fiori, Righetti, Pedrazzini, Grandi, Tomasini, Dalessi, Maghetti, Tonini, along with many others hailing from Ticino, including Natale Giacomini and James Bloom, the young men who had accompanied Virgilio on the long trip from Ticino to California. Many other Swiss Italians ranched in the nearby regions of Tomales, Nicasio, Bolinas, Olema Valley, Point Reyes, Two Rock and Bodega.[7]

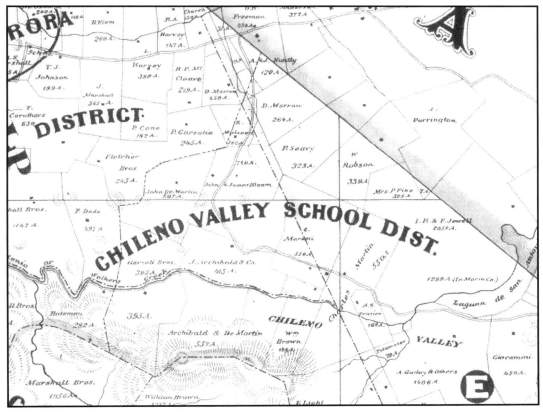

Chileno Valley, 1873

The small villages in the Vallemaggia, some with only three hundred inhabitants, made for close connections. As a district judge, Luigi had acquaintance with many of the families throughout the valley. He knew

Caterina Traversi's family in Cevio, and probably also the Martinoia and Moretti families. This knowledge may have reassured Luigi that Virgilio's decision to join Martinoia was sound.

Early in 1868, Martin partnered with Henry Cohn, a young man from Petaluma who owned a San Francisco commission merchant firm specializing in eggs and dairy. Now instead of paying a fee to middlemen, Martin pocketed the profit when selling his dairy products and those of his fellow dairymen. Virgilio, educated and entrepreneurial, showed enough promise that Martin brought him into his new firm of Cohn, Martin & Co. Recommended to Martinoia by friends and associates, Virgilio once again jumped at opportunity without caring for details. Would he have a salary or be a partner? He didn't know, but he couldn't miss out on this latest chance for success. With Martin's support, Virgilio hoped he had finally found his way over mountains of debt and onto a smooth path to fortune.

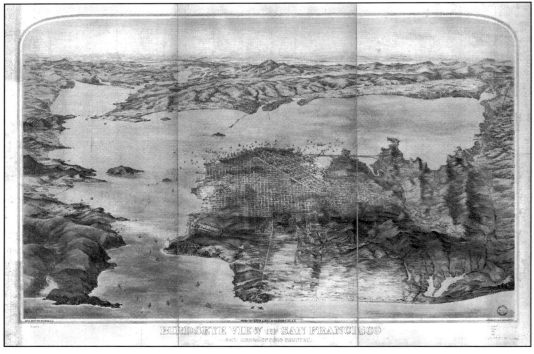

Birdseye View of San Francisco and the Bay, 1876

SIXTEEN

"Fortune for me has been uneven . . . "

May 30, 1869—Letter from Virgilio in San Francisco to Luigi in Peccia

Despite hopes for a promising future with Martinoia, Virgilio could not avoid misfortune. In the last days of May 1869, Virgilio wrote to Luigi a long letter informing him that he had been severely ill.

> It's been about one year now since I got a strong cold that took me to bed for four days, and then I healed well. I didn't feel badly until last autumn, then a cough and inflammation of the lungs started to torment me, and I coughed blood because of the irritation. This last phase stopped by using good precautions but from January to May the cough kept me from sleeping many nights and in March I was worse. I felt exhausted. I am cured, with the expense of medicine and also by putting a man at my post to do my work for some time.
>
> But I believe that the only thing that helped is the change of the seasons, the heat. All this May I was getting better, regained strength and now I am well advanced in recovery. The thing most adverse with a sickness like this is the cold, but now that it is summer it's helped me reestablish myself so I don't fall back at the first change of the season. I have good and well-paid employment, and I work with good people. In the end, all goes well enough so I can't complain.

Virgilio's symptoms resembled those common to phthisis, pronounced "tai-sis" or "thai-sis," a disease now known as tuberculosis. Glossing over the illness with hopes that warm weather would bring back his strength, he went on to inform Luigi that he had sold his store in Petaluma and moved to San Francisco after buying into the commission house owned by Charles Martin and Henry Cohn. He paid $1250 for a quarter interest in the company,

127

with Martin owning a quarter, and Cohn one-half.[1] Martin worked from his ranch in Chileno Valley, some fifty miles from San Francisco, minding his dairy business and building relationships with fellow ranchers. He left day-to-day activities in San Francisco to his partners and agreed to pay Virgilio fifty dollars a month to work at the firm. A presence in both city and countryside well-positioned the company to sell agricultural products for the region's ranchers.

Virgilio's other partner, Henry Cohn, a young man in his early twenties, had been born in Alabama, then moved to Petaluma with his family in the early 1850s. Henry's father, Isaac H. Cohn, a Jewish immigrant from Bavaria, also sold wholesale eggs, butter, and cheese on commission. Henry had first worked as bookkeeper for the family business, then split off to create his own firm, H. Cohn & Co. When Charles Martin purchased an interest, the company's name changed to Cohn, Martin & Co., and that name remained after Virgilio joined the business, replacing partner D.R. Foss.

California's dairy and egg industry had grown rapidly. In San Francisco's early days, milk, butter and eggs were in such high demand that companies gathered and sold murre eggs from the Farallon Islands, twenty-five miles off San Francisco's coast.[2] The Pacific Egg Company's mostly Greek and Italian employees, wearing shirts with large pockets to hold their harvest, clambered over desolate, perilous island cliffs to gather eggs deposited by seabirds in crags and ledges. In 1863, in a gun battle over gathering rights, the Pacific Egg Company managed to hold position, after losing one man and shooting several attackers.[3] With chicken eggs scarce, murre eggs brought exorbitant prices, and between 1851 and 1863, over five million murre eggs were sold in San Francisco.[4]

San Francisco also lacked good cheese and butter. In the long sea voyage to California, dairy products imported from Boston, New York and Chile arrived spoiled and nearly inedible. Despite poor quality, prices during the 1850s soared: three dollars an egg, twenty dollars per pound of butter and twenty-five dollars per pound of cheese.[5]

Dairy ranches in the North Bay began to fill the demand. In 1857, contention over ownership of the Point Reyes Peninsula resulted in a lawsuit, one of many in California resulting from disputes over enormous ranchos originally conveyed by Mexican land grants. Attorneys Oscar and James Shafter won the suit for their client, then purchased the entire Point Reyes Peninsula for less than eighty-five thousand dollars.

The Shafters sold a portion of the peninsula at Tomales Point to Solomon Pierce, a family friend from Vermont. With Charles Webb Howard, a wealthy San Franciscan who had married Oscar Shafter's daughter, they split the remaining land into more than thirty dairy ranches, naming each ranch with a letter of the alphabet, the A Ranch, B Ranch, and so on. They rented them out to the Steeles, the Lairds, and other producers whose dairies benefited from the highly desirable location.[6]

Ranches on the Point Reyes Peninsula came to dominate butter and cheese production statewide. In 1861, Steele Brothers Dairy became the largest cheese producer in California with an output of forty-five tons, producing 640 pounds of cheese and seventy-five pounds of butter per day.[7] The success of the Point Reyes dairies and their high-quality butter, known as "Point Reyes Gold," inspired others to begin dairy ranching in the North Bay's grassy countryside. Many immigrants, particularly from Ticino, Ireland and the Azores, began ranching in the area.

By 1866, Marin County ranches produced more butter than any other California county. Schooners hauled North Bay butter and cheese to San Francisco from Petaluma and the coastal points of Tomales Bay, Drakes Bay and Bolinas. The temperate climate and vast stretches of hearty grasses bathed in misty ocean fog suited dairy farming well. In 1861, the *Marin Journal* extolled the coastal hills that supported great numbers of cattle. Within ten miles of the town of Tomales, 2,420 cows were milked twice a day.[8] That included the sixty-five milk cows grazing on Charles Martin's 550-acre Chileno Valley ranch.[9]

In the decade from 1860 to 1870, San Francisco's population nearly tripled from 57,000 to 150,000 residents. Demand for dairy products grew. In 1850, California dairies annually produced 702 pounds of butter and 150 pounds of cheese; by 1860, production had increased to over three million pounds of butter and 1.3 million pounds of cheese.[10] With butter and cheese sales skyrocketing, Virgilio, as a partner in Cohn, Martin & Co., seemed positioned to prosper.

The firm could also capitalize on the need for greater quality. In 1862, the *Santa Cruz Sentinel* lamented that "our people are content to eat Isthmus grease" brought on steamers from the East Coast. It encouraged local dairymen to produce butter: "Look into any butter depot in the city, and you find much of it oily, white, sometimes with hairs in it…The best butter makers can sell their product faster than they can make it without going any distance for a market."[11]

Charles Martin aimed to profit from the demand. Soon after purchasing his partnership from Henry Cohn, he began advertising the benefits of "YELL-OH BUTTER!" from "Celebrated Swiss Dairies of Marin County."[12]

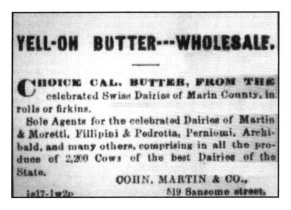

Daily Alta California, **June 19, 1868**

In October 1870, he placed a full-column advertisement in the *Daily Alta California*. It looked and read much like a news article, describing the poor quality of early dairy products produced in California: "a fat, greasy abomination, which entered our market under the name of Butter, and a wavy, leathrey [sic] compound called Cheese, which, when placed beside the imported Butter and Cheese, shamed the home-producer."

Shouldn't California be able to provide its own quality dairy products? Martin announced that Cohn, Martin & Co. could do just that. Declaring that he had established the first Swiss Dairy in California,[13] he claimed that he had also "assisted and induced several hundred skilled and intelligent Swiss dairymen to follow his example . . . " Martin asserted that his firm had affiliations with nearly all the Swiss dairies in the State, an aggregate of over ten thousand cows.[14] Cohn, Martin & Co. could provide "Fresh, golden-hued butter, with a rich, rosy flavor, of surpassing consistency, firm and choice."

130

Through his connections with fellow Swiss-Italian immigrants, Martin had indeed created an informal conglomerate of dairymen across the state. Although a herd of only sixty-five cows grazed on his ranch, his commission firm gathered products from many other Swiss dairymen. Dairies affiliated with Cohn, Martin & Co. also began manufacturing Gruyere cheese, which Martin claimed to be "equally excellent as the best imported, with the advantage of being fresh, and not transported across an ocean, one continent, and part of another."

Gruyere cheese had been made in the French-speaking region of Switzerland since the twelfth century. Gruyere's distinctive nutty flavor comes from the quality of local raw milk, unique native grasses, brine used to rub the cheese during months of aging, and the expertise of cheesemakers who have learned over generations how best to manage the aging process. Although Martin's Swiss dairymen could not possibly reproduce authentic Gruyere, the goal of producing a California cheese using traditional Swiss practices provided another selling point for the firm.

Virgilio surmised that Luigi did not know much about commission houses, so he took satisfaction in describing his new enterprise in detail.

> The business works like this: we receive products from the country, principally butter, cheese, eggs, chickens, veal, leather, tallow, etc., that is, products that can be consigned for which there is a market. They are sold for the producer's account or for whomever sent it, deducting the cost of transport and we receive 5% of the amount as payment for the effort and service of selling it. This is called selling by commission. The commission is a percentage that is deducted and must be paid to execute the sale of the merchandise; a firm that makes business in this way is called a "Commission House."

> The firm opened February 1868. It has been making progress and all goes well. Last year it made sales of around 15,000 dollars per month, and this year it will be around $20,000 per month. Now from April to July is the best season, and I calculate the monthly sales at about $30,000.

Virgilio jumped at the chance to buy into this promising enterprise.

Perhaps to impress Luigi on the firm's potential, he had quoted gross sales figures, which did not account for the amounts paid to producers. Based on Virgilio's calculations, monthly profits prior to expenses would amount to five per cent of the gross, or about $1,500.[15] If they kept expenses down, the partners would do very well. Martin could add to his considerable wealth and expand his dairy operations in Chileno Valley. With his earnings, Henry Cohn could continue living at the prestigious five-story Nucleus Hotel, the largest brick structure on Market Street.[16]

Virgilio envisioned paying off his debts with the large returns from his new investment. He earned a salary of fifty dollars a month, a sum far exceeding the fifteen dollars he had earned in Ghirardelli's soda factory. His compensation seemed reasonable given he had no experience in the commission business.[17] He described his job to Luigi:

> My work starts at 7 am and ends at 6 pm. It's my duty to receive and register the merchandise that comes in, sell and buy merchandise to send to the ranchers when orders are received, and deliver them the accounts and explanations of transactions made for them. The most important part of my duties is to correspond with our clients and supervise the affairs of the firm in general. For this last part I am earning the good esteem and appraisal of my parners.

Virgilio had reason to be proud of his step up in status. His new position required considerable skill and knowledge. West Coast commission

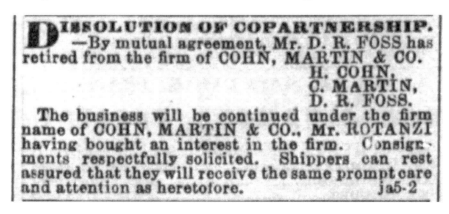

Daily Alta California, **January 6, 1869**

merchants also brokered goods from East Coast and overseas firms, shipped goods by steamship to California's Central Valley and stored surplus items until the market improved. Virgilio needed to build good relations with ranchers, other merchants, shippers and the bankers who lent the company money to import goods. He had to be aware of money exchange rates and the fluctuating value of gold, bills of exchange and other credit instruments and also understand government import/export tariffs and regulations. Virgilio had a lot to learn.

He emphasized to Luigi that his shop in Petaluma had been doing well. Its sale yielded enough money to pay off his creditors in California. With the remaining proceeds, rather than resolve his debt to Bagnovini, he had decided to buy into Martin's firm. Hopeful about his new prospects, Virgilio looked forward to a good income. "Now I can earn in a year what then I earned in three or four."

Virgilio had also used proceeds from his Petaluma sale to open a provisions shop in San Francisco with a partner, Omero Medici, probably related through Virgilio's mother, Caterina Medici. Their Swiss Store appeared in the Italian language newspaper *L'Unione Nazionale* in an ad:

L'Unione Nazionale, **November 1870**

"Merchants and Brokers, Wholesale and Retail, Commissions, Wines, Liquors, etc. Every ability to provide all varieties of the said items at the most liberal terms and all orders entrusted to us will be fulfilled promptly and at REMARKABLY LOW PRICES."

Virgilio's shop at 1115 Dupont Street between Pacific and Broadway stood on the edge of Chinatown in the heart of the Barbary Coast, a six-to-eight-block area well-known as a red-light district.[18] Walking between home and shop, Virgilio passed hustlers hanging around gambling houses and loose ladies selling their wares in tawdry concert saloons and dance halls. During the day, Virgilio would have to make his way past opium dens and Chinese porters who swayed from side to side as they carried heavy loads of produce in baskets balanced on bamboo poles over their shoulders.

DuPont Street, 1865

At night, the streets came alive with corruption. Seeking lurid excitement in the city, ranchers and miners crowded the area during the rainy season. Chronicler Benjamin E. Lloyd sensationalized the dark side of San Francisco, describing the Barbary Coast as "the haunt of the low and vile of every kind. The petty thief, the house burglar, the tramp, the whoremonger, lewd women, cut-throats and murderers, all are found there . . ." As if these degradations were not enough to warn readers to stay away, he continued, "The licentiousness, debauchery, pollution, loathsome disease, insanity from dissipation, misery, poverty, wealth, profanity, blasphemy and death, are there. And Hell, yawning to receive the putrid mass, is there also."[19]

Lloyd's exaggerations contained some truth. Crowded quarters, contaminated water and unsanitary conditions made for unhealthy living and may have contributed to Virgilio's illness. The location did offer Virgilio proximity to the Italian-speaking community. He and many of his Swiss-Italian countrymen resided with French, Basque, Italian and South American neighbors just north of Broadway in what came to be called the Latin Quarter, now known as North Beach.

Although Omero tended to the shop, Virgilio had taken on a heavy workload as both commission merchant and store owner. Hoping for some help, he persisted in encouraging Francesco to immigrate to California.

> I must write to Cecchino. It's already been some time, and I
> really want to try to get him to come here. From what I can tell,
> California would be somewhat better than Australia, even though
> he's had good employment there. If he comes here, he can find
> excellent employment easily, and if nothing else, there is always
> a position beside me to keep the books of our firm for $100
> per month.
>
> I also find that I am very able to make good business with a little
> shop here in San Francisco and supporting each other we could do
> better than with him being so far away. For him to come here now,
> it's not like it was when I arrived or when he arrived in Australia
> when we had to start at the bottom of the ladder. His experience
> and what he has learned in Australia can serve him here by all
> means as well. You also see that he has made bad deals once more
> and must start all over again! I would like to start again here in
> California at a good pace without falling back. Hope gives me
> thoughts of a good future for both of us.

Although his new venture with Martin seemed promising, Virgilio admitted to his father: "Fortune for me has been uneven and I have found it fickle after spending energy and hard work trying various things." His bouts of ill-health during the past year had forced him to face his mortality. He thought of subscribing to La Solidarité Mutual Protection Association, a newly formed insurance plan. He notified Luigi: "I sent you a booklet of its policies; I have tried to join it but since it was presented to me when I was ill, I could not be accepted. Now that I am well, I want to try another time and when you get the card, it will be the pledge of my health." According to the association's guidelines, Luigi would receive, on Virgilio's death, in gold or silver coin "a cash payment of as many dollars as there are members; number of members, one thousand."[20]

Like his brother in Australia, Virgilio actively engaged in community activities. While living in Petaluma, he and partner Orazio Franzoni joined the Petaluma Fire Department's newly formed Young America Engine Company No. 3, one of Petaluma's several volunteer fire companies. Each potential member of the Young America Engine Company No. 3, if not well known to its membership, underwent an investigation by committee regarding the applicant's character. With the committee's approval, all members then voted to allow Virgilio and Franzoni to join the company. Once initiated, they had to commit to attend meetings and to fight the frequent fires that often threatened wooden buildings in the rapidly growing town.

One of thirty-one members of this volunteer fire company, Virgilio both contributed to the community good and benefited from the group's many social activities—holiday balls and fundraising events, banquets to honor company leaders and athletic events, where members challenged other volunteer firemen in races, hose-laying and pumping contests. Of course, the company marched in the Fourth of July parade.

In September 1868, Virgilio had joined the crowd in Petaluma's Plaza for firing of a salute celebrating Swiss National Independence Day.[21] Along with other Swiss Italians, he then marched in a long procession westward out of town, walking several miles through the grass-covered, rolling hills surrounding Chileno Valley to a ranch site prepared for the large picnic festivities. There with over three hundred fellow Swiss Italians, Virgilio heard orations in Italian by community leaders amidst the rousing cheers of his countrymen celebrating Ticino. He enjoyed plenty of food, drink and dancing to a band brought from San Francisco.[22] Songs from his homeland brought back to Virgilio memories of the alpine village he had left behind. Expecting Luigi would be interested in how his countrymen celebrated their homeland abroad, Virgilio sent his father a souvenir, perhaps a program listing the day's officers, orators, literary exercises and musical selections.

Daily Alta California, 1870

Virgilio enthused to Luigi about taking a prominent role in forming a Swiss military company called the Swiss Guards. In 1850, California's first Legislature had authorized independent groups of volunteers formed along military lines, each with a constitution, by-laws and rules for administration. In 1871, San Francisco had over thirty-seven such military companies, many organized by ethnicity or nationality, including the San Francisco Hussars, the German Schuetzen Verein, Irish Wolf Tone Guard, Irish Montgomery Guard, African-American Brannan Guards, Irish Hibernian Rifles, French Zouaves and the Italian Garibaldi Guard.[23] Men flocked to join these companies, which, despite their uniforms, armories and military equipment, primarily served as fraternal and social clubs.

Justly proud to have written statutes for the Swiss Guard and pleased to have joined his compatriots representing Switzerland, Virgilio explained his activities to Luigi.

> Also here in San Francisco a Swiss military company is being organized. I am sending you a copy of the letterhead that I have written and printed in Italian and French. I haven't altered even an accent from my manuscript that I sent to the printing office. The German part was written by someone else. I am also sending you a copy of the statutes; the compilation of them is my work, at least four-fifths of it. I was vice-president of this company and after having resigned from this post, I couldn't refuse being made treasurer. It is loosely organized, but it is progressing very well. The expenses are already almost all covered and for the Fourth of July holiday, the anniversary of American independence, all the company will sortie for the first time.

I am happy because it reflects honor on me for what I have done
to organize this company. I don't make any money from it,
even though I have expenses. It is pride in one's nationality and
patriotism and mainly an instructive and lawful diversion.

Virgilio joined other Swiss immigrants at the Guard's armory to take part in military drills. As the group's treasurer, Virgilio accounted for funds raised at banquets and balls, picnics and other festivities featuring singing and dancing, games, target shooting and raffles. He also arranged payment for sharpshooter uniforms and imported Swiss rifles, the same weapons used by the Swiss Army.[24] In 1869, the Guard had sixty members from every region in Switzerland. To support his military activities, Virgilio asked Luigi to send a book of military theory.

Virgilio's long letter continued with even more demands, including requests for a geography book and maps he might sell in his store.

You have already asked me more than once if I received the
geography of Balbi[25] and I don't know if I have answered you
about it. I received it but it stayed in my possession just a short
time. It was delivered to Lamberti in San Jose when I came to
Petaluma several years ago and returned to me, but I no longer
know how to account for it. It would make me very happy if you
sent me another of the same, or one more recent, and one or more
maps of Switzerland, big ones to put on the walls. If you have
the opportunity to send them, send me half a dozen maps of
Switzerland, and if you buy them, tell me the price.

With his social circles expanding, Virgilio once again inquired about the Rotanzi/Rottanzi family genealogy, curious to know whether he shared family ties with the very influential Dr. Antonio Rottanzi, physician for San Francisco's Italian Mutual Benevolent Association. Virgilio also asked Luigi to send certain other items that he might sell in his store:

With the ease of transport and so many of our countrymen coming
often, you can also arrange to send items that can bring good
earnings. When you have a good opportunity, put my schoolbooks
in a bundle and send them to me. I would like to review them and
copy them all.

Another of Virgilio's requests involved Rotanzi relatives Carlo and Atanasio Patocchi. Twenty years older than Virgilio, Carlo Patocchi had spent many years in California. He had long since given up his store in Placerville, which he had claimed was worth more than the family house in Ticino. After several years working in San Jose for the Yocco brothers, who had taken in and cared for Alessandro when he was ill, Patocchi had now moved to San Francisco.

San Francsico from Russian Hill looking down Vallejo Street, 1866

Seven years back, in September 1862, Carlo Patocchi had written to his cousin Luigi, asking him to manage affairs after his mother's death. Now in 1869, he once again asked Luigi, through Virgilio, to sort out questions of his family and inheritance.

> Carlo Patocchi is here in San Francisco with his wife, and his brother Atanasio works for us as a cart driver. We are all together in the same firm. I have been asked by both of them to ask you for accounts of their interests back home, giving them the best possible idea of the state of affairs of their family, and doing it without making it obvious to anyone in the village.

The Patocchi brothers expected that nothing much remained from their parents' estate, which had been encumbered for their trip to California. They offered to pay what they owed for their passage by deducting that amount from the inheritance, but they did not want to overpay. Acting as an intermediary, Virgilio took this opportunity to give his father instructions on how to handle the business: "try not to rely on the information of those people who may be partial to one or the other." As a district judge, Luigi had significant experience discerning interests and making fair judgements.

Virgilio lived on Telegraph Hill at the southeast corner of Vallejo and Kearny Streets. Carlo Patocchi lived with his wife up the street at the rear of 431 Vallejo.[26] Telegraph Hill had become a "Little Italy," described in 1867 in the Italian newspaper, *La Voce del Popolo,* as a "model colony" of Italians in the United States, thanks to its successful, law-abiding residents.[27] Virgilio and Patocchi found familiarity in the small enclave of Italian speakers who lived on the hill overlooking the Bay.

Brimming with news, Virgilio allowed himself a moment of regret.

> I go to Petaluma often and also to the ranches where I often
> find almost all of those who are from our area. This year those
> ranches did well, better still than the year before. When I sold the
> produce garden in San Jose, had I gone to Petaluma as my idea
> had been then, wanting to be truly happy, I would certainly not
> have needed to stay in this country. I would have been helped by
> all of our countrymen who were on the way to making it and as
> the ranches in the Petaluma area have always done well, perhaps I
> wouldn't have missed out on making a fairly good fortune.

Virgilio could not overlook the fact that he had started out on the same foot as his travel companions James Bloom and Natale Giacomini, who now operated their own dairy ranches in the Chileno Valley.[28] In 1868, Giacomini had sold his ranch of about one thousand acres for $6,500.[29] Virgilio still carried heavy debts. After briefly revealing bitter regrets, Virgilio recovered quickly. After all, now he owned a shop on Dupont Street and a quarter interest in a commission merchant firm that promised good profits. Surrounded by folks from home, he seemed grateful for their support, goodwill and esteem. In a year, if all went well, he should be debt-free.

SEVENTEEN

"A badly cared for cold can lead to the tomb!"

July 4, 1869—Letter from Luigi in Peccia to Virgilio in San Francisco

Disturbed by news of Virgilio's illness, Luigi did not believe that Virgilio was past the danger point. He understood how serious such an illness could be. He wrote back the very day after he received Virgilio's letter.

> My poor and Dear Virgilio!
> I have read with bitter pain your beloved letter of May 30th, received yesterday, to which I can now give due. I wish to reply, and I am pressed to tell you quickly and urgently that if you don't soon see yourself safely healed from the bad dangers that can destroy your life, repatriate while there is still time to save yourself and be with your father.
>
> A badly cared for cold can lead to the tomb! Take good care, oh dear one, my dearest son, of what you are doing: If your health is restored, I beg you to always take good care of yourself: never drink cold drinks and never too hot, don't drink spirits, or strong drinks of any sort, drink instead dairy products, broths, veal, with fresh bread or rye, or pancotto [a soup of broth and bread] with fresh butter. Don't drink or eat salty things; use salt sparingly.

Luigi spelled out a long list of time-honored home remedies, favoring them above all else. His anxiety for Virgilio's recovery seeps through each detailed prescription.

> From time to time the inevitable weakness requires a little good wine, old, not manipulated or adulterated, and if that doesn't go well, at the point that a little bit of old wine doesn't help you, it's a sign that the illness still exists, and therefore [you need] a new cure. Don't take irritating medicines but only those from oils, teaspoons of castor oil or other soothing oils. These are the

simplest remedies and cures that have helped me recover so much and so many times from the sickness that assaults you, and because of such cures, it's now been two years that I haven't been attacked.

Sweating is an excellent remedy, even in travel, as long as you have the means to stay heated, and change the shirt that becomes warmed up and the shirt should not have holes, and then keep well away from any cold, and cold air, and always take care of yourself and keep yourself from anything that can take over all your energy and normal hardiness.

An excellent remedy is to put flax seed or some hot polentina [a poultice made of linseed] on the stomach and lungs, repeating enough times, and don't ever let it lose heat; but after some of these external applications, it's necessary to keep it hot and keep it from the air and from the cold, with patches on the stomach for a long time and even for years. The patches for the stomach must be made so that if the season's heat greatly increases, you can take off the cloth for a time; if instead it grows colder, gradually add a cloth for a time. You then also need to have physical and mental rest, a total and long rest, where you can remain in the warmth of your bed until it is over. In sum, either come home, or assure yourself of being able to take good and complete care; the cause of your sickness is nothing other than the effect of the sufferings and stresses that you continually bear.

Write me right away about whether your illness is getting better or worse without keeping anything from me.

Luigi promised that he would follow up on Virgilio's many requests from his last letter, but only "afterwards, if God agrees to your recovery." He mentioned that Virgilio's sister had married and that Francesco's boss, probably referring to Fabrizio Crippa, was visiting. He ended his letter entreating Virgilio to do nothing but "recover and that is all."

In his last letter to Luigi, Virgilio had waved aside his illness and written mostly of his achievements, his volunteer activities and details of his new firm. Luigi had replied with no words of praise or encouragement. He made no mention of Virgilio's new partnership with Charles Martin, nor did he comment on work Virgilio had done for the Swiss Guard. He glossed over

Virgilio's desire that Francesco join him in California. Luigi suspected that the illness was worse than Virgilio claimed. Coughing blood, after all, does not accompany a common cold. Luigi had already lost one son, Alessandro, dead and buried in a land far beyond reach. He dreaded losing another.

**Coat of arms painted on exterior of a
Rotanzi house in Peccia**

EIGHTEEN

"The way things are going is promising…"

October 24, 1869—Letter from Virgilio in San Francisco to Luigi in Peccia

After nearly six months without a response to his many requests, Virgilio acknowledged in a letter to Luigi dated October 24, 1869 that he had asked for too much. In response to his requests, all he had received were warnings and suggested remedies for his illness.

> You haven't replied to my letter of May 30th other than that you received it. I burden you too much and because of that you haven't been in a hurry to respond and by looking to do all that I ask of you, you haven't been able to bring yourself to write me again up until now.
>
> I have asked you for so many things, not because they are necessary, but only for my curiosity and only because you might fulfill those requests that come easily. I asked you for so many things as if you don't have anything to do other than to attend to my little requests. I ask you to excuse me. I don't wish to bother you.
>
> If it's not too much trouble to send me what I have asked, you could do it, but don't go out of your way to do it.

Despite this apology, Virgilio made yet another demand on Luigi, this one coming as a statement rather than a request:

> I have received a letter from Guscetti and Company from Magadino [a small town near Locarno] from which they look to develop a business relationship with this firm. They will probably make a trial shipment to import cheese, salami etc. If it turns out that they make substantial shipments, this firm intends to appoint you to buy the merchandise to ship.

144

Perhaps Virgilio assumed that Luigi would be eager to earn money by procuring goods for Cohn, Martin & Co. As a district judge, Luigi earned more than most villagers, but supporting a family in the Vallemaggia, one of the poorest regions in Switzerland, could try even those in the professions. "In no part of Switzerland," commented one scholar about Ticino, "is there more poverty, bordering on wretchedness, so much idleness, and so little industry."[1] Educated professionals found it hard to survive elsewhere in Switzerland too. Reporting on the cost of living in 1873, the U.S. Consul in Zurich noted that a teacher could barely provide for a family of five, even with his wife working.[2] Luigi may have welcomed the chance to earn some income from Virgilio's firm in San Francisco.

Virgilio hoped Luigi would be impressed by his company's relocation to a new building.

> On the first day of this month we changed store locations and
> have taken an elegant building in the commercial center of this
> city. The way things are going is promising. Little is happening
> now, but we are waiting to make the most business in the next
> season, which starts reviving in February.

The firm had moved from 519 Sansome Street to 315/317 Clay Street, two blocks closer to the wharves. San Francisco's busy waterfront hosted ships and steamers from all parts of the world. From every street leading to the east shore, wharves bustling with stevedores, sailors and laborers extended into the Bay. There schooners arriving from Petaluma brought cheese and butter from North Bay ranches for sale in San Francisco's markets.

Virgilio's new building was built on landfill. The spot had once been underwater in the Bay. Down the street from Virgilio's workplace on the corner of Sansome Street stood the Niantic Hotel, built on ruins of a ship that had brought gold seekers to San Francisco in 1849. Deserted by crew members who had rushed off to the mines on arrival, the Niantic was brought to shore and transformed into a hotel and shipstore, a place to warehouse and auction off goods delivered to the wharves. As the city grew, builders moved the shoreline farther east by filling in the area around the Niantic and similar shipstores with "made-ground."

Although he reported to Luigi news of his firm's move, Virgilio made no mention of the devastating natural disaster that had led to construction of the company's new building. On October 28, 1868, at seven minutes before eight o'clock in the morning, a massive earthquake lasting about one minute shook the San Francisco Bay Area. It was later estimated by seismologists to measure 7.0 on the Richter scale. The Hayward Fault in the East Bay had shifted, causing a deep fissure in the earth, a crack from six inches to two feet wide. Tremors were felt around the Bay.[3] At the time of the 1868 quake, Virgilio lived in Petaluma, where the earthquake destroyed many brick buildings and chimneys. The disaster came to be known as the Great San Francisco Earthquake. Although it did not cause fires that ravaged the city, as did the disaster of 1906, it shook the area with the most severe tremors experienced to date.

The day after the quake, the *Morning Call* described ruins throughout the city and reactions of residents during the quake:

> A gentleman who was on Clay-street wharf at the time, and whose
> business is connected with the wharf, informs us that the scene
> from where he stood was grandly terrible. The ships alongside
> the wharves swayed to and fro like they do when in the trough
> of the sea, with the waves rolling mountain high. The wharves
> shook and trembled with great force; piles of wheat and bricks
> were thrown down, and in some instances into the Bay. The horses
> in the drays and trucks became panic-stricken, and reared and
> plunged in mad fury. But during all this time, while everything
> on shore was trembling with terror, the waters of the Bay were as
> placid as upon the calmest Summer's day.[4]

The earthquake damaged many buildings in the East Bay but created more harm to structures in San Francisco, with its greater density and many brick buildings. San Francisco's Customs House and City Hall, both poorly constructed, shut down due to fears of collapse. The area west of Montgomery on Clay Street sustained the most severe damage because its buildings sat on made-ground. Two structures on the 300 block of Clay Street suffered near total destruction.[5]

146

Virgilio's new workplace, constructed on the site of a quake-ruined Clay Street structure, sat in the heart of San Francisco's commercial produce district. Commission houses clustered near the waterfront to handle shipments of goods on the wharves. Virgilio didn't have to go far from his office to shop for produce for his provisions store. Down the street, vendors at the Clay Street Market and the New Market sold fresh meat and fish. Just around the corner, the Washington Market occupied an entire block. Built in 1854, it held over sixty stalls selling fish, game, poultry, eggs, oysters, fruits and vegetables. Butchers offered huge sides of beef and lamb hanging on racks, pork sausages and massive hams. Customers could purchase giant firkins or rolls of golden butter piled high in pyramids, bushels of eggs and rounds of cheese from the dairymen of Marin and Sonoma Counties. Stalls offered a wide array of fresh fruits and vegetables from Italian truck farms south of San Francisco.[6]

Post-earthquake, Railroad House, Clay St., October 21, 1868

If Virgilio needed a break from work, he could cross the street to visit the Exhibition Rooms of the *California Farmer and Journal of Useful Sciences*, which claimed to be the only agricultural journal in California. There he could peruse samples of agricultural products representing California's bounty, from "a fine bunch of tobacco" to a parcel of sixteen-rowed white flint corn, and from a box of native walnuts to a collection of copper ores from Mount Diablo's mines. The producer's name, town, and county and the details of production accompanied each item in the collection.[7]

For a hearty meal at lunch or dinner, Virgilio could walk two blocks from his office to Campi's Italian and Swiss Restaurant, a favorite gathering place for Italian-speaking businessmen since its founding in 1859. For a fixed price of two-bits or twenty-five cents, he could feast on a full meal of salad, pasta, entree, sourdough bread, wine and coffee. He also might greet the Swiss-Italian owners, Giuseppe Campi and Natale Giamboni.[8]

Virgilio informed Luigi that he had written to Francesco but that he hadn't heard from Bagnovini regarding his debts. He seemed assured that "there will be a way for us to agree smoothly." He had sent Luigi local newspapers, including one featuring Petaluma's Swiss Festival, although Luigi had not acknowledged receipt. He went on in his letter to inform Luigi of the many relatives and acquaintances whose ties to home and to each other made life in California more tolerable, stating, "At last almost all my acquaintances are in this area." In particular, he gave news of Luigi's cousin Carlo Patocchi who was back working at Yocco's store in San Jose, and Patocchi's brother Atanasio, who had for a time worked with Virgilio at Cohn, Martin & Co.

Virgilio pointed out to Luigi the generous donation his new partner Charles Martin had offered to villagers in his hometown of Cevio.

> You have heard news of the offer of 100,000 francs that Carlo Martinoja has made to the town of Cevio to be used for the benefit of the town.
>
> This is a great idea, and the goal is to help the town in the same way that Martinoja has helped so many here. Those from Cevio here already owe him and are very obliged for so many favors

he has done for many of them. He is a rich man, a just man and a benefactor. Haven't I done well to have him as a partner? Even though back home some individuals think the idea impossible, if such a proposal is accepted, it will be a great benefit for the town. Consider only that the money would be put to good use instead of used in speculation in ranches, it would render 200 per cent more than expenses, and it could be used in secure investments. Another benefit is the employment it would create for various friends and relatives.

After giving scores of fellow countrymen a start in California dairy ranching, Charles Martin now aimed to help villagers back home. It's understandable that villagers might wonder at his large donation. They knew only the subsistence economy that had forced many of their fellow villagers to emigrate. In 1850, Cevio had a population of 927 inhabitants. Now twenty years later, due to massive migration, it was reduced to about 550 residents.[9] Those left behind in Ticino greatly benefited from the altruism of relatives and friends abroad. As immigrants gained wealth in California, signs of their generosity appeared in villages and churches throughout

Bust of Luigi Filippini in Cevio Main Square

Ticino. Parishioners of Cevio's church mounted a plaque announcing that the church had been restored in 1875 thanks to benefactors in California.[10] Over time, the emigrants' strong ties to home resulted in hospitals, schools and a rail system in the Vallemaggia that allowed villagers to transport goods to market by train.[11]

Although some villagers appreciated such bounty, others resented

the good fortune of those who had emigrated. Wealthy returnees built distinctive homes much grander than the typical rustic village structure. Some of these houses, easily distinguished from the simple stone cottages of most villagers, became known as *le case degli emigranti*, the emigrants' houses. Two-story stucco houses built in prime locations, they featured symmetrical facades, iron railings and a heading over the front door designating the date and initials of the proud owner. This flagrant display of wealth doubtless created envy in some of those left behind.

Virgilio could not pay off his debts, let alone shower benefits on villagers back home, but after suffering so many failures, he proudly wrapped himself in the

S. Maria Assunta e S. Giovanni Church in Cevio acknowledges benefactors in California, 1875 in this wall plaque

prestige he had gained through his partnership with Charles Martin. He begged for Luigi's approval, posing the question "Haven't I done well to have him as a partner?"

Despite Virgilio's craving for praise, Luigi made no mention of Virgilio's new position. Could he have felt a tinge of jealousy that his son had found such opportunities? Perhaps he was annoyed that Virgilio had deferred his debt payments to Bagnovini. He may have been offended that Virgilio ignored his request for emancipation, which would have freed him from responsibility for Virgilio's financial quagmire. Virgilio's presumption that Luigi would take on duties for Cohn, Martin & Co. may also have irked Luigi. What father likes to take orders from a son?

Emigrant Houses, Brontallo

On the whole, Virgilio assured Luigi that he was satisfied with how things were going. "I am in good health. I live my life in contentment, contemplating the way time passes quickly and things change rapidly so that one day you see yourself unhappy and soon after you're on the road to fortune and prosperity."

With his new partnership, Virgilio had risen from the depths of despair to see a future full of promise. He made no further mention of his illness. He knew how quickly circumstances could turn for the worse, but for now, he would not give that a thought.

NINETEEN

So much time lost…"

April 29, 1870—Letter from Francesco in Hepburn to Luigi in Peccia

While Virgilio relished the promise of his new partnership, Francesco had steady work in a supportive community. Despite his relative success, he lamented to Luigi the time he had wasted in Australia. He had not written to his father for nearly a year, neglecting to reply to three letters from Luigi. He told his father that he had put off writing until he could report some success in his mining ventures.

Luigi, having yearned for the return of his son for more than a decade, would rather have heard bad news than none at all. He learned something about Francesco's life in Australia from friends and acquaintances returning to Ticino, but second-hand stories could not replace words straight from the pen of his beloved son. With feeble excuses, Francesco informed Luigi of his current unhappy state of affairs:

> . . . right now I am not much better off than when I landed here more than 14 years ago. It's painful to consider so much time lost and so many ardent hopes destroyed! My dear father! You have written that no matter the circumstances, you want nothing better than to receive frequent news from me. At times I was going to write, but then I thought that I'd have good news to communicate at any moment. Thus I could have made up for the long silences with joyful news. Having only forlorn news is very sad, both for me and you.

Luigi had always urged Francesco to return home to family, with or without wealth, but Francesco had used his failure to strike it rich as a feeble excuse for not writing. He had been employed for about the last four years as a legal manager for two mining companies: Lady Darling Quartz Mining

Company and Swiss Mountains Quartz Mining Company. As manager, Francesco was responsible for keeping company books and reporting results to shareholders and the public. He announced company meetings, calls to shareholders, and auctions for forfeited shares in local newspapers. Francesco also tracked royalties paid to the companies by "tributers," teams of miners contracted by mining companies to work in exchange for a percentage of the gold they extracted.

A supportive infrastructure had developed along with Australia's mining industry. With mining companies needing ever more capital, stock exchanges were formed to trade in company shares. At the height of Victoria's gold craze, the Bendigo Stock Exchange, one of the largest gold exchanges in the world, listed over thirteen hundred companies. In the latter half of 1870, investors speculated in mining stocks both within and outside the stock exchange building. Out on the street, traders often blocked traffic in the market frenzy.[1]

To draw investors, some companies issued shares that required only a partial payment. Then, as they required more capital for deeper drilling, they would issue calls to investors for payment of unpaid balances. Shareholders had to pay the call no matter what the company's financial state, whether the stock had gained or lost value or whether the company needed to liquidate.

A good part of Francesco's job involved publishing notices of these calls and accounting for resulting transactions. Mining company notices filled pages of local newspapers. Although legally responsible to pay full price for their shares, some investors refused. Others registered under false names when purchasing shares. If the company was doing poorly, they could simply ignore calls, but if the company's prospects looked promising, they would pay up.[2] These subterfuges added to the complexity of Francesco's work. For each of his companies, he also published biannual reports of assets and liabilities in the *Victoria Gazette.*

In 1871, the Victoria Parliament passed the No Liability Act. This legislation aimed to provide more capital for the mining industry by making investments less risky. The Act specified that shareholders could lose only their original investment and were not legally bound to pay a call. They could walk away and forfeit their shares, which were then sold at auction. This act enabled mining companies to attract investors reluctant to lose all they owned in speculative ventures.

Francesco had invested in at least two mining companies, having purchased two shares of the Garibaldi Gold Mining Company, which mined at Kidd's Gully near Daylesford, and three shares of the Swiss Mountain Quartz Mining Company, started by Pietro Lucini at Doctor's Gully. Italian speakers, many of them Francesco's friends and associates, including Leonardo and Stefano Pozzi, made up the bulk of the thirty or so shareholders in this company. Lucini owned the most shares, while Francesco, as manager, owned the fewest.[3] He was also paid an annual manager's salary of over one hundred pounds sterling.

Francesco didn't bother to describe to Luigi the details of his mining losses, but in the risky business of digging up the earth for precious metal, failure came frequently. Francesco also did not mention in his letter that a few years back he had entered local politics, running in an 1867 election for a position on the Yandoit and Franklin Road District Board. Many of Francesco's associates, including Michele Bedolla, currently served or had served on the Board. Francesco lost the election in a very close race, sixty-five to sixty-two, but two years later, he joined the Board as an employee, its first hired clerk.

Road district boards, an early form of local government in Victoria, built and maintained roads and bridges in rural areas. They set up toll booths and collected taxes from district landowners to pay for infrastructure projects.[4] Formed in 1860, the nine-member Yandoit and Franklin Road District Board met in Hepburn. As Clerk, Francesco was responsible

Shire of Mount Franklin

NOTICE IS HEREBY GIVEN that a General Rate of One Shilling in the Pound for the year 1881, and payable on the 1st day of January next, has this day been made on all the Ratable Property within the Shire. The statement of such rate is open to the inspection of any person interested, at the Shire Office, Hepburn. If any person think himself aggrieved on the ground of unfairness or incorrectness in the valuation of any ratable property included in such rate, or in the amount assessed thereon, he may at any time within one month from this date, appeal to the Justices at the Court of Petty Sessions held at Yandoit, but no such appeal will be entertained by the said Justices, unless Seven Days' notice (in writing) of such appeal be given by the aggrieved party to the Council of the Municipality.

F. ROTANZI, Secretary.

Shire Office, Hepburn,
13th December, 1880.

Mt. Alexander Mail, **December 13, 1880**

for collecting rates from property owners along roads in the district's approximately one hundred square miles. He also published requests in local newspapers for bids from contractors for road work.

Rural roads in Victoria required constant attention. Winter rains made them impassable, preventing transport of goods and causing prices to rise. In 1861, a local newspaper reported that roads were worse that season than they had been for many years. On one road, the bodies of three bullocks lay stuck in quagmire, while horses and drays had bogged down in frequent intervals.[5] Such road conditions were not only dangerous, they made transportation extremely time-consuming. Francesco's position on the road district board put him front and center of one of his community's greatest concerns.

Francesco also omitted telling Luigi that he had been severely ill in the past year, instead writing, "With it all, my health has been generally good, and at present it is excellent." But a local newspaper in February 1869 reported that "Gastric fever seems to be prevalent in the Daylesford district. Mr. Rotanzi, clerk of the Yandoit and Franklin Road Board, is just recovering from a severe attack, and Mr. Bedolla, a neighbor, is now suffering from the disease."[6] Gastric fever, also known as typhoid fever, resulted from food or water tainted by salmonella bacteria. The cause was not known at the time. The disease could be life-threatening, but Francesco chose to keep this bout of illness from Luigi. It was long past.

Francesco turned his attention to health of his family members:

> I was sad to hear from you that Virgilio had been seriously ill for a long time without knowing if he would recover. Afterwards in one of your letters I learned of his recovery and after that by one of his [letters] that he wrote after a rather long silence.
>
> As for you, I would like to be satisfied with your assurances that you are now well and that you have little suffering. But I have no illusions that you are the same father. Don't try to lighten the fact so you don't cause too much worry! I hope that you find yourself in as good health as I would like you to be. That would greatly please me. So be it!
>
> At least take care to conserve your precious life and fulfill your

firm and my fervent vow of 100 years. I am also unhappy to know
that brother Alessandro was sick and suffered for so long! Really I
can't imagine the wretched trials that weigh upon our poor home!

How removed Francesco must have felt from his family, from his
brother and father, each in separate far-off corners of the world. He received
news of them just a few times a year, if that. At a time when the average life
span for an Australian male was about forty-five years, Francesco, now in
his early thirties, vowed to live to one hundred years and urged Luigi to do
so as well.

On a somber note, Francesco reflected on the passing years, recalling
Alessandro, who had been dead now for about six years. He expressed hopes
for one of his three sisters, Angelica, who had found a husband: "I wish
happy days to our dear Angelica in her new state, and I only wish that she
has met a good husband: I prefer to see a contented poverty than a splendid
fortune with days embittered by discord..."

Eighteen months earlier, Francesco's family had survived a massive
deluge, which in October 1868 had raged through Ticino and Northern
Italy, sweeping away entire villages, roads and bridges, drowning livestock,
damaging crops and killing villagers. "The bells from the church towers
were tolling, as we were solemnly assured, to drive away the storm," a
traveler reported of the disaster. "The precipices on either side of the valley
were streaming with countless and almost continuous waterfalls, and we
met on all sides families flying to secure refuges, wretched, half-clothed
men and women dragging along their shrieking children, and tottering
under the burden of such household goods as could be snatched up."[7]
The calamity drove another wave of immigrants, not to Australia, but to
California, where the refugees hoped to find a better life after their villages
had been destroyed.

The *Marin Journal* reported on the disaster: "The sheep and goats,
which formed the chief wealth of the region, were drowned in flocks, and
nothing remains for the wretched population but help from other countries,
starvation or exile." It put out an appeal for donations: "The Swiss are a very
thrifty, frugal and industrious class of people, and deserve the sympathy

of the charitable. Many of them will probably be forced to emigrate to this country where they can all find farms better than the best in Switzerland."[8]

Aid poured into Ticino, including funds from Francesco's community in Victoria. The local Daylesford newspaper reported that "subscription lists have been opened at the business places of the principal Swiss residents."[9] A Mr. Rotanzi had been appointed secretary to the fund. Francesco deplored the flood's damage in his letter to Luigi and wrote of the aid fund, but he didn't acknowledge that he had been placed in charge.

> I have received your news about the floods: we have taken up a collection here and sent an aid fund of 1425 francs. In the *Gazetta Ticinese* that is received here from the Italian Society, of which I am a member, there were descriptions of what happened. Poor Peccia, I imagine that it will not be left in peace until it is buried under ruins and rubble.

Likely Luigi would have been proud to learn of Francesco's role in the flood relief fund and even prouder of the great honor accorded his son when Francesco was chosen to welcome an Italian Admiral to Melbourne. In May 1867, Francesco had represented Victoria's Italian community in a delegation welcoming Admiral Vittorio Arminjon and his small warship *Magenta* to

The Magenta, **July 1870**

Melbourne. The Admiral had made treaties with Japan and China for the newly formed Kingdom of Italy and had stopped in Melbourne before continuing a circumnavigation of the globe.

The Consul General for His Majesty the King of Italy had introduced Francesco and other delegation members to Admiral Arminjon. The delegation had congratulated the Admiral on treaties he had negotiated, then requested that Italy begin direct trade with Melbourne. It concluded with an exuberant cheer: "Long live the King! Long live Italy!"[10]

Francesco was not a citizen of the new Kingdom of Italy, the Italian flag was not his country's flag, nor was King Vittorio Emmanuel II his king. Francesco was a Swiss citizen. That the Italian nationals in the Daylesford-Hepburn community chose Francesco to represent them at this event reflected the great respect they accorded him and the close ties between Italian speakers regardless of nationality.

Francesco hadn't heard from Virgilio for about six months. Once again, Virgilio had urged Francesco to come to California. Francesco told Luigi that it was "an excellent offer" in which he could partner with Virgilio in a store or work for one hundred dollars a month. He considered that Virgilio's "recommendation is very good, considering that I would go home on the way, and that is exactly what I would intend to do."

Francesco seemed to consider Virgilio's offer seriously, then he pulled back, citing his mining ventures as reasons to stay in Australia. Virgilio had informed Luigi about Francesco's mining losses, expecting those failures would motivate Francesco to join him in California, but Francesco was not ready to give up on finding fortune in the mines of Victoria. He explained to Luigi that he had lost his savings on a new venture.

> I must put off Virgilio's invitation until next year. I still have some interest in two mine works that do not require any expenses from me. If things go well, I could leave here sooner than I think, and if they go poorly, I would leave here by '71 and come for a visit to all of you dear ones at home, then go on to join brother Virgilio. And even now, after more than 14 years of deceptions and vanished illusions, and after being at the point of leaving the country, I am full of hope and grand certainties. I feel still an unstoppable

confidence in a successful outcome. I am still likely to realize my
aspirations in this country.

In this letter full of contradictions, Francesco no longer wrote of
returning home for good. If he joined Virgilio, he would visit on his way
to California. He continued in his letter deploring the petty inheritance
squabbles and narrow-minded disputes that troubled Luigi. Referring to
unnamed persons with whom Luigi, likely in his judicial role, had conflict,
Francesco compared Ticino's imbroglios with Australia's orderly society.

> I am sure that I would not be able to adapt myself to living in a
> country where one only sees envy, vendettas, egoism, in sum all
> that one can imagine, but what can one expect from a country
> that is called Liberal in ideas and action? In this regard, we here
> in Australia are able to have a happy life! As long as we do our
> duty and act honestly, we are always secure of our position. A
> great feature of this country is that the administration of justice
> is separate from any political influence. Once the judges are
> appointed, they can't be removed except for very serious
> reasons, and they must rigorously refrain from meddling in
> any political affairs.

Francesco was well aware of the bloody battles between conservatives
and liberals that had plagued Ticino for decades. Political differences over
major issues such as secular versus religious education and centralized
versus federal government resulted in armed conflicts. Federal authorities
were called in to maintain order in 1870 and several more times over the
next twenty years.[11] Francesco knew from first-hand experience how the
Australian system differed from practices in Ticino. He had seen Luigi,
subject to political whims, forced to curry favor to retain a judgeship. As a
local government clerk, Francesco took comfort in knowing that "As long as
we do our duty and act honestly we are always secure of our position."

Comparing politics and justice in Ticino and Australia, Francesco
revealed his true feelings. Having experienced government under British
rule, he refused to go back to the political vagaries of his homeland. Francesco
had adapted very well to life in Australia. In May 1868, Francesco had become a
naturalized citizen of the United Kingdom. At that time, he "swore to be faithful

and bear true allegiance to Her Majesty Queen Victoria, as lawful Sovereign of the United Kingdom of Great Britain and Ireland, and this Colony of Victoria." Under oath in front of a Justice of the Peace, he vowed that he wanted to settle in Victoria and become a British subject. He most likely did not inform Luigi of this significant change in his status.

Francesco was entrenched in a community whose members valued his friendship and contributions. Although he had lost savings in mining investments, he was still "full of hope and grand certainties" that his gold mining prospects would come through. Virgilio would have a very long wait for his brother to accept his call to California. After nearly fifteen years in Australia, Francesco had become Francis.

Shire of Mount Franklin, 1876

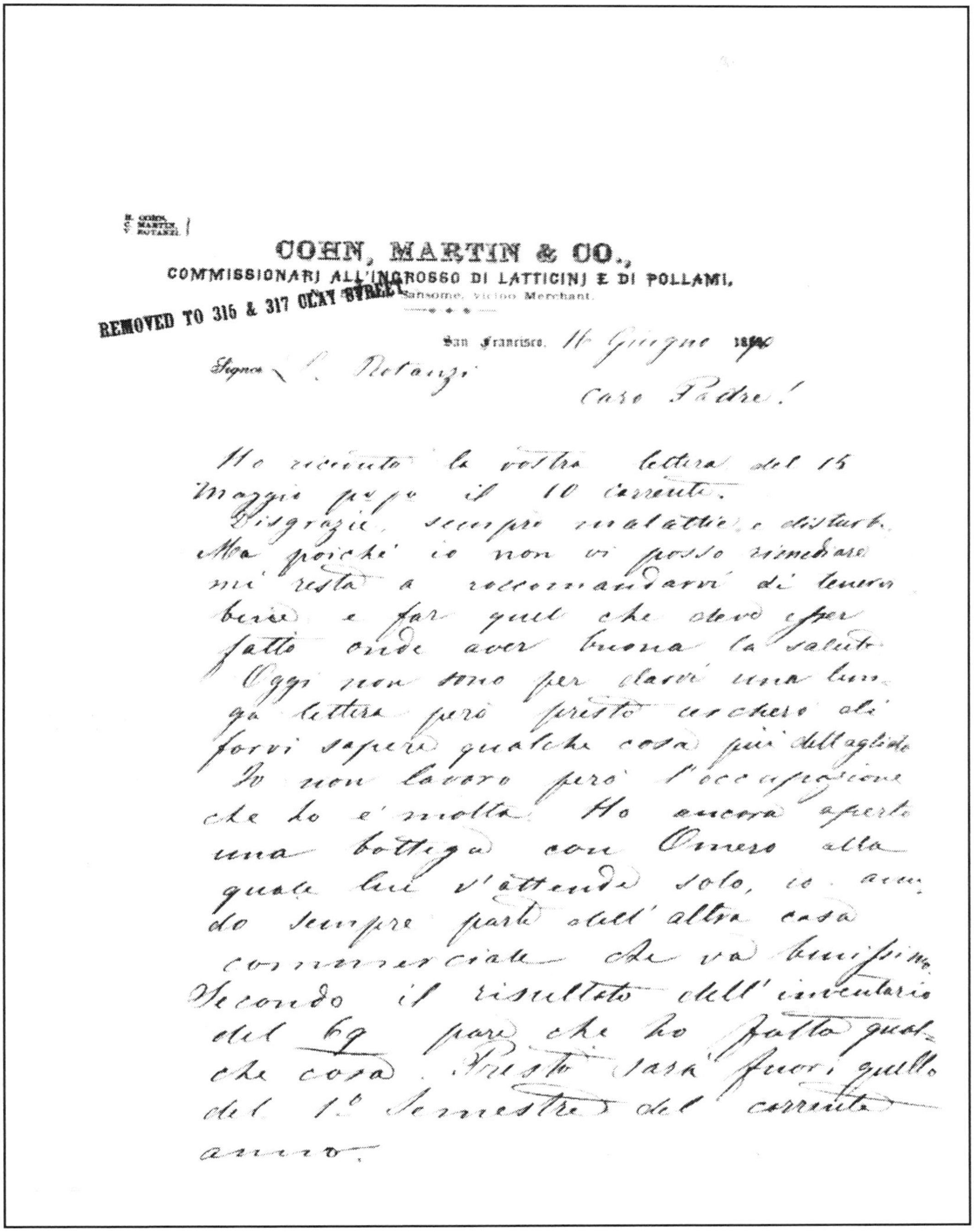

COHN, MARTIN & CO.,
COMMISSIONARI ALL'INGROSSO DI LATTICINJ E DI POLLAMI.
Sansome, vicino Merchant.
REMOVED TO 316 & 317 CLAY STREET

San Francisco, 16 Giugno 1870

Signor L. Rotanzi

Caro Padre!

Ho ricevuto la vostra lettera del 15
Maggio p.p. il 10 corrente.
Disgrazie, sempre malattie e disturbi.
Ma poichè io non vi posso rimediare
mi resta a raccomandarvi di tenervi
bene e far quel che deve esser
fatto onde aver buona la salute.
Oggi non sono per darvi una lun-
ga lettera però presto cercherò di
farvi sapere qualche cosa più dettagliato.
Io non lavoro però l'occupazione
che ho è molta. Ho ancora aperto
una bottega con Omero alla
quale lui s'attende solo, io aven-
do sempre parte dell'altra casa
commerciale che va benissimo.
Secondo il risultato dell'inventario
del 69 pare che ho fatto qualche cosa. Presto sarà fuori quello
del 1° Semestre del corrente
anno.

Letter from Virgilio to Luigi, June 16, 1870

TWENTY

"…if Cecchino really knew how it is here, he would come."

June 16, 1870—Letter from Virgilio in San Francisco to Luigi in Peccia

In June 1870, Virgilio wrote a brief, jumbled letter to Luigi. He seemed overwhelmed with business matters.

> Today I am not going to give you a long letter, but I will quickly give you some details.
>
> I don't do physical work but I am very busy. I still have the shop I opened with Omero, but only he attends to it. I still own part of another commercial house that goes extremely well. According to the inventory of '69, it seems that I have done well.

Perhaps to avoid worrying Luigi, Virgilio did not mention that in March a fire had broken out at 1111 Dupont Street, two doors down from his shop. The fire damaged the two-story frame building occupied by a saloon and a shoe shop upstairs, and also severely burned the building next door at 1113, which housed the Railroad Saloon and a lodging house. Virgilio could be grateful that his shop at 1115 Dupont was spared, as damage amounted to about five thousand dollars, and many occupants of the burned building lost everything in the fire.[1]

Virgilio still hoped to lure Francesco to California. He felt sure his older brother would fare well in San Francisco's booming economy.

> I have written so many times to Cecchino but it seems that he hasn't ever received my letters and not yours either. Now I write him with every steamer that leaves here, which is monthly.
>
> Various arrivals from Australia make me think that if Cecchino really knew how it is here, he would come. Send word that I do

know something about California, of that he can be the judge.

Apparently he has a good business but he can't make it with the economy. I wait for the schoolbooks, but I am not so anxious for all the other things that I have requested.

In contrast to Francesco, who downplayed his achievements, Virgilio made sure Luigi knew that he was no longer working as a laborer. He had substantial responsibilities. Having failed with a ranch laden with liabilities, Virgilio now aimed to profit from selling cheese and butter produced by his compatriots. He proudly informed Luigi that "The activity from the commission firm is between 60 to 70 thousand dollars, and the major part of its management is entrusted to me." Too busy to give details of his ventures, he deferred to his partner Omero, "who perhaps has more time and will give a better report."

Chinese Market, Sacramento Street, 1866

Virgilio also claimed that he had too many obligations to contact Bagnovini, who still waited for the money he had lent Virgilio for his ranch purchase. "I must write to Bagnovini. I would have done it already, but I don't know where to start with having so much to do these days. If butter sells at a pretty good price, I believe I'll do very well this year."

Once again, Virgilio asked, or rather directed, his father to take care of some business for him in Ticino.

> I have not written to Guscetti from Magadino, but you could do a favor by giving him an option for the purchase of 200 dozen dry calf stomachs.
>
> Send them immediately, making an account of all your travels and expenses and troubles. If you are not able to do this, employ some individual whom you can trust. We must send them in the fastest way possible, by steamship, not by sailboat, to the firm in New York (the address I have put here at the end). From that firm they will be sent here by railroad in the most affordable way.
>
> You need to put them in a large case (or two) of hermetically sealed tin, with wood on the outside, strong but not heavy.
>
> New York has already been sent a telegram that 60 dozen will arrive first – a while back here they were worth $3.50 per dozen. Now that they are scarce they are valued at $10.00 – so it's greatly important to receive them before other cases of them arrive.

Virgilio's shipment of dry calves' stomachs would end up on North Bay dairy ranches where they would be used to make cheese. The stomachs, a veal byproduct, contain rennet, an enzyme complex produced by unweaned calves to help digestion. Rennet, an essential ingredient in cheesemaking, causes proteins in milk to coagulate and form curds.

Virgilio knew that he could sell two hundred dozen dried calf stomachs, but he had to get them before his competitors. He had taken a risk, given many known and unknown shipping hazards. If the shipment arrived late, damaged, or not at all, Virgilio stood to lose his market advantage and jeopardize his business relationships.

Just as Virgilio had initially seen great promise for the ranch he purchased, Charles Martin, Virgilio's new partner, saw enormous potential in California's vast coastal dairy lands. His vision for California's dairy industry grew from his origins in the Vallemaggia, which produced

164

excellent cheeses from small numbers of cows herded high in the Alps over craggy trails from one meadow to another, following seasonal grasses. California had vastly more land and a perfect climate. Martin and his Swiss compatriots had the expertise. Martin envisioned an illustrious future for himself, his fellow Swiss Italians and for their herds grazing on ranches covering California's coastland.

In an ad placed in the *Marysville Daily Appeal*, Martin reminded readers that the Netherlands, with less land than San Bernardino County, exported butter worth eight million dollars in 1868. Why couldn't California, with its enormous acreage, compete with the world-renowned dairy produce of the Netherlands and Switzerland? Martin's grandiose vision for Cohn, Martin & Co. encompassed the globe:

> Were the great natural capabilities of California in the Dairy
> Produce line worked onto the same pitch of perfection as those
> of the Netherlands and Switzerland, we could furnish ample
> supplies for India, China, Japan, Mexico, the Amoor country[2]
> [Eastern Siberia], Alaska, and the Isles of the Pacific. And it is
> the intention of this firm to elevate the character of our Dairy
> Products, extend the field of production, and secure for them a
> reputation which will make them coveted at home and abroad.[3]

Henry Cohn, son of a veteran commission merchant, knew the business, but it was Martin, not Cohn or Virgilio, who had formed strong business relationships with Swiss-Italian dairymen. With the firm for just over a year, Virgilio appeared to have little to do with Martin's marketing efforts, although he claimed to be responsible for most of the firm's management. Along with Henry Cohn, Virgilio handled day-to-day operations in the San Francisco office while Martin, from his Chileno Valley ranch, mapped out the firm's long-term strategies and alliances with dairies operated by relatives, friends and acquaintances—Tognazzini, Fiori, Bloom, Garzoli, Codoni, Cheda, Giacomini, deMartini, Martinelli and a host of others.

Swiss-Italian ranchers gained leverage from the firm's distribution channels and marketing efforts as Martin positioned Cohn, Martin & Co. as a large, geographically diverse and distinctive association of expert Swiss dairymen. What specifically distinguished Swiss dairy practices from others at the time is unclear, but by extolling Swiss expertise, Martin intended to heighten his firm's market value and compete against well-known dairy producers like the Pierce Point dairy ranch and the Steele Brothers.[4]

The *Marin Journal* in 1871 noted that "there are now about 600 Swiss in the county, nearly all of whom are engaged in dairying. The great majority of them commenced poor, on leased land, and nearly every one of them has made money." It reported that land around Tomales was worth $30 to $45 an acre, but the Swiss were buying elsewhere as land was becoming scarce in Marin and Sonoma counties.[5] Swiss-Italian ranchers migrated to dairy land farther south on California's coast, to San Mateo and Santa Cruz counties, then to San Luis Obispo. When land there became unavailable, they bought in Santa Barbara County and up the coast in Mendocino, Humboldt and Del Norte Counties. Ultimately, Martin's vast, informal network of Swiss dairymen covered the length of California's coastal range, from the north in Crescent City to the south in San Diego.

In his ad, Martin mentioned that his firm owned an enormous ranch, a "splendid tract" over "five miles in extent," in Santa Cruz County. Martin likely referred to the spread purchased by Giuliano Stefano Moretti and his son-in-law Jeremiah Respini, who, like Martin, hailed from Cevio. This vast coastal property amounted to over forty thousand acres near Punto Año Nuevo south of Pescadero, where the Steele Brothers had also purchased large dairy holdings.[6] Bound together with Moretti and Respini by financial and possibly familial ties, Martin likely felt justified in claiming this land as part of his firm's holdings.

When Giuliano Moretti first immigrated to California, he had worked as a laborer on Martin's ranch in Chileno Valley. Martin helped him get a start and may have helped finance the Santa Cruz ranch purchase. The Martin-Moretti family partnership remained strong over decades. In the mid-1850s, the two men bought land together in Chileno Valley. Nearly four decades later, in 1893, Charles Martin and Giuliano Moretti, with several other Swiss Italians, including Joseph Traversi, purchased the Santa Ysabel dairy and cattle ranch, nearly eighteen thousand acres in San Diego County, expanding their operations to California's southernmost county.

The full-column ad placed by Charles Martin to promote Cohn, Martin & Co. may have skipped readers' attention, but sensational front-page headlines in both Omaha and San Francisco newspapers featuring Henry Cohn and the law likely did not. On May 5, 1870, the *San Francisco Chronicle*'s front page announced: "The Zamit-Cohn-Omaha-Complication—How a Maltese Poultryman Fell Among Thieves."[7]

The incident began in April 1870 when Cohn filed a complaint against a fellow poultry and egg dealer Frank Zamit, a Maltese immigrant, claiming that Zamit had taken goods worth six hundred dollars under false pretenses from Cohn, Martin & Co. On learning that Zamit had headed out of state for New York, Cohn took his complaint to California's Governor Henry Huntley Haight, who, under law enforcement practices unheard of today, appointed private citizen Cohn to bring Zamit back to California to face charges.[8]

Telegraphed of Zamit's potential arrival, sharp-eyed Omaha Marshal William G. Hollins captured Zamit in Omaha's train station and took him into custody along with a buckskin bag of gold amounting to fifteen hundred dollars. Just after Cohn arrived in Omaha to bring Zamit back to California, a Nebraska judge revoked the warrant for Zamit, ruling it a civil case to collect a business debt rather than a criminal case involving theft. Marshal Hollins, however, confiscated the fifteen hundred dollars in gold he had collected from Zamit and gave a portion of it to Cohn, who went to the bank and used it to pay for a $1450 draft on a bank in San Francisco in favor of Charles Martin.

Zamit's attorney immediately claimed that Marshal Hollins and Cohn had conspired to steal the fifteen hundred dollars when Zamit only owed Cohn, Martin & Co. six hundred. The attorney, charging that Hollins had stolen Zamit's money, had the funds recovered from the bank and secured a warrant for the arrest of both Cohn and Hollins on charges of larceny.

After several days of court hearings and lengthy testimony from a number of witnesses, the judge released both Cohn and Hollins from jail, ruling that they had committed no crime, after which Cohn's attorney accused the Omaha City Attorney and the District Attorney of false imprisonment. Next the District Attorney put out a warrant for Cohn on a charge of perjury.

Accusations flew back and forth. The *Omaha Republican* stated that "the case is the principal topic of conversation on the streets…"[9] The *San Francisco Chronicle* poked fun at the fiasco, describing the day when Cohn appeared in court on charges of perjury: "Everybody arose at an early hour, and when asked by the gentlemanly barkeeper at the neighboring "grocery," "what's yourn?" absently replied, "Fifteen hundred, gold, in brown buckskin bag—I mean, whisky cocktails."[10]

Cohn resolved this messy incident by skipping town. As reported in the *Chronicle*: "He had availed himself of the darkness…to cross the river in a small boat to Council Bluffs, and was not afterward heard from."[11] Omaha authorities documented the incident for Governor Haight, hoping that the Governor would make Cohn and Zamit answer for their actions.

News coverage of this imbroglio cast doubt on Henry Cohn's integrity and on the good name of his firm. Charles Martin, aspiring to earn a reputation for a sterling company offering superior products, must have recoiled in alarm at news of the fiasco. A few months later, two inventors sued Cohn, Martin & Co. for twenty thousand dollars in damages, alleging that the firm infringed its patent for egg packing boxes.[12] Notice of this suit did not nearly approach the negative publicity of articles dwelling on "The Buckskin Bag of Gold—Robbery, False Imprisonment, Habeas Corpus, Perjury, and Everything Else."

Virgilio did not write home about the Cohn/Zamit brouhaha. It did not speak well of his firm, and it would mean nothing to Luigi. Yet he also failed to tell his father of even more shocking news, sure to cause Luigi to worry. He had become entangled with a sixteen-year-old Corsican girl named Elisa. Soon he would become a father. Virgilio could not count on his compatriots to refrain from gossip in their reports home, but in his hasty letter to Luigi, Virgilio made no mention of Elisa or of his baby, due in just two months.

TWENTY-ONE

"How much wretchedness has happened…"

December 18, 1870—Letter from Virgilio in San Francisco to Luigi in Peccia

Where had Virgilio met Elisa? Unlike girls who hung about the bars and brothels of Virgilio's Barbary Coast neighborhood, Elisa came from a reputable family. At sixteen, she no longer attended school and was considered of marriageable age. The daughter of Corsican immigrants Francisco (Francois) Giacobbi and Marie Francoise Salicetti Giacobbi, Elisa was born in Paris in 1853 and had immigrated with her parents to Mayfield, California as a tiny infant. Francisco and Marie may have chosen to settle in Mayfield because Marie's brother Joseph lived there. By 1870, Elisa's father, sixty-year-old Francisco, had moved his family to San Francisco where he worked in the wine industry.[1] Elisa, the eldest child, had two younger sisters and a younger brother, all still in school.[2]

Notre Dame des Victoires

Cosmopolitan San Francisco offered numerous opportunities for young people to gather together. The city's residents, with their mixtures of language and culture, had enjoyed revelry since Gold Rush days, gathering in French cafes, and German concert and beer halls. Charitable institutions held gala balls, such as that taking place in July 1860 for the Asylum of the Deaf, Dumb and Blind, where "Three or four thousand persons were present, including a great number of pretty ladies, and many of a class of steady people rarely seen at the theaters and other places of light amusement."[3]

Public celebrations took place, not only on the American Fourth of July and Admission Day, but on the holidays celebrated by each immigrant group: Swiss Independence Day, Irish St. Patrick's Day, French Bastile Day, Italian Columbus Day, German May Day, Latin Carnevale and others. Summertime picnics held by fraternal societies and militia groups like the Swiss Guard offered chances for young people to meet and mingle in the countryside.

San Francisco's freewheeling spirit placed young people in peril of breaking taboos. In 1869, journalist John S. Hittell remarked, "In no part of the world is the individual freer from restraint. Men, women, and children are permitted to do nearly as they please. High wages, migratory habits, and bachelor life, are not favorable to the maintenance of stiff social rules..."[4] Chronicler Benjamin E. Lloyd, commenting on the city's dissolute social conduct, warned:

> . . . we would say to the parents of San Francisco to look closer to
> their daughters, for they know not the many dangers to which
> they are exposed—know their associates, guard their virtue—and
> to mildly counsel their sons, for when upon the streets of this gay
> city they are wandering amid many temptations.[5]

Virgilio had been raised in a small village where the priest threatened damnation for the sins of pre-marital sex. The Catholic Church also condemned contraception, yet contraceptive devices were not hard to find in San Francisco. After 1844, the year Charles Goodyear patented the rubber vulcanizing process, condom production increased. By 1870, condoms, known as "rubbers," could be readily purchased from doctors, pharmacies, dry-goods stores and mail-order houses. Advertisements for protective devices, such as "Dr. Reynolds Patent French Safe—Prevention Better than Cure," frequently appeared in newspapers.

Far from the priest's censure and watchful eyes of fellow villagers, in a wide-open, cosmopolitan city known for its wild spirit, Virgilio had violated the codes of conduct with which he had been raised. He had ignored warnings on the clock face of the Cathedral of St. Mary of the Immaculate

Conception on the corner of Dupont and California Streets, a few blocks from his store. It admonished young men to avoid the Barbary Coast's wicked temptations with the words: "Son, Observe the Time and Fly from Evil" (Ecclesiasticus 4:23).

Virgilio's son, Joseph Jean Virgil, was born on August 26, 1870. Just about three weeks later, on September 17, Virgilio and Elisa married in Eglise Notre Dame des Victoires, the church serving San Francisco's large French-speaking community. The event is listed in the church registers. The Roman Catholic Church required that wedding banns, announcements of upcoming marriage celebrations, be read and published at least three Sundays in advance of the wedding ceremony to allow for any possible objections. No such banns were published for Virgilio and Elisa.[6] Given the circumstances, it's unlikely that Elisa walked down the aisle in a lacy white gown and a crown of orange blossoms, followed by the customary entourage of bridesmaids and flower girls.[7]

In his letter dated December 18, 1870, Virgilio wrote as if he were still single, making no mention of Elisa or the baby.[8] Despite, or perhaps because of, his new familial obligations, Virgilio's optimism had dimmed. For the first time since leaving the Vallemaggia, he complained to Luigi about the hard life of an immigrant, the foreign language and culture, the unfamiliar surroundings, the health hazards and the struggle to survive.

> It's true that the only good on this earth is to hope for the best and accept and resign oneself to what comes. Now it's been 10 years since I have left home and in that time we have carefully followed each other in each passage of our lives. How much wretchedness has happened in between the little bits of goodness, still always hoping that the future would be better.

Like Francesco, who also expressed that time had taken its toll, Virgilio no longer exuded the energy that had driven him in the past to succeed.

> I have always improved my state, it's true, but health and activity and ten years of work with the fixed goal of saving have led me to an old age compared to when I started to seek my fortune. It's enough to make anyone recognize that I would also have been

rewarded for my work and my efforts in a different country.

In his mid-twenties, Virgilio felt disheartened and disillusioned. His enthusiasm may have been waning, but he was not destitute. He rented living space at 930 Montgomery Street, likely in one of the many widow-run boarding houses found throughout San Francisco. The 1870 census does not indicate that Elisa lived with him. He is listed as a grocer, with no real estate, but with personal property worth one thousand dollars.[9] This amount may have been his half of Rotanzi & Company which he co-owned with Omero Medici, and which had assets worth two thousand dollars.[10] He remained a partner at the commission firm, as did Henry Cohn, who had returned from his imbroglio in Omaha apparently unscathed. But when Virgilio compared his state with those of some compatriots who had gone into dairy ranching, he fell far short.[11]

Virgilio questioned the choice he had made when, ten years earlier, full of hope and enthusiasm, he had set out for California.

> I don't wish to say that I regret coming here. Now I must find my-
> self content, but at home perhaps I would have been able to learn
> and perhaps have success in a fine career, one more limited in
> allure, more limited in earnings, but more steady and more secure
> and happier and healthier than that of the immigrant.

Virgilio had fallen into a trap about which the California Immigrant Union warned potential immigrants. Its promotional brochures advised new arrivals on what to expect and how to navigate the pitfalls that could destroy inexperienced newcomers:

> The man who is making a start should be content with slow and
> sure profits. There is so much wild speculation in California, that
> strangers often imagine it is necessary for them to take part in
> it, and they lose their money before they suspect that they are
> in peril, and perhaps at the very time when they fancy that they
> are on the road to fortune. There is no country in which close
> attention to the strictest rules of business prudence pays better
> than in California.[12]

Lured by a dream that had turned into a nightmare, Virgilio had succumbed to California's high-stakes fever when he made his rash ranch purchase. Twenty-five years old, laden with debt and a young family to feed, he looked back on his efforts with regret. In hindsight, he wondered if steady employment, close family support, and the familiarity of home may have been a better choice. San Francisco's aura, formed since the Gold Rush by venturers and gamblers, nurtured only its winners.

Speculative frenzies made Virgilio's fellow San Franciscans giddy with dreams of riches. San Francisco's forty-niner gold hysteria had subsided, but the 1859 Comstock Lode discovery had brought new waves of wealth and ruin. Silver stock trading became the foremost financial activity in San Francisco.[13] Nearly everyone joined in the silver stock delirium. Joseph King, former chairman of the San Francisco Stock Exchange, described the stock transactions taking place each morning outside the exchange even before it opened: "And the street business! The first session was at 11 A.M. Before that hour we would congregate on the north side of California street, on the corner, and below Montgomery. And what sales we made!" A policeman managed the scores of buyers and sellers so that passersby could squeeze through the crowds.[14]

"Speculation went mad," wrote Mark Twain, who spent eighteen months in San Francisco during the 1860s. "Bankers, merchants, lawyers, doctors, mechanics, laborers, even the very washerwomen and servant-girls, were putting up their earnings on silver stocks, and every sun that rose in the morning went down on paupers enriched and rich men beggared. What a gambling carnival it was!"[15]

The city's residents saw immense fortunes materialize overnight. For some, the wealth evaporated just as quickly. Many, to be sure, made vast fortunes in the silver mines. James Flood, William O'Brien, John MacKay, and James Fair, Bonanza Kings of the Consolidated Virginia Silver Mine, became some of the richest men in the United States. Others grasped for fortune's ring in a whirling merry-go-round that left them dizzy and distraught.

A lottery to fund the Mercantile Library Association offered another chance to get rich quick. In 1852, a group of wealthy, civic-minded citizens had founded the library, intending to "make our infant city as distinguished for literature and science as it already is for its commerce and wealth."[16] Without public funding, such private associations established subscription or membership libraries, opening their doors to dues-paying members. Mercantile library associations, intended to broaden the horizons of men engaged in commercial enterprises, had already formed in other cities across the nation, including New York, Boston, Cincinnati, Baltimore and St. Louis.

In 1868, the San Francisco Mercantile Library Association erected a large three-story building on Bush Street in the heart of the commercial district. In its elegant facilities, members could read, play chess, hear lectures and dine together. The well-used library made newspapers available from as far away as the Sandwich Islands and the Cape of Good Hope and managed an average yearly circulation of eighty thousand volumes.[17]

Camilla Urso, 1883

Expenses for the new building and its extensive collections far exceeded the Association's reserves. In 1869, creditors threatened to close the library. In February 1870, to help the Association pay off its debts, the California State Legislature passed the Mercantile Library Gift Concert Bill, allowing the Association to hold a lottery despite passage of an 1861 Act to Prohibit Lotteries.

As a fundraiser and promotion for the lottery, the world-famous violinist Camilla Urso donated her services to produce a three-day grand music festival. The renowned Urso served as main attraction, financier and producer. She planned to put on the largest musical extravaganza ever held on the Pacific Coast, a "monster concert" to rival Boston's 1869 Grand National Peace Jubilee celebrating the end of the Civil War. Such enormous productions drew throngs of participants with big-name performers, thousands of singers and massive orchestras.

Holding her concerts over three afternoons in February, Urso performed at the Mechanics' Pavilion on Union Square, possibly the largest wooden building then standing in America, covering two and one-half acres.[18] She supervised the remodeling of this enormous building for the concerts, including a deluxe private viewing box for which banker and financier William Ralston offered three thousand dollars and San Francisco Mayor Selby outbid him with thirty-two hundred dollars.

Urso's agent traveled throughout the state gathering musicians. Children were released from school to rehearse and sing in the event.[19] The first Grand Concert included an orchestra of two hundred instruments, a chorus of twelve hundred voices from every singing society in California, a full military band, the city militia drum corps, one hundred San Francisco uniformed firemen beating on anvils, the ringing of city fire bells and the firing of cannon. Urso gave her net profits of nearly twenty thousand dollars to the Mercantile Library Association, whose officers held a grand ball for her on the festival's final day.[20]

Three fund-raising concerts led with a crescendo to the grand lottery ticket sales on June 1, when two hundred thousand lottery tickets were offered to the public at five dollars apiece, a significant amount, as schoolteachers earned about forty-five to sixty dollars per month.[21] The big prize was one hundred thousand dollars, with over six hundred lesser prizes. The total of all prizes amounted to half a million dollars in gold coin.[22]

The prospect of winning the lottery cast a spell nationwide. Orders arrived even before the lottery office opened to sell tickets. The public became so enthused by dreams of winning that some tickets, especially those considered lucky numbers, were sold at a premium of fifty cents to ten dollars. The office received nearly one hundred and fifty orders, many by telegraph, for the ticket number 1849, the year of California's Gold Rush, and one buyer offered a fifty-dollar bonus for it. A New York buyer ordered one thousand tickets and offered to purchase more tickets worth one hundred thousand dollars if given a suitable discount. Scalpers tried to hijack the lottery by buying all or a large portion of the tickets at a discount, then selling them at full price or a premium for a ten to twenty-five percent gain on their investment.[23]

A chance at the lottery promised big wins, at five dollars in gold coin per ticket, less than half the price of an annual subscription to the *Daily Alta California*.[24] Ten thousand tickets sold on the first day of sales, five thousand the next, and on the third day, sales were suspended because not enough tickets had been printed. The *Sacramento Daily Union* lamented:

> The worst anticipations as to the demoralizing effect on the comunity are more than realized. Servant-girls and their employers, clerks, schoolboys, day laborers, merchants and church dignitaries crowd each other in the scramble for tickets. All brokers have them in their windows for sale, and men are walking all around with handsful of tickets retailing them.[25]

Large buyers threatened that if they did not win they would sue on the grounds that the lottery was unconstitutional.[26]

On October 31, 1870, in front of fifteen thousand eager spectators in the immense Mechanic's Pavilion, twelve blind persons from the Deaf, Dumb and Blind Asylum drew the numbers. J.W. Stow, a wealthy board member of the Mercantile Association, announced winning tickets. The drawing lasted nearly fourteen hours, starting at nine in the morning and ending at half past ten at night.[27] As soon as Stow called out the numbers, they were telegraphed to the *Daily Alta California*, which printed extra editions listing the winning numbers every twenty minutes until the close of the drawing, finally printing a comprehensive list of all winning numbers and prizes.[28]

The announcer's wife Marietta L. Stow described the scene as "a seething, bellowing, heaving multitude. The elegant, in fine, sweet-scented raiment, hobnobbed with the unwashed, uncombed, and unkempt. The millionaire and Barbary-Coaster sat down together, awaiting the turn of

Fortune's wheel."[29] On the way home after the drawing, Mrs. Stow asked her husband why he looked so pale. He showed her two revolvers he had placed in his pockets in case the crowd grew out of control. With relief, he exclaimed, "I thank God it's over! I would not pass through another such ordeal for the price of my life, and I'm no coward."[30]

For a very few, the lottery made dreams come true. Had Virgilio purchased a ticket or split a chance with friends, he most likely would have joined the many losers. The following day, the *Daily Alta California* reported that "The disappointment has been almost general, for, although there are many who have enough cheerful philosophy to be prepared to receive either blank or prize with equanimity, the mass of humanity are not so constituted."

One such desolate loser was Emil Hirsch, one of Virgilio's employees at Cohn, Martin & Co. Hirsch's sobering story, described in lurid detail, made the front page of the *San Francisco Chronicle*: "Suicide of Emil Hirsch—Supposed Cause, Losses in Lotteries." Hirsch, "the young German well known in the business and social circles in this city," had "staked all the money he could raise in these wild lottery schemes as a last hope of retrieving his altered fortune."[31]

Emil Hirsch had indeed overextended himself. The *Sacramento Daily Union* reported that Hirsch had lost about $2,900 in mining stocks.[32] The *Sacramento Bee* reported that Hirsh was "the first victim of the Mercantile Library lottery, but he will not be the last. We may look for a round of suicide from this cause, and a large addition to the inmates of the Insane Asylum."[33] At least one other such suicide followed.[34]

Chloroform and laudanum, the two narcotic substances used in these suicides, were popular drugs to relieve pain and stress. Laudanum, a tincture of opium mixed with water or wine, was a widely used painkiller. A main ingredient in many patent medicines, it could be purchased without a prescription at local apothecary shops to ease a wide range of ailments.[35]

Virgilio and Hirsch, both in their twenties, had worked together at Cohn, Martin & Co. Hirsch had been the company's bookkeeper. Young Hirsch's suicide must have given Virgilio pause. As he continued his letter to Luigi, Virgilio now made it clear that he wanted to come home.

> Your letters and thoughts of my dear father, of my brothers and
> sisters, of the country of my innocent youth made me cry in 1861,
> [the year Virgilio left home] and renew hot tears when writing
> these words. But I thought less of you [then] than in these times.
> Yes, I will do what I can to come home; the lure of money loses its
> force when I think of seeing my good father again, getting older
> from aggravation that his sons are absent when they could
> console him.

Virgilio desperately seemed to be searching for a way out, a way home.
In his anxiety, he once again turned to thoughts of Francesco, proposing a
plan that, based on Francesco's past reluctance to leave Australia, had no
basis in reality.

> Yes, I must look to come home and avoid the fates of two brothers
> and an uncle.[36] But it hasn't been totally like that for Cecchino, at
> least he is alive. As for him, what does he have to do at home? He
> needs to come try in California. In this way we could trade places,
> and I would be able to come home as I want so much to do.

Death loomed in Virgilio's thoughts as he referred to the passing of his
brother Alessandro and his uncle Giacomo. Without explicitly stating that
he feared for his own life, Virgilio hinted that he suffered ill health, with
consequences far greater than his financial struggles.

He did not answer questions Luigi had posed in his previous letters,
questions which may have related to his finances, his new family or his
future. In an odd reversal, Virgilio wrote to his father the very words of
praise and love that he wished Luigi would offer him. He wanted to hear
an absolution. He yearned for Luigi to tell him that he had no need to be
ashamed of his failures.

> Excuse me for not replying to each and every principal point in
> your letter. It's too hard to do it because I am too agitated. I have
> already told you not to put yourself down in your way of writing
> to me; You do not have to ask to be excused and to make apologies
> as if you lacked something. You know how much I love you and
> hold you in esteem and how well you proved yourself, so that I
> could never doubt you in any way.

Virgilio's letter is fraught with anxiety and regret. He still owed money for his failed ranch purchase, but Bagnovini had died before Virgilio could pay him back. Virgilio assured Luigi that he still intended to pay off Bagnovini's heirs, then took a moment to wonder how things would have been different with his older brother working with him in California. Despite years of begging Francesco to come to California, Virgilio could not let go of the thought that his brother might come to help him.

> Perhaps if Cecchino had come earlier, I would have been spared
> the losses that come pressing on me now. I have written to him
> five or six times and haven't ever had a reply.

> If I knew that he was not going to come, I would sell my part of
> the commission firm, because if I must abandon San Francisco, I
> wish to liquidate everything first.

Virgilio then abruptly switched to business, once again ordering Luigi to quickly arrange a shipment of goods. The first transcontinental railroad had been completed in the prior year, allowing Virgilio to receive his shipment from New York in days rather than months.

> In the quickest way possible, send 150 or 200 dozen calves'
> stomachs in the manner that I have already written, that is: to
> New York by steamer, and not by sail, and from New York to
> San Francisco by train—in that way if they are received soon
> it's possible to sell them well. Make an invoice against our firm
> (Cohn, Martin & Co.) at about 3 francs per dozen. Include the
> delivery costs and put it together with the shipment papers. This
> will serve to pay a little here to the custom office. The amount we
> must pay you, the real amount, make it so you gain at least a franc
> per dozen beyond what they cost you; in that way the profits will
> remain with you. Here we will earn still more—at least ten francs
> per dozen—now we are selling them at six dollars —they are
> valued always from $3.50 to $4.00.

> I salute you from my heart saying I am your most affectionate son,
> Virgilio.

Virgilio's anxiety leaped out from the pages as he bounced from one topic to the next, from regrets to wishes, from doubts to shipping details. He ended it hastily with a business order and a perfunctory salutation.

These words were likely the last Luigi had from Virgilio. Just four months later, on April 1, 1871, a little over ten years after arriving in California, Virgilio succumbed to phthisis, as tuberculosis was called at the time. The disease, also known as consumption, had been slowly wasting away his body, causing him to lose energy and motivation.[37]

Virgilio's death notice described him as a twenty-four-year-old merchant, born not in Switzerland, but in France, a result of Elisa or one of her Corsican family members providing information to the authorities.[38] Like Francesco, Virgilio had joined a Masonic Lodge. He was buried in San Francisco's Masonic Cemetery, a cemetery in the city's western region.[39]

In the early twentieth century, the cemeteries once located on the city's western perimeter now stood near the city center. To make way for housing, buried bodies were dug up from these cemeteries and moved to Colma, a town south of San Francisco.[40] With no relatives to claim his body and pay for its removal, Virgilio's remains were exhumed and re-buried in a mass grave at Colma's Woodlawn Cemetery. The San Francisco Public Works Department repurposed his tombstone, with so many others, using some for landfill or gutters, others for seawalls along the Great Highway, the Marina and approaches to the Golden Gate Bridge.

Repurposed headstone, San Francisco's Buena Vista Park

TWENTY-TWO

"They say he was an imposter…"

February 26, 1872—Letter from Elisa in San Francisco to Luigi in Peccia
January 6, 1875—Letter from Elisa in San Francisco to Luigi in Peccia

With Virgilio gone, Elisa, not yet twenty, found herself a widow with a tiny infant in her care. In February 1872, nearly a year after Virgilio's death, Elisa wrote a letter in Italian to Luigi, with whom she had already corresponded:

> Dear Father!
>
> I have received your letter and read it with much pleasure. After waiting a long time for it, and seeing that you didn't respond to me, I didn't know what to think.
>
> I am sorry to hear that you do not have good health, and this needs to be taken care of more than any other thing. If health isn't good, our road is most sad.
>
> Up to now my health hasn't been good. After his death, I wasn't well. You told me to be resigned, but if I resign myself to one thing, I am tormented by another. After he died I assure you that I had nothing but anguish. If I didn't have those at home, I wouldn't have known where to find help. I am left with nothing.

Elisa could be thankful she was a widow and not an unwed mother on whom stigma cast a dark shadow. Some women resorted to suicide or infanticide to escape the shame of their plight. Abortions were dangerous and illegal. Those arrested for performing them were charged with murder.

San Francisco offered some help to unmarried or single mothers. The San Francisco Lying-In Hospital and Foundling Asylum had been formed to care for unwed women and their children. The institution was usually

Francois Giacobbi, date unknown

full with about one hundred children born at the asylum or left at its door each year.[1] At the San Francisco Female Hospital, founded in 1868, over seventy-five children were born each year, more than half illegitimate. The institution was said to have saved many fallen women from killing their newborn children.[2] The Magdalen Asylum for Wayward Girls, an institution founded in 1867 by the Sisters of Mercy, took in delinquent and rebellious girls, some sent by the city court and others by parents. In 1874, the Asylum housed a total of 150 women and girls.[3]

Fortunately, Elisa had her parents, Francisco and Maria Giacobbi, who sheltered their daughter within the family both before and after the birth of their grandchild. In June 1870, Elisa, unwed and over six months pregnant, lived with her parents and her two younger sisters, Emily, fourteen years old, Sophia, seven years old, and her brother Louis Agassio, twelve years old.[4] She continued to stay with her family after the birth of her baby.

Bereft from Virgilio's death, Elisa suffered yet another trauma. Announcing the shocking blow to Luigi, she revealed her helplessness and outrage.

> Martinoja [Charles Martin] wants to give me nothing of what I
> expected from Rotanzi's share.

Chapter Twenty-Two

> He told me that the firm had losses and that Rotanzi's part was
> 7,800 pounds sterling, and that I had nothing to see in stock. He
> has done all as he wants. He has acted as he pleased without
> asking me my wishes. He sold Rotanzi's share, without coming
> to ask me if I wanted to sell. In sum he has cheated me.

The amount Martin quoted Elisa, 7,800 pounds sterling, was a very large sum, about $43,000 in 1870 dollars.[5] If indeed that were Virgilio's share of liabilities, his initial investment of $1,250 had amounted to a loss of $43,000 in just a couple of years, and, once again, he had made a very poor investment.

Martin may have told Elisa the truth regarding the company's losses, but given the high demand for dairy products, the firm's excellent ranching connections and Martin's business acumen, it is unlikely that the firm was losing money, particularly such an enormous amount. What's more, Martin had no trouble finding a new partner. On May 5, 1871, Cohn and Martin placed a notice in the *Daily Alta California* announcing that the co-partnership was dissolved due to Virgilio's death.

Almanacco Italosvizzero Americano, **1881**

One week later, on May 12, a notice in the same newspaper announced that "Mr. Camil Steffani has been admitted a partner in the firm of COHN, MARTIN & CO." Sometime later, Martin also offered shares of the business to Natale Giacomini, one of Virgilio's traveling companions to California.[6]

Martin had chosen a well-connected partner with Camillo (Camil) Steffani, who owned a hardware store at 1006 Dupont Street, just a block away from Virgilio's Swiss Store. Prominent in the Swiss-Italian community, Steffani served as an officer of the Swiss Benevolent Society and the Swiss Rifle Club and became a founding member of the Speranza Italiana Lodge, the Masonic Lodge formed by and for Italian speakers.[7]

In her letter, Elisa continued to vent her frustration to Luigi:

> Poor Rotanzi had named him [Martinoja] executor in his will
> believing that he would treat me well. He had such faith in
> him, but poor Rotanzi didn't know that he would treat me in
> this manner. If it's true that the dead see everything always, he
> [Virgilio] will suffer a second time, to see the manner in which he
> [Martinoja] operates.
>
> I gathered together the will and put it in the hands of Martinoja. It
> was well sealed. I let him keep it 37 days to have time to put all the
> books to his liking, then he sent it back, without troubling to put it
> in an envelope as if it were just a piece of paper picked up off the
> street! Thus seeing the way in which he treated me, I was obliged
> to bring a lawsuit.

Martin's crass handling of Virgilio's papers fell far outside the bounds of good manners. Elisa could barely contain her rage and anxiety, denouncing Martin as a heartless thief. She found Martin's treatment of Virgilio's will especially appalling.

> I assure you that to him, it means very little, because he is wealthy,
> and in this country that is what always rules. Even this wicked
> man with all his wealth is jealous of what poor little Rotanzi
> gained with the sweat of his brow and what caused him to die.
> Now you imagine my position: to see all these lawsuits on one
> side, tears on the other. It's true that a plight never comes alone.

Elisa understood the power Martin's affluence afforded him. He had indeed joined the ranks of the wealthy. In 1876, his name appeared in the *Marin Journal* on a list of taxpayers assessed ten thousand dollars or more entitled "The Heavy Men of Marin County." Appearing with him, along with many of Marin's wealthiest pioneers such as George McNear and Albert Kent, were several Swiss-Italian compatriots.[8] In just fifteen to twenty years, through hard work and ingenuity, they had transformed themselves from penniless immigrants to some of the county's richest men. The list included Benedict Sartori, possibly the Sartori with whom Virgilio had quarreled over his unfortunate ranch purchase.

It was clear to Elisa that the enormous strain of Virgilio's two businesses had caused his death. She had seen his health compromised by his relentless striving in pursuit of success. Most people infected with tuberculosis bacteria do not develop the active illness. His resistance low, Virgilio succumbed to a disease from which few recovered. In his final days, he still believed that Francesco might come to his aid in California.

In 1869, Virgilio had subscribed to La Solidarité, a mutual insurance company. One month after Virgilio's death, a listing appeared in the *San Francisco Bulletin* to the members of La Solidarité announcing Virgilio's death and assessing one dollar from each member to be paid to his designated heir.[9] A few days later, a notice announcing the termination of Virgilio's co-partnership with Henry Cohn and Charles Martin appeared in the *Daily Alta California*.[10]

Perhaps Virgilio had exaggerated the extent of his partnership in Cohn, Martin & Co. On joining the firm a year earlier, he had written to his father that he had invested $1250 from the sale of his half of the Petaluma store for one quarter of the company. Virgilio had praised Martin to Luigi: "He is a rich man, a just man and a benefactor. Haven't I done well to have him as a partner?" Yet despite Virgilio's quarter interest, the firm's name never changed to include him. Craving approval and blinded by opportunity, Virgilio may have inflated his share in the company to Luigi and Elisa.

Yet Charles Martin could easily have cheated Elisa. She was a very young woman with no business experience. The model woman of the time was a domestic creature who knew nothing of crude commerce. She was charged with creating a comfortable refuge from the brutal world of business for her hard-working husband. Etiquette books advised women: "In conversing with professional gentlemen, never question them upon matters connected with their employment."[11] What did Elisa know of Virgilio's business? A cunning businessman might easily have taken advantage of a defenseless, young widow.

Mid-nineteenth century etiquette guides admonished women to avoid showing negative emotions: "If a lady has cares, let her conceal them from the world, or not go into it. Whatever be her merit, let her not forget that she may be a man in the superiority of her mind and decision of character, but that externally she ought to appear a woman!"[12] Women should be docile and retiring, showing "An affectionate, complying, and almost timid aspect, a tender solicitude for those who are about her . . . Her face should breathe hope, gentleness, and satisfaction; dejection, anxiety, and ill humor should be constantly banished."[13]

In her letter to Luigi, Elisa did not hold back expressing her fierce anger at how Martin had treated her. However, she may have misrepresented the situation, perhaps exaggerating in hopes of gaining monetary or moral support. Her accusations of theft against Martin contrasted sharply with his excellent reputation in the Swiss-Italian community. Unfortunately, all records of Elisa's lawsuit and its outcome have disappeared.

Elisa's predicament was not an unusual one for widows. One of her contemporaries, an older, more experienced woman, also struggled to gain her rightful inheritance in ways that flaunted social norms for women. The forthright Mrs. Marietta L. B. Stow, whose prominent husband, Joseph W. Stow, had announced the winning numbers in the Mercantile Lottery, brought the issue of probate for widows to the attention of the nation.[14] Mrs. Stow had enjoyed privileges of the wealthy elite as wife of a well-known member of San Francisco's high society. In 1872, on returning to San Francisco from a trip abroad, Mrs. Stow learned that her affluent husband

Marietta Stow in her Equal Rights Costume

had died suddenly. Instead of inheriting Mr. Stow's assets, the wealth she was due as Mr. Stow's wife, Marieta Stow found herself destitute while the will was held up in probate court. Just as Elisa blamed Charles Martin, Mrs. Stow accused the will's executors of fraud. Widows had the right to inherit property, but both Elisa and Mrs. Stow had to take their struggle to court.[15]

Marieta Stow's outrage drove her to mount a nationwide campaign to repeal probate laws. She traversed the United States, making speeches in a relentless push for widows' rights. In her book *Probate Confiscation: the Unjust Laws which Govern Women*, she advocated for reform of California's marital property law. Inflamed by injustice, she drafted a "Bill for the Protection of Widows and Orphans" and lobbied to pass it in the California State Legislature without success. In 1878, she spoke at the State House in Boston of the widow's plight: "You may claim, gentlemen, that, in case of malfeasance, a widow has legal redress. Ah Yes! She has in one sense; but litigation is an expensive luxury, and she has no money perhaps to prove that the executors are derelict in duty."[16] Riled by injustices she suffered in a male-dominated society, Mrs. Stow took an active role in the suffragist movement, running for Vice President of the United States in 1884 on the Equal Rights Ticket.[17]

Elisa lacked Marieta Stow's feminist zeal and political ambitions. She only wanted what she felt was rightfully owed from Virgilio's share of Cohn,

Voting Ballot for Presidential Election, 1884

Martin & Co. Likely her father had hired and paid an attorney to handle the lawsuit for her. She continued to lament her losses in her letter to Luigi.

> My youth has passed for a life full of thorns. The little happiness I have enjoyed was in the brief time when I was with him [Virgilio]. God makes me pay most dearly these days. I believe that there are very few at my age that have had so many troubles.
>
> I have written a letter to my brother-in-law in Australia, [Francesco], but I have not had an answer up to now. It's been already 3 or 4 months, but as I don't have his address, perhaps the letter didn't reach him. I believe that he intends to come to California. I would be greatly pleased to know him.
>
> Don't forget to respond to me. You don't know the pleasure that I get in reading your letters. Receive my greetings and share them with your daughters. You say that you have a very tiring life. I will pray then that your daughters will answer me without waiting.
>
> If you write to Australia, ask him [Francesco] if he has received my second letter, and tell him to write me and send me his address.
>
> I send you this prayer, take courage and don't be unhappy. Think that you still have a son near you [Marino] who can console you even though you have two sons who have died. My only consolation is going to visit the grave, to be able to make you imagine how beautiful it is. It's all full of flowers because he was still young. I have put nothing but white flowers there and a heart of greenery.
>
> One thing that would give me great pleasure is you sending a portrait of your family which is so dear to me. My father, it's been already 2 years since he [Virgilio] departed, leaving me in anguish; keeping my pledge to him I will find myself crying in pain and sadness the months of April and May; poor father, you were so pleased by my contentment when I wrote to you that Rotanzi made me so happy.
>
> I am always your affectionate daughter,
> Elisa Rotanzi

Three years after announcing to Luigi that she planned to sue Martin, Elisa's litigation still had not been resolved. On January 6, 1875, Elisa wrote again to Luigi, this time in French.

> Dear Father-in-law! You must be very surprised with my long silence, and you must think badly of me. You have reason to complain, for I realize it's bad on my part to have stayed so long without writing you, but I hope that you will excuse me when you know the reason for my negligence.
>
> When I received the letter from Isolina [one of Virgilio's sisters] dated March 6th, I was going to answer it, but there were only a few days until the third anniversary of Rotanzi's death. I wished to wait to go to the grave of my poor Rotanzi to take all kinds of flowers and send them to you. It was April 1st and the following day I became sick from poison oak. That lasted more than 20 days. Cured from that, a sickness came over my body and my eyes that made me stay in bed. I feared for my sight. I don't know how long I had to rest without being able to see light. I stayed in bed more than 4 months without getting out.

Elisa's bout of poison oak might seem like a feeble excuse for not writing, but severe attacks were not uncommon, some causing eye damage. The cursed plant still grows rampant throughout California's countryside, twisting up tree trunks and entwining its dense, shrubby branches with look-alike blackberry bushes. Contact with the sap-like oil secreted by the plant's leaves and stems causes skin to erupt in an itchy, painful rash, possibly a dangerous affliction. In 1857, *Hutchings' California Magazine* warned that "there are some afflicted so severely, as to induce protracted illness, often blindness, and sometimes even death."[18]

Elisa continued recounting to Luigi her excuses.

> You will tell me that since I have been cured I have been able to write, that's true, but I also wanted to see the end of my lawsuit in order to be able to tell you something of it, and it never came. From when it started in December up to today, it hasn't yet ended, but I hope that it won't be long.
>
> But if you knew how these miserable ones fight it, as they falsely swear about everything related to Rotanzi; oh, it's unbelievable.

They have forged the books in order to make me see losses, and well, they say that it was Rotanzi who forged them, they say that he wasn't honest, they say that he was an imposter. Finally they say all that they can against him, because they know that he isn't here to respond. I don't know why God lets such creatures exist on this earth.

I will let you know about it when it is finished.

Since Virgilio's death, the nation's economy had faltered. Following a period of post-Civil War economic expansion, a world-wide depression beginning in 1873 had been triggered by a number of factors, including "railroad mania," a wild speculation by banks in railroad construction. The economic collapse, known as the "Long Depression," lasted until 1879. During this six-year period, thousands of businesses went bankrupt, unemployment surged, and economic activity shrank.

San Francisco was not immune to the effects of this slump. Many Easterners headed West where they believed they would find better opportunities. Resentment against cheap Chinese labor burgeoned anew during this period of extreme job scarcity. Businesses clawed and scraped to stay alive. Many went under. This massive economic downturn likely made Charles Martin even less willing to cooperate with Elisa.

Other concerns that plagued Cohn, Martin & Co. would add to Elisa's troubles. In a sudden break with Henry Cohn on September 16, 1873, Charles Martin and Camillo Steffani placed an announcement in the *Daily Alta California* dissolving the firm of Cohn, Martin & Co. and forming a new firm called Martin & Steffani.

Five days later on September 23, 1873, the front page of the *San Francisco Chronicle* disclosed the cause of the break-up in the headlines: "ABSCONDED. Henry Cohn Perpetrates a Financial Stratagem and Goes East . . . How He Gave his Partners the Slip - The Money He Has Taken With Him." Cohn had skipped town:

It leaked out yesterday that Henry Cohn, of the produce firm of Cohn, Martin & Co., had closed up his business in this city in a manner more summary than legitimate, and stolen off to the East

with a nice little stake raised on the credit of the firm. The house
of Cohn, Martin & Co., the place of business of which was at 309
to 313 Clay street, was composed of the distinguished financier,
Henry Cohn himself, Charles Martin, who resides near Petaluma,
and Camilo Steffani, of this city. Cohn had been in the house five
or six years. Mr. Steffani bought in two years and a half ago.

Cohn left San Francisco in the middle of May saying he would be back
in two weeks, but he failed to return. Before leaving, he had withdrawn five
thousand dollars from Anglo California Bank as the firm's partner, making
Cohn, Martin & Co. liable for the loan. On learning of this fraud, Martin and
Steffani dissolved their partnership with Cohn.

Steffani misled the press, stating that "Cohn never contributed any
money to the partnership and really owns no interest therein," whereas
Cohn had actually founded the firm. Martin, Virgilio, and later Steffani
had bought into Cohn's business. According to the news article, Cohn had
caught the partners off-guard. They "were not aware that Cohn had any bad
habits that might tempt him to the commission of his crime, but have been
told since his departure that he was addicted to gaming . . . No attempts are
being taken for his pursuit and capture."[19]

This fiasco lent credence to Elisa's complaints against Martin. Henry
Cohn was an acknowledged gambler and thief, and both Martin and Steffani
lied to the press by stating that Cohn had no interest in the firm.[20] With the
economy depressed and the company plundered by one of its partners, Elisa
faced even lower odds of a satisfactory settlement.

In 1874, further complicating Elisa's chances to obtain Virgilio's fair
share of the company, Martin took on another partner, Louis Feusier, forming
the company Martin, Feusier & Steffani.[21] A wealthy French immigrant,
Feusier had found his way from France to the Mother Lode in 1852, settling
in silver-rich Virginia City, Nevada, where he operated a grocery store. He
was an original town trustee, its treasurer, and a developer, building many
stone structures, including the Wells, Fargo & Company building. While in
Virginia City, Feusier made the acquaintance of former California governor
Leland Stanford and Samuel Clemens, the future Mark Twain.[22]

In 1867, Feusier returned to San Francisco to engage in the wholesale produce business.[23] With Feusier joining his company, Charles Martin could well ask, as Virgilio had when he joined with Martin, "Haven't I done well to have him as a partner?"[24]

Elisa concluded her letter with a second request to Luigi for Rotanzi family photographs.

> I end my letter wishing you good health, a happy year. I hope
> that God will fulfill my prayers and make you all happy. I miss
> portraits of all your family in my album. I wish very much to
> have them . . .

Like many other young women of her time, Elisa collected and exchanged small photographs called cartes de visite for her album. For the first time, photographic images had become affordable for more than the privileged few. Photographers made multiple paper prints cheaply from glass negatives, enabling them to sell a dozen for a few dollars. Exchanging and collecting cartes de visite became known as "cardomania," a type of social media in the 1870s.[25]

Elisa may have had another motive for requesting that Luigi send family photographs. They could give her son, Jean Joseph Virgil Rotanzi, the only glimpse he might ever have of his father's boyhood, of his grandfather Luigi, his aunts and uncles, and of Peccia, the alpine village Virgilio had loved and left to find fortune in California.

TWENTY-THREE

"I surely expected better success…"

June 12, 1875 - Letter from Francesco in Hepburn to Luigi in Peccia

Although Elisa imagined that Francesco intended to come to California, Francesco had made no moves in that direction. By 1875, Francesco Rotanzi had become a respected figure with some status not only with Italian-speaking immigrants, but also in the larger community. With a group of fellow Italian speakers, he had become interested in developing the Daylesford-Hepburn economy through a project to establish a silkworm industry.

Albino Paganetti and Stefano Pozzi, owners of the Italian Hill Long Tunnel Company, along with Francesco and several other associates, envisioned the Daylesford-Hepburn area as a perfect place for raising silkworms. The men had grown up in Lombardy and Ticino, regions renowned for centuries as excellent silk-producing centers. Having applied their native expertise to establishing vineyards, orchards and olive groves in Victoria, the Italian speakers now sought to bring sericulture, the production of silkworms, to their adopted land.

In March 1874, at a meeting of the Daylesford town council, Francesco read a proposal by Albino Paganetti to select about forty acres of land close to Daylesford on which to begin growing silkworms. Paganetti aimed to use this operation as a showcase for obtaining a government grant of one thousand acres and a subsidy for importing mulberry trees from Italy. He estimated that, four years after planting, the operation would yield twenty-five thousand pounds per year. The *Daylesford Mercury* reported that the council agreed to the proposal: "It will be a good day for Australia when silkworm culture occupies a front place in the industries of the land."[1]

Several months later in June, at another Council meeting, Francesco

193

presented Paganetti's plans. Mrs. Sara Florentia Bladen Neill, founder of the Victorian Ladies' Sericultural Company, offered a different proposition. The wealthy widow of a prominent military officer, Mrs. Bladen Neill had formed this company as a cooperative to "provide gentle employment for indigent ladies of a higher class of education" through teaching them how to raise silkworms.[2] As sericulture did not require heavy labor, Bladen Neill and her friend and project director, Jessie Grover, saw sericulture as a way to help rural women gain financial freedom through small-scale cottage operations. They agreed with Anne Timbrell, author of *A Treatise on Sericulture in Queensland*, that "a clever quiet girl of ten is not only as fit but fitter to manage silkworms than a man."[3]

With disease devastating Europe's silk industry, global demand for healthy silkworm eggs had surged. Mrs. Bladen Neill had traveled to England and Europe to learn the intricacies of silk production and to import worms and various species of mulberry trees to Victoria. She claimed to have obtained disease-free "grains," as silkworm eggs were known, for the start of her company. A government grant of six hundred acres near the Mount Alexander diggings enabled her to plant thousands of mulberry trees on the property.

In her proposal to the Daylesford town council, Mrs. Bladen Neill suggested that Paganetti's group of investors form a branch of her company and designate a young lady to be trained to handle silkworm production. The Victorian Ladies Sericulture Company articles of association stipulated that "No person but a woman shall be eligible as a Director."[4] After Mrs. Bladen Neill presented her proposal, the Daylesford competitors explained that they were not interested. They wished to invest in silk production to benefit themselves and the Daylesford area, to serve as "a source of wealth of the district, employing its people and improving the value of its property." Her Mount Alexander plantation "might as well be 1,000 miles away so far as any advantage was likely to be derived by Daylesford." The newspaper report of the meeting noted that "After a further conversation, Mr. Rotanzi, in graceful terms thanked the ladies for their courtesy and kindness, and the gentlemen withdrew."[5]

The Italian speakers had a clear advantage over Mrs. Bladen Neill, despite her social connections and research visits to silk producers throughout Europe. They had grown up surrounded by mulberry trees, cocoons and silkworms. These enterprising men were not inclined to turn control of their dreams for a local silkworm industry over to a company operated by females. A campaign to better the lives of rural women did not interest them. They were businessmen, not philanthropists.

In October 1877, three years after he first proposed the silkworm project in Daylesford, Albino Paganetti remained resolute, but he was clearly frustrated with lack of support from the government of Victoria. Expressing surprise that sericulture had not become one of Australia's major industries, in a letter to the *Melbourne Leader*, he touted its success in Ticino and Northern Italy: "Forty-one years ago, in Italy and part of Switzerland, the value of silk produced was £8,000,000 sterling, and at the present time it is valued at £60,000,000 sterling per annum. Now, Sir, do not these figures show that real wealth [is] to be derived from cultivating the silkworm, and why should it not be started in this colony?"[6]

Despite such intense efforts, silkworm production in Victoria did not take hold.[7] Paganetti failed to convince the government to grant funds for his project, which was too costly for his group of private investors. Mrs. Bladen Neill's Mount Alexander venture also failed, largely because that area's climate proved unsuitable for mulberry trees and silk worms.[8] Mrs. Bladen Neill attributed the failure of sericulture in Victoria to the reluctance of Australians to try anything new. They didn't see themselves raising silkworms and, unlike Paganetti and the Italian speakers who had first-hand knowledge of the industry, they couldn't imagine its possibilities.[9]

Returnees to Ticino had likely told Luigi tales of Francesco's many civic contributions, including his role as Secretary to the Board of the Daylesford Hospital and Benevolent Asylum. This institution, founded in 1862, not only provided medical care, but, in its capacity as a benevolent asylum, provided lodging for indigent and destitute persons. Members of the Swiss and Italian Association, recognizing that the well-being of the community depended on the availability of a local hospital, took on the Daylesford hospital as their organization's major beneficiary. Dr. Severino Guscetti, Francesco's good friend, served as the hospital's honorary surgeon.[10]

In 1871, the community held the first fundraising event for the hospital. Residents who had migrated from around the globe to Daylesford and Hepburn Springs joined in the festivities. As Commander-in-Chief, Francesco headed up the Italian-speaking contingent. He led a large group of about three hundred Swiss and Italians, many of them his friends, including Joseph Righetti dressed as Swiss folk hero William Tell.[11] The group organized along military lines, with lieutenants and captains, colonels and majors, all carrying muskets and outfitted in military regalia.[12]

The Daylesford Hospital Fete, 1877

The Chinese contingent also numbered in the hundreds. More than twenty years after the first Chinese miners had arrived in Victoria, Chinese culture still remained strange to the Europeans. In 1877, a reporter described the annual Daylesford Hospital Fete:

> Inside the ground about 4,000 people were assembled, all kinds of sports having been provided for their amusement, not the least of which was a large number of Chinese, clad in gorgeous array, and carrying banners of all shapes, sizes, and colours bearing arms of extraordinary shape and make, and headed by a band of musicians who made the day hideous with what they termed music, but which principally consisted of the beating of drums and gongs.[13]

Despite Chinese participation in Daylesford's civic festivities, the Chinese continued to be targets of discrimination. In 1868, a *Report on the Condition of the Chinese Population in Victoria* provided statistics to Parliament for each district in Victoria. It vilified "the two greatest curses to Chinamen:" gambling and opium. The report condemned the "opium shops which stud the Chinese camp so thickly" and in which could be found "abandoned European women, who sell themselves to do wickedly…" The report raised concerns that opium addiction could spread rapidly to the general population. Non-Chinese players also flocked to Chinese gambling houses where "night after night, assemble young men and boys, eager to risk their money in the most bare-faced gambling."

Member, Swiss and Italian Association

The report noted that Daylesford and Hepburn had a total Chinese population of 1,021. Of those, 765 were miners and eighty-five were fossickers, those who sifted through waste piles for remaining gold. The Daylesford and Hepburn District had four active gambling houses and six opium shops. Eighty Chinese were jailed in 1867 for offenses including "vagrancy, burglary, manufacturing spurious gold, gambling, violent assault, contempt of court, stabbing, mining on a reserve, disorderly behavior in the street, fighting, manslaughter, escaping from prison, and hawking without license."[14]

Chinese thieves targeted the Italian Hill-Long Tunnel Mine in a series of sluice box robberies. Due to these thefts, Stefano Pozzi and his partners kept a twenty-four-hour watch at their mine. Twice in 1882, Pozzi shot Chinese thieves aiming to steal from his mine. In the early hours of the morning on March 28, Pozzi heard noises that sounded like someone tampering with a sluice box. After shouting out, he shot into the dark with his double-barreled shotgun. The next day, learning that a Chinese man had been hospitalized with gunshot wounds, Pozzi turned himself in to the police. He was charged with shooting with intent to maim.

In court, Hock Sim, the man Pozzi had shot, blew out a match, the customary Chinese method of taking an oath in Victoria's courts.[15] He stated that he made his living by gambling and that after smoking some opium the night of the incident, he went to see a friend. He swore he never touched the sluice box. However, Hock Sim's injuries and blood on the sluice box suggested that he was guilty of attempted theft. Within his rights to protect his property, Pozzi was released.[16] Later that year, Pozzi once again shot at another sluice box thief. Searching Chinese huts in the vicinity, police found an opium-smoking Chinese man whose boots and foot, riddled with gunshot, pointed to his guilt."[17]

A paid interpreter helped Chinese immigrants communicate in court. The Chinese community was not the only group facing language barriers. In 1860, so many residents of all nationalities were unable to read English that Daylesford employed a town crier to announce the news and publicize events.[18] The crier gained attention with a handbell and the cry "Oyez,

Oyez, Oyez!" In a booming voice, the crier yelled out this French-Norman expression meaning "Hear Ye, Hear Ye," then announced proclamations, market days, new laws and advertisements for all in earshot to hear.[19]

In 1863, the *Daylesford Express* had reported the need for a paid Italian interpreter: "It is, we confess, a matter of astonishment to us that there is no official interpreter of the Italian language attached to our courts of justice . . . the presiding magistrate or Warden, as the case may be, could arrive at a far more satisfactory decision if the evidence of natives of Italy are invariably translated by a recognized paid interpreter."[20] In April 1864, Francesco posted a notice in Italian in the *Daylesford Express and Hepburn Advertiser* announcing interpreter services.[21] Francesco helped Italian speakers in the courtroom, in business transactions and in writing home to relatives. He had become a well-known and respected community resource whose services were reliable and trustworthy.

Group of Diggers, 1858

Francesco was surrounded by opportunities to invest in the mines, any of which could strike it big. He naturally gravitated to the Italian Hill Long Tunnel Gold Mining Company, a company operated by Italian speakers. By 1857, gold seekers had dug tunnels through much of Italian Hill. When the first owners were forced to sell the mine to pay creditors, three partners, Stefano Pozzi, Albino Paganetti, and Christian Fumberger, purchased it and continued to dig. By 1870, their company had drilled down 1515 feet. The partners kept burrowing until the tunnels reached two miles long, creating a seemingly endless maze of passages under the town of Daylesford. In 1874, they laid down a substantial tramway through the tunnels.[22]

By January 1875, Francesco had become legal manager of this company, registering it as a limited liability company with offices at Stefano Pozzi's rooms on Vincent Street, Daylesford.[23] The company's thirty-two shareholders included many Italian speakers, among them Francesco. To keep investors and the general public apprised of mining activities, the Victoria Department of Mines published a quarterly report by the Surveyors and Registrars of each mining district. The *Mining Registrar's Report* for the last quarter of 1874 commented on the progress of the company mining Italian Hill. It employed six men, excluding timber fellers, carters, and other auxiliary workers. The company was doing well.[24]

Italian Hill-Long Tunnel Mine's largest investors grew wealthy from their gold finds. With his earnings, Stefano Pozzi built a fine residence he dubbed "The Vallemaggia." Entrance to the Long Tunnel Mine stood behind his home. Surrounding it, Pozzi planted a vineyard, an orchard and extensive vegetable and flower gardens, encircled by a wall of quartz extracted from his mine. Embedded in the quartz were shiny gold bits until thieves snatched away the gold-laden chunks.[25]

Francesco owned one hundred shares of the Italian Hill Long Tunnel Company. Despite Long Tunnel's good earnings,[26] Francesco wrote to Luigi that his investments "never up to now have produced a single cent." He was an accountant trusted with managing the portfolios of several mining companies, yet he claimed to have run through his personal earnings, investing whatever gains he made in new ventures that ultimately failed.

Nearly twenty years had passed since the discovery of gold in Victoria, but lust for the metal continued to incite miners to a frenzy. In October 1873, a local newspaper announced that "A beautiful alluvial nugget weighing 44 oz. was dug up recently at Blanket Flat, near Daylesford."[27] Miners scrambled to the area. Such massive finds boosted Francesco's hopes.

Occupied with his work, his mining ventures and his many community activities, Francesco had put off writing home. When he finally did send a letter to Luigi in June 1875, he once again attributed his negligence to his floundering mining company investments.

> My dearest Father,
> I have no excuses for my long silence; I must confess that the delay was generally caused, as was my past procrastination from one month to another, by the delusive hope of having better news to give you from one month to another. Thus the time passed, and I find myself here with nothing favorable to tell you.

Having lost Alessandro and Virgilio far from home, Luigi craved any news of his remaining immigrant son. Francesco consoled himself that returnees to Ticino had kept Luigi updated. News must have reached Luigi of Francesco's solid employment and his many community activities. From this knowledge, perhaps Luigi understood that Francesco had assimilated into Daylesford-Hepburn's social network and that he would not return soon, if at all. Francesco wrote that he would not come home until he had success in the mines.

> Many times I would be at the table and abandon the idea, disgusted with myself that I had not better news to give you, which I so wanted to do! It's a hard thing that after so many years I can't have the pleasure of announcing to you a good success, and that waiting month after month, I can't find myself in a better place! It's only this that gives me heart to expect indulgent consideration from you, my dear Father, for my otherwise unpardonable silence.
>
> I have been here around twenty years, and surely I expected better success . . . during this time I didn't take many holidays, but surely I could have saved money that I threw away. I could have had the money I wanted and at the same time continue to invest in the mines that up to now have never produced a single cent. I waited a long time for an excellent result from the last business that I wrote you about. I spent 3 years with the thought that it

would produce in four or five months. Now after all the time that
has passed, 4 or 5 more months are needed to obtain gold. The
signs are exceptionally good, and I don't doubt of great success,
but the incalculable delays and enormous expenses are enough to
discourage anyone.

Francesco assured Luigi that he was healthy and well-employed, and
that his job was comfortable, except for a period when he was over-worked.
He wrote that his work did not require physical strength, stating, "I only
apply for positions that call for using my head." Continuing his long letter,
Francesco warned Luigi to discount glowing reports from friends and
acquaintances returning to Ticino.

I find that, as usual with all the repatriates, Martino Respini of
Cevio has exaggerated news of my status: it's very true that I am
well and I am well thought of, even if fortune hasn't worked out.
At least I have always earned some little thing, but I have always
spent it in vain attempts to improve things.

On March 23, 1873, Francesco had written to Luigi that "as soon as
finances permit, I want nothing else than to come and see you all." As a
result, Luigi apparently had offered to send Francesco money to return
home. Now in his long letter, Francesco assured Luigi that he did not need
Luigi to send money. He estimated that for the next four or five months,
he must put all his earnings into the tunnel mine. Then when it started to
produce, he would be able to save his profits.

Francesco, a competent accountant, appeared unable to manage his
own finances. It's not surprising that Luigi seemed confused about his
son's financial needs. Francesco was sending mixed messages. Apparently
Francesco could not find a way to let Luigi know that he did not want to leave
his secure life in Daylesford and Hepburn Springs, not even for a visit home.
Vacillating, as he had in response to Virgilio's calls to California, Francesco
could not bear to tell his father that he wanted to stay in Australia for good.

Some immigrants who had made the long and arduous trip to Australia
resisted returning home without the fortunes that had lured them away. In a
letter to his brother, Pietro Scazighini expressed sentiments very similar to

those Francesco shared with Luigi:

> I tell you truly that it has always been my thought to come home,
> but after I have made this long journey and lost so much time in
> this country I don't want to come home with just the money I paid
> for the journey or a little more; I'll continue mining and always
> hope that some day God gives me the good fortune to make some
> good money, then I would come home right away to find you with
> all the relatives . . .[28]

Francesco wrote that he had been following events in Ticino, reading
Swiss newspapers at the Hepburn Springs Italian Library for notice of Luigi's
re-election as a district judge.

> I marvel at the result of the Canton appointments: I had read a
> partial list in the *Gazetta Ticinese*: and I wanted to find the names
> of the candidates to the Tribunal, but they were missing, although
> I have no doubt that your success was secure.

In 1875, Luigi had been able to keep his position, but the conservative
political climate led to his demotion in 1887.[29] Francesco went on in his letter
to address legal documents, including his will, in which he was leaving
everything to Luigi, then equally to his siblings if Luigi predeceased them.
Luigi had also written of how he intended to distribute his assets to his heirs,
including Francesco. Gone from Peccia for twenty years, years in the prime
of his life when he could have been at home supporting his father, Francesco
understandably questioned whether he deserved Luigi's generosity.

> Now I pray you to not make distinctions in my favor, because
> I don't deserve it. If I did something that you saw merited
> approval, that's for me a more acceptable reward than any man
> could wish for.
>
> In fact, thinking that the brothers and sisters at home have been
> able to give you help while I have been absent during the time that
> I could have been of some use to you, it seems to me that I am not
> entitled to participate in the inheritance of your wealth.

What painful feelings must have surfaced when writing of these
bequests and legacies. Luigi had lost his son the day Francesco took off for

Australia. For twenty years, they knew each other only through infrequent letters and second-hand reports. What did Luigi imagine about his son's life? He had seen a fifteen-year-old youth leave Peccia. Now Francesco was a thirty-five-year-old man who apologized for being unable to help from afar.

Francesco continued his long letter with news of villagers who had immigrated, including Maria Giovanettina, a woman with whom Luigi had grown up. Now both Luigi and Maria were in their sixties, but Luigi was better off, having stayed in Ticino where his family could care for him.

> No other news of merit: at this moment as I'm writing, it's pouring down rain and it's icy cold. Maria Giovanettina is totally blind and finds herself in the government prison, not as a criminal, but because she doesn't have means of sustenance and no one gives her help . . .

Daylesford Hospital, 1872

Maria Giovanettina, one of the few early women immigrants from Ticino, had been born in 1812 in Peccia and arrived in Australia in 1855 when she was already in her mid-forties.[30] Today an historic plaque marks the location on Hepburn Spring's Main Road where Maria owned a lemonade shop. More likely, she had sold liquor without a license. Alcohol was prohibited in gold fields, but miners could find it in sly grog shops.

Such enterprises could bring up to two hundred pounds per day in gold-rich areas. If caught, sly grog shop owners could easily recoup the fifty-pound fine for operating without a license.[31] Now old, blind, destitute and alone, Maria's fortune had waned.

Few social institutions existed as a safety net for the sick and poor.[32] Victorian law imprisoned vagrants and other individuals who had no means of support. Prisoners who had committed the crime of poverty crammed the jails. As Secretary to the Board of the Daylesford Hospital and Benevolent Asylum, Francesco may have been in a position to help Maria by facilitating her admission to this institution, but that did not happen.

In 1871, Francesco's civil service job expanded when the Yandoit and Franklin Road Board became the Mount Franklin Shire, which included the towns of Daylesford and Hepburn. The shire, similar to a county government, had responsibility for tax collection, electoral rolls, public health, business licenses, weights and measures, slaughterhouse inspections and dog catching. In 1873, Francesco became the shire's secretary, then in 1874, his responsibilities again increased. He described these changes to Luigi.

> Last October the Municipal government resolved that the job of Secretary be merged with that of Engineer and Evaluator and that training be offered to Secretary Rotanzi. I did not want to accept the job because I would have to pay an engineer at my expense when necessary, while the responsibility would still rest with me. But since it was decided to merge the three posts, my choice was to take it or to leave my position as secretary. Therefore, I accepted it. The budget is 250 pounds sterling per year for public works, streets and bridges, etc., all planned and estimated by the engineer and submitted to the inspection of the Government.[33]

> The work of the Secretary is also very heavy. All must be done according to the most minute formalities; Not a cent is spent if it's not authorized in writing and without formal receipt. All this precision is for the best. Each year a rigorous examination of all the operations in the accounts and all the other transactions is made by two people nominated by the town's government; and I have always passed these exams with credit.

Francesco had taken on important roles in local government, assuming responsibility for a large budget. With a penchant for records and figures, he was good at what he did. His temperament fit his job's exacting nature, and he took pride in doing it with precision. Working with numbers was confined and predictable. Fortunately, Francesco could make a good living with his accounting skills, because his gambling for gold consistently failed.

Elisa hoped that her brother-in-law might still come to California, but now with Virgilio gone, Francesco had even less reason to leave Australia and start over in another country. He was entrenched in Australia, and, although he claimed that he wanted to return to Peccia, his actions showed that he was not eager to leave. Knowing how much his father wanted him to come back, especially with Alessandro and Virgilio gone, how could he tell Luigi that Australia had become his permanent home?

TWENTY-FOUR

"Tell Grandma that I also expect to see her again…"

March 22, 1876—Letter from Francesco in Hepburn to Luigi in Peccia

In March 1876, Francesco returned to Hepburn after attending an annual meeting of the Odd Fellows, Manchester Unity IOOF, in New South Wales.[1] He had risen from Hepburn Lodge secretary to Provincial Grand Master, requiring attendance at quarterly and annual meetings. Nineteen passengers had traveled in steerage on the steamer *Rob Roy,* but Francesco had gone in style in the steamer's saloon.

Ever busy, Francisco took a few moments after returning from his trip to write a brief note to his father. Once again, he lamented his investment losses, announcing to Luigi that one of his mining company ventures had totally failed and was in liquidation.

> The loss is great, but regrets are useless. I am determined to meddle with the mine no more. This venture was one of those considered to produce certain excellent results. In any case, in a few months it will have an outcome and finally be over.
>
> Results of this kind are discouraging; and now after more than twenty years of trying it seems the rise to eventual success has stopped. So many trials and failed hopes should be reasons to curb experience and abandon other risks. Adding to these thoughts is that after so many years of sacrificing, not only do I have to lay aside the hope of recuperating the losses, but also of compensating for the time spent in vain. This thought is the hardest when I think of wanting to leave the country and addressing myself to the possibility mentioned in your letter of January 16th of the security that comes with good employment.

Apparently Luigi had again urged Francesco to come home with the lure of steady work, but Francesco already had secure positions, both as a civil service clerk with the local government and as a legal mining manager for several mining companies. Moreover, Francesco had found another source of income. He had become an agent of the National Insurance Company of Australasia, selling fire and home insurance from his office on Daylesford's main street.

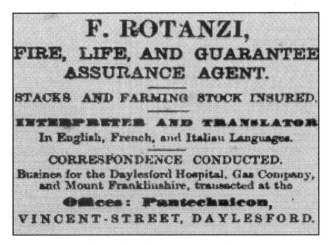

Daylesford Advocate, March 15, 1879

In 1876, extreme flooding once again inundated Ticino and devastated other parts of Switzerland. In Australia, Francesco took control of the Swiss Inundation Relief Fund in his area, announcing in a letter to the editor of the *Mercury and Express* newspaper that over thirty-six pounds sterling had been raised, which he had sent, after subtracting for printing and postage, to the Swiss consul in Melbourne. The newspaper later announced that "Mr. Frank Rotanzi" had received a letter from the Swiss consul thanking him, the committee and the donors for their response.[2]

As if his many employment, social and charitable activities were not enough, Francesco served with his friend Stefano Righetti on the local school board, the Board of Advice for Education. In 1878, as Board chairman, Francesco welcomed a group of government ministers to Daylesford for the opening of a new school.[3] The Melbourne *Argus* described a large contingent of government officials who, upon reaching Hepburn, were feted at a lunch enjoyed by at least seventy attendees. As host, Francesco proposed toasts to "The Queen" and "The Ministry," then led the officials to the schoolhouse accompanied by a large crowd of townspeople and school children.[4] Francesco, that is, Francis, had indeed become a full-fledged British citizen and a community leader of some local import.

Over the years, Francesco had purchased stock in several other mining companies besides the Italian Hill-Long Tunnel mine. His stake in the Enterprise Quartz Mining Company far exceeded all his others. By 1879, he had purchased two thousand shares in this company. At five shillings per share, Francesco's investment amounted to five hundred pounds, almost eighty thousand Australian dollars in 2019.[5] Despite lamenting to Luigi about his heavy losses and his desire to abandon risky ventures, Francesco persisted in investing with a gambler's false hopes of striking it rich.

> I will give it [coming home] all ample and serious consideration;
> I want to make the best decision: up to now, however, I still have
> faith in an ultimate success, and therefore I will keep your good
> suggestions in mind in case of need. So many betrayed hopes
> leave still new hopes, and just when you think it is not probable,
> the wheel takes a favorable turn and pays you back for all
> your efforts.

Francesco continued to send Luigi mixed messages. Now was not the right moment. He needed more time to make a decision. Although he told Luigi he would seriously consider returning, it didn't seem likely that he would make the move.

> Under the current circumstances, I can't say when I will be able
> to return home. I hope that things will change. I will wait and
> give myself some time to decide. My health is fine, and I lack no
> necessities. I would like you, my dear father, and Severina to be
> doing well. Tell Grandma that I also expect to see her again, many
> hugs to both.
> Your affectionate son,
> Francesco Rotanzi

One year after arriving in Australia, Francesco had written to Luigi, "Tell Grandma that I thank her with all my heart but for now it's not time for me to come home. I take her into my heart until I can see her again . . ." Now two decades later, he again expressed expectations that he would see his grandmother once more.

TWENTY-FIVE

"My dreams worry me..."

February 4, 1880—Letter from Luigi in Peccia to Francesco in Hepburn

Four years later, in 1880, Luigi sent Francesco the sad news that Grandma Medici had died. Francesco would never see her again. The death of Francesco's grandmother, the mother of Luigi's first wife Caterina Medici, must have caused Luigi to reflect on life's impermanence. Now in his sixties, he expressed to Francesco his intense fears and anxieties in a letter dated February 4, 1880.

> My good dear son!
> For several years, around these months, I have had the great
> pleasure of receiving some letters from you, my dear Cecchino, or
> at least, somebody gave me news of you.
>
> One way or another, I hunger for news of you. I am impatient.
> I crave it; but for a long time I have not been able to get around
> anymore, so I no longer have the satisfaction of having news of
> you, of hearing talk of you.
>
> The longer your silence draws out, the more anxiety grows in me
> each day, the anxiety of wanting to know how you are, what you
> are doing, if you are in good health, if you are happy, how you are
> doing; I think your health may be bad (or that something bad has
> happened to you.)

Haunted by deeply distressing nightmares, Luigi had a premonition that his son was in danger. He was so attuned to Francesco that he sensed threats to his son's well-being from halfway around the world.

> I have never been superstitious, but sometimes my dreams worry
> me. Two nights I saw in my dream: you were writing, looking

the same as when you left, and I saw some men with serious, almost threatening, faces. I don't know what they wanted. You answered to them: "Leave me in peace, I am writing to my father. Afterwards I will be with you." And you were crying. At this point I awoke, I also was all in tears! It's a dream, I know. But it made such an impression on me that I had no more rest. I had to write to you to get a little relief. And if, God wishes, as I hope, that you, dear son, have not fallen into misfortune, I can only blame my continuing fears on the weakness of my body and mind, both physically and mentally.

Francesco was, in fact, severely ill. The *Daylesford Advocate* had announced in October 1879 that "it is with deep regret that we have to state that Mr. Frank Rotanzi, the respected secretary of the Mount Franklinshire, is so seriously ill as to cause the greatest anxiety to his friends. He has now been confined to his home for some time, and though until a few days ago he has been able to get up, he has at last been compelled to take to his bed."[1]

Had Luigi been aware that Francesco was indeed ill, he would have written a very different letter. Luigi had no way of knowing that Francesco had been bedridden since October of 1879. He could only intuit that Francesco was in danger from his two dreadful dreams. Thus, Luigi spent a good part of his letter bitterly complaining of his reduced professional status.

Since 1849, he had been a member of *La Società degli amici dell'educazione del popolo*, an organization that promoted secular education, democratic ideals, rationalism and scientific investigation. He had held on to his district judgeship due to his liberal leanings. Now the political pendulum had swung far to the right. The Conservatives, aligned with the Catholic Church, had won heated elections in 1875 and 1877. Stripped of his prestigious position as District Court Judge, Luigi was shunted to the bottom rung as an alternate, cast aside in an intolerable reversal of fortune. He wrote in rage of his diminished status:

> I am not sick, but not healthy either. I have been nearly always close to the stove or the *pigna* this winter from November 19th to today, except for a brief time when I was called to Cevio to sit as an alternate! What humiliation! I, the first President, find myself there as a substitute, under the disparaging sneers of 90% of the *Orecchioni*?

[adherents to the conservative-Catholic party]. Everywhere they spark only poison, injustice, hatred and vendettas! Poor Canton Ticino, where those in command are ambitious loafers, criminals, liars, rascals, priests and women!

The women of Ticino were anything but ambitious loafers. With so many men gone abroad, women had been left to do hard labor: hauling lumber and hay, caring for animals and children, tending both house and field. At an early age, most girls knew they were destined for marriage and children, following the narrow paths of their mothers and grandmothers.[2]

Women Gathering Hay, Vallemaggia

Pushed aside, stripped of his position of authority, Luigi kept to himself. Huddling by the stove in the depths of snowy winter, he wrote: "All is calm, almost like death; and I have only melancholy and sadness for company."

Voicing contempt for the *Orecchioni* and the political reversals that had brought him shame and humiliation, Luigi's revulsion seethed through his letter as he condemned those clamping down on the secular movement and bringing religion back into schools.

The *pigna*, a traditional stove/heater

Continuing on, Luigi spelled out a very long list of villagers who had died in the past few months and named for Francesco the few elders who remained alive. "Now the oldest residents in Peccia are three women: Patronzina, Costantina and Morganta." Grandma Medici's generation was dying. Luigi's would be next. Luigi bemoaned the handling of Grandmother Medici's inheritance, prone to the meddling of "an imprudent conniver without a shadow of scruples . . . I will have to accept it, inasmuch as to litigate for such a small amount would eat up 10 times as much."

Luigi sent Francesco greetings from all remaining family members: Francesco's sisters, Clorina and Angelica, their husbands and children, and from Severina, who had been a toddler when Francesco left home but who was now a thirty-year-old spinster. Luigi made sure to include greetings from Maria, Francesco's stepmother, and his half brothers and sisters: "all make vows to see you again, or to see you for the first time." Back in 1856, after just a year in Australia, Francesco guessed that he would first see his half-sister Isolina "when she is almost grown." Now she was a twenty-five-year-old married woman. Given his ill-health, he might never meet her nor see his father again either.

TWENTY-SIX

"I have seen the false road traveled…"

March 8, 1880—Letter from Francesco in Hepburn to Luigi in Peccia

Luigi's nightmares mirrored serious threats to Francesco's well-being. His illness prompted him to respond almost immediately to his father's letter, apologizing for his long silence and explaining that he had hoped to recover rather than worry Luigi with news of his poor health. One month after Luigi wrote of foreboding nightmares, Francesco took pen to hand and described his condition to Luigi.

> At the end of January 1879, I neglected a bad cold, and consequently it went into my lungs. I healed very well, but unfortunately I had a relapse and in October I broke a vein in my lungs. It was a miracle from God that I was saved.
>
> Afterwards I improved, but now sometimes I feel better and sometimes worse. I can't use my head so I have a man who works for me and another who also does things for me. I can't go around inspecting things, so I keep these employees because they like me and they are diligent.[1] The doctor told me it's going better considering the danger I escaped, but it will take a rather long time to recover completely.
>
> The cough is rather a discomfort. I take cod liver oil continually, and I take medicines of all sorts, those that make me feel better and those that don't. Here I can't have the best Rooslo and Crosby. [Possibly a reference to Crosby's Balsamic Cough Elixir, widely advertised and recommended by a Dr. Rooke.]
>
> You are worried, my dear father, and you have reason considering your precarious health and poor Severina's illness, but what to do? We must trust in God, putting ourselves with faith in the hands of our Redeemer.

Having earned a good living and reputation with his brains, now Francesco was unable to think clearly. Humbled, he took refuge in spiritual teachings. Reevaluating time spent in Australia, he regretted that he had not given more thought to Luigi and his family back home. Francesco had good cause to feel guilty. He had worked long and hard, volunteered many hours for civic and charitable causes, speculated in numerous mining ventures and built strong bonds with community members, all the while only rarely taking a few moments to connect with his family in Peccia.

Francesco's intense remorse may have grown even stronger when he considered Luigi's yearnings for accounts of his life in Australia and the poor excuses he had offered over the years for not writing. When Virgilio had begged him for help in California, Francesco appeared to consider the possibility of joining his brother, but his actions spoke otherwise. He offered weak excuses, claiming he had to see about one thing or another.

Francesco's friend Stefano Pozzi expressed a sentiment in a letter back home that explained one reason why many of his fellow immigrants remained in Australia: "I am happy to be here for the great freedom above all. You sing, speak, do anything and no one can stop you. You work, as is the duty of man. No one obeys or is master; everyone is master and no one a servant."[2] Tiny Peccia, perched high in the Alps, surrounded by steep cliffs, bound villagers tightly in centuries-old cultural and religious traditions. Daylesford-Hepburn's wide-open fields and low rolling hills offered space to breathe.

In Australia, Francesco had forged a new career, broader and more substantial than that of a village schoolteacher. He had thrived in the comradeship of both his fellow Swiss and Italians and the members of his friendly societies, the Odd Fellows and the Masons. Many of his highly educated friends included refugees from the struggle for Italian unification. They shared political ideals and worked together for civic good. What similar outlet would Francesco have had back home? In 1870 and 1876, political turmoil in Ticino grew so fierce that federal forces were needed to restore order.[3]

Now chastened by illness, Francesco made no mention of mining investments, ever his focus in previous letters. Gold's lure had gone dull in the dark shadows of his close call with death.

> My affliction has been a great blessing. It has got me thinking:
> I have seen the false road traveled when neglecting solemn
> religious duties and my duties towards you—my indifference and
> my lack of writing to you and not helping you more than I have.
> I hope that God welcomes me back into his Grace. I observe the
> Gospel and all the Testament the best I can, and I read and listen
> to the precious words and the consolation contained therein.

Finding solace in religion, Francesco still deplored church hierarchy, writing: "But I can't conform to the precepts and ordinances established, not by our Lord, but by the various dominant heads of the church, for motives not necessarily for the salvation of souls." Despite distrusting priestly authority, Francesco had shown his generous spirit to a Catholic clergyman in Daylesford-Hepburn. When the local Benedictine priest needed to visit sick parishioners and celebrate mass in churches throughout the area, traveling on roads that were often barely passable, Francesco, with another volunteer, collected enough donations to present the Father with a buggy.[4]

With his usual kindness, Francesco occasionally visited Giuseppe Sartori, an acquaintance who had been brought into the Aradale Insane Asylum.[5] This asylum, built in 1863, was located in Ararat, about eighty miles from Francesco's home in Hepburn Springs. A model mental health institution at a time when country quiet and rest were thought to help cure mental illness, Ararat was a self-sustaining village for over one thousand patients and five hundred caregivers, including sixty-three buildings, an orchard, gardens, vineyard, dairy and pigsties. It provided a chapel and workshops for carpentry, engineering, printing and upholstery, along with a fire station and a morgue.[6] Once patients were brought into the institution, it was difficult for them to get released. Sartori was fortunate to land in this bucolic setting instead of prison where so many poor and sick people like Maria Giovanettina were held captive.

After years of neglecting family, Francesco, chastened by illness, now hoped to change, aiming to write to Luigi more often. Forced to acknowledge his death as a real possibility, he had made arrangements.

I am sorry that my sickness has prevented me from sending you some money. However I have never lacked for anything, and the Borsa family has always treated me like a son in their house. I made a will last July covering a few things in order to avoid legal issues, but I hope it won't be needed now. Almost nothing is left or just a few crumbs because of my expenses. I have assigned upright people, Michele Bedolla as negotiator and the banker Thomas Cotton as executor. If I die, I leave everything to you, and in case of your death to Maria and all the brothers and sisters equally.

Francesco chose Michele Bedolla, a long-time friend and associate, as his estate's executor. Owner of the Bedolla Hotel and a former Justice of the Peace, Bedolla was a well-respected community member with whom Francesco had worked at the Mount Franklin Shire. As co-executor, Francesco selected Thomas Cotton, manager of the Daylesford branch of the Colonial Bank of Australia and a fellow Shire Board member who had served as treasurer. Although Francesco hoped to no longer need these men's help soon, his chances for a much longer life were about as certain as his gold mining ventures.

Francis Rotanzi's Will and Codicil

TWENTY-SEVEN

"At present the shares aren't worth anything…"

May 4, 1881—Letter from M. Bedolla in Hepburn to Marino Rotanzi in Peccia

Francesco revised his will again in July 1880. He could see the end coming. He died a few months later, the day after Christmas, 1880. He had suffered a slow, progressive wasting away of his body. Noted on his death certificate, the cause of his death was phthisis.

Although this term described tuberculosis, the disease that had killed Virgilio, Francesco's death may have been caused by silicosis, also called miner's phthisis, a lung disease common to many workers digging for gold in the mines. Miner's phthisis ravaged the mining communities of Victoria, wiping out miners in their thirties and forties, leaving widows to fend for themselves and their children. Incidents increased after pneumatic drills were introduced in the late 1860s.[1]

Francesco spent most of his life in administrative positions, but his early labors in damp, dusty mines may have caught up with him. He had worked as a miner for about a year and a half when he first arrived in Australia. It takes only a small amount of fine silica dust from grinding quartz to create conditions for chronic silicosis. Tiny particles of silica embedded in lungs remain there for decades. No symptoms might appear for ten years or more, but damaged lungs eventually cause a chronic cough, shortness of breath, and susceptibility to other lung diseases such as tuberculosis.

Many in the Daylesford-Hepburn community deeply mourned Francesco's death. On December 30, 1880, the *Daylesford Advocate* announced his passing. Customarily, newspaper death notices amounted to a line or two. The unusually long obituary devoted to Francesco speaks to how highly the community held him in esteem. For many years, Francesco had been ailing, taking short trips along the sea coast to improve his condition with only temporary relief. He spent the last months of his life at home, eventually confined to his room. The Borsa family, with whom he had boarded for years, took care of Francesco at the end. The newspaper notice, entitled "Death of Mr. Francis Rotanzi," commented on his last days:

> His demise was not unexpected, as it was painfully apparent
> to his attendants that for the past week or two he was hovering
> between life and death. Indeed, had it not been for the devoted
> attention with which he has been nursed by his immediate
> friends, his life would not have been spared so long. Such was
> the deep respect felt for the deceased gentleman by those among
> whom he lived, that no trouble or expense was spared in battling
> with the illness...

The notice attributed Francesco's death to "a naturally delicate constitution" shattered by overwork and "over study." While noting the loss to the community institutions with which Francesco had been involved, the notice acknowledged the great loss to Swiss and Italian residents, for whom Francesco had served as a "guide, philosopher, and friend." It commented on his business expertise: "the deceased was so fully conversant with all that appertains to English commercial and general pursuits, that in all transactions of any moment his countrymen had constant recourse to his advice and assistance." And it praised his generosity: "to his unfortunate brethren his purse was ever open, and indeed at times when he had not the wherewithal to relieve their pressing necessities, he found means to do so."

The obituary described how Francesco had come to master the English language "by means of great perseverance and close study outside his ordinary working hours, which were necessarily long." It discussed at length his community work and business associations such as the Odd Fellows and Masonic Lodges, the Yandoit and Franklin Road Board, and the Daylesford Hospital and Benevolent Association. After extolling Francesco's community contributions, the notice went on to describe his funeral:

> The funeral took place on Tuesday last, and it was the largest and
> most imposing cortege witnessed in Daylesford, notwithstanding

the limited publicity which could be given it. The brethren of the Masonic Lodge turned out in good numbers, as did also the members of the Hepburn Lodge, and these are joined by members of the Forester's Court, to which the deceased belonged. Behind the hearse followed a large number of private friends, and then came the nearly forty vehicles, and a number of mourners on horse-back.

Daylesford's cemetery is divided into sections according to religious and ethnic classifications: Catholic, Church of England, Wesleyan, Presbyterian, Methodist, Independent, Chinese and others. Francesco was buried in the Church of England section with services read by a pastor of the Church of England and brothers of the Masonic and Odd Fellow lodges.

> **NOTICE.**
>
> ALL SWISS AND ITALIANS are invited to attend a MEETING, to be held at Pozzi's Rooms, Vincent-street, Daylesford, on SATURDAY, 8th January, 1881, at 8 o'clock p.m., for the purpose of devising the best means raising a Subscription to erect a suitable Monument over the grave of our late lamented friend and patriot, FRANCIS ROTANZI.
>
> VINCENT PERINI.

Announcement in Daylesford newspaper

None of his pall-bearers, most of them Masons and Odd Fellows, was Swiss or Italian, reflecting Francesco's strong ties with the dominant Anglo community. Yet Francesco's Italian-speaking friends did not forget him. As Francesco had no family members to pay for his headstone, they stepped up to honor him. Shortly after Francesco's death, the *Daylesford Advocate* reported on a meeting of the Swiss and Italian Association to plan fundraising for Francesco's monument.[2]

Five months later, in May 1881, executor Michele Bedolla wrote to Marino Rotanzi regarding Francesco's estate. Marino, born two years after

Francesco had left Peccia, knew his half-brother Francesco only by name. Bedolla informed Marino that Francesco had £164 at the time of his death, but his outstanding bills amounted to a little over £110. Moreover, Bedolla wrote that Battista Borsa, with whom Francesco had boarded, claimed £50 and that "Mr. Borsa refused to give me the details of what remains in his house that belonged to the deceased and to give me his watch with the gold medallion that was awarded to the deceased by the Society of Mutual Help, of which he was one of the most active members."[3]

Bedolla continued to describe the condition of Francesco's estate:

> He held 2000 shares in a mine that cost him £58. Up to now they haven't found gold so that at present the shares aren't worth anything, but I hope that shortly it will produce at least something.

> Moreover he held credits for money lent at £255.7 and in his will he left them to the local Hospital.[4] I believe they won't be able to collect many of them as they will find them in the hands of the indigent. The poor Deceased was always ready and had a large hand to help those who asked for help.

Probate paper, Francis Rotanzi

Bedolla finally obtained Francesco's watch from Borsa, but he had to take Borsa to court over the claim of £50. He promised to inform Marino of the court's decision and the final disposition of Francesco's affairs.

After twenty-seven years in Australia, years of hoping to strike gold in one mine after another, years of waiting to tell Luigi that he had hit a bonanza, Francesco's unfulfilled dreams went with him to his grave. The Swiss and Italian Association paid for Francesco's gravestone, an impressive monument, the top of its tall stone column broken and ragged to mark a life cut short.[5] Buried next to Francesco is Nellie (Ellen) Borsa, daughter of Battista and Ellen Walton Hill Borsa.

Monuments of Francesco Rotanzi and Nellie Borsa, Daylesford Cemetery

Nellie died three years after Francesco at the age of 21. Francesco and Nellie must have shared a close relationship as they are buried side by side within a wrought iron fence that frames their graves, just the two of them, and links them together for posterity. Imagining this connection helps to soften the jagged edges of Francesco's life, a life of hard work and civic contribution, yet a life without wife and children, far from the family he left in Peccia as a youth.

TWENTY-EIGHT

"Bitterly tried by misfortune"

Luigi lived another twenty years after Francesco's death. He died in 1901, outliving six of his ten children, including his three sons who had emigrated from Ticino in their youth. *La Società degli amici dell'educazione del popolo* published an obituary for Luigi, a long-time member, in its journal:[1]

> Slowly fading away in Peccia at the beginning of last October, at
> the advanced age of 87 years, [was] the old teacher and magistrate
> Luigi Rotanzi. He was a member of the Society of the Friends of
> the People's Education for more than half a century, for which,
> even in the saddest times, he always retained a particular
> preference; perhaps it brought back sweet memories of his youth
> and happier times.

The obituary described Luigi's early years as an educator and praised the qualities that made him a respected judge. "Honesty, perspicacity, integrity, and a rare diligence were the imprint of his every act, together with a conciliatory manner and the utmost thoughtfulness and judgment."

However, it made no attempt to hide the misfortunes that befell Luigi in his later years, describing how, when the Conservative government took over, "he was subjected to ostracism, and words can barely express how much his good-natured and modest spirit remained disheartened from it…" The ruin of Luigi's career weighed little compared to the heartache of his family life.

> But new pains were added to the old—because, in private life, he
> was bitterly tried by misfortune. Father of numerous children for
> whom he had sacrificed to give them the benefits of education, he
> saw six of his children die in the prime of life, including the last,
> Professor Marino, just a few years ago. With so much torment, his
> father's heart would have been broken if, raised in the school of

pain, he had not been able to rise above the miseries of this world
and yield himself to the bittersweet balm of resignation.

Emigration had ravaged Luigi's family. Before his three sons left Peccia, Luigi had lost his only brother, Giacomo, who died in 1852 in Sacramento, California, shortly after arriving on the steamship *Columbia*. Giacomo's wife, Innocenta Mattei, pregnant at the time her husband left Ticino for California, became a single mother struggling to raise her two infant children, Emilia and Seraphino.[2]

Despite the tragedy of his brother's death, Luigi made it possible for his sons to follow their dreams in Australia and California. As best he could, he traced the highs and lows of their daily lives and offered support from afar, always reminding them that they were loved and missed back home. Luigi's obituary ended by highlighting his notable strength of character and good judgment: "His honored name will be fondly remembered by all who were close to him, and especially by those who found in his counsel strength in adversity and a guide through tribulations."

One can only imagine the depth of Luigi's heartache when, one by one, his sons died half a world away. Unable to see them again, he could only conjure up images of their youth and visions of what their futures might have been. What did Luigi gain in return for helping his sons emigrate? Their ventures brought him dreadful worries and sorrow.

He mourned Alessandro, whose brief life ended far too soon. He feared gullible Virgilio's rash judgments, his impulsive leaps into bad business deals and his abrupt marriage to a Corsican girl. To the extent that he knew of them, Luigi could take pride in Francesco's civic contributions, the roads he built, the mineral springs he saved, the leadership he provided and his charitable offerings to the poor. Although Luigi had reason to be gratified by his son's achievements and generosity to others, how could Francesco's failure to write even occasionally and his tenuous promises to return home not have stung deeply?

In his final days, sitting bundled in blankets by the *pigna,* Luigi must have wandered in his musings back to the days of his prime when he meted out justice in the Vallemaggia district court, when his young sons, spirited and hopeful, left home for the unknown, vowing to return soon with fortunes. He may well have mused about Alessandro's brief sojourn in a place named San Jose, about Francesco's life in a small Australian mining town called Hepburn Springs, and on Virgilio's highs and lows in the cities and dairy lands of Northern California. With many of his children gone, along with most villagers of his generation, Luigi fortunately still had relatives to care for him. Offspring from his second wife, those "lively little rascals" about whom he had written decades earlier, had married and borne children of their own, allowing him to live his later years in the land of his birth, "withdrawn in the comfort of his family."

Cherub on ceiling of the Ossuary, Church of Santa Maria del Carmelo, Coglio

EPILOGUE

The Rotanzi brothers left no offspring bearing their name. Their bloodlines were cut off at their deaths, with the exception of Virgilio's son, Joseph, who, raised as a Giacobbi, never learned of his biological father. Many questions in this story are unanswerable. Was Luigi ever told of his grandson Joseph Virgilio Giacobbi? Did Charles Martin cheat Elisa of her inheritance? Was Elisa's lawsuit against Charles Martin successful? Did Virgilio exaggerate the extent of his partnership with Martin?

Those answers are unknown, but it is certain that none of Luigi's three sons found the fortune they had sought when they left Peccia. Some of their friends, relatives and associates who also emigrated from Ticino became extremely wealthy. Others, like Alessandro, died destitute. Many settled down to raise families that, over generations, still celebrate their Swiss-Italian origins. The following stories of individuals who touched the lives of the Rotanzi brothers cover a wide range of immigrant experiences, some whom fortune favored, others whom it abandoned.

Elisa Giacobbi Rotanzi Mortier (1854–1897)

The 1906 earthquake and fire destroyed court papers, so nothing is known of Elisa's lawsuit against Charles Martin, but not all of Elisa's records were lost in that disaster. As flames encroached the Eglise Notre Dame des Victoires, the priest had the presence of mind as he fled the fire to take the books recording births, marriages and baptisms, saving them from destruction.[1] Those records document a few vital details of Elisa's life.[2]

Seven years after Virgilio died, Elisa, then twenty-four, married Joseph Pierre Marie Edward Mortier, a thirty-eight-year-old immigrant from

Bordeaux, France. They wed on May 4, 1878 in the Eglise Notre Dame des Victoires, the same church in which Elisa had married Virgilio.

Elisa did not attempt to conceal her previous marriage. The church records list her as Elisa Rotanzi, born Elisa Giacobbi in Paris. Yet it's doubtful that Joseph Mortier or anyone beyond Elisa's immediate family knew that she had given birth to Virgilio's child. Elisa's parents, Francisco and Marie Giacobbi, had been raising her boy, Joseph Virgilio, as their youngest son.

Elisa made a promising match with Mortier. He was a winemaker and close friend of Camille Aguillon, a well-known vintner from Sonoma. Aguillon served as witness to the couple's wedding. By marrying Mortier, Elisa's life became linked with the French emigrés, orchardists and vignerons who helped build California's early fruit and wine industries.

In 1882, Elisa settled with Mortier in the Livermore Valley, about thirty miles east of the coastal foothills surrounding San Francisco Bay. Farmers in the area raised cattle and farmed wheat and hay. Mortier saw great potential for growing grapes. He planted vines for Cresta Bianca Winery, one of the original Livermore Valley wineries.[3] He also planted his own small vineyard and built a house he named "Maison Mortier," which served both as the Mortier's residence and a lodge.[4] That same year, Elisa gave birth to the couple's first child, Emily.

Mortier's friend Camille Aguillon had arrived in California from France in 1851. After a brief stint in the mines, he grew produce in San Francisco, making a fortune at a time when scarce fresh fruits and vegetables brought astronomical prices. With his profits, Aguillon purchased vineyard land from General Mariano Vallejo, who, as the Mexican commander of Northern California, had laid out Sonoma pueblo, the last Mexican colonial settlement formed in California. From the General's brother Salvador Vallejo, Aguillon bought an adobe building on Sonoma plaza where he established his wine cellars. The first French winemaker in Sonoma, Aguillon grew his winery into the town's largest.[5] In 1865, Aguillon made over ten thousand gallons of wine, one of Sonoma Valley's top ten producers.[6]

Winemaking brought Mortier and Aguillon in business together. Following Mortier's lead, Aguillon also bought land in the Livermore Valley, building on it the valley's first large winery.[7] He put his friend Mortier in charge.[8] As head winemaker, Mortier purchased most of the grapes grown in the area and oversaw production of enormous quantities of wine. Aguillon took on partner Gottardo Bustelli and in 1884, its first year of operation, their winery produced sixty thousand gallons.[9] Reporting on one of the winery's thirty-thousand-gallon tanks, a local newspaper claimed that "two sets of quadrilles (a square dance) could be formed on the bottom of the tank."[10]

In 1885, after managing Aguillon's winery for about a year, Mortier resigned to build a winery of his own. That same year, Elisa gave birth to a second daughter whom they named Olivette. Elisa took care of her family in the new home Mortier had built for his family on their ranch. There she helped Mortier raise grapes, stone fruit, figs and olives. Mortier kept ever busy, advertising Picholine olives and White Adriatic Fig trees, along with Aguillon's wine in the local newspaper.[11]

But Mortier did not confine his large ambitions to the Livermore Valley. He envisioned vineyards in Tulare County, south of Fresno,

California. He joined the West Coast Fruit and Wine Growers Association, an entity incorporated in 1886 to purchase agricultural land in California. As the association's superintendent, Mortier had a significant role in the organization, traveling to Tulare to assess the area's promise for orchards and vineyards. By 1889, Mortier's gamble in Tulare County had failed. The one thousand acres purchased by the association proved unsuitable for fruit and grapevines. The West Coast Fruit and Wine Growers Association dissolved, along with Mortier's investment.[12]

That same year, due to mismanagement, the Livermore Farmers' Union collapsed. This large enterprise, formed in 1874, had bought and sold nearly all the grain and produce in the Livermore Valley, along with managing real estate and railroad operations.[13] Its unexpected demise shocked the community. The *Livermore Herald* reported that "The failure of the Farmers' Union is a severe blow to our valley. The creditors will lose nothing, but many of our own people—farmers, business men and others—are heavy losers, and will be financially crippled for years by their losses."[14]

None of Mortier's enterprises, not his ranch, nor his vineyard, nor the French Liquor Store he operated near the Livermore Hotel on Main Street, could stave off financial ruin.[15] Newspaper notices in March and April announced that Mortier's debts had been assigned to the sheriff, his liabilities ranging between twenty-five hundred and three thousand dollars, his assets nominal.

Joseph and Elisa, their ranch and vineyard sold off at a sheriff's sale, moved with their two daughters across the Bay to Mountain View in the Santa Clara Valley, where they may have had a summer home. Known as the Valley of Heart's Delight, the verdant valley brimmed with the earth's bounty. Acres of vineyards supplied grapes to the many wineries surrounding the region's small towns. A skilled vintner and orchardist, Joseph quickly found work, first as ranch foreman on the Scott Ranch, later as manager of the Collins Ranch on the valley's west side, an area known because of its beauty as "Paradise Corner."[16]

In 1892, the California wine industry suffered from lack of capital. Winegrowers at the State Viticultural Commission convention debated whether an exhibit at the 1893 Chicago World's Fair would help boost the industry. The group agreed to sponsor an exhibit and appointed Mortier, an acknowledged expert, on a committee to test and select quality wines for the Chicago exhibition.[17]

Like most women of that time, Elisa lived in her husband's shadow. Although Mortier's expertise as a vigneron who knew how to grow grapes and make excellent wines was well recognized by his peers, details of Elisa's life as wife, mother and homemaker have disappeared. Yet her surroundings had allure: peach, prune, cherry and apricot trees blossomed each spring in delicate shades of cream and pink, vines dripped with thick clusters of grapes ripening for autumn's harvest. Elisa had only a few seasons to enjoy them. Her life ended in 1897, eight years after moving to the Santa Clara Valley. She died after a long illness at age forty-three.[18]

Joseph Mortier lived another seven years in Mountain View with his two daughters. He died in 1904 at age sixty-five. Like many of his contemporaries, Mortier engaged in a variety of occupations, from vigneron to orchardist, carpenter to inventor.[19] Later in life, he began manufacturing the "Mortier ladder," used to pick fruit in the valley's ubiquitous orchards. At his death, the *San Francisco Chronicle* reported the passing of a "Pioneer Fruit-Grower of Mountain View."[20]

All traces of Mortier's ladder have vanished, along with Santa Clara Valley's vast expanse of orchards, now smothered by Silicon Valley's asphalt expressways. Blossoms flower each spring in just a few precious acres of heritage orchards preserved as reminders of the valley's past bounty. Yet across the Bay in the Livermore Valley, many more vineyards and wineries still thrive where Mortier, recognizing the region's potential for producing fine quality wines, planted some of the first grape vines.

Joseph Jean Virgil Giacobbi (1870–1948)

Virgilio and Elisa's son Joseph Virgil grew up on Powell Street in San Francisco with his grandparents Francisco and Maria Giacobbi, whom he believed to be his parents. He was seven years old when Elisa left home to marry Joseph Mortier. Many years separated him from the Giacobbi children. He was thirteen years younger than his uncle Louis Agassi and eight years younger than his aunt Sophie.[1]

l. to r. the Giacobbis: Sophie, Francois, Louis Agazzi, Joseph, Maria, Elisa, c.1875

In 1882, Elisa and Joseph brought their two-year-old daughter Emily to the Eglise Notre Dame des Victoires to be baptized. Twelve-year-old Joseph Virgil was baptized that same day.[2] The Catholic Catechism teaches that infants should be christened in the first few weeks after birth, yet Joseph Virgil was nearly old enough for confirmation.[3] Giacobbi family history holds that Francois Giacobbi was an avid socialist who wrote political treatises which his son-in-law Joseph Mortier burned after Giacobbi's death. Perhaps

Giacobbi also objected to the Church, causing Elisa to wait until after her father's death to have her daughter and Joseph Virgil baptized.[4]

At the time, Joseph Virgil was attending St. Ignatius College, a large and well-known preparatory school founded in 1855 by the Jesuits. In the baptismal records, Joseph Virgil's mother is recorded as Maria Salicetti Giacobbi, (actually his maternal grandmother), but his father's name is left blank. Mortier's friend and employer Camille Aguillon and Camille's daughter Elise witnessed the event as Joseph's godparents.[5]

Francois Giacobbi died in 1881. Marie died three years later. Her death notice perpetuated the pretense of Joseph's birth, citing her as mother of Joseph Virgil.[6] At some point in the early 1880s, the boy left St. Ignatius and moved to Livermore to live with his sister (mother) Elisa and Joseph Mortier.[7] With both grandparents gone, he became the ward of his uncle Louis Agassi, who administered Joseph's assets amounting to $1,633.06, worth roughly forty thousand U.S. dollars in 2018.[8] When Elisa and Mortier moved from Livermore to Mountain View, Joseph moved with them.

Louis Agassi greatly influenced Joseph's choice of occupation. In 1886, after learning the jewelry trade at the Pacific Jewelry Company, Louis founded his own company L.A. Giacobbi, located in San Francisco's financial district.[9] He traded in jewelry, diamonds and gemstones, importing precious stones and selling them wholesale. Joseph became a lapidary, cutting, polishing, and engraving gemstones. Likely the two worked together, Louis importing the stones and Joseph polishing them to increase their beauty and value.[10]

Louis married and had two sons, Elvin and Lloyd, who joined their father in the business. In the 1920s, Elvin Giacobbi merged the business with Joseph N. Wineroth, Sr. Together they created a partnership with Granat Retail Jewelers and began selling to individual clients as well as to retailers. Eventually L.A. Giacobbi & Co. moved to its current location on San Francisco's Maiden Lane, where the company, now owned by Joseph N. Wineroth III (Joel), continues to sell precious gemstones as it has since Louis Agassi Giacobbi founded the business in 1886.

At age thirty-three, Joseph married Gertrude Skinner and settled down in Oakland. They had met at a picnic in Tiburon. A year later, Gertrude gave birth to their first and only child, Ruth Louise Giacobbi. Joseph partnered in the lapidary firm of Giacobbi & Keller in San Francisco and continued to operate this business until it failed in the Great Depression. He and Gertrude retired to their summer cottage in Stevens Creek in Santa Clara Valley. Stevens Creek Dam construction forced them to move again, although not far, to Monte Vista, an idyllic rural area in the hills of Mountain View.

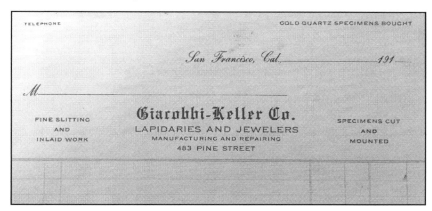

Letterhead of Joseph Giacobbi's firm

Joseph is remembered by his family as brilliant but somewhat eccentric. He loved to tinker with tools and engines but showed little business acumen. A member of the Corinthian Yacht Club, he rowed on the Bay every Sunday. Spending whatever money came in, he fortunately had financial support from his brother (uncle) Louis Agazzi through gifts of stock over the years.[11] Although he did not seem troubled in his early days, later in life Joseph suffered from mental illness. In 1948, at the age of seventy-seven, Joseph took his own life after wounding his wife Gertrude with a gunshot to her throat. Joseph had been under a physician's care for mental instability and had expressed concerns that he would hurt himself and others.[12] Although the injury to Gertrude was not fatal, the shock triggered an existing kidney problem that resulted in her death three days later.

The Giacobbis never told Joseph about his father Virgilio, his grandfather Luigi, and his uncle Francesco in Australia. Growing up with the Giacobbis, Joseph Virgil traced his family roots to Corsica, a craggy Mediterranean island that had been conquered many times over the centuries. His maternal ancestors spoke French and the Corsu dialect. Joseph may have been told of the Giacobbis' life in Corsica and in Paris before they came to California, but he did not know that the sister he lived with for so many years was actually his mother. He also had no clue that he was kin to Swiss-Italian dairymen ranching up and down the California coast. Cut off from his father's roots, Joseph Virgil lost his Swiss-Italian family connections, half of his rich heritage and a large part of his self.

Bay Man Wounds Wife, Kills Self

SAN JOSE, May 29. — (P) — In what the sheriff's office termed a suicide and attempted murder, Joseph B. Giacobbi, 75, retired San Francisco jewel cutter, was found dead yesterday in his Monte Vista home and his wife seriously wounded.

Lowell Bradford, criminologist for the district attorney, said powder burns on Giacobbi's hand indicated he had shot himself through the head and his wife, Gertrude, 74, through the throat.

Mrs. Clarabelle Pompella, a Monte Vista neighbor, said she was awakened by Mrs. Giacobbi about 6:30 A. M. when the woman came for help. She quoted Mrs. Giacobbi as saying she did not know she was wounded until she awakened, but remembered hearing two shots during the night and thought she was dreaming. A pistol was found beside her husband's bed.

Mrs. Giacobbi was taken to the hospital, where her condition was reported fair.

Giacobbi's son in law, James S. Norris, told officers Giacobbi had been under a physician's care and had worried that he might injure someone. His condition appeared to have been improved lately, Norris said.

The Fresno Bee · **May 29, 1948**

234

Charles Martin (Carlo Martinoia) (1830–1905)

From all outward appearances, Charles Martin led an exemplary life. After Virgilio's death, Martin's wealth and status continued to grow. Following years of making informal loans to fellow immigrants, Martin turned to banking, founding and directing several local banks.[1] By providing credit to ranchers and small businessmen, Martin and his fellow bankers helped grow the agricultural economies of Marin and Sonoma counties.

In the 1880s, sales of margarine, largely produced by East Coast manufacturers, threatened to cut into dairy producers' profits. Makers of oleomargarine, or "bull butter," as it was called, passed off the concoction made from animal fat as butter. Dairymen, a good number of them Swiss-Italian immigrants, united throughout the state to protect California's dairy industry. Martin became actively involved, representing Marin County at the 1892 State Convention of Dairymen.

Sausalito News, **December 1892**

Recognizing that strength comes from unity, some dairymen decided to outdo commission merchants like Martin who had become rich distributing their produce. In 1891, they formed the Dairymen's Union, a cooperative organization that sold members' products directly, bypassing commission houses. The union also advocated for high quality dairy standards and monitored the market for fraudulent merchandise. By this time, Martin, Feusier & Co. had diversified beyond wholesale dairy product sales, trading in canned salmon from Alaska and fine clarets and brandies from its local Sebastopol Winery.

Charles Martin Jr. on his Chileno Valley ranch, date unknown

In 1896, setting his sights beyond local banking, Martin went international. He partnered with Henry Brunner, a banker who had emigrated from Switzerland, and Antonio Tognazzini, a Swiss-Italian rancher from San Luis Obispo, to form the multi-national Banca Svizzera Americana of Locarno, Switzerland, with branches in San Francisco and San Luis Obispo. To secure funding, the organizers met with Swiss-Italian ranchers up and down the California coast and obtained the backing of what the *San Francisco Call* termed "145 Swiss of means."

Martin headed up the San Francisco branch, while Tognazzini managed the San Luis Obispo office. The bank made low interest loans, helping ranchers build and improve dairy operations. Remittances flowed into the Locarno headquarters in Switzerland, funding infrastructure projects, including the funicular railway from Locarno to the Madonna del Sasso Sanctuary and the ValMaggina electric railway that ran the length of the Vallemaggia.[2] In 1920, the Union of Swiss Banks acquired the Banca Svizzera Americana.[3]

In 1885, Martin purchased the Santa Ysabel Ranch, nearly eighteen thousand acres of cattle and dairy property fifty miles east of San Diego. According to the news article announcing the sale, he partnered with James Bloom (Battista Fiori), one of Virgilio's travel companions to California, and Petaluma rancher J. S. (Joshua) Brackett to purchase the former Mexican land grant for seventy-five thousand dollars. As with many of his ventures, Martin also offered partial interests to relatives, including nephew Joseph Traversi and niece Matilda Respini Ricioli.[4]

One of Martin's many properties throughout California, Santa Ysabel

Charles Martin, c.1900

Ranch became a successful San Diego dairy operation under the management of Samuel Rotanzi, Luigi's nephew and a cousin of the Rotanzi brothers. The enormous ranch provided a home in 1906 for Martin's daughter Ermelinda and her husband Fiorenzo Moretti. Descendants of the original Swiss-Italian owners still live on the ranch land today.

Some years before his death, Martin formed a corporation, Charles Martin Company, to manage his interests. He served as president with his children as officers. After his death, one of his sons, Charles G. Martin, headed up the family firm and oversaw its substantial interests throughout the state.

Martin never forgot his origins, donating funds to Cevio to make improvements for the village. He also gave large amounts to build a new church, the Church of the Assumption, in Tomales, a town near his ranch in Chileno Valley. The congregation, many of them Swiss-Italian immigrants, had outgrown their small, wooden-frame chapel. In 1899, the cornerstone of the new church was laid "in the presence of thousands," according to the *San Francisco Call*, with Archbishop Riordan of the San Francisco Archdiocese presiding, assisted by priests from several towns along the North Pacific Coast Railroad line.[5]

Church of the Assumption, Tomales, c.1901

Parishioners volunteered many long hours to gather materials from quarries throughout the area, some hauling Marin County blue stone with ten-horse teams from a quarry located twenty miles away in San Rafael. Having worked as a mason in his youth, Martin knew how to build with stone. Observing the church after construction was well underway, Martin is said to have remarked that the mortar was inadequate and that the foundation did not provide enough support. The supervisor was fired, but building continued to completion.[6] Martin imported a marble altar and railings from Carrara, Italy to enhance the church interior. Reporting on the dedication ceremony, the *San Francisco Call* dubbed the new church "the most beautiful house of worship in California."[7] Martin had been right about the Church of the Assumption's faulty construction, but he did not live to see the earthquake of 1906 reduce to rubble the place of worship he had painstakingly helped create.[8] In 1905, Martin died at home on his ranch in the Chileno Valley at the age of seventy-five.

Church of the Assumption post-earthquake

On his death, Martin's estate was reported to be worth one million dollars. *La Nuova Elvezia* commented that Martin "made fortunate speculations in land in such a way that within a quarter of a century he was reported to be the richest member of the Ticinese Colony." The *Marin Journal* gave an account of his funeral, "probably the largest in the history of Petaluma . . . by actual count 160 vehicles followed the hearse to Calvary cemetery." Local banks closed in Martin's honor. The *Marin Journal* continued, ". . . the community loses one of its oldest and best-known citizens and probably the wealthiest man in Sonoma and Marin counties."[9]

Arriving in California in 1852 with just a few coins in his pocket, Martin reached the pinnacle of wealth after fifty years in his new home. Yet his legacy is far greater than his pile of riches. He sparked the flow of Swiss-Italian immigrants to California, fostering them in a dairy industry they made robust through decades of hard work and determination.

Despite his many business dealings, Martin spent much of his time with family on his Chileno Valley ranch and made sure each of his children settled on ranches of their own. Anita, one of Martin's daughters, married Peter Dolcini, a young man from Cevio who worked on her father's ranch. Today descendants of Charles Martin through Peter and Anita Martin Dolcini continue to graze cattle and operate dairy ranches throughout vast rolling grasslands of West Marin and Sonoma counties.

Carlo and Caterina Martinoia, c.1900

Pietro and Anita Dolcini, c.1884

Charles Michael (Carlo Michele) Patocchi (1825–1900)

Luigi Rotanzi's cousin Carlo Patocchi resolved to stay in the Golden State, struggling to make a living in many different ventures: he owned a butcher shop in Marysville; he worked alongside Virgilio at Cohn, Martin & Co. in San Francisco; he clerked for the Yocco Brothers Grocery in San Jose; in 1876, he opened the William Tell Market on San Jose's First Street; he operated another butcher shop in San Jose, then another in San Francisco, then another in Petaluma, where he also opened a saloon.

Despite these many attempts to get ahead, Carlo Patocchi ended his life in poverty. In 1900, after forty-one years of ups and downs in California, he died penniless at age seventy-five, an inmate of the San Francisco City and County Almshouse.[1]

San Francisco Almshouse, c.1880

James B. Bloom (Battista Fiori) (1842–1893)

Battista Fiori arrived in New York City with Virgilio Rotanzi and Natale and Antonio Giacomini on March 31, 1861, after a thirty-seven-day Atlantic crossing. They arrived in San Franciso on May 6, 1861. Heady dreams of riches inspired all four youths, yet fate led them to wildly different ends.[1]

On leaving Brontallo at the age of eighteen, Battista Fiori could not have imagined the wealth his efforts would garner. Not long after arriving in California, he anglicized his name to James Bloom, a loose translation of *fiori*, which means "flowers" in Italian. He barely escaped being hanged as a thief just six months after his arrival, but despite that misadventure, he did not discourage his younger brother Joseph from joining him in California. Unlike Virgilio, who failed to lure Francesco to his side, Bloom thrived in partnership with his brother, who left Brontallo a year after James at age fourteen.

He first worked on a dairy in Tomales, then five years after his arrival in 1866, Bloom became a neighbor of Charles Martin when he purchased a ranch of about seven hundred acres in Chileno Valley. By 1869, he was doing well enough to return to Brontallo to marry Lucy Fiori, a girl from his village. They settled on the home ranch in Chileno Valley, where they raised a family of eleven children.

In 1870, Bloom bought a 1150-acre ranch near Olema from Giuseppe Fiori, who may have been a relative or, at the least, a fellow villager from Brontallo. Fiori had partnered on the ranch with Levi K. Baldwin, a well-known dairy rancher and three-time Marin County supervisor. James Bloom had the good fortune to purchase Baldwin's large, productive property. He sold a half-interest to his

James Bloom in *History of California, Coast Counties*

242

brother Joseph, who worked the Baldwin dairy while James managed his ranch in Chileno Valley.[2]

By 1872, just eleven years after arriving in California, Bloom had become wealthy. As a taxpayer with property assessed at twenty thousand dollars or more, he was one of "the rich men of Marin County."[3] Bloom continued to purchase ranch land and to diversify his investments. In 1875, he and his brother, along with Andrew DeMartin, bought the Washington Hotel in Petaluma.[4] In 1885, he partnered with Charles Martin and J. S. Brackett to purchase the Santa Ysabel Ranch in San Diego County.

Bloom also took an active role in politics, serving as a delegate from Sonoma to California's Democratic Convention in 1884. With fellow dairy ranchers, he co-founded the Dairymen's Union in 1891 to protect dairymen's rights and fight the influx of oleomararine.

Swiss-Italian Celebration, James Bloom Ranch, July 6, 1890

Despite his success, Bloom didn't forget his origins. Returning to visit Brontallo while on a tour of Europe in 1889, he donated to his hometown "a public fountain at a considerable cost, which bears his name and perpetuates his memory."[5] Bloom's children strengthened family ties to the Swiss-Italian community through marriage, as, for example, when Amelia married Michael DeMartin, Leopoldina married J. J. Dado, Clorinda married S. J. Maggetti, Claudina married A. A. Dado and Americo married Vivian Filippini.[6] Of his eleven children, sons Adolph and Americo carried on their father's business under name of Bloom Brothers, then incorporated as the Bloom Company with their sister Lucia. Together they operated "some of the largest and best ranches in Marin county."[7] Many Bloom descendants remain living in the area, including Dennis Rodoni, who was elected to the Marin County Board of Supervisors in 2016.

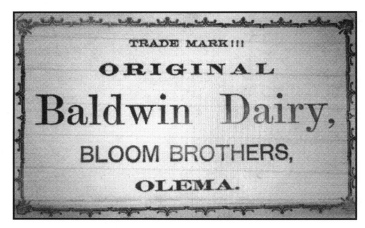

Trademark for the Bloom Brothers' Baldwin Dairy

Guido L. Rotanzi (1887–1921)[1]

In 1904, three years after Luigi's death, his grandson, Guido Rotanzi, seventeen years old, left Peccia for California. Guido's father, Marino, had died when Guido was nine years old. On arrival in California, Guido first lived with his uncle, Theodore Medici, who operated the Swiss Hotel on Market Street in San Jose. In prior years, this hotel had been run by Luigi Giannini, a Genoese immigrant and father to the banker A. P. Giannini, who was born in the hotel.

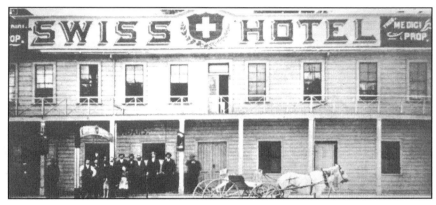

Swiss Hotel, San Jose, c.1895

Guido became a soft drink merchant and operated a business at 702 S. First Street.[2] In 1920, the first year of Prohibition, Guido was arrested in a raid on his saloon while trying to pour liquor down a clogged sink.[3] Luigi Rotanzi was spared the anxiety of trying to guide his grandson through this adversity half a world away. It would have sorely tried his equanimity.

Guido lived the first half of his life in Ticino, the second half in San Jose, California. He died the year after his arrest at the age of thirty-three and is buried in the Santa Clara Mission Cemetery. After his death, his wife Henrietta continued to sell sodas in the former saloon, now an historic landmark of old San Jose.

Dr. Antonio Rottanzi (c.1817–1892)
Giosue Rottanzi (1826–1899)
Leopold Rottanzi (1834–1900)

Dr. T. A. Rottanzi (1867–1911)

Virgilio had entrusted his medical care when he became ill to Dr. Antonio Rottanzi. Despite Virgilio's attempts to find a linkage, the two families were not related.[1] Dr. Rottanzi had emigrated from Faido, Switzerland, where his family had operated a large lace factory.[2] As a prominent San Francisco physician, Dr. Rottanzi lived well. In 1870, with assets of about twenty-four thousand dollars, he lived in a spacious house with his wife Caroline, their six children, his brother Giosue, a cook and a domestic servant.[3] He died in 1892, leaving a considerable estate and a fine reputation for having served his community well.[4]

The doctor's younger brother Giosue partnered in the family's pharmacy and operated a liquor store on Market Street. He produced and sold a medicinal liqueur called "Long Life Bitters," likely made with grapes from his vineyard on the San Francisco Peninsula. Younger brother Leopold manufactured punch beverages and also ran a saloon, later working as a clerk in Giosue's liquor store.

The Rottanzi winery south of Market Street drew attention at crushing time. A neighbor who grew up in the area recalled that "During the wine season the Rotanzis (sic) would receive a couple of tons of grapes on the sidewalk, which they would have crushed in the basement, and what a feast we would have after grabbing bunches of grapes from the boxes . . . "[5]

Antonio Rottanzi's son Tulio Antonio "T.A." Rottanzi became a physician like his father and, with his uncle Giosue, operated the pharmacy on Third and Folsom Streets, one of the first commercial establishments south of Market Street in San Francisco.

T.A. had political ambitions. In 1896, he was elected to the San Francisco Board of Supervisors and soon became known for his "High Hat Ordinance," which banned women's extravagantly large hats in theaters.

The *Sausalito News* thanked T.A. for opposing the objectionable hats: "If we desire to study birds, we naturally go to an aviary or museum, and we seek nodding flowers and buds at the florist or in the garden; they are out of place at the theatre or opera."[6] Dr. T.A. Rottanzi later became acting mayor and the official physician for the City of San Francisco.[7]

A cartoonist's response to SF Supervisor T.A. Rottanzi's Hat Ordinance

Samuel (Seraphino) Rotanzi (1853–1929)

Luigi Rotanzi's nephew Seraphino began life without a father. In 1869, despite his father Giacomo's ill-fated attempt at immigration, seventeen-year-old Seraphino also made the trip to California, where he eventually purchased a ranch near Petaluma.[1]

In 1889, Charles Martin and his partners hired Seraphino, his name anglicized to Samuel, to manage their vast Santa Ysabel Ranch.[2] In his new job, Samuel had charge of a large cattle operation, several ranch buildings and three dairies. By 1895, he was running the largest dairy in Southern California for Martin and his investors.[3] For many years, he managed both his own holdings and the large Santa Ysabel dairies until Fiorenzo Moretti, husband of Charles Martin's daughter Ermelinda, took over in 1923.[4]

Like Martin, Samuel became a businessman, banker and civic leader. Rotanzi Street in the nearby city of Ramona recalls Samuel's thirty-three years as superintendent of the Santa Ysabel Ranch. Helvetia, William Tell and Ticino Streets in the small town of Santa Ysabel evoke the many Swiss Italians drawn to work on the ranch. In 2001, San Diego County created the Santa Ysabel Open Space Preserve, saving thirty-eight hundred acres of the land from development.[5] Descendants of the original Swiss-Italian owners still ranch on the remaining property.

Santa Ysabel Dairy, c.1895

Antonio Germano Tognazzini (1846–1906)

When Antonio Tognazzini, Charles Martin's partner in real estate and banking ventures, left his village of Someo for California in 1861 at the age of sixteen, he could not possibly imagine the wealth and status he would enjoy in his later years. He began as a milker on a ranch in Nicasio, Marin County. As years passed, Tognazzini continued to grow his family and his financial assets. In 1872, he purchased a seven-hundred-acre ranch near Cayucos, north of Morro Bay in San Luis Obispo County. He continued to add to his ranch properties in San Luis Obispo and Santa Barbara counties, becoming an affluent dairy rancher and community leader.

In 1881, he bought 3,200 acres of the Rancho Casmalia, a former Mexican Land Grant in Santa Barbara County.[1] Anticipating the railroad, Tognazzini built a hotel and a store, founding a town he named Someo to honor the village he had left over thirty years earlier.[2] The town grew as railroad and oil company employees moved in. When the post office opened in 1896, the town's name changed from Someo to Casmalia, but its Someo and Ticino Streets still recall Tognazzini's beloved village in the Vallemaggia.

Emigrants from Someo who had done quite well in California returned to their village to build homes, ten stately houses in a row, in an area of their native village that came to be called the *Quartiere Californiano*, the California District. These houses, built in late nineteenth-century San Francisco style by Tognazzini and other wealthy immigrants, including the Righettis, Muscios and Perinonis, stand in stark contrast to Someo's humble stone cottages.

One of these buildings, the Palazzo Tognazzini, currently houses a home for the elderly. Plans are underway to transform the site into an Emigration Center to preserve and make public research materials on the Vallemaggia, including thousands of documents donated by Professor Giorgio Cheda. The institute will serve as a museum, archive, library and comprehensive resource on Ticinese emigration.[3]

Along with their elegant villas, Tognazzini and his fellow Californians created a cemetery befitting their riches. Today Someo has two cemeteries. *Il*

Cimitero degli Americani, the American Cemetery, contains massive, intricately carved monuments reflecting the wealth of the emigrants from Someo who made fortunes in California.

Like Charles Martin, Tognazzini became a banker. With Henry Brunner, he founded the Commercial Bank of San Luis Obispo and in 1896 joined Martin and Brunner in founding the Swiss American Bank of Locarno.

Oil, not dairy, drove some of Tognazzini's later real estate purchases. At the turn of the century, in pursuit of liquid black gold, prospectors and investors rushed to lease land from dairy ranchers for drilling rights. They erected a "forest of derricks," digging deep down to probe for petroleum. The Casmalia Oil and Development Company drilled down one thousand to twelve hundred feet before finding oil on Tognazzini's Casmalia Ranch in 1902.[4]

Tognazzini died in San Luis Obispo in 1906, one of the richest men on the central California coast and a recognized leader of its Swiss colony.[5]

American Cemetery, Someo, 2015

Giuliano Stefano Moretti (c.1821–c.1896)
Jeremiah Respini (1852–1912)
Louis Moretti (1876–?)

Giuliano Moretti and Charles Martin jointly purchased ranch land in Chileno Valley in 1856.[1] A few years later, a number of emigrants from Cevio, including Moretti, moved south to Santa Cruz.[2] There Moretti purchased forty thousand acres of coastal property which Charles Martin, in his newspaper ads for Cohn, Martin & Co., touted as "a splendid tract five miles in extent."[3]

Moretti's purchase, about eleven miles north of Santa Cruz, had been the Rancho San Vicente, a large Mexican land grant spanning five miles of rocky coastline. It was bordered on the south by another former land grant, the Rancho Arroyo de la Laguna, and on the north by San Vicente Creek. From the ocean shore, it stretched high into the Santa Cruz Mountains, an area rich in timber, lime deposits and other natural resources.

Moretti and Respini in Cevio's Piazza, pre-1900

In 1867, a few years after Moretti started ranching on his huge spread north of Santa Cruz, Jeremiah Respini, who eventually became his son-in-law, joined him. Sometime in the 1880s, Respini wed Moretti's daughter Jeconia, a marriage tightly binding father and son-in-law together in both family and business affairs. In 1890, Moretti and Respini returned to Cevio. With the wealth they had gained in California, the men purchased and restored a seventeenth century villa in Cevio's historic district.[4] Known as the Casa Respini-Moretti, today the building forms part of the Museum of the Vallemaggia.

By the turn of the century, many early immigrants had died or returned to the Vallemaggia, some to retire in comfort. Moretti lived out the rest of his life in the Vallemaggia. Respini stayed for at least ten years, serving as Cevio's mayor from 1890 to 1900, all the while overseeing management of his California properties from abroad.

Then a new generation arrived bringing a whirlwind of change that forever disrupted Santa Cruz County's peaceful dairy lands. Most of the early immigrants had been satisfied to make a very good living raising cows and selling dairy products. Louis Moretti, Giuliano's son, looked to capitalize on his family's extensive land holdings in ways that went far beyond milk, butter and cheese.

In about 1900, Louis Moretti moved to California to manage his father's enterprises.[5] Unlike members of the prior generation who had left Cevio with barely an elementary education, Louis was trained as an electrical engineer. With him came another relative, attorney Eliashin Moretti. They first stayed on Respini's Yellow Bank Ranch, along with about twenty other laborers, nearly all from Ticino.[6]

Oil exploration became the first of many attempts at new land use. In 1900, the State Mineralogist inspected the Respini ranch with favorable reports that oil could be found on the property, resulting in the local Santa Cruz Oil Company leasing land from Respini and two of his neighbors. Oil rigs sprung up along the coast. The local paper surmised, "With good oil and coal prospects in this county who knows but what Santa Cruzans may yet reap fortunes rivaling those of the Coal Barons of Pennsylvania and the Oil

Kings of Southern California."[7] The company found oil, but not enough to be profitable. By 1902, the oil boom had gone bust.

But the resource-rich land offered other opportunities. In 1901, Louis Moretti and Jeremiah Respini joined their two vast land holdings in a corporation they named the Coast Dairies & Land Company.[8] Although the company included five separate dairies that shipped products to San Francisco, this new business entity set the stage for a dramatic change to the once bucolic coast north of Santa Cruz.[9] A Coast Dairies Property plan prepared for the Trust for Public Land describes the impact:

> The story of the North Coast is really two histories, before
> and after the incorporation of the Coast Dairies & Land Co.
> in 1901. The combination of the Moretti and Respini family
> assets, together with the leadership of Louis Moretti, provided
> a catalyst for an explosion of activity more like the booms of the
> gold fields or Silicon Valley than the pastoral landscape we value
> today. The Coast Dairies Corporation was the major agent for
> change in the early twentieth century.[10]

Museo di Valmaggia, Cevio

253

In 1905, James Filippini, director of the Coast Dairies & Land Company for Respini and Moretti, handled the sale of ninety-seven acres of the San Vicente Ranch to the Standard Portland Cement Company, which planned to build the second largest cement factory in the country on the coast. Coast Dairies also sold 101 acres to Southern Pacific for a Coast Line Railroad to carry cement to San Francisco.[11]

Through Coast Dairies & Land Company, Moretti and Respini owned and managed three company towns and all supporting infrastructure for the cement factory. A town called Bella Vista formed near the quarry to house mine workers. To accommodate about seven hundred cement factory workers, many of them Greek immigrants, Louis Moretti built a larger company town with two hotels, a post office, general store (known as the Cash Store), barber shop, butcher shop, livery stable, blacksmith shop, public hall and public school, all managed by Moretti and his fellow Swiss Italians.[12] Initially named San Vicente, the town eventually become known as Davenport.

When the 1906 San Francisco earthquake and fire caused brick and mortar construction to fail and wooden buildings to burn to the ground, Davenport cement and lumber felled from the Moretti-Respini property helped rebuild the city. Coast Dairies & Land Company property, spanning six watersheds, had abundant water sources. The company sold a spring to the city of Santa Cruz, providing the city with a sorely needed water supply. Today the spring still provides about twenty percent of the city's water.[13]

When it appeared that the United States would enter World War I, the Respini and Moretti families returned to Ticino, although they continued to hold their properties as absentee landlords.[14] The absence of Moretti and Respini did not stop the Coast Dairies & Land Company from starting new businesses.[15] In 1904, Half Moon Bay sent the first carload of artichokes from California to markets on the East Coast.[16] From there, artichoke fields expanded up and down the coast, north to Marin and south to San Mateo, Santa Cruz, Monterey and San Luis Obispo.

The Coast Dairies & Land Company leased land to farmers to grow artichokes and other produce. Swiss-Italian Louis Poletti became a leader in the agricultural community, forming the Davenport Producers Association and serving as a commission merchant, annually distributing 650 carloads of brussels sprouts, artichokes and other produce nationwide for growers, mostly Italian immigrants, who farmed over two thousand acres on the Santa Cruz Coast.[17]

The Moretti and Respini families owned and operated their massive land holdings for over a century. Their land represented the third-largest privately held California coastal property from San Francisco to the Mexican border.[18] In 1998, the Trust for Public Land purchased the property to preserve it for open space. Over four hundred acres of its coastal cliffs and beaches became public property in 2006 as the California Coast Dairies State Park. In 2014, President Obama designated the Moretti-Respini former dairy ranch part of the Cotoni-Coast Dairies National Monument.

Coast Dairies State Park

Battista Giovanni Borsa (c.1832–1889)

Born in Bellinzona, Switzerland, Battista Giovanni Borsa landed in Victoria in 1852 to try his luck in the mines. Four years later, he married Ellen Walton Hill, with whom he had one son and eleven daughters. Five of the daughters died in infancy. Francesco Rotanzi kept the books for Borsa's butcher shop and lodged with the Borsa family for many years.

To accommodate the growing crowd of vacationers who came to Hepburn Springs to enjoy the waters, Borsa opened the Bellinzona Guest House, named for his birthplace, the largest city in Ticino. Two Borsa daughters married into the Zelman family of artists and musicians.[1] After Borsa's death, his daughters took over management of the Bellinzona.

The Bellinzona, c.1915

In 1906, a bush fire ravaged nearly all of Hepburn Springs. Homes, farmhouses, miners' huts, stores, hotels and guesthouses burned to the ground. The fire engulfed the Chinese camp, destroying all structures except the Joss House, the Chinese temple.[2] In a massive reconstruction, the Zelmans rebuilt a grander Bellinzona Guest House to accommodate the crowds of Melbourne's Jewish emigrés who flocked to Hepburn Springs to take the waters and socialize in an atmosphere vaguely recalling their European homelands.[3]

After a period of decline in the 1960s and 1970s, the region made a comeback as Victoria's Spa Country, a weekend getaway destination for Melbourne city dwellers. Today it offers luxury spa resorts, wine tours and gourmet restaurants while retaining historic buildings harkening back to its gold-country heritage. In Hepburn Springs, Borsa Crescent, a small semi-circular street, and Borsa Hall, a community center, still carry Battista Borsa's name, and his Bellinzona Guest House, renamed the Bellinzona Resort, continues to welcome visitors to the hot springs.

Hepburn Mineral Springs, Daylesford, 1903

The Pozzi Brothers
Guiseppe (1818–1897)
Twins Alessandro (1831–1868) and Leonardo (1831–1908)
Stefano (1833–1922)

Australia dealt the four Pozzi brothers vastly varied fortunes, from kind to cruel. Twins Leonardo and Alessandro, their older brother Giuseppe and younger brother Stefano, immigrated at separate times to Australia from Giumaglio, a village of about four hundred people in 1850.[1] Their parents herded goats and raised a family of ten children.

On arriving in Victoria, Alessandro first worked as a stonemason in Melbourne, then headed for the Hepburn/Daylesford gold country. Despite struggling to make a living in the mines, Alessandro encouraged his younger brother Stefano to join him in Australia. Alessandro's twin brother, Leonardo, a fellow passenger with Francesco Rotanzi on the *Agen und Heinrich*, arrived in Australia a year later in 1855.

By 1856, the three Pozzi brothers had earned enough to open a business—a bakery, grocery and liquor store at Old Racecourse in Hepburn. Stefano added to his earnings by working as a jeweler, locating his shop, "Up a Tree," on top of a large, tall stump to better secure his precious materials.

The Pozzi Brothers Store at Jim Crow

Giuseppe, the oldest and the last Pozzi brother to immigrate to Australia, arrived in 1861. By that year, almost one-quarter of Giumaglio's population had left for Australia.[2] Giuseppe, a baker and miller, bought land for a vineyard and established a successful flour mill at Franklinford that he operated until his death in 1897.

In 1869, Stefano invested as one of the main shareholders in the Long Tunnel Mine. At the time, that mine had already carved out eighteen hundred meters of tunnel from the earth underneath the streets of Daylesford. Stefano's gamble paid off. By 1886, he had made enough from mining to build a new home he called "the Vallemaggia," including a lavish garden fronting the entrance to the Long Tunnel Mine. With his wealth, Stefano lived a comfortable life in Daylesford. He died in 1922 at age ninety, one of Daylesford's oldest residents.

In 1866, Alessandro opened the Daylesford Bakery, but he lost everything when a fire destroyed his store. At Alessandro's death in 1868 at the age of thirty-seven, the *Mercury* reported, "by his energy and intelligence he had paid off his outstanding liabilities, and was again making a position for himself when carried off by disease."[3] At the time of his death, Alessandro held IOUs amounting to about two thousand pounds from loans he had extended to his friends and acquaintances.

Of the four brothers, Leonardo lived the most varied and adventurous life. After failing with a series of bars, hotels and mining investments, Leonardo headed off to New Zealand, later sending for his family. He settled in Christchurch, the largest city in New Zealand's South Island, where, after losing money in a hotel business, he opened a gunsmith shop that provided him and his family enough to live on.

Ever industrious, Leonardo invented and patented "Pozzi's Pen Ink Feeder," considered the precursor to the fountain pen. He advertised that it would "enable the writer to write from 150 to 450 words with one dip of the pen."[4] He achieved little success with this invention, nor with Pozzi's Climax, his patent for light and fast roller skates.[5]

Leonardo also turned his mind to the economic and political issues of his day. In 1887, New Zealand was suffering from a severe depression that lasted for over a decade. Leonardo took up the working man's cause, addressing disgruntled crowds at weekly protests in Christchurch's Cathedral Square. He lectured and published pamphlets arguing against free trade, decrying unemployment in a "land flowing with milk and honey."[6] In 1888, he published a book of his views called *Modern slavery and civilization: dialogue on the industries & toilers of New Zealand.*[7]

Leonardo Pozzi

In 1890, after twenty years in New Zealand, Leonardo returned with his family to Victoria. He claimed he had been unable to make a good living in New Zealand, blaming the "misruling of the money bags."[8] In Melbourne, he opened a gunsmith shop called the Swiss Arms Depot.

In New Zealand, Leonardo had tried, with little success, to start up a silk industry. Back in Melbourne, he became a founder of the Victorian Silk Culture Association. Promoting the economic advantages of cultivating silk as a cottage industry, he published a book in 1894 on the how-to's of sericulture.[9]

Leonardo also continued as a labor activist in Melbourne, becoming a Socialist Party member and giving lectures to various trade groups to encourage the formation of unions. He complained that the labor market, controlled by the English ruling class, was unfair to foreign immigrants.

Traveling to Australia at age twenty-five, Leonardo had intended "to stay three years, make a fortune in gold mining, and then go back home again." Fifty years later, three years before his death, he recalled his youthful optimism, writing, "I must confess that I have made a very bad calculation."[10]

Leonardo died from diabetes in 1908. The leftist periodical *The Socialist* reported on the funeral and legacy of "Comrade Pozzi," stating that "As a mechanic, he was one of the finest that ever lived in Australia," and that during the fifty-three years Leonardo had been in the Southern Hemisphere, "he had all through this period worked actively for the cause of the people."[11]

TWO PROVERBS OF TICINO

I sòld i fa sòld,
i pioeucc i fa pioeucc

.

Money makes money,
lice only make lice.

Maasg succ gregn per toeucc.

Dry May, grain for all.

ROTANZI FAMILY MEMBERS

Luigi (Aloysius) Rotanzi (1814–1901) A teacher and judge from Peccia in the Vallemaggia District of Ticino. Luigi lent three of his sons the funds to immigrate to California and Australia.

Francesco Rotanzi (1839–1880) Oldest son of Luigi Rotanzi and a teacher by training, Francesco was the first of the Rotanzi brothers to leave Peccia, heading for Australia in 1855.

Alessandro Rotanzi (1843–1864) Second son of Luigi Rotanzi and the last son to leave Peccia, following Virgilio to California in 1862.

Virgilio Rotanzi (1845–1871) Luigi Rotanzi's third son, Virgilio, arrived in California in 1861.

Elisa Giacobbi Rotanzi Mortier (1854–1897) Born in Paris of Corsican parents, Elisa married Virgilio Rotanzi when she was about sixteen years old. She later married Frenchman Joseph Mortier.

Joseph Virgil Giacobbi (1870–1948) Baptized as Joseph Jean Virgil Giacobbi. Son of Elisa and Virgilio Rotanzi.

Caterina Medici (?–?) Luigi Rotanzi's first wife and mother of the three brothers who emigrated from Peccia.

Luigi Rotanzi's daughters born of his first wife Caterina Medici:
Carolina (1842–?) Also known as Clorina.
Luigia Angelica (1848–?).
Severina (1850–?) Never married. Suffered from a long illness.

Luigi Rotanzi's children born of second wife Maria Moretti:
Filomena (1855–?) Also known as Isolina.
Marino Rotanzi (1857–1895) The fourth son of Luigi Rotanzi.
Albina (1860–1895).
Bernardino (1862–?).

RELATIVES, FRIENDS AND ACQUAINTANCES

Camille Fortune Aguillon (1828–1906) Vintner from France who established a winery on the town plaza of Sonoma, California. Aguillon employed Joseph Mortier, Elisa Rotanzi's second husband, to manage his Livermore vineyards.

Bagnovini (?–?) First name unknown. An emigrant from Peccia who lent Virgilio Rotanzi funds to invest in a California ranch deal that turned sour.

Michele Bedolla (1831–1916) Friend and compatriot of Francesco Rotanzi, Bedolla immigrated to Australia in 1855 from Russo, Ticino and served as an executor of Francesco's will.

Sara Florentia Bladen Neill (?–1884) Enterprising founder of the Victorian Ladies' Sericultural Company, which aimed to assist indigent women through teaching them small-scale silk production.

Adolph J. Bloom (1872–1937) Son of James B. Bloom. A poultry rancher and co-owner with Charles Martin in the Santa Ysabel Ranch in San Diego County.

James B. Bloom (1842–1893) Also known as Battista Fiori, he accompanied Virgilio Rotanzi from the Vallemaggia to San Francisco in 1861, along with Natale and Antonio Giacomini. Partner with Charles Martin in Santa Ysabel Ranch near San Diego.

Battista Borsa (c.1831–1889) A butcher in Hepburn, born in Bellinzona, Switzerland. Borsa partnered with Fabrizio Crippa in a butcher shop, employing Francesco Rotanzi as bookkeeper and accountant.

Nellie (Ellen) Borsa (c.1862–1883) A daughter of Battista Borsa. She is buried in Daylesford Cemetery next to Francesco Rotanzi.

Joshua Barney Brackett (1868–1933) Born in Petaluma, California, Brackett invested with Martin, Bloom and others in the Santa Ysabel Ranch.

Henry Brunner (1857–1921) A native of Schmiedrued, Switzerland, Brunner founded nineteen banks in California, including the multi-national Swiss-American Bank of Locarno with Charles Martin and Antonio Tognazzini.

263

Henry Cohn (c1846–?) A partner with Charles Martin and Virgilio Rotanzi in the San Francisco commission merchant firm Cohn, Martin & Co.

Fabrizio Crippa (1819–1892) An immigrant from Monza, Italy, Crippa built an award-winning vineyard and estate in Victoria's gold country. He partnered with Battista Borsa in a butcher shop and employed Francesco Rotanzi as a miner and a bookkeeper.

Louis Feusier (1825–1917) A partner with Charles Martin and Camille Steffani in a San Francisco commission merchant and import firm.

Luigi Filippini (1846–1892) An immigrant from Cevio, Filippini joined his brother Charles to ranch in California. Never marrying, he left a large donation to his village. A bust of Filippini stands in Cevio's main square.

Battista Fiori (1842–1893) See James B. Bloom. Accompanied Virgilio Rotanzi from the Vallemaggia to San Francisco, along with Natale and Antonio Giacomini.

Foscalina (?–?) An associate of Bagnovini who sold Virgilio Rotanzi a ranch that did not live up to its promises. This person's identity remains a mystery. The surname may have been scrambled in the process of transcription.

Orazio Franzoni (1834–?) A partner with Virgilio Rotanzi in a hardware store in Petaluma, California.

Christian Fumberger (1841–1892) An immigrant to Australia from the Swiss Canton of Grisons, Fumberger partnered with Albino Paganetti and Stefano Pozzi in the Italian Hill-Long Tunnel Mine in Daylesford.

Domingo Ghirardelli (1817–1894) Born Domenico Ghirardelli in Liguria, Italy. Founder of a successful chocolate factory, Ghirardelli gave Virgilio and Alessandro Rotanzi their first jobs in California.

Dominic Giacobbi (1850–1930) Nephew to Francois Giacobbi and rector of the Jesuit Novitiate of the Sacred Heart in Los Gatos, California from 1888 to 1905. On seventy acres of the novitiate's grounds, he planted a vineyard whose grapes made altar wines the Jesuits sold to the public after retaining sacramental portions.

Francois Giacobbi (1813–1881) Also known as Francisco or Francis Jacoby. A Corsican-born vintner who immigrated to California shortly after the Gold Rush. Father of Virgilio Rotanzi's wife Elisa.

Louis Agassi Giacobbi (1858–1950) Son of Francois Giacobbi. Started L.A. Giacobbi & Co. specializing in fine jewelry in San Francisco.

Marie Salicetti Giacobbi (1830–1884) Corsican-born mother of Elisa Giacobbi.

Antonio Giacomini (c1840–?) A native of Brontallo, Antonio Giacomini made the trip with Virgilio Rotanzi from the Vallemaggia to San Francisco.

Natale Giacomini (1842–1923) Also a native of Brontallo, Natale Giacomini travelled with Virgilio Rotanzi to San Francisco in 1861.

Marianna Giovanettina (1812–?) A villager from Peccia and one of the few women to immigrate to Australia in the early years of the Swiss-Italian migration. She owned property and ran a business in Hepburn Springs.

Severino Guscetti (1816–1871) A Swiss-Italian physician who had represented Ticino in the Swiss Parliament and who immigrated to Australia when his political party suffered defeat. He became a prominent member of the Italian-speaking community in Daylesford-Hepburn and one of Francesco Rotanzi's close friends.

Giacomo Lucini (1831–1896) A political refugee and immigrant to Australia from Intra on the shores of Lake Maggiore in Italy where his family manufactured linen and lace textiles. With his brother Pietro, he built the Lucini and Company Macaroni Factory, the first pasta factory in Australia. On its walls and ceilings, he painted images reflecting patriotism for a united Italy.

Pietro Lucini (1825–1893) Also an Italian political refugee from Intra, Pietro Lucini employed newly-arrived Francesco Rotanzi as a delivery man for his shop. Behind their home and macaroni factory in Doctor's Gully, the Lucini brothers also operated the Lucini Reef-Swiss Mountain Reef Gold Mine.

Carlo Martinoia (1830–1905) Surname also spelled Martinoja or Martinoya. Known as Charles Martin in the United States. Emigrating from Cevio as a young boy, Charles Martin became a wealthy dairyman and businessman in California. He took on Virgilio Rotanzi as partner in his San Francisco commission merchant firm and served as executor of Rotanzi's estate.

Angelo Mattei (c1844–?) Mattei traveled to California with Alessandro Rotanzi and remained friends with the Rotanzi brothers in California.

Omero Medici (?–?) Also known as Homer Medici. He partnered with Virgilio Rotanzi in a grocery and liquor store on Dupont Street in San Francisco.

Giuliano Stefano Moretti (1828–c1906) A native of Cevio, Moretti purchased land in Chileno Valley in 1856 with Charles Martin. Later, with his son-in-law, Jeremiah Respini, he purchased a vast stretch of land in Santa Cruz on which he operated a large dairy.

Joseph Mortier (c1839–1904) The second husband of Elisa Giacobbi Rotanzi. A vintner from France who managed Camille Aguillon's wineries in Livermore.

Padovani (?–?) A youth who accompanied Alessandro Rotanzi and Angelo Mattei from Ticino to California. He may have been Giovanni Padovani, a friend of the Rotanzi brothers in California.

Albino Giacomo Paganetti (1836–1924) An emigrant from San Nazzaro on the shores of Lago Maggiore, Paganetti owned the Italian Hill-Long Tunnel Mine with Stefano Pozzi and Christian Fumberger. He promoted efforts to establish a sericultural (silk) industry in Victoria.

Atanasio Patocchi (?–?) Cousin of Luigi Rotanzi and brother of Carlo and Domenico Patocchi. He worked for a time at Cohn, Martin & Co. with Virgilio Rotanzi.

Carlo Patocchi (c1825–1900) Cousin of Luigi Rotanzi, Patocchi immigrated to the Mother Lode in California during the Gold Rush and planted roots despite severe hardships. One of his many jobs involved working for the Yocco brothers' grocery store in San Jose, California.

Domenico Patocchi (?–?) Brother of Carlo and Atanasio Patocchi, and cousin of Luigi Rotanzi.

Louis Pellier (1817–1872) A immigrant from Saint-Hippolyte, France, Pellier partnered with Gioachino Yocco in a San Jose plant nursery, then gave birth to Santa Clara Valley's prune industry by planting the valley's first french prunes. With his brother Pierre, he founded the Mirassou Winery.

Vincenzo Perini (1832–1862) An immigrant to Australia from Mergoscia, Switzerland, Perini operated the Commissioners Reef Gold Mine and opened the Locarno Guest House, named for his home in Ticino.

Carlo Petar (1834–1890) A partner with Domingo Ghirardelli in the wholesale and retail liquor business.

Alessandro Pozzi (1831–1867) One of four brothers from Giumaglio, Ticino who settled in Australia. Twin to Leonardo Pozzi, Alessandro co-owned a store with his brothers, then opened a bakery and a wine shop in Daylesford.

Giuseppe Natale Pozzi (1818–1897) Last of the four Pozzi brothers to arrive in Australia, he opened a flour mill in Daylesford.

Leonardo Pozzi (1831–1908) A fellow passenger with Francesco Rotanzi on the ship *Agen Und Heinrich* to Australia. Twin brother of Alessandro Pozzi, he worked in the mines, spent years in New Zealand, then returned to Melbourne to open a gunsmith shop.

Stefano Pozzi (1833–1922) One of the four Pozzi brothers from Giumaglio. A jeweller, he opened a store and bakery in Daylesford with his brothers and later became co-owner of the Italian Hill-Long Tunnel Mine. A close colleague of Francesco Rotanzi.

Jeremiah Respini (1852–1912) An immigrant from Cevio to Marin County where he bought acreage in Chileno Valley with Charles Martin, then moved to Santa Cruz to manage vast coastal dairy lands with his father-in-law Giuliano Stefano Moretti.

Francesco Rossetti (1825–1904) A physician born in Biasca, Switzerland. He was one of the first doctors in the Jim Crow gold fields and later served as honorary physician for the Daylesford Hospital. He operated a store in Hepburn Springs which he sold to Michele Bedolla, who transformed it into the Savoia Hotel.

Eligio Gaetano Rotanzi (1871–1944) Son of Gaetano Rotanzi, a cousin to Luigi Rotanzi. Eligio arrived in California in 1890 and eventually became foreman on Antonio Germano Tognazzini's ranch in Cayucos.

Norman Rotanzi (1913–1992) Son of Eligio Gaetano Rotanzi, Norman became head groundskeeper for William Randolph Hearst's renowned Castle in San Simeon, California.

Serafino Abele Rotanzi (1852–1929) Also known as Samuel A. Rotanzi. Luigi Rotanzi's nephew and cousin to Francesco, Alessandro and Virgilio. Samuel worked for Charles Martin and his associates, managing their Santa Ysabel Ranch before starting his own dairy.

Giosue Rottanzi (1826–1889) A prominent druggist and brother of Dr. Antonio Rottanzi. Giosue owned a pharmacy on Third and Folsom Streets in San Francisco with his brother, Dr. Antonio Rottanzi. He was also a wine dealer and produced a health-promoting patent medicine called "Long Life Bitters."

Dr. Antonio Rottanzi (1817–1892) A physician and prominent member of San Francisco's Swiss-Italian community, originally from Faido, Ticino. Dr. Rottanzi operated a hospital under the auspices of *La Società Italiana di Mutua Beneficenza* (the Italian Mutual Benevolent Association of San Francisco) and offered health insurance and medical services at his pharmacy and clinic.

Sartori (?–?) First name unknown. Sartori partnered with Bagnovini to sell a ranch to Virgilio Rotanzi, a sale that thrust Virgilio into heavy debt. The first name is not mentioned in the Rotanzi letters. He may have been Benedetto Sartori from Giumaglio, the eldest of several brothers who operated dairies in the Bodega area of Sonoma County.

Camillo Steffani (1839–1883) A hardware dealer and partner with Charles Martin and Louis Feusier in their San Francisco commission merchant firm. Vice-President of the Swiss Mutual Benevolent Society and Founder and Treasurer of the Freemason Loggia Speranza Italian, No. 219, Steffani married Leopoldina Rottanzi, daughter of Dr. Antonio Rottanzi.

Antonio Germano Tognazzini (1846–1906) A native of Someo, Tognazzini worked as a milker on dairies in Marin County, then bought land in Cayucos near San Luis Obispo, California, later purchasing additional dairyland near Santa Barbara. With Henry Brunner and Charles Martin, Tognazzini established the Swiss-American Bank of Locarno.

Carlo Traversi (1831–1872) Traversi brought his viola from Cevio to Daylesford where he started an orchestra and operated a dance hall on Howe Street.

Caterina Traversi (1833–1897) A native of Cevio, Caterina Traversi married Charles Martin and settled with him on a ranch in Chileno Valley, Marin County where they had seven children.

Gioachino Yocco (c1822–1889) Also known as Joaquin Yocco. An Italian from Ossola, a village near the Swiss border, Gioachino Yocco partnered with Louis Pellier in a San Jose nursery and established a San Jose grocery store with his brother Clementi. He helped with food and shelter when Alessandro Rotanzi became ill.

ENDNOTES

ABBREVIATIONS FOR FREQUENTLY USED SOURCES:

ANC—Ancestry, https://www.ancestry.com/
ARCH—Internet Archive, https://archive.org/
CDNC—California Digital Newspaper Collection, https://cdnc.ucr.edu/
HATH—Hathitrust Digital Library, https://www.hathitrust.org/
GOOG—Google Books, https://books.google.com/
NCOM—http://www.newspapers.com
TROVE—National Library of Australia, https://trove.nla.gov.au/

PROLOGUE

1. Bridget Rachel Carlson, *Immigrant Placemaking in Colonial Australia: the Italian-speaking Settlers of Daylesford* (Melbourne: Victoria University of Technology, 1997), 25, http://vuir.vu.edu.au/15416/1/Carlson_1997compressed.pdf.
2. Jean G. Vaucher, "Emigration from Switzerland," https://www.iro.umontreal.ca/~vaucher/Genealogy/Documents/Emigration1.html.
3. Giorgio Cheda, *Maggia: Brief Report on Emigration in California in the Second Half of the 18th Century*, trans. Jay Grossi, Summary from Maggia Viva (Locarno: Pro Vallemaggia, 1974), 147-171.
4. Carlson, *Immigrant Placemaking*, 30.
5. *The Straits Times*, May 3, 1853, http://eresources.nlb.gov.sg/newspapers/Digitised/Article/straitstimes18530503-1.2.20.
6. Carlson, *Immigrant Placemaking*, 31.
7. Luigi Jorio, "Leaving the poverty behind," Jan. 7, 2009, SWI Swissinfo.ch, https://www.swissinfo.ch/eng/culture/leaving-the-poverty-behind/76144.
8. La Società Genealogica della Svizzera Italiana, "20 anni di Genealogica nella Svizzera Italiana," Biblioteca Cantonale, Bellinzona, June 2017.
9. From 1870 to 1915, a wave of Swiss-Italians immigrated to Buenos Aires. They originated mainly from the area around Lugano and Mendrisio. May 4, 2009, SWI Swissinfo.ch, https://www.swissinfo.ch/eng/argentina/6786958.
10. Dale Bechtel, "Finding the 19th century mystery man," Oct. 20, 2011, SWI Swissinfo.ch, https://www.swissinfo.ch/eng/finding-the-19th-century-mystery-man/31204128.
11. Maurice E. Perret, *Les colonies tessinoises en Californie* (Lausanne: Rouge, 1950), 33.
12. Giorgio Cheda, "Le lettere degli emigranti al servizio della storia" in *Un altro Veneto.*

Saggi e studi di storia dell'emigrazione nei secoli XIX e XX, ed. E. Franzina (Abano Terme: Francisci, 1984), 339.

13. Perret, *Les colonies tessinoises en Californie*, 41.

14. Perret, *Les colonies tessinoises en Californie*, 33.

CHAPTER ONE

1. John Ball, *An Alpine Guide: the central alps, Including the Bernese Oberland, and All Switzerland . . . ,*part 2 (London: Longman, Green & Co., 1873), 306, GOOG.

2. Samuel Butler and R. A. Streatfeild, *Alps and sanctuaries of Piedmont and the canton Ticino* (New York: E.P. Dutton & Co., 1913), 39, ARCH.

3. Regione Lombardia, Direzione Generale Istruzione Formazione e Cultura, Archivio di Etnografia e Storia Sociale (AESS), Intangible Search: Inventario del Patrimonio Immateriale delle Regioni Alpine, http://arm.mi.imati.cnr.it/aess/intangible_wrk/show_ich_detail.php?db_name=intangible_ich&lingua=inglese&idk=ICH-MBS01-0000000617.

4. In 1850, the Vallemaggia district's administrative center, Cevio, had 927 inhabitants. Maggia and Someo, the next two largest towns, had 641 and 633, respectively. The remaining nineteen villages had five hundred residents or less, some much less. Confederazione Svizzera, Ufficio federale di statistica, Ticino Population Figures, 1850-2000, https://www.bfs.admin.ch/.

5. Cheda, "Le lettere degli emigranti," 166.

6. This tradition reaching back to the Swiss Confederacy still survives today in Ticino, although newcomers to a village may apply to be accepted into this group. "Il passato del nostro territorio splende negli archivi patriziali," ALPA, Associazione dei Patriziati Ticinesi, Alleanza Patriziale Ticinese, https://www.alleanzapatriziale.ch/wp-content/uploads/testi/stampa/2017/2017_cdt.pdf.

7. J. Gentilli, *The Settlement of Swiss Ticino Immigrants in Australia* in Geowest, No. 23, Third Edition (Nedlands: University of Western Australia, 1988), 42.

8. Battista Strozzi, letter dated Mar. 26, 1855, in Cheda, *L'emigrazione ticinese in Australia*, vol. 2, 429.

9. Edmund Burke, ed., *The Annual Register*, vol. 121, *The Times* (London), Jan. 29, 1879 (London: Rivingtons, 1880), 16, GOOG.

10. Ticino Canton government statistics published in *The Freeman's Journal* (Sydney), Jun. 4, 1870, TROVE.

11. In December 2016, trains began running at full schedule through the new Gotthard Base Tunnel, the world's longest at over thirty-five miles. Opening ceremonies included performers dancing in devilish and goatish costumes harkening back to the Devil's Bridge legend. Where Francesco faced an extremely perilous crossing, now passenger trains zip through the tunnel at about 125 miles per hour. "The Gotthard in Newspapers and Periodicals," Swiss National Library, https://www.nb.admin.ch/snl/en/home/publications-research/dossiers/gotthard-periodicals.html.

12. Leonardo Pozzi, letter dated Sep. 24, 1855, Cheda, *L'emigrazione ticinese in Australia*, quoted in "We were transported to shore by the lice, "SWI Swissinfo.ch, http://www.swissinfo.ch/eng/-we-were-transported-to-shore-by-the-lice-/6783584.

13. Pozzi, letter dated Sep. 24, 1855.

14. Pozzi, letter dated Sep. 24, 1855.

15. Paul P.J. Sheppy, *Death Liturgy and Ritual: Volume II: A Commentary on Liturgical Texts* (Ashgate Pub Ltd, 2003), 19, GOOG.

16. The ship departed on May 13, 1855, arriving on Oct. 4, 1855.

17. In a letter dated Nov. 10, 1855, Alessandro Brocchi, an immigrant from Ticino wrote home of the arrival: "On October 5, the Robert Society, the shipping agent for the *H. Ludwina* debarked at the port of Sydney, Australia a group of 176 passengers so thin, hungry and miserable that we . . . no longer recognized our dear compatriots, and we all began to weep to see them so miserable." Carlson, *Immigrant Placemaking*, 103.

18. "Italian Migration Stories," New South Wales State Archives and Records, https://www.records.nsw.gov.au/archives/collections-and-research/guides-and-indexes/stories/italian-migration-stories.

19. Leonardo recalled this voyage decades later, writing through the rosy lens of recollection in the broken English learned in his fifty years abroad. Pozzi, letter dated Sep. 24, 1855.

20. Carlson, *Immigrant Placemaking*, 100.

21. The *Heinrich und Agen* arrived Sept 21, 1855. *The Cornwall Chronicle*, Sep. 26, 1855, TROVE.

CHAPTER TWO

1. Cliff Judge and Roma Emmerson, "Some Children at Risk in Victoria in the 19th Century," *Children Australia*, Vol 2, No. 1 (Cambridge Univ. Press: 1977), 7–13. https://www.cambridge.org/core/journals/children-australia/article/some-children-at-risk-in-victoria-in-the-19th-century/2E984ECECCCC811A30017DA982945B32.

2. *Australia Gazette*, Sep. 6, 1852 quoted in Victorian Cultural Collaboration, Gold! SBS Special Broadcasting Services, Melbourne, http://www.sbs.com.au/gold/story.php?storyid=49.

3. "The Gold Metropolis Overview," eGold, Electronic Encyclopedia of Gold in Australia, Univ. of Melbourne, http://www.egold.net.au/biogs/EG00013b.htm.

4. Manning Clark, *History of Australia* (Melbourne University:1993), 222.

5. Bruce Mitchell, "Hargraves, Edward Hammond (1816-1891)" *Australian Dictionary of Biography*, http://adb.anu.edu.au/biography/hargraves-edward-hammond-3719.

6. Population increased from 29,000 in 1851 to 123,061 in 1861. eGold, "The Gold Metropolis Overview."

7. Alessandro Brocchi in Carlson, *Immigrant Placemaking*, 107.

8. "By the *Ludwina* last week we received another batch of Italian immigrants, who appear to be for the most part healthy able bodied men, and suitable for any agricultural and pastoral pursuits, but almost every one of them is unable to speak a word of English; this is a grievous circumstance, and as I remarked in your issue of 5th May last, 'the importance of a little English seems to be overlooked by those gentleman who send out these foreign labourers, since no provision is made to instruct them in our language, during the several months occupied by the voyage to this country . . . " *Empire* (Sydney), Oct. 13, 1855, TROVE.

9. The name Jim Crow may have originated in a contemporary rhyme or in a corruption of "jumcra," the indigenous name for the area. Victorian Places, Monash University and the University of Queensland, http://www.victorianplaces.com.au.

10. Edward Wishart and Maura Wishart, *Spa Country: Victoria's Mineral Springs* (Melbourne: Dept. of Sustainability and Environment in conjunction with Victorian Mineral Water Committee, 2010), 162.

11. Stefano Pozzi, letter dated Aug. 24, 1854, Cheda, *L'emigrazione ticinese in Australia*, quoted in Carlson, *Immigrant Placemaking*, 468.

12. "To the Diggins," Gold! http://www.sbs.com.au/gold/story.php?storyid=18.

13. "People are flocking in from all countries now, and there is not accommodation for a tenth of them. Some have to sleep in sheds, &c., who never knew anything but a feather-bed in England. We have had very heavy rains lately; several people have been drowned on their way to and from the diggings in attempting to swim the creeks, as the Government does not think of putting any bridges where required; indeed, the people are beginning to murmur against the abominable way in which our government is carried out." Letter to *Australia Gazette*, Aug. 31, 1852, "The Immigration Rush," quoted in Gold! http://www.sbs.com.au/gold/story.php?storyid=49.

14. "The very significant and varied roles Indigenous guides fulfilled especially in the initial alluvial gold rush period when vast tracts of Victoria remained trackless or at best rudimentary is monumental—showing new goldfields, rescuing, providing food, liaising, warning, trading and naming features in the landscape, determining the most direct and easily traversable route (often along traditional pathways) and locating food, medicine and water in order to sustain their non-Indigenous companions, safely conveying gold seekers and others by fording rivers safely, preparing temporary shelters, acting as diplomats and interpreters, negotiating passage through the country of resident clans met on the line of march and locating precious waterholes for horses and other stock." "Aborigines & the Gold Rush," State Library of Victoria, http://ergo.slv.vic.gov.au/explore-history/golden-victoria/life-fields/aborigines-gold-rush.

15. Carlson, *Immigrant Placemaking*, 41.

16. William Craig, *My Adventures on the Australian Goldfields* (London: Cassell, 1903), 66, ARCH.

17. Andrea Ferrari, "History of Hepburn" (Unpublished Notes), Daylesford & District Historical Society.

18. Mining equipment: a whim is a vertical horse-powered drum used as a hoist in a mine; a whip is a rope and pulley hoist; a puddler is a piece of equipment used to separate gold from clay. It consists of a pit shaped like a donut with a rake that is pulled through a sludge of clay, gold and water to break up the clay and allow gold to separate from it; poppet heads are frames above mine shafts used to haul ore buckets. Wishart and Wishart, *Spa Country*, 163.

19. Henry T. Maddicks, and Keith H. Butler, *100 Years of Daylesford Gold Mining History, August 1851 to 1951* (Daylesford, Vic.: Daylesford & District Historical Society, 1981), 39.

20. Craig, *My Adventures on the Australian Goldfields*, 55, ARCH.

21. William Howitt, *Land, labour, and gold: two years in Victoria: with visits to Sydney and Van Diemen's Land* (London: Longman, Brown, Green, and Longmans, 1855), 282, ARCH.

22. Pozzi, letter dated Sep. 24, 1855.

23. Pozzi, letter dated Sep. 24, 1855.

24. Vincenzo Perini, letter dated Aug. 8, 1859 in Cheda, *L'emigrazione ticinese in Australia*, vol. 2, 218, quoted in Carlson, 182.

25. Vincenzo Perini, letter dated Aug 8, 1859, Cheda, *L'emigrazione ticinese in Australia* quoted in "Letters from Swiss-Italian Immigrants to Victoria in the 19th Century" by Tony Pagliaro in Newsletter of the Italian Historical Society, Jan–Feb–Mar 1991, vol. 2, no 1, Italian Historical Society—COASIT, https://www.coasit.com.au/images/ihs/newsletters/IHSN_vol2_no1_1991.pdf.

26. Heritage Council of Victoria, Victorian Heritage Database Report, "Former Macaroni Factory," http://vhd.heritagecouncil.vic.gov.au/places/592/download-report.

CHAPTER THREE

1. Natural disasters ravaged Ticino in 1834, 1839 and 1840. Luigi Lavizzari, *Escursioni nel cantone Ticino* (Ticino: Valadini e comp., 1863), 431, GOOG.
2. Carlson, *Immigrant Placemaking*, 78.
3. *La Democrazia*, April 17, 1856. In 1850, for instance, 146 men and 148 women lived in the village of Corippo in Val Verzasca; twenty years later, 54 men and 108 women remained. Giorgio Cheda quoted in Stefania Summermatter, "Women were the 'Stationary Engine' of Migration," Jan. 23, 2009, SWI Swissinfo.ch, http://www.swissinfo.ch/eng/women-were--stationary-engine--of-migration/6782948.
4. Gender demographics changed radically during the years of emigration. In 1850, the ratio of males to females in the Vallemaggia was approximately 50%: 3,511 males to 3,971 females. In 1870, there were 2,506 males to 4,157 females (36.7%), and in 1900, 1,909 males to 3,289 females (63.3%). Cheda, *L'emigrazione ticinese in Australia*, 151.
5. Vanoni's painting lists names of passengers: Lorenzo Debernardi, Celestino Debernardi, Costantino Boneti, Abondio Martinelli, Basilio Garzoli, Maurizio Tomasi, Costanzo Martinelli from Maggia. Giovanni Antonio Vanoni, Ex-Voto of Emigrants to Australia, dated Apr. 5, 1868. Chiesa di Santa Maria delle Grazie, Maggia, Ticino.
6. "Religiosità e vita quotidiana" Archivio Patriziale di Cevio-Linescio, http://www.patriziatoceviolinescio.ch/ita/contents/view/religiosit_e_vita_quotidiana.
7. Giuseppe Strozzi and Oliveto Rodoni, *Diario d'Australia: quando si andava per oro* (Locarno: A. Dadò, 1992), 33.
8. Marco Marcacci, "Stefano Francini, 150 anni dopo," SWI Swissinfo.ch, https://www.swissinfo.ch/ita/stefano-franscini--150-anni-dopo/6010546.

CHAPTER FOUR

1. Two years earlier, *Harper's Weekly* had described crafty swindlers on the Atlantic's far side. "From the hour of his departure to the hour of his settlement on his final resting-place, the emigrant is a prey to human vultures. At the great ports where emigrants embark in the Old World—Liverpool, Limerick, Glasgow, Belfast, Bremen, Amsterdam, Havre—a brood of hungry rascals earn a fat livelihood by cheating them." *Harper's Weekly*, Jun. 26, 1858, GOOG.
2. Before Haussmann, most buildings in Paris were made of brick or wood and covered with plaster. Haussmann required that the buildings along the new boulevards be either built or faced with cut stone, primarily local cream-colored limestone, which gave harmony to the boulevards.
"Story of cities #12: Haussmann rips up Paris—and divides France to this day," *The Guardian*, https://www.theguardian.com/cities/2016/mar/31/story-cities-12-paris-baron-haussmann-france-urban-planner-napoleon.
3. The *Bavaria* originally carried "packets" of mail to and from British embassies and colony outposts. "Days of the Old Packet," The ShipsList, http://www.theshipslist.com/accounts/packets.shtml.
4. "Le Havre as emigration port," Genealogical Historical Services, http://www.genhist.

org/ghs_Havre_eng.htm.

5. Tyler Anbinder, *City of Dreams* (NY: Houghton, Mifflin, Harcourt, 2016), 264.

6. From August 1, 1855 to April 18, 1890, Castle Garden was New York State's immigration center, after which the U.S. government took over immigration processing. "Castle Garden: America's First Immigration Center," The Battery Conservancy, http://www.castlegarden.org.

7. On the ship's manifest, the original handwritten image, Virgilio appears as a 19-year-old female farmer from Italy. The ship's master recorded Virgilio's gender as female, despite attesting with his signature that the list "truly designated the age, the sex and the occupation of each passenger." Digitized records often reflect errors due to the difficulty of transcribing handwritten script. Virgilio's name is listed as "Virginio" and "Virgilia Rottanze" in digitized versions of this manifest.

8. Bartholomew Benvenuto's boarding house on 13 Crosby Street in New York City was listed as Benvenuto B. & Co. in *Trow's New York City Directory*, 1861. New York City Public Library Digital Collections, https://digitalcollections.nypl.org.

9. Alison Leigh Cowan, "A Guide to Houses No Gentleman Would Dare to Frequent," City Room: Blogging from the Five Boroughs, *New York Times*, Jan. 26, 2011, https://cityroom.blogs.nytimes.com/2011/01/26/on-the-records-a-well-preserved-roadmap-to-perdition/.

10. Parks, Recreation and Cultural Affairs Administration, Landmarks Preservation Commission, City of New York, SOHO Cast Iron Historic District Designation Report, 1973, http://sohobroadway.org/wp-content/uploads/2018/08/LPC-SoHo-CastIron-Historic-District-Designation-Report_1973.pdf.

11. Giosue Gianini is listed in *Trow's New York City Directory* for 1863 as Josiah Giannini, a glazier, living with his brother Peter at 187 Mott Street. *Trow's New York City Directory*, 1863, ARCH.

12. Also called a Napoleon, a Marengo is a gold coin issued by Napoleon Bonaparte after winning a battle against the Austrians near the Italian village of Marengo.

13. Steamers left New York for Panama on the 1st, 11th, and 21st of each month.

14. David Thomas Valentine, *Manual of the Corporation for the City of New York*, part 2 (New York: Common Council, 1859), 584, HATH.

15. "Barnum's American Museum Illustrated," The Lost Museum, City University of New York, http://lostmuseum.cuny.edu/archive/assets/images/archive/barnum_american_museum_illustrated.pdf.

16. William Henry Aspinwall founded the Pacific Mail Steamship Company and built the Panama Railroad. The Panama Railroad, http://www.panamarailroad.org.

17. "Steamships at San Francisco," The Maritime Heritage Project, http://www.maritimeheritage.org/ships/Steamships_N-to-O.html.

18. *New York Herald*, Nov. 11, 1863, in John Haskell Kemble, *The Panama Route 1848-1869* (Columbia, S.C.: University of South Carolina, 1990), 149.

19. James Dawson Burn, *Three Years Among the Working Classes in the United States During the War* (London: Smith, Elder and Co., 1865), 131, 133, ARCH.

20. Launched in 1853, the *SS Sonora* was 269 feet long and weighed 1,616 tons. "Steamships at San Francisco," The Maritime Heritage Project.

21. Bruce C. Ruiz, Sr., "The Isthmian Crossing—The Argonauts," Panama History, http://www.bruceruiz.net/PanamaHistory/isthmus_crossing.htm.

22. "The *SS Sonora* took 15 days and 12 hours to arrive in SF on May 6, 1861. It left Panama

April 21st with New York mail of April 1st and arrived at half past seven o'clock in the evening. She brings 750 passengers and $67,000 in treasure from Manzanillo. Off Santa Barbara she experienced a terrific gale of wind, with heavy head sea, which lasted forty-eight hours." *Sacramento Daily Union*, May 7, 1861, CDNC.

23. John S. Hittell, *A History of the City of San Francisco and Incidentally of the State of California* (San Francisco: A.L. Bancroft, 1878), 135, HATH.

24. "About the Wharves, San Francisco News and Stories," The Maritime Heritage Project, http://www.maritimeheritage.org/news/wharves.html.

CHAPTER FIVE

1. Carlo Petar, a Swiss Italian, partnered with Ghirardelli for several years.

2. Sidney Lawrence, *The Ghirardelli Story* (California History, UC Press: 2002), ARCH.

3. Ghirardelli interned with Pietro Romanengo fu Stefano, a high-end sweet shop started in 1780 and still in business in Genoa today. Italy on this Day, "Domenico Ghirardelli—chocolatier," http://www.italyonthisday.com/2018/02/domenico-ghirardelli-Italian-chocolatier-San-Francisco-Ghirardelli-Square-Rapallo-Genoa.html.

4. Lawrence, *The Ghirardelli Story*.

5. Henry Halleck was a partner in the law firm of Halleck, Peachy and Billings. This firm handled over half the land grant claims coming before the U.S. Land Commission, the entity responsible for deciding land ownership in the transition from Mexican to U.S. governance. Many Mexican land grantees lost their property in lengthy court battles, wherein much of the disputed land ended up in the hands of attorneys. Halleck gained ownership of a large portion of West Marin property, which later became home to many Swiss-Italian dairy families. During the Civil War, Halleck quit the firm to join the Union Army as a major general. He was later made chief of staff of the Union Army.

6. Ann Shumard, "Domingo Ghirardelli: Chocolate in the Golden State," facetoface (blog), National Portrait Gallery, http://npg.si.edu/blog/domingo-ghirardelli-chocolate-golden-state.

7. Angela Ghirardelli Jorgensen, one of Ghirardelli's daughters, described the gardens: "Mr. G. being an Italian, felt that his place would not be complete if he had not something in it from his native land—so in 1858 he sent for marble statuary—marble dogs, urns for plants, fountains, life sized statues of Washington, Columbus, Count Cavour, Mercury, Agriculture, etc. These were placed all through the garden, with Columbus and Washington in front of the house on either side of the steps, with the two dogs at foot of steps." Polly Ghirardelli Lawrence, *The Ghirardelli family and chocolate company of San Francisco* (Berkeley, Calif: Regional Oral History Office, Bancroft Library, University of California, 1985), http://digitalassets.lib.berkeley.edu/roho/ucb/text/lawrence_polly_ghiradelli.pdf.

8. Metropolitan Transportation Commission, Association of Bay Area Governments, *The Bay Area Census*, http://www.bayareacensus.ca.gov/historical/historical.htm.

9. I. J. Benjamin, *Three Years in America, 1859-1862*, vol. II (Philadelphia: Jewish Publication Society of America, 1956), 111., HATH.

10. Hans-Jurgen Krackher, "Discover the Chapter of Marketing before Coca Cola," SpiritSchweppes, https://spiritschweppes.com.

11. "Explosion of a Soda Bottle with Fatal Results. While Fortunato Vilar, of the San Jose French Soda Works, was filling a bottle with soda this morning, the bottle burst, a portion striking his neck and cutting the carotid artery. He was attended by several physicians, but

expired in half an hour. He leaves a mother and brother." *San Francisco Chronicle*, Aug. 21, 1869, NCOM.

12. *Sacramento Daily Union,* Oct. 11, 1861, CDNC.

13. *Marin Journal*, Oct. 12, 1861, CDNC.

14. *Marin Journal*, Nov. 2, 1861, CDNC; Marin Journal, Nov. 23, 1861, CDNC.

15. Anti-Chinese sentiment intensified over the next decade as California's economy fizzled. After Chinese workers completed the trans-continental railroad in 1869, they returned to San Francisco in large numbers. Militant groups formed to force them from the region. At the height of the frenzy, the Swiss Italians formed a brigade, the Swiss-Italian Anti-Chinese Dragoons, numbering forty members. The group resolved to help "remove the Chinese nuisance from the heart of this city." *San Francisco Chronicle*, Feb. 22, 1880, NCOM.

16. Benjamin, *Three Years in America*, 70.

17. *Daily Alta California*, May 12, 1861, CDNC.

18. Hinton Rowan Helper, *The Land of Gold: Reality Versus Fiction* (Gale, Sabin Americana, 1855), ARCH.

19. *New York Times* writer Horace Greeley came up with the terms "bear market" and "bull market" to indicate stock market conditions after observing a bull and bear fight in California's Mother Lode district in 1850. The bull hooks upward, as does a rising stock market, and the bear swipes down, as when stocks fall. Mary Hall, "Where Did the Bull and Bear Market Get Their Names?" https://www.investopedia.com/ask/answers/bull-bear-market-names/.

20. *Daily Alta California*, Jul. 26, 1860, CDNC.

21. More comparisons come from a blurb in the *Richmond Dispatch*, Mar. 21, 1861, describing "Wages in San Francisco, Cal.," NCOM. "The average wages of day laborers, in San Francisco, Cal., is $2 a day, with board, or $2.50 without; of carpenters, $4 a day, without board; of female domestics, $7.50 to $8 a week, with board. The average price of board, for laboring men, is $5 per week."

22. National Bureau of Economic Research, Wages and Earnings in the United States, 1860-1890: Wages by Occupational and Individual Characteristics, Outrun Change, http://outrunchange.com/2012/06/14/typical-wages-in-1860-through-1890/.

23. "Military Pay," Civil War History, American Battlefield Trust, https://www.battlefields.org/learn/articles/military-pay.

CHAPTER SIX

1. Andrew Ward, *Daylesford and Hepburn Springs Conservation Study* (Shire of Daylesford and Glenlyon, Victoria: 1985).

2. Ward, *Daylesford and Hepburn Springs Conservation Study*.

3. "qualcosa di piu, che il semplice baretto dove si beve un bicchiere" (something more than a place where one comes to drink). Leonardo Pozzi, letter dated Sep. 7, 1857, Cheda, *L'emigrazione ticinese in Australia,* quoted in Carlson, *Immigrant Placemaking*, 47.

4. *Daylesford Advocate and Hepburn Courier*, May 3, 1860, TROVE.

5. Justin Stafford, "Indigenous History: The Dja Dja Wurrung," Victorian Cultural Collaboration, SBS, Special Broadcasting Service, slideplayer.com, http://www.sbs.com.au/firstaustralians/.

6. Cate Elkner, "Not just Bewildered Onlookers: Aboriginal Participation in the Goldrushes," A Nation's Heritage, eGold, Electronic Encyclopedia of Gold in Australia,

Univ. of Melbourne, http://www.egold.net.au/biogs/EG00045b.htm.

7. H. N. Nelson, "Parker, Edward Stone (1802–1865)," *Australian Dictionary of Biography*, National Centre of Biography, Australian National Univ., http://adb.anu.edu.au/biography/parker-edward-stone-4363/text7093, 1974.

8. Ferrari, *History of Hepburn*.

9. Nelson, *Australian Dictionary of Biography*.

10. Carlson, *Immigrant Placemaking*, 254.

11. Australian Bureau of Statistics, "Land Tenure and Settlement. Yearbook Australia, 1911," http://www.abs.gov.au/AUSSTATS/abs@.nsf/DetailsPage/1301.01911.

12. *Mt. Alexander Mail*, Oct. 2, 1857, TROVE.

13. *Daylesford Express*, Feb. 6, 1864, TROVE.

14. Villa Parma is listed in the Victorian Heritage Database as an important heritage site. Heritage Council Victoria, Victorian Heritage Database, https://vhd.heritagecouncil.vic.gov.au.

15. Bull boar sausages have a unique flavor that makes them still popular today. In 2005, the Slow Food Movement named Bull Boar an endangered recipe and included it in the Ark of Taste project, a catalog of endangered heritage foods. Slow Food Foundation for Biodiversity, "Bull boar Sausage," https://www.fondazioneslowfood.com/en/ark-of-taste-slow-food/bull-boar-sausage/.

16. Wishart and Wishart, *Spa Country*, 164.

17. Still standing today, the Lucini pasta factory, Australia's oldest Italian building, is registered by Heritage Victoria and classified by the National Trust, https://vhd.heritagecouncil.vic.gov.au.

18. *Daylesford Mercury*, Feb. 1864, TROVE; John Butler, *Birtchnell's Daylesford directory* (Ballarat, Vic: S. L. Birtchnell, 1865), GOOG.

19. *Daylesford Express*, Oct. 22, 1864, TROVE.

20. *Daylesford Mercury*, Feb. 1864, quoted in Ward, *Daylesford and Hepburn Spring Conservation Study*.

21. Roslyn Maguire, "Italians in Evidence in 19th Century Australia," https://swissitalianfesta.com/wp-content/uploads/2020/09/Italians-in-evidence-in-19th-Century-Australia.pdf.

22. J. Ulysses Browne, *Age* (Melbourne), Apr. 11, 1936, TROVE.

23. Maddicks and Butler, *100 Years of Daylesford Gold Mining History*, 45.

24. Antonio Ghidossi, letter 1881, in Pagliaro, "Letters from Swiss-Italian Immigrants to Victoria in the 19th Century."

25. An herbalist named Sing Song lived in Hepburn and treated Chinese clients. Carol Holsworth, "Chinese Herbalists 1850s-1930s" Rural Victoria, https://chineseruralvictoria.wordpress.com/chinese-herbalists-1850s-1930s/.

26. Ferrari, *History of Hepburn*.

27. "Chinese Immigration Act 1855," Documenting a Democracy. Museum of Australian Democracy, https://www.foundingdocs.gov.au/item-sdid-18.html.

28. "Daylesford," *Sydney Morning Herald*, Feb. 8, 2004, http://www.smh.com.au/news/Victoria/Daylesford/2005/02/17/1108500206394.html.

29. *Mount Alexander Mail*, Aug. 27, 1862, TROVE.

30. *Observer* (Adelaide), Mar. 28, 1857, TROVE.

31. *Southern Australian Register*, Aug. 3, 1857, TROVE.

32. The 1861 Daylesford census reveals only 658 females in a population of 1,919. Carlson,

Immigrant Placemaking, 311.

33. In the Vallemaggia, 1341 of the 1534 couples who wed between 1855 and 1875 were born in the same village. In Verzasca, the figures were similar, with 884 out of 944, or 93 percent. Cheda, *L'emigrazione ticinese in Australia*, quoted in Carlson, *Immigrant Placemaking*, 369.

34. *Mount Alexander Mail*, Jun. 4, 1858, TROVE.

35. *Mount Alexander Mail*, Aug. 6, 1862, TROVE.

CHAPTER EIGHT

1. Likely a reference to St. Anthony Head near Falmouth in Cornwall.

2. In her autobiography, Louisa Christina Rollfing described steerage on the steamship *Nurnberg*, which left Bremen for Galveston on October 18, 1880. Rollfing as quoted in "The Trip to Texas," Piwetz Family, http://freepages.rootsweb.com/~piwetz/genealogy/.

3. *Pall Mall Gazette*, Aug. 9, 1879, as quoted in "Steerage Class—Accommodations — Cunard Steamship Line—1879," Gjenvick-Gjonvik Archives: Social and Cultural History, http://www.gjenvick.com/Steerage/1879-SteerageAccommodations-Cunard.html#ixzz3gfGX3HND.

4. The gold and silver from the western mines carried by the Pacific Mail steamships helped fund the Union war efforts. The ships were at times threatened by Confederate raiders attempting to steal the valuable cargo. Ellyse Stauffer, "Making Way: Steamship Mail in the 19th Century," Smithsonian National Postal Museum, https://postalmuseum.si.edu/research-articles/making-way. The *Golden Age* would return to Panama on May 16, loaded with a treasure shipment of $811,138.83. Henry G. Langley, *The San Francisco Directory for 1862 . . .* (San Francisco: S.D. Valentine & Son, 1862), 26, https://sfpl.org/locations/main-library/magazines-newspapers-center/bay-area-city-directories-and-phone-books/san-0.

5. Bill of Fare for the Pacific Mail Steamship Company's Steamer *Golden Age*, Saturday, Jul. 26, 1863, Buswell & Co., printer, University of California, Berkeley, Bancroft Library, Online Archive of California, https://oac.cdlib.org/ark:/13030/tf6n39p4fx/?brand=oac4.

6. *Daily Alta California*, May 6, 1862, CDNC.

7. Alessandro wrote to Luigi that he had traveled with 1012 passengers from New York to Aspinwall and 1600 from Panama to San Francisco.

CHAPTER NINE

1. Carlo Michele Patocchi was born in August 1825 in Switzerland. According to the 1900 U.S. census, he immigrated to California in 1859, but Patocchi puts the date earlier in his letters. U.S. Census Bureau (1900), ED 421 City and County Alms House, San Francisco city, San Francisco, California, digital image s.v. "Charles Pattocchi," http://www.family-search.org.

2. Adams & Co's Express (Nov 1849 - Feb 1855) was the first shipping company serving California's mining region and became the leading company shipping gold between California and New York with a banking department that purchased gold dust. Calvet M. Hahn, "Adams' Express and Independent Mail," Carriers and Locals Society, *The Penny Post*, 1990, https://www.pennypost.org/ pdf/Adams-Express-by-Hahn-1990.pdf.

3. *Sacramento Daily Union*, Feb. 23, 1855, CDNC.

4. William Tecumseh Sherman (1820-1891) was a businessman, speaker and writer who served as a general in the Union Army during the American Civil War (1861–65). "The Civil War in America: Biographies. William T. Sherman," Library of Congress.

5. William Tecumseh Sherman, *Memoirs of General William T. Sherman: With an Appendix, Bringing His Life Down to Its Closing Scenes, Also a Personal Tribute and Critique of the Memoirs,* vol. 1 (New York: D.A. Appleton, 1886), 109, HATH.

6. "Mary Aaron Museum, "About Marysville, California," https://maryaaronmuseum.com/about-marysville-california/.

7. Cheda, *L'emigrazione ticinese in California*, Vol. 2, table 1.

8. Noah Chittenden Fassett, "The Fassett Letters: The Gold-Rush Fassetts from Licking Co., Ohio," http://physics.clarku.edu/~rkohin/Fassett.html.

CHAPTER TEN

1. The Yocco store was located at 292 Market Street, north of Santa Clara Street in downtown San Jose. *Bishop's directory of the city of San Jose for 1876* (San Francisco: B. C. Vandall, 1876), GOOG.

2. The fruit, the Prune d'Ente, originates from a variety brought back to France from Damascus by the Crusaders in the 12th century and grafted by Benedictine monks onto local plum trees. Florence Fabricant, "In France, the Prune Holds a Noble Station," *The New York Times*, Oct. 31, 2001, https://www.nytimes.com/2001/10/31/dining/in-france-the-prune-holds-a-noble-station.html.

3. Sara Humber, "Overseas Property: The Plum Location in France," *The Sunday Times*, May 15, 2005, https://www.thetimes.co.uk/article/overseas-property-the-plum-location-in-france-t50wp8vqxn3.

4. "By 1939, San Jose, with a population of 57,651, was the largest canning and dried-fruit packing center in the world, with 18 canneries, 13 dried-fruit packing houses, and 12 fresh-fruit and vegetable shipping firms.
"Economic History," Santa Clara County: California's Historic Silicon Valley, National Park Service's National Register of Historic Places, the City of Santa Clara, the California Office of Historic Preservation, and the National Conference of State Historic Preservation, https://www.nps.gov/articles/economic-history.htm.

5. Michael A. Shea, "Nineteenth Century Medicine in the Santa Clara Valley" (San Jose: California Pioneers of Santa Clara County, 2012), California Room of the Martin Luther King/San Jose State Library, San Jose, CA.

6. A belief popularized by Dr. Benjamin Rush, one of the country's most celebrated physicians. Shea, "Nineteenth Century Medicine."

7. Linnæus Smilax, *Sarsaparilla, and Sarsaparilla so-called: a popular analysis of a popular medicine; its nature, properties, and uses* (London: Aylott, 1854), 26, GOOG.

CHAPTER ELEVEN

1. The identities of Bagnovini and Delponte are unknown. Delponte is referred to elsewhere in Virgilio's letters as "the blacksmith." He likely came from Bignasco. Bagnovini was a villager from Peccia. The only Bagnovini documented in California at the time is Jacque (Giacomo) Bagnovini, listed as a laborer in living on Taylor Street between Lombard and Chestnut Streets in San Francisco. Henry G. Langley, *The San Francisco Directory for 1858 . . .* (San Francisco: S.D. Valentine & Son, 1858), 57, https://sfpl.org/locations/main-library/magazines-newspapers-center/bay-area-city-directories-and-phone-books/san-0.

2. Ten years later, San Jose's population had tripled. By 1867, it had a population of about

nine thousand residents. Metropolitan Transportation Commission, Association of Bay Area Governments, *The Bay Area Census*, http://www.bayareacensus.ca.gov/historical/historical.htm.

3. J.P. Munro-Fraser, *History of Santa Clara County, California, including its Geography, Geology, Topography, Climatography and Description* (San Francisco: Alley, Bowen & Co., 1881), 420-421, ARCH.

4. "Grand Celebration of the Opening of the San Jose Railroad," *Daily Alta California*, Jan. 17, 1864. CDNC.

5. Virgilio paid fifteen dollars for a peddler third-class license, which allowed him to peddle with a one-horse cart, and twenty-five dollars for a second-class license, which allowed him two horses. In November 1863, he paid $4.17 in taxes, assessed at fifteen percent for a third-class peddler, on earnings of $27.80 per month. "United States Internal Revenue Assessment Lists, 1862-1874." Familysearch.org.

6. Craig Thornber, "Glossary of Medical Terms Used in the 18th and 19th Centuries," History of Medicine, https://www.thornber.net/medicine/html/medgloss.html.

7. Alfred Hudson, *Lectures on the Study of Fever* (Philadelphia: Henry C. Lea, 1869), 145–46, GOOG.

8. An 1864 report to the Italian Ministry of Foreign Affairs by Giovanni Battista Cerruti, the first Italian consul in San Francisco, in Alessandro Baccari and Andrew Canepa, Olga Richardson, "The Italians of San Francisco in 1865: G.B. Cerruti's Report to the Ministry of Foreign Affairs," *California History Quarterly*, 60:60:350–369.

9. The Swiss Benevolent Society met for a time in the Helvetia Hotel on Pine Street between Montgomery and Kearny Streets and maintained an office at 309 Clay Street, also home to the commission merchant firm of Martin, Feusier and Steffani. Camille Steffani, an officer of the Society, may have shared his office with the organization. Langley, *San Francisco Directory, 1884*, https://sfpl.org/locations/main-library/magazines-newspapers-center/bay-area-city-directories-and-phone-books/san-0.

10. *Daily Morning Chronicle*, Feb. 2, 1869, NCOM.

CHAPTER TWELVE

1. Intercolonial Exhibition of Australasia, Melbourne, 1866-67 Official Record (Melbourne: Blundell & Co.,1867), 200, State Library of Victoria, http://digital.slv.vic.gov.au/.

2. Official Catalogue of Exhibits, Essays, etc., Prepared for the Philadelphia Centennial Exhibition, 1876 (Philadelphia: Commissioners, 1875), 114, HATH .

3. International Exhibition 1876 Official Catalogue, U.S. Centennial Commission (Philadephia: John R. Nagle & Co., 1876), 164, ARCH.

4. *Victoria Government Gazette*, (Melbourne: Government Printer, Jan. 1867), 158, State Library of Victoria, *Victoria Government Gazette*, Online Archive, 1836-1997, http://gazette.slv.vic.gov.au.

5. Of forty-four emigrants from the town of Vogorno, twenty-three signed their loan contract with a cross. Carlson, *Immigrant Placemaking*, 298.

6. Clare Gervasoni, *Macaroni & Mineral Water, Spa Country's Swiss Italian Story* (Hepburn Springs: Hepburn Springs Swiss Italian Festa Inc., 2005), 97.

7. *Dizionario Storico della Svizzera*, Accademia svizzera di scienze umane e sociali, s.v. "Severino Guscetti," http://www.hls-dhs-dss.ch/i/home.

8. *The Assassination of Abraham Lincoln* . . . United States Department of State, U.S.

Government Printing Office, 1867, HATH.

9. John Martin Vincent, *State and Federal Government in Switzerland* (John Hopkins Press, 1891), 94, HATH.

10. A news report regarding the Swiss and Italian Association, which established the library, announced: "Our Italian population—probably the largest on the gold-fields, if not in the colony—have a well-supported public library of books in their own beautiful language. The annual meeting was held last week at Spring Creek, when the report showed the institution to be flourishing . . . " It cited "Mr. F. Borsa, an old companion in army of the general when he fought in South America. Other vieux moustaches who have seen service under the hero of Caprera are now peacefully employed either in the cultivation of the grape or in mining." The Borsa referenced may have been either Battista, Antonio, Serafino or GianBattista. There was no F. Borsa in the Daylesford region. The term "vieux mustaches" refers to veteran soldiers. Garibaldi retired to the Island of Caprera in Sardinia after his mercenary days were over. *Argus* (Melbourne), May 8, 1865, TROVE.

11. Unable to afford a complete military uniform, volunteers in Garibaldi's forces wore red shirts and eventually came to be called "Redshirts."

12. In the mid-1880s, a mine tunnel beneath Daylesford's St. Peter's Catholic Church collapsed, damaging the church's spire and walls. "History of St. Peter's Daylesford," https://www.ballarat.catholic.org.au/pnews/history-of-st-peters-daylesford-1865-2015/.

13. A sluice-head is a unit of flow used in apportioning water among miners equal to one cubic foot of water per second. Sizes, https://sizes.com/units/sluice_head.htm. *Age* (Melbourne), Jun. 30, 1865, TROVE.

14. Susan Lawrence and Peter Davies, Striking Gold in Water Management, LaTrobe University, http://www.latrobe.edu.au/our-work/water-and-land-management/striking-gold-in-water-management.

15. Howitt, *Land, labour, and gold*, 205.

16. Committee members were Dr. Severino Guscetti, Fabrizio Crippa, Pietro Lucini, Michele Bedolla, Vincenzo Perini, Pitcher, Walter Hutton, Stephens and Mantica with Francesco Rotanzi as secretary. Gervasoni, *Bullboar, Macaroni & Mineral Water*, 71.

17. Hepburn Mineral Springs Reserve, Heritage Council Victoria, Victoria Heritage Database, http://vhd.heritagecouncil.vic.gov.au/places/1993.

18. *Daylesford Mercury* as quoted in the *Argus* (Melbourne), Mar. 31, 1869, TROVE.

19. Carlson, *Immigrant Placemaking*, 54.

20. Lodge Devotion 723, "Masonic Buildings—Daylesford Masonic Centre & its Craft Lodge," http://www.lodgedevotion.net/devotionnews/masonic-buildings---articles-editorials-and-histories/masonic-buildings/masonic-buildings---daylesford-masonic-centre-its-craft-lodge.

21. *Inside the Freemasons: The Grand Lodge Uncovered*, directed by I. Michael Toth, (Reality Films, 2010), Netflix.

22. Carlson, *Immigrant Placemaking*, 245.

23. George Neil Emery and J. C. Herbert Emery, *A Young Man's Benefit: The Independent Order of Odd Fellows and Sickness Insurance in the United States and Canada, 1860-1929* (McGill-Queen's Press, 1999), 126, GOOG.

24. *Star* (Ballarat), Apr. 13, 1866, TROVE.

25. In comparison, a married caretaker couple on a farm earned from 50 to 55 pounds per year including rations, about 10 lbs of flour, 12 lbs of meat, 2 lbs sugar and 1/4 lb tea, each, per week. *Geelong Advertiser*, Apr. 28, 1866, TROVE.

26. "Life Expectancy at birth (years) by sex, Queensland and Australia, 1881-1890 to 2015-2017," Queensland Government Statistician's Office, http://www.qgso.qld.gov.au/products/tables/life-expectancy-birth-years-sex-qld/index.php.

CHAPTER THIRTEEN

1. "Charcoal has been burned since the early fifties, and is produced chiefly by Italians, from oak and partly from willow. San Francisco used in 1881 120,000 sacks of 60 lbs. each, or 3,600 tons, worth about $65,000." Hubert Howe Bancroft, *The Works of Hubert Howe Bancroft: History of California*, vol. 7 (San Francisco: The History Company, 1890), 77, ARCH.
2. J. Charles Whatford, *Fuel for the Fire: Charcoal making in Sonoma County: An Overview of the Archaeology and History of a Local Industry* (Society for California Archaeology, California Office of Historic Preservation, 1994), https://www.scahome.org/publications/proceedings/Proceedings.13Whatford.pdf.
3. U.S. Census Bureau (1870), San Antonio Township, Marin, California, s.v. "Natale Giacomini," http://www.familysearch.org.
4. Cheda estimates that of the 27,000 immigrants to California, only 1,000 of the men established ranches. Dale Bechtel, "Migrations interview: Part Five," Jan. 7, 2009, SWI Swissinfo.ch, https://www.swissinfo.ch/eng/migrations-interview--part-five/7135364.
5. *Pacific Rural Press*, Jul. 6, 1872, CDNC.
6. *Marin Journal*, Jan. 8, 1870, CDNC.
7. *Marin Journal*, Apr, 30, 1870, CDNC.
8. *Sonoma Democrat*, Dec. 31, 1881, CDNC; *Sonoma Democrat*, Jan. 21, 1882. CDNC. The article was signed by G. Tomasini, Victor Sartori, Antonio Bassi, Victor Piezzi, G. Bassi, Vincenzo Bassi and John Gicaomini.
9. *Marin Journal*, Aug. 16, 1883, CDNC.
10. *Marin Journal*, Jul. 24, 1883, CDNC.
11. J. Netten Radcliffe, "Report on cholera in 1867," in *Reports of the Medical Officer of the Privy Council and Local Government Board with Regard to the year 1874* (London: Privy Council, 1875), 81, HATH.
12. Sir William Tennant Gairdner, *Public Health in Relation to Air and Water* (Edinburgh: Edmonston and Douglas, 1862), 15, ARCH.

CHAPTER FOURTEEN

1. August Hirsch, *Handbook of Geographical and Historical Pathology*, Volume 1 (London: New Sydenham Society, 1883), 419, ARCH.
2. Charles Jules Armand Bioche, and Charles Goujet, *Dizionario generale ragionato della procedura civile e commerciale*. s.v. "emancipazione," (Palermo: Pietro Pensante, 1854), 640, GOOG.
3. Munro-Fraser, *History of Sonoma County [Cal.]* (San Francisco: Alley, Bowen & Company, 1880), 344, ARCH.
4. Munro-Fraser, *History of Sonoma County*, 303.
5. *Petaluma Journal and Argus*, Nov. 22, 1866, GOOG.
6. A hod carrier is a worker who supports bricklayers, stonemasons, cement finishers, or plasterers by preparing and carrying supplies.
7. Chris Carlsson, "Eight Hour Day Movement," FoundSF, http://www.foundsf.org/index.

php?title=Eight_hour_day_movement.

8. Carlsson, "Eight Hour Day Movement."

9. "The worthy steam farmer will be a sort of factory owner and engineer-in-chief, and many of his men will be mechanics, engine drivers, and stokers (persons who tend furnaces to produce steam) . . . There are many recorded instances of steam-ploughed fields yielding 2 or more quarters of wheat per acre more than fields of the same character of soil alongside but cultivated by horses." *California Farmer and Journal of Useful Sciences*, Feb. 25, 1869, CDNC.

10. James B. Hume, *Wells, Fargo & Co. Stagecoach and Train Robberies, 1870–1884* (North Carolina: McFarland, 2010), 22.

CHAPTER FIFTEEN

1. This surname is variously written with a 'j' as in "Martinoja," with a "y" as in "Martinoya," or most commonly with an 'i' as in " Martinoia."

2. *La Nuova Elvezia*, Apr. 1905. Translated by Emilie Martin, from the files of Sally Gale.

3. The Swiss Republic Restaurant was located on the Long Wharf. Also known as Central Wharf, it extended nearly three thousand feet into San Francisco Bay, serving as a wharf for Pacific Mail Steamers and other vessels. "Long Wharf Site," San Francisco Landmarks, NoeHill in San Francisco, https://noehill.com/sf/landmarks/cal0328.asp.

4. San Antonio Township was an unincorporated area on the border of Sonoma and Marin counties in western Marin County. It was originally part of the Mexican land grant Rancho Laguna de San Antonio. Chileno Valley was named for Chilean immigrants who settled in the area. Martin purchased the property from the Bojorquez family, which had inherited the land originally granted by the last Mexican governor of California, Pio Pico. John Anderson, "Chileno Valley History as Seen by A. Nielsen," *Petaluma Argus-Courier*, Jun. 17, 1954, NCOM.

5. U.S. Census Bureau (1860), San Antonio Township, Marin, California, s.v. "Charles Martin," ANC.

6. Martin was not the only Swiss Italian to anglicize his surname. Other examples include Fiori (Bloom), Adami (Adams) and DeMartini (DeMartin).

7. U.S. Census Bureau, Selected Federal Census Non-Population Schedules (1850-1880), s.v. "Charles Martin," ANC.

CHAPTER SIXTEEN

1. The newspaper announcement noted that D. R. Foss had retired from Cohn, Martin & Co. and Virgilio Rotanzi had purchased an interest in the firm. *Daily Alta California*, Jan. 5, 1869.

2. Common murres, also known as common guillemots, live in dense colonies and lay pear-shaped eggs on cliff ledges. Audubon, "Why are Murre Eggs So Pointy," https://www.audubon.org/news/why-are-murre-eggs-so-pointy-new-research-debunks-prevailing-theory.

3. *Daily Alta California*, Nov. 25, 1863, CDNC.

4. *California Farmer and Journal of Useful Sciences*, May 15, 1863, CDNC.

5. "Gold Rush Prices Worksheet," PORTS-Parks Online Resources for Teachers and Students, California Department of Parks and Recreation, https://www.parks.ca.gov/pages/22922/files/worksheet-goldrushprices.pdf.

6. Carola DeRooy and Dewey Livingston, *Point Reyes Peninsula: Olema, Point Reyes Station and Inverness* (Charleston, SC: Arcadia, 2008), 28.

7. "Two Centuries of Prominence and Personalities," California's Dairy Industry: the Early Years 1769-1900, California Milk Advisory Board, http://www.californiadairypressroom.com/press_kit/history_of_dairy_ndustry.

8. *Marin Journal*, May 11, 1861, CDNC.

9. U.S. Census Bureau (1860), San Antonio, Marin, California; Schedule Type: Agriculture, digital image s.v. "Charles Martin," ANC.

10. U.S. Census Bureau, Agriculture of the United States in 1860 (Washington D.C.: U.S. Government Printing Office, 1864), 12, https://www2.census.gov/library/publications/decennial/1860/agriculture/1860b-05.pdf#.

11. *Santa Cruz Sentinel*, Jul. 25, 1862. CDNC.

12. *Daily Alta California*, Jun. 19, 1868, CDNC.

13. Charles Martin's early Chileno Valley land purchase supports his assertion that he started the first Swiss dairy in Chileno Valley. His claim as the first in California is unverified.

14. Martin may not have exaggerated the number of cows in his Swiss-Italian ranching network. The 1870 U.S. census counted 164,151 milk cows in California, 18,655 in Marin County, 14,960 in Sonoma County and 9,370 in Monterey County, home to Giuliano Moretti's forty thousand acres on the Santa Cruz coast.

U.S. Census Bureau Agricultural Schedules, Compendium of the Ninth Census, https://www2.census.gov/library/publications/decennial/1870/compendium/1870e-35.pdf?#.

15. In comparison, average monthly salary for a manufacturing wage earner in 1870 was thirty-two dollars. Clarence D. Long, *Wages and Earnings in the United States* (National Bureau of Economic Research, Inc., 1960), 48, https://www.nber.org/chapters/c2497.pdf.

16. The Nucleus Hotel was also home at the time to William Haas, a wholesale grocer who became a wealthy philanthropist and built in 1886 what is now known as the Haas-Lilianthal House, a Queen Anne mansion and museum on Franklin Street. Langley, *The San Francisco Directory for 1869*.

17. Virgilio was not receiving room and board, so his earnings were less than that of bakers, who earned from thirty to fifty dollars per month "found," that is, including room and board, and dairymen, who earned thirty to forty-five dollars found. Edward Young, *Annual Report of California Labor Exchange*, May 1869 in "Special Report on Immigration Accompanying Information for Immigrants," (Washington: Government Printing Office, 1872), 221, HATH.

18. After the 1906 earthquake, Dupont Street was repaired and renamed Grant Avenue. Derek Strahan, "Lost New England Goes West: Dupont Street, San Francisco," Lost New England, Jun. 1, 2016, http://lostnewengland.com/2016/06/lost-new-england-goes-west-dupont-street-san-francisco/.

19. Benjamin E. Lloyd, *Lights and Shades in San Francisco* (San Francisco: A.L. Bancroft, 1876), 80, ARCH.

20. In 1886, the Association applied to dissolve the corporation. The dissolution was contested by a woman named Elisa Little in the Supreme Court of California. She contended that when her husband died on Jan 29, 1882, there were 355 members, but she was only paid 150 dollars. She did not receive a dollar for each member. The Association argued that not every member paid in, so she only received what the members contributed. The court ruled in favor of the Association, and it was allowed to disincorporate. *West Coast Reporter*,

vol. IX, Feb.-Mar. 1886, (A.L. Bancroft, 1886), GOOG.

21. *Daily Alta California*, Sep. 21, 1868, CDNC.

22. This holiday is traditionally celebrated on August 1, the date that the Federal Charter of 1291 was signed forming a confederation of three alpine cantons marking the beginning of the Swiss nation. *Marin Journal*, Sep. 26, 1868, CDNC.

23. Henry G. Langley, *The San Francisco Directory for 1871* . . . (San Francisco: S.D. Valentine & Son, 1871), 903, https://sfpl.org/locations/main-library/magazines-newspapers-center/bay-area-city-directories-and-phone-books/san-0. In contrast to the primarily fraternal and social groups, ranger militias, funded by state and federal officials, conducted expeditions to fight and kill Native Americans. Benjamin Madley, *An American Genocide: The United States and the California Indian Catastrophe* (New Haven: Yale Univ. Press, 2009), 174-5.

24. *Sydney Morning Herald*, Jun. 17, 1869, TROVE.

25. Eugenio Balbi was an Italian geographer, as was his son, Adriano. The book Virgilio referenced may have been *La nostra patria: brevi notizie di geografia italiana*, 1861.

26. Henry G. Langley, *The San Francisco Directory for 1869* . . . (San Francisco: S.D. Valentine & Son, 1869), 533, https://sfpl.org/locations/main-library/magazines-newspapers-center/bay-area-city-directories-and-phone-books/san-0.

27. Richard Dillon and Lynn Davis, *North Beach: the Italian heart of San Francisco* (Novato, CA: Presidio Press. 1985), 34.

28. Dairy ranching could be profitable. A local newspaper in 1869 noted that a rancher in Bodega "milked this year 25 cows and has made 218 pounds of butter from each cow. This butter he has sold at an average price of forty cents a pound. The cows brought him 25 calves. Ten of them he sold for $150 and the remaining fifteen are worth $300. So his account stands thus: Butter. $87.20 for each cow. $2180.00; 25 calves, $450.00; total, $2630 00." *Russian River Flag*, Oct. 28, 1869.

29. *Marin Journal*, Dec. 26, 1868, CDNC.

CHAPTER EIGHTEEN

1. Conrad Malte-Brun, Adriano Balbi, *System of Universal Geography* (Edinbugh: Black, 1842), 373, HATH.

2. Report of Consul Byers in 1873 in Edward Young, *Labor in Europe and America* (Philadelphia: U.S. Government Printing Office, 1875), 614, GOOG.

3. Abraham Hoffman, *California's Deadliest Earthquakes: A History* (The History Press, 2017), 36.

4. "Destruction of Property in Various Parts of the City," *San Francisco Morning Call*, Oct. 22, 1868, Virtual Museum of the City of San Francisco, http://www.sfmuseum.org/hist1/1868eq.html.

5. The event became known as "The Great Earthquake" until nearly forty years later when, in 1906, a quake estimated at 7.6–7.9 magnitude shook San Francisco. Timothy Swenson, "The Great Earthquake of 1868," 2006, http://museumoflocalhistory.org/wordpress2/wp-content/uploads/2014/10/Hayward1868.pdf.

6. *San Francisco Chronicle*, Jun. 25, 1916, Proquest Historical Newspapers, San Francisco Public Library.

7. Flint corn, also known as Indian corn, is grown largely in Central and South America for food and animal feed. http://www.history.com/news/hungry-history/indian-corn-a-

fall-favorite. *California Farmer and Journal on Useful Sciences*, Sep. 11, Oct. 30 and Nov. 27, 1863, CDNC.

8. Dillon and Davis, *North Beach*, 76.

9. Confederazione Svizzera, Ufficio federale di statistica, Ticino Population Figures, 1850-2000, https://www.bfs.admin.ch/.

10. Chiesa di Santa Maria Assunta e di San Giovanni Battista. The current structure was built in the 1700s and renovated in 1876. A placard on the wall is inscribed: "Ristauro...Benefattori di California . . . Anno MDCCCLXXV" (Restored . . . Benefactors in California . . . 1875).

11. Luigi Jorio, "A Home for the Family; a Church for the Parish Priest," May 11, 2009, SWI Swissinfo.ch, https://www.swissinfo.ch/eng/a-home-for-the-family--a-church-for-the-parish-priest/6795444.

CHAPTER NINETEEN

1. John Tilston, *Bull Market: The rise and eclipse of Australian stock exchanges* (Lulu, 2016), 31, GOOG.

2. Tilston, *Bull Market*, 30.

3. *Victoria Government Gazette*, (Melbourne: Government Printer, Oct. 1866), 158, State Library of Victoria Online Archive, 1836-1997, http://gazette.slv.vic.gov.au.

4. Norm Darwin, *Gold'n Spa: A History of Hepburn Shire* (Ballarat, Vic: H@nd Publishing, 2005), 97.

5. *Star* (Ballarat), Jul. 20, 1861, TROVE.

6. *Star* (Ballarat), Feb. 3, 1869, TROVE.

7. Frederic Harrison, *My Alpine Jubilee* (London: Smith, Elder, & Co., 1908), 94-95, HATH.

8. *Marin Journal*, Dec. 26, 1868. CDNC.

9. *Geelong Advertiser*, Dec 11, 1868, TROVE.

10. *Argus* (Melbourne), May 28, 1867, TROVE.

11. Federal authorities were required to maintain order in Ticino in 1870, 1876, 1889, and 1890-91. Leslie Friedman Goldstein, *Constituting Federal Sovereignty: The European Union in Comparative Context* (Baltimore: JHU Press, 2003), 132, https://epdf.tips/constituting-federal-sovereignty-the-european-union-in-comparative-context-the-j.html.

CHAPTER TWENTY

1. *Daily Alta California*, Mar. 27, 1870, CDNC.

2. Amoor Country is in Eastern Siberia. Published in 1860, *A Voyage Down the Amoor* by Perry McDonough Collins popularized the notion that Eastern Siberia provided opportunities for trade. World Digital Library, https://www.wdl.org/en/item/26/.

3. *Marysville Daily Appeal*, Nov. 27, 1870, CDNC.

4. During the Civil War, as a donation to the Sanitary Fund, a precursor to the Red Cross, the Steele Dairy made a massive 3,800-pound cheese wheel for exhibit at the Industrial Fair of the Mechanic's Institute in San Francisco. Fair attendees could glimpse the enormous mound for a quarter. After the fair ended, slices of the gigantic cheese were sent to the White House for President Lincoln, to General Grant and to General Frederick Steele, brother to dairyman Isaac Steele. The remainder was sold to San Franciscans, making about $2,820 for the Sanitary Fund by 1864. Myron Angel, *History of San Luis Obispo County,*

California; with illustrations and biographical sketches of its prominent men and pioneers (Oakland: Thompson & West, 1883), 40–41, ARCH.

5. *Marin Journal*, Oct 21, 1871, CDNC.

6. The Moretti and Respini families eventually formed the Coast Dairies and Land Company to manage their vast acreage on the Santa Cruz Coast. "Coast Dairies," The Trust for Public Land, https://www.tpl.org/our-work/coast-dairies#sm.0006rp86t11yzdx2 t7n2ej21u6gn2.

7. *San Francisco Chronicle*, May 5, 1870, NCOM.

8. *San Francisco Chronicle*, Apr. 20, 1870, NCOM.

9. *San Francisco Chronicle*, Apr. 28, 1870, NCOM.

10. *San Francisco Chronicle*, Apr. 20, 1870, NCOM.

11. *San Francisco Chronicle*, May 5, 1870, NCOM.

12. *Sacramento Daily Union*, Jul. 17, 1870, CDNC.

CHAPTER TWENTY-ONE

1. According to Giacobbi family history, Francisco never "did a lick of work," but lived off his wealthy wife Maria's inheritance. However, the 1870 U.S. census lists him as a "Wine Mfct." The 1880 U.S. census lists him as a retired farmer, so he may have been a viticulturist with vineyards on the San Francisco Peninsula. U.S. Census Bureau (1870 and 1880), San Francisco, California. ANC; Carol Voss, "Some Giacobbi History," 2009.

2. U.S. Census Bureau (1870), San Francisco, California, digital image s.v. "Francis Jacoby," ANC.

3. *Daily Alta California*, Jul. 7, 1860, CDNC.

4. John S. Hittell, *The resources of California: comprising agriculture, mining, geography, climate, etc., and the past and future development of the state.* 5th ed. (San Francisco: A. Roman, 1863), 364, HATH.

5. Lloyd, *Lights and Shades in San Francisco*, 81.

6. Interview with Fr. Etienne Siffert, Church of Notre Dame des Victoires, Oct. 2, 2009.

7. "Wedding Traditions and Fashion from the 1860s to the 1930s," The Lockwood-Matthews Mansion Museum, https://www.lockwoodmathewsmansion.com/exhibit/wedding-traditions-fashion-1840s-1930s/.

8. Virgilio may have told Luigi of his new wife and son, but the first part of the letter has been lost, and, in the remainder, he makes no mention of his new family.

9. U.S. Census Bureau (1870), San Francisco, California, digital image s.v. "Virgil Rotanzi," ANC.

10. Virgilio's store is noted as owning fifteen horses, very likely a recording error. U.S. Census Bureau (1870), Non-Population Schedule, Fourth Ward, San Francisco, California digital image s.v. "Virgil Rotanzi," ANC.

11. Natale Giacomini, one of Virgilio's travel companions to California, now owned a 396-acre dairy ranch in Chileno Valley valued at seventy-five hundred dollars, farm implements worth three hundred dollars, and livestock worth over four thousand dollars (sixty-three milk cows, three horses, fifteen other cattle and five pigs). U.S. Census Bureau (1870), Selected Federal Census Non-Population Schedules: Agriculture, s.v. "Natale Giacomini," ANC. In the 1870 U.S. census, Natale Giacomini's real estate assets are listed at twelve thousand dollars, his personal estate at five thousand dollars. U.S. Census, Bureau (1870), San Antonio Township, Marin, California, digital image s.v. "Natale Giacomini," ANC.

12. John S. Hittell, *All About California and the inducements to settle there. California as a Home to the Immigrant* (San Francisco: California Immigrant Union, 1874), 39, HATH.

13. John S. Hittell, *A History of the City of San Francisco and Incidentally of the State of California* (San Francisco: A.L. Bancroft, 1878), 429, HATH.

14. Joseph L. King, *History of the San Francisco Stock Exchange* (San Francisco: J. L. King, 1910), 76, ARCH.

15. Mark Twain, *Roughing and the Innocents at Home* (George Routledge & Sons: New York, 1882), 341. GOOG.

16. Constitution of the San Francisco Mercantile Library, in the Catalogue of the San Francisco Mercantile Library (San Francisco: Mercantile Association, 1854), 29, ARCH.

17. The building included a reading room, reference library, ladies' reading room, a parlor, a chess and smoking-room, a writing room, a museum and a store room for periodicals. The basement contained a spacious lecture-room and supper-room, with ladies' and gentlemen's dressing rooms. Its extensive periodical section included "one hundred and sixteen magazines, about twenty-five illustrated papers—some of which are foreign— over one hundred Atlantic and about one hundred and fifty Pacific Coast papers." Lloyd, *Lights and Shades*, 118.

18. A.L. Bancroft, *Bancroft's Tourist Guide. Yosemite. San Francisco and around the Bay* (San Francisco: A.L. Bancroft & Company, 1871), 155, ARCH.

19. *San Francisco Chronicle*, Feb. 6, 1870, NCOM.

20. Langley, *The San Francisco Directory for 1871*.

21. *Russian River Flag*, Feb. 3, 1870, CDNC.

22. *Russian River Flag*, Nov. 3, 1870, CDNC.

23. *Sacramento Daily Union*, May 27, 1870, CDNC.

24. *Daily Alta California*, Jul. 17, 1870, CDNC.

25. *Sacramento Daily Union*, Jun. 3, 1870, CDNC.

26. On June 14, ticket sales were enjoined. The issue went to a Grand Jury, which decided on August 3 to let the Mercantile Library Lottery proceed. Langley, *The San Francisco Directory for 1871*.

27. Thomas R. Jones, "October in California Fifty Years Ago - Big Lottery Drawing Holds States Attention," *The Grizzly Bear*, Official Organ Native Sons and Native Daughters of the Golden West, October 1920, 4, HATH.

28. *Daily Alta California*, Oct. 31, 1870, CDNC.

29. Donna C. Schuele, "In Her Own Way: Marietta Stow's Crusade for Probate Law Reform Within the Nineteenth-Century Women's Rights Movement," Yale J.L. & Feminism (1995). https://digitalcommons.law.yale.edu/yjlf/vol7/iss2/5/.

30. Mrs. J. W. Stow, *Unjust Laws which Govern Woman*, (Published and sold by the author. Place of publication not identified: 1877), 204, HATH.

31. *San Francisco Chronicle*, Nov. 4, 1870. Proquest Historical Newspapers, San Francisco Public Library.

32. *Sacramento Daily Union*, Nov. 4, 1870, CDNC.

33. *Sacramento Bee*, Nov. 4, 1870; "Obituaries and death notices, He-Hf," San Francisco Genealogy, http://www.sfgenealogy.org/sf/vitals/sfobihe.htm.

34. "William T. Britton attempted suicide this evening by swallowing two ounces of laudanum, on the corner of Bush and Sutter streets. The attempt was discovered in season and his life saved. He had written a note, sharing that he held thirty-five coupons in the Mercantile Lottery and hoped to win a prize, but luck was against him and had been for a

year." *Sacramento Daily Union*, Nov. 18, 1870, CDNC.

35. A useful anesthetic, chloroform also became a fashionable recreational drug, as it gave pleasurable sensations when inhaled. According to one source, the substance even gained use by brides at weddings. "Sentimental young ladies now use chloroform when the marriage ceremony is being performed. A white handkerchief saturated with chloroform, and applied to the mouth slides the 'dear creechar' [sic] into the blissful state. Oh, delicious!" *Sacramento Daily Union*, Apr. 20, 1852, CDNC.

36. With "two brothers and an uncle," Virgilio refers to his brother Alessandro, who died just a few years after arriving in California and to his uncle, Luigi's only brother Giacomo Rotanzi, who died shortly after arriving in Sacramento, California in 1852.

37. Although it was not known until the 1880s, phthisis is caused by bacteria spread through the air. Dampness, lack of ventilation and crowded living conditions helped spread the illness. In 1871, this contagious disease resulted in 518 deaths in San Francisco, the most common cause of death in the city in each of the previous four years. Municipal Government-San Francisco, *San Francisco Municipal Reports for the fiscal year 1870–71, ending June 30, 1871*, 311, ARCH.

38. Virgilio's name is recorded as first name "Rotanoza" and surname "Virgilio." Mortuary Record of the City and County of San Francisco, 1871. San Francisco Public Library History Center, San Francisco Mortuary Records, 1865–1873, Reel 1.

39. The Masonic Cemetery was located west of Masonic Avenue and bordered by Fulton and Turk Streets. Virgilio had probably joined the Masonic Lodge in Petaluma about the time he became a volunteer fire fighter and an active member of the Swiss Guard. "Old Cemeteries in the City," FoundSF, http://www.foundsf.org/index.php?title=Old_Cemeteries_in_the_City.

40. Home to many cemeteries, Colma is known as "the city of the dead," "the city of silence" or "the city of souls." Colma has more dead bodies than live residents, leading to the city's tagline: "It's great to be alive in Colma." "Ocean Beach gusts reveal headstones, S.F. history," *San Francisco Examiner*, Jun. 8, 2012, https://www.sfexaminer.com/news/ocean-beach-gusts-reveal-headstones-s-f-history/.

CHAPTER TWENTY-TWO

1. *Daily Alta California*, Dec. 3, 1875, CDNC.

2. *Daily Alta California*, Mar. 5, 1871, CDNC.

3. By 1895, the "inmates" spent their time toiling over needlework for San Francisco's wealthiest women. A San Francisco newspaper society page reported that "For several weddings in high society announced for this fall, the inmates are preparing dainty creations for the trousseaus of the brides, including Spanish drawn work in most intricate designs, each piece marked with the monogram of the bride to be. Society ladies of the City have placed a number of orders for table decorations for dinners and lunches when the season again opens." Embroidering finery for San Francisco's privileged society ladies must have rankled those girls, yet living in this charitable institution was bound to be better than living on the streets. *San Francisco Call*, Jun. 23, 1895, CDNC.

4. Listed as Francois and Marie Jacoby. U.S. Census Bureau (1870), San Francisco, California, digital image s.v. "Francois Jacoby," ANC.

5. The average value in 1870 of 7,800 pounds sterling was $5.588 per pound or $43,586 dollars. Measuring Worth, https://www.measuringworth.com/calculators/exchange/

result_exchall.php?action=&iyear=1870&dyear=1870&ival ue=7800&itype=pound.

6. John P. Grueningen, *The Swiss in the United States: A Compilation Prepared for the Swiss-American Historical Society As the Second Volume of Its Publications* (San Francisco: R and E Research Associates, 1970), 96.

7. The Speranza Italiana Lodge No. 219, a lodge established by and for Italian speakers, was not chartered in San Francisco until 1872, after Virgilio's death. Its name translates to "Italian Hope," affirming the dream for a new Italy. Many leaders of the Italian Risorgimento, the movement to unify Italy, were Masons, including King Victor Emanuele, Guiseppe Garibaldi, Camillo Benso di Cavour, and Giuseppe Mazzini. Golden Gate Speranza Lodge No. 30, F. & A.M., "History from 1852 to 2005," https://docplayer.net/62185372-Golden-gate-speranza-lodge-no-30-f-a-m-history-from-1852-to-2005.html.

8. Paul Dado, the De Martins, the Garzolis, Giuliano Moretti, Luigi Filippini, and Benedict Sartori were also listed as Marin County "Heavy Men." *Marin Journal*, Jul. 27, 1876, CDNC.

9. "To the Members of La Solidarité. You are hereby notified of the death of Mr. Virgilio Rotanzi. He was a regular member of the French Mutual Beneficial Association, La Solidarité, and an assessment of one dollar is due from you and payable to the Secretary of the Association within thirty days from this date . . . dated April 26, 1871." *San Francisco Bulletin*, May 1, 1871, CDNC.

10. "DISSOLUTION OF CO-PARTNERSHIP The copartnership heretofore existing between COHN, MARTIN & CO. has been dissolved by the death of V. ROTANZI. The firm will be continued by the undersigned under the old firm name. HENRY COHN/ CHAS. MARTIN." *Daily Alta California*, May 5, 1871, CDNC.

11. Florence Hartley, *The Ladies' Book of Etiquette, and Manual of Politeness, A Complete Handbook for the Use of the Lady in Polite Society* (Lee & Shepherd, 1872), 15, GOOG.

12. E. C. Calabrella, *The Ladies' Science of Etiquette, By a Lady* (Edinburgh: Paton and Ritchie, 1851), 24, GOOG.

13. *Etiquette for Ladies, with Hints on the Preservation, Improvement, and Display of Female Beauty* (Philadelphia: Lea & Blanchard, 1840), 34, GOOG.

14. Marietta Stow's husband, Joseph Washington Stow, does not appear to be related to William Walter Stow, a contemporary in San Francisco and a commissioner for Golden Gate Park for whom Stow Lake in that park is named. Wendy Chmielewski, Jill Norgren, Kristen Gwinn-Becker, Her Hat Was In The Ring, "Marietta Stow," http://www.herhatwasinthering.org/biography.php?id=7740.

15. Stow, *Probate Confiscation*, 31.

16. In 1881, Stow began publishing a monthly newspaper, the *Woman's Herald of Industry and Social Science Cooperator*, covering topics related to women's advancement, including equality of women, birth control and eugenics. She formed the Woman's Independent Political Party to encourage women to engage in politics, and in 1882, she became an independent candidate for governor of California. Two years later, she ran as an Equal Rights candidate for Vice-President of the United States. Chmielewski, Norgren and Gwinn-Becker, "Marietta Stow," Her Hat Was In The Ring.

17. Elisa exaggerates the length of time since Virgilio's death. He had died less than one year earlier in April 1871.

18. Although awareness of poison oak's painful effects was as pervasive as the plant itself, many picnickers returned to the city from weekend wanderings in the woods with prickling, red rashes. To assuage pleasure seekers' concerns, resorts and parks advertised terrain free of the noxious shrub. Newspapers and magazines published advertisements

and formulas for cures ranging from caustic potash baths to wild sunflower teas, vapor baths to a mixture of iron sulphate and laudanum. James Mason Hutchings, *Hutchings' California Magazine*, May 1857, 492, HATH.

19. Henry Cohn disappeared without a trace. No record of his subsequent adventures has been found.

20. When Charles Martin bought into Cohn's company, an ad appeared in the *Daily Alta California* of Feb. 13, 1868 announcing that "Mr. Chas. Martin has bought an interest in the firm of H. Cohn & Co., Choice Yellow Butter, Cheese and Egg Depot, 519 Sansom Strt." *Daily Alta California*, Feb. 13, 1868, CDNC.

21. Feusier joined the firm on June 4, 1874. *Daily Alta California*, Jun. 6, 1874, CDNC.

22. Twain mentioned Feusier in an article on teacher examinations. *Virginia City Territorial Enterprise*, March–April, 1863, reprinted in *The Works of Mark Twain; Early Tales & Sketches*, vol. 1, 1851–1864, (Univ. of California Press, 1979), 231–32, http://www.twainquotes.com.

23. Feusier joined in with other family members, including a nephew, Edward, who operated Feusier and Spafford, a commission merchandise firm that maintained a warehouse at 310 and 312 Clay Street, across the street from Charles Martin's company. This firm specialized in exporting salmon and fruit, including raisins, dried, preserved and canned, to Australia, Mexico and South America. *California Farmer and Journal of Useful Sciences*, Mar. 29, 1877, CDNC.

24. In 1870, Louis Feusier purchased an octagon house on Russian Hill as a wedding present for his bride, Louise Guerne. Louise's brother, George Emile Guerne, for whom the town of Guerneville, California was named, was a business partner of Thomas T. Heald, founder of Healdsburg, California. George Kenny, a clerk for the historian Hubert Howe Bancroft, built the octagon house at 1067 Green Street in 1858 according to recommendations put forth by Orson Squire Fowler in his book *A Home for All: The Gravel Wall and Octagon Mode of Building*. Fowler, a phrenologist and amateur architect, maintained that an octagon house cost less to build and promoted healthier living with more sunlight and better air circulation. One of only two octagon houses now remaining in San Francisco, Feusier's house was listed on the National Register of Historic Places in 1974. "Feusier Octagon House," San Francisco Landmarks, NoeHill in San Francisco, https://noehill.com/sf/landmarks/sf036.asp.

25. Especially popular at the start of the Civil War, cartes de visite provided soldiers and family members with an inexpensive way of sharing mementos with their loved ones. Along with those of family members and friends, photographs of celebrities, royalty, actors, politicians and military leaders were traded in huge numbers. Cards of the most famous personages sold over one hundred thousand copies. Cards were also used for promotional purposes. Actors advertised performances, abolitionists sold portraits of beaten slaves to fund anti-slavery campaigns, attorneys and physicians promoted themselves and their services. "Celebrity Culture: (Albumen Prints, Cartes de Visite and Cabinet Cards)," Dawn's Early Light, the First 50 Years of American Photography, Cornell University, http://rmc.library.cornell.edu/DawnsEarlyLight/exhibition/celebculture/.

CHAPTER TWENTY-THREE

1. *Daylesford Mercury*, Mar. 26, 1874, TROVE.
2. "Obituary for Mrs. Bladen-Neill," *Sydney Morning Herald*, Sep. 11, 1884, TROVE.
3. Adrienne Ferreira, "The Silk Road, Silk Farming" in *The Monthly*, June 2011,

https://www.themonthly.com.au/adrienne-ferreira-silk-farming-silk-road-adrienne-ferreira-3366.

4. Mrs. Bladen Neill, "Silk Growing Its Prospects and its Wants," *Journal of the Society of Arts, Royal Society for the Encouragement of Arts Manufactures and Commerce*, Vol. 24, London, April 28, 1876, 538, GOOG.

5. *Argus* (Melbourne), Jun. 23, 1874, TROVE.

6. *Leader* (Melbourne), Oct. 13, 1877, TROVE.

7. Sericulture did not take hold anywhere in Australia. The most successful attempt took place in New Italy, in New South Wales when, in 1891, Italian immigrants obtained government-funded loans to grow silk worms. Despite government support, the project was devastated by a fire that destroyed the New Italy colony and its silk worm equipment, causing the project to fail. Ferreira, "The Silk Road."

8. "Former Mount Alexander Silk Worm Farm," Heritage Council Victoria, Victorian Heritage Database Report, http://vhd.heritagecouncil.vic.gov.au/plac es/5256/download-report.

9. Stefano Pozzi's brother Leonardo returned to Victoria from New Zealand in 1890 and founded the Victorian Silk Culture Association. He picked up Paganetti's passion and created a model silk farm. Despite these efforts, the silk industry never caught on. "Silk Culturists Past and Present," *Herald* (Melbourne), Nov. 24, 1914, TROVE.

10. In Switzerland, Dr. Guscetti held a number of government positions, including Ticino's Minister of Education and Deputy in the Swiss Parliament. He authored a school textbook on grammar and a history of Switzerland. When his liberal principles conflicted with those of his political party, he immigrated with his family to Victoria. In Hepburn Springs, Dr. Guscetti led the campaign with his fellow countrymen to preserve the mineral springs. Francesco gave the eulogy at Dr. Guscetti's funeral in 1871. *Argus* (Melbourne), Apr. 24, 1871, TROVE; Carlson, *Immigrant Placemaking*, 273.

11. William Tell is a Swiss legendary hero whose resistance to an autocratic bailiff led to formation of the Swiss Confederacy. Tell and his cross-bow are well-known symbols of Swiss independence.

12. *Daylesford Advocate*, 1871, Daylesford & District Historical Society.

13. *Argus* (Melbourne), Mar. 2, 1877, TROVE.

14. The report concluded that "the wisest course would be to encourage their return to their country" by clamping down on opium dens and gambling houses. W. Young, "Report on the condition of the Chinese population in Victoria" (Melbourne: John Ferres, Government Printer, 1868), 11-13, https://www.parliament.vic.gov.au/papers/govpub/VPARL1868No56.pdf.

15. *Solicitors' Journal and Reporter*, Vol. 7 (Law Newspaper Co., Jul. 25, 1863), 726, GOOG.

16. Ruth Dwyer, "The Long Tunnel Mine, Italian Hill: Hands in the Riffles" *Italian Historical Society Journal*, Jan.-June 2002, vol. 10, no. 1), 26, http://coasit.com.au/IHS/journals/Individual%20Journal%20Extracts/Long%20Tunnel%20Mine%20from%20IHS%20Journal0028.pdf.

17. *Riverine Herald*, Echuca, Vic., Jul. 1, 1882, TROVE.

18. Maddicks and Butler, *100 Years of Daylesford Gold Mining History*, 45.

19. "Today the Ancient and Honourable Guild of Australian Town Criers keeps the tradition alive," Australian Towncriers, http://www.australiantowncrier.com.

20. *Daylesford Express and Hepburn Advertiser*, Apr. 5, 1863, TROVE.

21. "I would like to announce to all my fellow patriots and to Italians in general, who now

are residents in Daylesford, that I intend to act as interpreter for Italians and if it should happen, also for French. I hope to be able to profit with good service and to be a useful support to those for whom I will have the honor of facilitating negotiations, having a long experience in this colony and sufficient ability for such affairs. P.S. Secrecy is my principle in important business." *Daylesford Express and Hepburn Advertiser*, Apr. 1864, TROVE.

22. The Long Tunnel Company, Heritage Council Victoria, Victorian Heritage Database, vhd.heritagecouncil.vic.gov.au.

23. "In the early days of Victorian mining, in what Shakespeare would call its 'salad days, when the judgment was green,' parties of diggers were accustomed on Saturday nights to draw up their balance sheets on the first scrap of paper that came to hand, and after dividing their profits, to light their pipes with the document containing the account of the week's transactions. Limited liability, however, has very nearly swept away all such primitive fashions. We have now properly-formed companies looked after by properly-constituted legal managers, a very necessary class, and no one doubts that they are as useful to mining companies as book-keepers are to any mercantile firm.
The Act called Fraser's, under which so many associations have been incorporated, has made these gentlemen a power in the land. There can be no objection to this as long as the functionaries in question limit themselves to the duties of their office, and keep in remembrance that they are paid servants, and have a public duty to perform. A manager is not to barter away his own reputation to serve his company, nor the company's to profit his own purse." Thomas Dicker, *Dicker's Mining Record and Guide to the Gold Mines of Australia*, 5, Nov. 28, 1865 (Melbourne: Thomas Dicker, 1865), 350–351.

24. "The Great Tunnelling Gold Mining Company, at Italian Hill, are working in the faces at 4000 feet from the tunnel mouth at 180 feet from the surface; the wash is 2 feet deep, and the width 100 feet; 61 ozs. 14 dwts. 12 grs. have been obtained during the quarter, 6 men being employed in the work, exclusive of fellers of timber, carters, &c." Victoria Dept. of Mines, Ainsworth, A.B., Alderdice, A., Allen, G., Amos, M., Armstrong, . . . Wright, P. *Reports of the Mining Surveyors and Registrars quarter ended 31st March 1873* (Melbourne: John Ferres, Government Printer, 1874), https://www.parliament.vic.gov.au/papers/govpub/VPARL1873No22.pdf.

25. Carlson, *Immigrant Placemaking*, 57.

26. The Italian Hill-Long Tunnel mine was worked until 1912. Daylesford Mining Division, Historical Notes, Pandora, Australia's Web Archive, http://nla.gov.au/nla.arc-147062.

27. Michael Cannon, *The Australasian Sketcher with Pen and Pencil*, Oct. 4, 1873, 126. http://www.nla.gov.au/nla.news-title49.

28. Pietro Scazighini, letter dated May 20, 1864, quoted in "Emigranti Ticinesi in Australia," http://www.scuoladecs.ti.ch/emigrazione/materiali-didattici/Lettere_per_attivita_didattica.pdf.

29. *Gazzetta Ticinese*, Apr. 30, 1887.

30. Maria Giovanettina was born in 1812 and arrived in Australia on the *Lucie* in 1855. Two others with the surname Giovanettina immigrated to Australia: Bartolomeo and Giovanna, who may have been Maria's siblings. Gentilli, *The Settlement of Swiss Ticino Immigrants in Australia*, s.v. "Giovanettina."

31. Seweryn Korzelinski, (translated and edited by Stanley Robe) *Life on the goldfields; Memoirs of a Polish migrant; 1850s in Victoria*, Mentone Educational Centre, 1994, quoted in Gold! Victorian Cultural Collaboration, Special Broadcasting Services, Melbourne, Australia, https://www.sbs.com.au/gold/story.php?storyid=17#98.

32. Brandon Gleeson, "Backrooms, Wards and Backlanes: The Landscape of Disability in Nineteenth-Century Melbourne," Urban Research Program, Working Paper #64, Dec. 1998, Research School of Social Sciences, Australian National University Series Editor: R.C. Coles Canberra, https://openresearch-repository.anu.edu.au/bitstream/1885/116291/1/apo-nid120556-484351.pdf.

33. The public works budget of 250 pounds per year contrasts sharply with the 200 pounds per day earned by sly-grog owners in the 1850s. Korzelinski, *Life on the goldfields*. Gold!

CHAPTER TWENTY-FOUR

1. *Daylesford Mercury and Express*, Nov. 1, 1876, TROVE.
2. The Independent Order of Odd Fellows originated in England in the 18th century as a friendly society. These groups formed to provide support in times of illness and death to members and their families. The Manchester Unity Independent Order (MUIOOF) was formed in Melbourne in 1840. "Overview: Friendly Society History," Australian Unity, https://www.australianunity.com.au/about-us/our-history.
3. The school still serves Hepburn today.
4. *Argus*, (Melbourne), Sep. 14, 1878, TROVE.
5. Five hundred pounds in 1879 would be worth $80,511 AUD in 2019. Thom Blake Historian, How Much is it Worth, https://www.thomblake.com.au/calculator.php.

CHAPTER TWENTY-FIVE

1. *Daylesford Advocate* quoted in the *Kyneton Observer*, Oct. 11, 1879.
2. Anti-feminist views kept Swiss women without a political voice long after women's suffrage movements won the right to vote in other countries. In 1959, a referendum on women's suffrage lost with 67% of the vote against. Women in Switzerland didn't gain the right to vote on a federal level until 1971. History of Switzerland, "Switzerland's Long Way to Women's Right to Vote," http://history-switzerland.geschichte-schweiz.ch/chronology-womens-right-vote-switzerland.html.

CHAPTER TWENTY-SIX

1. James Young, a native of Sydney, became Francesco's assistant in about 1878. After Francesco's death, he took over the position of secretary to the Mount Franklin shire. Alexander Sutherland, *Victoria and its Metropolis, Past and Present* (Victoria: McCarron, Bird & Company, 1888), 258, GOOG.
2. Stefano Pozzi, letter in Cheda, *L'emigrazione ticinese in Australia*, quoted in Pagliaro, "Letters from Swiss-Italian Immigrants."
3. The federal government intervened to quell disorder in Ticino in multiple instances: 1870, 1876, 1889 and 1890–1891. Goldstein, *Constituting Federal Sovereignty*, 132.
4. *Advocate* (Melbourne), May 17, 1873, TROVE.
5. Giuseppe Sartori and his brother, Carlo, emigrants from Giumaglio, arrived in Australia on the *Agen und Heinrich* with Francesco in 1855. Gentilli, *The Settlement of Swiss Ticino Immigrants in Australia*. s.v. "Sartori."
6. Aradale Lunatic Asylum, http://aradale.com.au.

Endnotes

CHAPTER TWENTY-SEVEN

1. Beris Penrose, "The State and Gold Miners' Health in Victoria, 1870-1910." *Labour History*, no. 101, (2011): 35–52, doi:10.5263/labourhistory.101.0035. https://www.jstor.org/.
2. *Daylesford Advocate*, 1881, Daylesford & District Historical Society.
3. Francesco died with many awards, including the Past Master's Jewel presented to him by the Mount Franklin Lodge of Hiram.
4. 255 pounds sterling equates to $41,060 AUD in 2019. Thom Blake, https://www.thomblake.com.au.
5. The inscription reads:

> In memory of
> FRANCIS ROTANZI
> For many years secretary
> Of the shire of Mount Franklin
> Who departed this life
> Dec. 26, 1880
> Aged 41 years
>
> Erected by his numerous friends
> As a token of respect and esteem
> For his many private virtues
> And the faithful manner
> In which he discharged his duties
> As a public officer

CHAPTER TWENTY-EIGHT

1. *L'Educatore della Svizzera Italiana: giornale pubblicato per cura della Societa degli amici dell'educazione del popolo* (Lugano: Societa degli amici dell'educazione del popolo, Nov. 15, 1901, Anno LIII, N. 22), 347–348, ETHzurich e-periodica, https://www.e-periodica.ch/digbib/.
2. Luigi's nephew Seraphino (Samuel) Rotanzi also emigrated from the Vallemaggia, becoming Charles Martin's foreman on the Santa Ysabel Ranch in San Diego County.

EPILOGUE
ELISA GIACOBBI MORTIER

1. The earthquake and fire of 1906 destroyed the church, which was re-dedicated in 1915. In 1984, the City of San Francisco designated the church a historical landmark. Notre Dame des Victoires, "History," https://www.ndvsf.org/about/history.html.
2. Father Etienne Siffert, interview, Oct. 2, 2009.
3. Voss, "Some Giacobbi History," 2009.
4. *Livermore Herald*, Jul. 13, 1882, CDNC.
5. Lewis Publishing, *An Illustrated History of Sonoma County, 1889*. 707-708, ARCH.
6. *Daily Alta California*, Feb. 26, 1866, CDNC.
7. Frona Eunice Wait wrote of the two Frenchmen who pioneered winemaking in the

Livermore Valley: "Among the first to perceive the future prospects of these new fields was Mr. C. Aguillon, the experienced winemaker of Sonoma, whose knowledge of the prominent characteristics of French vineyards of renown caused him to plant a branch establishment at Livermore for the purchase of the first grapes produced. He was preceded in a less conspicuous manner, but with no less intelligent appreciation, by Mr. J. Mortier, a gentleman whose home had been among the noblest vineyards of Bordeaux;"
Frona E. Wait, *Wines & Vines of California: Or, a Treatise on the Ethics of Wine Drinking* (Berkeley: Howell-North Books, 1973), 155, GOOG.
8. The *San Francisco Merchant*, advertised as "the only viticultural paper in the state," reported that Aguillon was "induced by his friend, Mr. J. Mortier to purchase a site for a winery and contract for all the main crops of this vintage that he could get at the rate of $30 per ton." *San Francisco Merchant*, Oct. 24, 1884, ARCH.
9. "Their [Aguillon & Bustelli] output of wine in 1884 was 60,000 gallons. Since then they have made 70,000 to 80,000 gallons annually, and this year (1890) their product will exceed 100,000 gallons, the most of which will be disposed of by wholesale, a few thousand gallons being consumed by the local trade." Lewis Publishing Company, *A Memorial and Biographical History of Northern California* (Chicago: The Lewis Publishing Company, 1891), 348, HATH.
10. Livermore Heritage Guild, *Early Livermore* (Charleston, SC: Arcadia Pub.: 2006), 22.
11.Aguillon partnered with Swiss-Italian winemaker Gottardo Bustelli to create the Pioneer Winery. He became wealthy producing large quantities of wine marketed as "claret." Shipping crushed grapes from Livermore to Sonoma for processing, he enlarged his Sonoma cellars with an additional building now known as the Aguillon building, located next to the Salvador Vallejo Adobe on the Sonoma Plaza. Aguillon and his family, his wife and three daughters, lived upstairs from the wine cellars.
Aguillon became so wealthy that he was able to save the city of Sonoma from financial ruin. In 1887, General Mariano Vallejo's profligate son, Uladislao Vallejo, the marshal and tax collector for Sonoma, ran off with the city's entire annual tax revenues. Instead of turning the income over to the City Treasurer, Vallejo absconded for Mazatlan, Mexico on the steamer *Costa Rica* with twelve hundred dollars of Sonoma taxpayer money. The *Sacramento Daily Union* reported: "The old General and his venerable wife are bowed down with grief . . . The city will not lose anything, as the money will be made good by Vallejo's bondsmen C. Aguilllon and F. Clew, both wealthy men." *Sacramento Daily Union*, Dec. 1, 1887, CDNC.

The earthquake and fire of 1906 severely damaged Camille Aguillon's Sonoma winery. He died of a stroke a few months later at the French Hospital in San Francisco. Aguillon's daughters did not continue their father's business. They placed an ad in the *San Francisco Call* that ran throughout August 1907: "50,000 GALLONS cooperage and all implements necessary for wine making for sale: also cellar for sale or rent; living apartments above. Miss Aguillon. Sonoma City, Sonoma county, Cal." Today the Aguillon building is listed on the National Register of Historic Places. *San Francisco Call*, Aug. 17, 1907, CDNC.
12. "West Coast Fruit and Wine Growers Association," *United States Investor*, Vol. 16, Issue 26, Nov. 18, 1905, (Investor Publishing Co., 1905), 1860, https://books.google.com/books?id=4k3_y4_wOfQC.
13. *Oakland Tribune*, Mar. 6, 1889, NCOM.
14. *Livermore Herald* in the *Oakland Tribune*, Apr. 3, 1889, NCOM.

15. *Livermore Herald*, Aug. 1, 1889, CDNC.
16. Seonaid McArthur and David W. Fuller, *Cupertino Chronicle* (Cupertino: California History Center, De Anza College, 1975), 83.
17. *San Francisco Call*, May 19, 1892, CDNC.
18. *San Francisco Call*, Apr. 8, 1897, CDNC.
19. Mortier was listed in the *1900 San Jose Directory* as a "Ladder Manufacturer." *San Jose City Directory, 1900-1901* (San Jose: Mrs. F. M. Husted, 1901).
20. *San Francisco Chronicle*, May 7, 1904, Proquest Historical Newspapers, San Francisco Public Library; *San Francisco Call*, May 7, 1904, CDNC.

JOSEPH VIRGILIO MORTIER

1. In the 1880 U.S. census, nine-year-old Virgil Jiacobi is listed as son of Francisco and Marie Jiacobi, a brother to his uncle, Louis Agassi Jiacobi, age 22, a jeweler at the Pacific Jewelry Company, and to his aunt, 17-year-old Sophie, an apprentice milliner. United States Census Bureau (1880), San Francisco, California, digital image s.v. "Virgil Jiacobi," ANC.
2. Aug. 13, 1882 as Joseph Jean Virgilio Giacobbi. Eglise Notre Dame des Victoires records, translated by Father Etienne Siffert.
3. Cathy Caridi, "Canon Law Made Easy," http://canonlawmadeeasy.com/2009/10/01/how-soon-should-a-baby-be-baptized/.
4. Voss, "Some Giacobbi History," 2009.
5. Eglise Notre Dame des Victoires records, translated by Father Etienne Siffert.
6. Marie Giacobbi died on March 12, 1884. The death notice reported her as "mother of Louis A., Joseph Virgil, Sophie Giacobbi and Mrs. E. Mortier." *Daily Alta California*, Mar. 14, 1884, CDNC.
7. Voss, "Some Giacobbi History."
8. This amount, $1633, is equivalent to $44,815.60 in 2020. https://www.officialdata.org/1886-dollars-in-2018?amount=. Joseph may have inherited this amount from Virgilio, if Elisa's lawsuit was successful, or from his grandfather, Francisco Giacobbi. *Daily Alta California*, Nov. 18, 1886, CDNC.
9. The Pacific Jewelry Company was a firm founded in the 1870s by Elias Nathan and Moses Samuel.
10. Joseph partnered with Leonard R. Keller. They operated their business at 483 Pine Street in San Francisco.
11. Voss, "Some Giacobbi History."
12. *Fresno Bee*, May 29, 1948, CDNC.

CHARLES MARTIN

1. Martin became director of the Hill Bank of Petaluma, and the Bank of Sebastopol as well as president of the Petaluma National Bank and the Marin Bank of San Rafael.
2. The ValMaggina operated from 1907 to 1965. The funicular still operates in 2020.
3. Pietro Nosetti, "La Banca Svizzera Americana (1896-1920) : une Immigrant Bank multinationale active entre le Tessin et la Californie," in *Rivista storica svizzera*: 64:111-119. The Swiss History Society, Bern, 2014, https://www.e-periodica.ch/cntmng?var=true&pid=szg-006:2014:64::394.
4. In 1923, Matilda and Achille Ricioli and Joseph and Benjamin Traversi sold a one-quarter undivided interest (more than four thousand acres of the total 17,719-acre Santa Ysabel

Ranch) for seventy-five thousand dollars to George Sawday, a local rancher. *Blade-Tribune* (Oceanside), Mar. 3, 1923.
5. *San Francisco Call*, Jul. 31, 1899, CDNC.
6. Charles Martin File, Tomales Regional History Center, Tomales, CA.
7. *San Francisco Call*, Jun. 16, 1901, CDNC.
8. Rather than rebuild the church, the parishioners decided to make do with their old church which had been built in 1860. Today Catholic churchgoers in Tomales still worship today in this small historic wooden structure.
9. *Marin Journal*, Apr. 13, 1905, CDNC.

CARLO PATOCCHI

1. U.S. Census Bureau (1900), ED 421 City and County Alms House, San Francisco city, San Francisco, California, digital image s.v. "Charles Patocchi," http://www.familysearch.org. The Almshouse was located on the site of the current Laguna Honda Hospital.

JAMES BLOOM

1. Three of the four youths did well;. It appears that Antonio Giacomini became a successful dairy farmer in Humboldt County. Relative and fellow travel partner Natale Giacomini joined him in Humboldt County after many years in Marin.
2. D.S. (Dewey) Livingston, *A good life: dairy farming in the Olema Valley: a history of the dairy and beef ranches of the Olema Valley and Lagunitas Canyon, Golden Gate National Recreation Area and Point Reyes National Seashore, Marin County* (San Francisco: National Park Service, Dept. of the Interior, 1995), 248.
3. *Daily Alta California*, Aug. 5, 1872.
4. *Russian River Flag*, Jul. 1, 1875.
5. *Sonoma Democrat*, Oct. 28, 1893.
6. Tom Gregory, *History of Sonoma County, California with Biographical Sketches* (Los Angeles: Historic Record Company, 1911), 440, HATH.
7. *Press Democrat* (Santa Rosa), Oct. 6, 1918.

GUIDO L. ROTANZI

1. Not to be confused with Guido Henry Rotanzi, son of Eligio and Carolina Giovanetti Rotanzi, who settled in Cayucos, California. Eligio (1871–1944) worked as foreman on Antonio Tognazzini's ranch. Another of Eligio's sons Norman Rotanzi became head gardener at Hearst Castle, San Simeon, working for William Randolph Hearst to create gardens for the estate. Eligio's father Gaetano Rotanzi was Luigi Rotanzi's cousin.
2. U.S. Census Bureau (1920), San Jose, Santa Clara, California, s.v. "Guido Rotanzi," http://www.familysearch.org.
3. *Oakland Tribune*, Mar. 19, 1920.

THE ROTTANZI FAMILY

1. Social ties, not blood relations, connected Virgilio obliquely to the Rottanzis. Leopoldina, one of Dr. Rottanzi's daughters, married Camille Steffani, who partnered with Charles Martin after Virgilio's death.

2. *San Francisco Call*, Nov. 22, 1900, CDNC.

3. U.S. Census Bureau (1870), San Francisco, California, digital image s.v. "Antonio Rottanzi," ANC.

4. *San Francisco Call*, Feb. 17, 1892, CDNC.

5. South of Market Boys, *South of Market Journal*, vol. 4-5, Dec. 1928-Dec. 1930, 269, ARCH.

6. *Sausalito News*, Jun. 19, 1897, CDNC.

7. *Registry and Directory of Physicians and Surgeons in the States of California, Oregon and Washington*, Medical Society of the State of California, 1905, GOOG.

SAMUEL ROTANZI

1. J. M. Guinn. *A History of California: Extended History of Its Southern Coast Counties Containing Biographies of Well-Known Citizens of the Past and Present*, vol. II (Los Angeles: Historic Record Company, 1907), 1739, ARCH.

2. Another ranch named Santa Ysabel is located near Templeton, California in San Luis Obispo County.

3. *Los Angeles Times*, Aug. 25, 1895, NCOM.

4. John Steven McGroarty, *California of the South*, vol. II (Chicago, Los Angeles, Indianapolis: Clarke Publ.,1933), 283, HATH.

5. San Diego Parks and Recreation, "Santa Ysabel County Preserves," https://www.sdparks.org/content/sdparks/en/park-pages/SantaYsabel.html.

ANTONIO TOGNAZZINI

1. Shirley Contreras, "Small towns of Casmalia, Guadalupe all started from land grants, The Heart of the Valley," *Santa Maria Times*, Feb. 24, 2013.

2. *Morning Tribune*, San Luis Obispo County, California, 1896, San Luis Obispo County Genealogical Society, http://www.slocgs.org/Tog.100/Tog-1896.html.

When Tognazzini chose the site for Someo, the *San Luis Obispo Morning Tribune* of March 1896 commented that "The location of the proposed new town is said to be good. There is a gradual slope which will permit of the best and simplest methods of drainage and will leave the people free from that every perplexing question of sewerage." *San Luis Obispo Morning Tribune*, Apr. 19, 1896.

Tognazzini would have been dismayed to learn of problems caused one hundred years later by a hazardous waste landfill site located about a mile north of Casmalia. From 1973 until its closing in 1989, the 252-acre dump received 5.6 billion pounds of toxic materials, contaminating Casmalia's soil and groundwater with PCBs, motor oil and pesticides. In 2001, the Environmental Protection Agency (EPA) designated Casmalia as a Superfund cleanup site. By 2018, the EPA had stabilized the site and drawn up a final five-year cleanup plan. Razi Said, *Santa Maria Times*, Jun. 28, 2018, https://santamariatimes.com/news/local/final-cleanup-plan-outlined-for-casmalia-superfund-site/article_64f0e43f-3de7-5d93-bb47-ea126ddd2026.html.

3. Nadia Fischer, "Il sogno americano revive a Maggia," *Corriere del Ticino*, Jul. 30, 2019, https://www.cdt.ch/ticino/locarno/il-sogno-americano-rivive-a-maggia-MJ1478691.

4. *Pacific Oil Reporter*, Nov. 30, 1900, 16. Dec. 7, 1900, 14, ARCH;

Paul Dvorkovitz, ed., *Petroleum Review*, vol. 7, London: 1902, HATH.

5. *San Francisco Call*, Jul. 20, 1906, CDNC.

THE RESPINIS AND MORETTIS

1. Grueningen, *The Swiss in the United States*, 95.
2. Some of the families from Cevio who settled in Santa Cruz: Mattei, Gianone, Filippini, and Scaroni. Local place names include Scaroni Road and Gianone Hill.
3. *Daily Alta California*, Oct. 26, 1870, CDNC.
4. The villa was built by the powerful Franzoni family who ruled the region from 1503 to 1798. During those three centuries, bailiffs from the Swiss Confederacy controlled Ticino.
5. Louis was Giuliano Moretti's son, although he is described as Respini's nephew in the 1900 U.S. Census. Guinn, *History of Coast Counties*, 600.
6. Fiorenzo Moretti was the future husband of Charles Martin's daughter Ermelinda. By 1900, he had become a manager of the Yellow Bank Dairy in Santa Cruz. U.S. Census Bureau (1900), Santa Cruz, California, digital image s.v. "Fiorenzo Moretti," ANC.
7. *Santa Cruz Evening Sentinel*, Dec. 19, 1900, CDNC.
8. Coast Dairies & Land Company officers were L. Moretti, president; D. Morelli, vice–president; and A. E. Morelli, secretary–treasurer. Fiorenzo Moretti lived with Jeremiah Respini and Louis Moretti. After he married Ermelinda Martin, the couple relocated to the Santa Ysabel cattle ranch near San Diego. U.S. Census Bureau (1900), Santa Cruz, California, digital image s.v. "Fiorenzo Moretti," ANC.
9. "Yellowbank," Santa Cruz Trains, http://www.santacruztrains.com/2014/07/yellow-banks.html.
10. Trust for Public Land, "The Coast Dairies Long-Term Resource Protection and Use Plan," http://cloud.tpl.org/pubs/local_ca_coastdairies2003_allchapters_merged.pdf, 2001, 1–6.
11. Another rail company, the Ocean Shore, also attempted to create a line from Santa Cruz to San Francisco, but it failed after the 1906 earthquake. Trust for Public Land, "Coast Dairies Long-Term Resource Protection and Use Plan."
12. Dorillo Morelli managed the Cash Store in Davenport for over twenty years. He came to California from Cevio in 1887, worked on Charles Martin's Santa Ysabel ranch in San Diego, then moved to Santa Cruz in 1900 to work at Respini's Yellow Bank Dairy. *History of Monterey and Santa Cruz Counties, California* (Chicago: S.J. Clarke Pub. Co., 1925), GOOG.
13. Trust for Public Land, "Coast Dairies."
14. The Moretti and Respini families entrusted oversight of the Coast Dairies & Land Company to a series of managers that included James Filippini, A.E. Morelli, Louis Poletti and Fred Pfyffer.
15. Michael Svanevik and Shirley Burgett, *Mercury News* (San Jose), Jan. 4, 2017, https://www.mercurynews.com/2017/01/04/matters-historical-the-kingdom-of-the-artichoke-and-the-battle-for-its-profits/.
16. *Santa Cruz Evening News*, May 13, 1935, CDNC.
17. Trust for Public Land. "Coast Dairies," https://www.tpl.org/our-work/coast-dairies#sm.0013rtuk21cytfd7wj32kud8azly1.
18. Over 1,665 acres on the Mendocino Coast, property once farmed by descendants of Antonio and Raimondo Stornetta, emigrants from Ticino, have also been made part of the California Coastal National Monument. Larry Stornetta, great-grandson of Raimondo, continues to ranch on part of the property today. *Corriere del Ticino*, "Obama: 'Stornetta, Good Job,'" Apr. 26, 2014, https://www.cdt.ch/ticino/obama-stornetta-good-job-DRCDT105547.

BATTISTA BORSA

1. Blanche married Ernest Zelman, and her sister, Clara, married Ernest's brother Victor, an acclaimed painter known for his plein-air landscapes of the Victoria countryside. A third Zelman brother Alberto founded the Melbourne Symphony Orchestra. DayGet, "Zelman Cottage, Art, Music and Love in Hepburn Springs," https://www.dayget.com.au/explore/zelman-cottage-home-art-history/.
2. *Mount Alexander Mail*, Jan. 25, 1906, TROVE.
3. Heritage Council Victoria, Victorian Heritage Database Report, "Hepburn Springs Swimming Pool," http://vhd.heritagecouncil.vic.gov.au/places/5639/download-report.

THE POZZI BROTHERS

1. Swiss Confederation, Federal Statistical Office, https://www.bfs.admin.ch/.
2. Carlson, *Immigrant Placemaking*, 50.
3. *Argus* (Melbourne), Aug. 25, 1868, TROVE.
4. *Mercury and Weekly Courier*, Nov. 13, 1890, TROVE.
5. *West Coast Times*, Feb. 16, 1889, TROVE.
6. Robert E. Weir, *Knights Down Under: The Knights of Labour in New Zealand* (Newcastle upon Tyne: Cambridge Scholars Pub, 2018), 5, HATH.
7. Leonard Pozzi, *Modern slavery and civilization: dialogue on the industries & toilers of New Zealand*, Christchurch: "*Lyttelton Times,*" 1888.
8. Pozzi, "I made a very bad calculation," SWI SwissInfo.ch.
9. Leonardo Pozzi, *Silk culture: practical instruction on silk culture, from the planting of the mulberry leaves up to the production of the cocoons and silk-worm eggs, or so called graine for the following season* (Fitzroy [Vic.]: Robert Barr, Printer, 1894).
10. Pozzi, "I made a very bad calculation," SWI SwissInfo.ch.
11. *The Socialist*, Mar. 27, 1908, TROVE.

BIBLIOGRAPHY

Accademia svizzera di scienze umane e sociali (ASSU). *Dizionario Storico del Svizzera (Historical Dictionary of Switzerland)*. http://www.hls-dhs-dss.ch/i/home.

Alley, Bowen & Co. *History of Sonoma County [Cal.]: Including Its Geology,Topography, Mountains, Valleys and Streams.* San Francisco: Alley, Bowen &Company, 1880.https://archive.org/details/historyofsonomac00alle/page/n8/mode/2up.

American Battlefield Trust. "Military Pay, Civil War History." https://www.battlefields.org/learn/articles/military-pay.

Anbinder, Tyler. *City of Dreams.* (NY: Houghton, Mifflin, Harcourt, 2016).

Angel, Myron. *History of San Luis Obispo County, California; with illustrations and biographical sketches of its prominent men and pioneers.* Oakland: Thompson & West, 1883. https://archive.org/details/historyofsanluis00ange/.

Annuario della Repubblica e Cantone del Ticino: per l'anno 1859-1860. Bellinzona, Ticino: Cancelleria dello Stato, 1860. https://books.google.com/books/about/Annuario_della_Repubblica_e_Cantone_del.html?id=a0JCAAAAcAAJ.

Aradale Lunatic Asylum. http://aradale.com.au.

Archivio Patriziale di Cevio-Linescio. "Religiosità e vita quotidiana." http://www.patriziatoceviolinescio.ch/ita/contents/view/religiosit_e_vita_quotidiana.

Association of Bay Area Governments. Metropolitan Transportation Commission. The Bay Area Census. http://www.bayareacensus.ca.gov/historical/historical.htm.

Associazione dei Patriziati Ticinesi, Alleanza Patriziale Ticinese. https://www.alleanzapatriziale.ch.

Audubon. "Why are Murre Eggs So Pointy." https://www.audubon.org/news/why-are-murre-eggs-so-pointy-new-research-debunks-prevailing-theory.

Australian Bureau of Statistics. "Land Tenure and Settlement. Yearbook Australia, 1911." http://www.abs.gov.au/AUSSTATS/abs@.nsf/DetailsPage/1301.01911.

Australian Towncriers. http://www.australiantowncrier.com.

Australian Unity. "Overview: Friendly Society History." https://www.australianunity.com.au/about-us/our-history.

Baccari, Alessandro and Andrew M. Canepa, Olga Richardson, G.B. Cerruti. "The Italians of San Francisco in 1865: G.B. Cerruti's Report to the Ministry of Foreign Affairs." *California History Quarterly*, Winter, 1981/1982, vol. 60, no. 4.

Ball, John. *An Alpine Guide; The central alps, Including the Bernese Oberland, and All Switzerland Excepting the Neighbourhood of Monte Rosa and the Great St. Bernard; with Lombardy and the*

Adjoining Portion of Tyrol … , part 2. London: Longman, Roberts & Green, 1864.

Bancroft, A. L. *Bancroft's Tourist Guide. Yosemite. San Francisco and around the Bay.* San Francisco; A.L. Bancroft & Company, 1871. https://archive.org/details/bancroftstourist00albarich/page/n6/mode/2up.

Bancroft, Hubert H. *The Works of Hubert Howe Bancroft: History of California,* vol. 7. San Francisco: The History Company, 1890. https://archive.org/details/histofcalif00bancroft/page/n10/mode/2up.

Battery Conservancy. "Castle Garden: America's First Immigration Center." http://www.castlegarden.org.

Bechtel, Dale. "Finding the 19th century mystery man." Swissinfo.ch, Swiss Broadcasting Corporation (SBC). Oct. 20, 2011. https://www.swissinfo.ch/eng/finding-the-19th-century-mystery-man/31204128.

Benjamin, I. J. *Three Years in America,* vol. II, 1859–1862. Philadelphia: Jewish Publication Society of America, 1956, HATH.

Biétry-Salinger, Jehanne. *Le guide franco californien du centenaire; notre centenaire.* San Francisco, 1949.

Bill of Fare for the Pacific Mail Steamship Company's Steamer Golden Age. Saturday, Jul. 26, 1863. Buswell & Co., printer, UC Berkeley, Bancroft Library, Online Archive of California, https://oac.cdlib.org/ark:/13030/tf6n39p4fx/?brand=oac4.

Bioche, Charles Jules Armand and Charles Goujet. *Dizionario generale ragionato della procedura civile e commerciale.* Palermo: Dalla stamperia di Pietro Pensante, 1854. https://books.google.com/books?id=HztdzDB73foC.

Bishop's directory of the city of San Jose for 1876: containing a general register of the names of all residents, and a classified business directory . . . San Francisco: B. C. Vandall, 1876. http://books.google.com/books?id=lpMtAQAAMAAJ.

Bladen Neill, Sarah. "Silk Growing Its Prospects and its Wants." *Journal of the Society of Arts, Royal Society for the Encouragement of Arts Manufactures and Commerce,* vol. 24. London: April 28, 1876. https://www.google.com/books/edition/Journal_of_the_Society_of_Arts/u7VJAAAAYAAJ?hl=en&gbpv=1.

Blake, Thom. Thom Blake Historian, How Much is it Worth. https://www.thomblake.com.au.

Bosshart-Pfluger, Catherine. *The Swiss Experience in San Francisco: 150 Years of Swiss Consular Presence in San Francisco.* San Francisco: Time & Place, 2006.

Burke, Edmund, ed., The Annual Register, 121, *London Times,* Jan. 29, 1879. London: Rivingtons, 1880. https://play.google.com/books/reader?id=37JBAAAAYAAJ&hl=en&pg=GBS.RA1-PA16.

Burn, James Dawson. *Three Years Among the Working Classes in the United States During the War.* London: Smith, Elder and Co., 1865. https://archive.org/details/threeyearsamong00burnrich.

Butler, John W. *Birtchnell's Daylesford directory* . . .Ballarat, Vic: S. L. Birtchnell, 1865.https://books.google.com/books/about/Birtchnell_s_Daylesford_Directory.html?id=DjzpNQAACAAJ.

Butler, Samuel and R. A. Streatfeild. *Alps and sanctuaries of Piedmont and the canton Ticino.* New York: E.P. Dutton & Company, 1913. https://archive.org/details/alpssanctuarieso00butl/page/38.

Buttke, Judy and Joyce Leveroni. *Dairy Families: 75 Years, Sonoma and Marin Counties.* Petaluma: North Bay Dairy Women, 2011.

Cahir, Fred. "Are you off to the diggings?" *La Trobe Journal*, Melbourne: State Library of Victoria Foundation, vol. 85, 2010.

Calabrella, E. C. *The Ladies' science of etiquette.* Philadelphia: T.B. Peterson, 1851. https://books.google.com/books?id=Y8VYAAAAcAAJ.

California Department of Parks and Recreation. "Gold Rush Prices Worksheet." https://www.parks.ca.gov/pages/22922/files/worksheet-goldrushprices.pdf.

California Insurance Commissioner. *Second annual report of the Insurance Commissioner of the state of California, year ending 1869.* San Francisco. https://catalog.hathitrust.org/Record/006257530.

California Milk Advisory Board. "California's Dairy Industry: the Early Years 1769-1900." http://www.californiadairypressroom.com/press_kit/history_of_dairy_ndustry.

Cannon, Michael. *The Australasian Sketcher with Pen and Pencil,* Oct. 4, 1873. http://www.nla.gov.au/nla.news-title49.

Carlson, Bridget Rachel. *Immigrant Placemaking in Colonial Australia: the Italian-speaking Settlers of Daylesford.* A PhD thesis. Victoria University of Technology: Melbourne, 1997.

Carlsson, Chris. FoundSF. "Eight Hour Day Movement." http://www.foundsf.org/index.php?title=Eight_hour_day_movement.

Centennial Exhibition. International Exhibition, 1876: official catalogue, part I. Philadelphia: Published for the Centennial Catalogue Co. by John R. Nagle and Co. 1876. http://catalog.hathitrust.org/api/volumes/oclc/78569511.html.

Chandler, Robert J. and Stephen J. Potash. *Gold, silk, pioneers & mail: the story of the Pacific Mail Steamship Company.* San Francisco: Friends of the San Francisco Maritime Museum Library. http://books.google.com/books?id=AC9PAQAAIAAJ.

Cheda, Giorgio. "Le Lettere degli emigranti al servizio della storia" in *Un altro Veneto. Saggi e studi di storia dell'emigrazione nei secoli XIX e XX*, ed. E. Franzina, Abano Terme: Francisci, 1984.

Cheda, Giorgio. *L'emigrazione ticinese in Australia: Epistolario.* Locarno: A. Dadò, 1976.

Cheda, Giorgio. *L'emigrazione ticinese in Australia.* Locarno: A. Dadò, 1979.

Cheda, Giorgio, *L'emigrazione ticinese in California.* vol. I, Locarno: A. Dadò, 1981.

Cheda, Giorgio. *L'emigrazione ticinese in California, Epistolario,* vol. II. Locarno: A. Dadò, 1981.

Cheda, Giorgio. *L'emigrazione ticinese in California: I ranceri*, vol. I and II, Pregassona-Lugano: Fontana, 2005.

Chmielewski, Wendy, Jill Norgren, Kristen Gwinn-Becker. Her Hat Was In the Ring. "Marietta Stow." http://www.herhatwasinthering.org/biography.php?id=7740.

City University of New York. The Lost Museum. "Barnum's American Museum Illustrated." http://lostmuseum.cuny.edu/archive/assets/images/archive/barnum_american_museum_illustrated.pdf.

Clancy, Mrs. Charles. *A Lady's Visit to the Gold Diggings of Australia in 1852-53. Written on the Spot.* London: Hurst and Blackett, 1853. https://archive.org/details/ladys_visit_gold_diggings_0811_librivox.

Clark, Manning. *History of Australia*. Melbourne University: 1993.

Collins, Perry McDonough. *A Voyage Down the Amoor.* D. Appleton & Co. New York, 1860. World Digital Library. https://www.wdl.org/en/item/26/.

Confederazione Svizzera, Ufficio federale di statistica. Ticino Population Figures, 1850–2000. https://www.bfs.admin.ch/.

Convert Units—Measurement Unit Converter. https://www.convertunits.com.

Cornell University. Dawn's Early Light, the First 50 Years of American Photography. http://rmc.library.cornell.edu/DawnsEarlyLight/exhibition/celebculture/.

Cowan, Alison Leigh. "A Guide to Houses No Gentleman Would Dare to Frequent," City Room: Blogging from the Five Boroughs, *New York Times.* (Jan. 26, 2011). https://cityroom.blogs.nytimes.com/2011/01/26/on-the-records-a-well-preserved-roadmap-to-perdition/?mcubz=3&_r=0.

Craig, William. *My Adventures on the Australian Goldfields*. London: Cassell, 1903. https://archive.org/details/myadventuresonau00craiiala.

Cresciani, Gianfranco. *The Italians in Australia*. New York: Cambridge University Press, 2003.

D'Aprano, C. *From goldrush to federation: Italian pioneers in Victoria 1850–1900*. INT Press, Melbourne, 1995.

Darwin, Norm. *Gold'n Spa: A History of Hepburn Shire*. Ballarat, Vic: H@nd Publishing, 2005.

DayGet, "Zelman Cottage, Art, Music and Love in Hepburn Springs," https://www.dayget.com.au/explore/zelman-cottage-home-art-history/

Daylesford Mining Division, Historical Notes, Pandora, Australia's Web Archive, http://nla.gov.au/nla.arc-147062.

Department of State. *The Assassination of Abraham Lincoln . . .* U.S. Government Printing Office, 1867. https://catalog.hathitrust.org/Record/000567848.

DeRooy, Carola and Dewey Livingston. *Point Reyes Peninsula: Olema, Point Reyes Station and Inverness*. Charleston, SC: Arcadia, 2008.

Dicker, Thomas. *Dicker's Mining Record and Guide to the Gold Mines of Australia*. Melbourne: Thomas Dicker, 1865.

Dillon, Richard H., and Lynn L. Davis. *North Beach: the Italian heart of San Francisco*. Novato, CA: Presidio Press, 1985.

Dvorkovitz, Paul, ed., *Petroleum Review*, vol. 7. London: 1902. https://babel.hathitrust.org/cgi/pt?id=uc1.c2622062;view=2up;seq=4.

Dwyer, Ruth. "The Long Tunnel Mine, Italian Hill: Hands in the Riffles." *Italian Historical Society Journal*. vol. 10, no. 1 (January-June 2002). http://coasit.com.au/IHS/journals/Individual%20Journal%20Extracts/Long%20Tunnel%20Mine%20from%20IHS%20Journal0028.pdf.

L'Educatore della Svizzera Italiana: giornale pubblicato per cura della Societa degli amici dell'educazione del popolo e d'utilita pubblica. Lugano: November 15, 1901, Anno LIII, N. 22. https://www.e-periodica.ch/digbib/vollist?UID=esi-001.

Elkner, Cate. "Not just Bewildered Onlookers: Aboriginal Participation in the Goldrushes, Indigenous Peoples, A Nation's Heritage." eGold, Electronic Encyclopedia of Gold in Australia, University of Melbourne. http://www.egold.net.au/biogs/EG00045b.htm.

Emery, George Neil and J. C. Herbert Emery. *A Young Man's Benefit: The Independent Order of Odd Fellows and Sickness Insurance in the United States and Canada, 1860–1929*. McGill-Queen's Press: 1999. https://www.google.com/books/edition/Young_Man_s_Benefit/RXweSVVTL2EC?hl=en.

Etiquette for Ladies, with Hints on the Preservation, Improvement, and Display of Female Beauty. Philadelphia: Lea & Blanchard, 1840. https://books.google.com/books/_/G8FAAAAAYAAJ?sa=X&ved=2ahUKEwj3hMyJ4srwAhWeGDQIHZScAOkQre8FAgcECw.

Fassett, Noah Chittenden. "The Fassett Letters: The Gold-Rush Fassetts from Licking Co., Ohio." http://physics.clarku.edu/~rkohin/Background.htm.

Ferrari, Andrea. "History of Hepburn," Manuscript. Daylesford & District Historical Society, Daylesford, AU.

Ferreira, Adrienne. "The Silk Road, Silk Farming." *The Monthly*, June 2011, https://www.themonthly.com.au/adrienne-ferreira-silk-farming-silk-road-adrienne-ferreira-3366.

FoundSF. "Old Cemeteries in the City." http://www.foundsf.org/index.php?title=Old_Cemeteries_in_the_City.

Gairdner, Sir William Tennant. Public Health in Relation to Air and Water. Edinburgh: Edmonston and Douglas, 1862. https://archive.org/details/publichealthinre00gair.

Genealogical Historical Services. "Le Havre as emigration port." http://www.genhist.org/ghs_Havre_eng.htm.

Gentilli, J. *The Settlement of Swiss Ticino immigrants in Australia*. Nedlands: University of Western Australia, 1988.

Gervasoni, Clare. *History of Hepburn*. Ballarat, Vic: Ballarat Heritage Services, 2003.

Gervasoni, Clare. *Italian Speakers in the News, 1855–1872: Selected Newspaper Articles Relating to Italian Speakers Covering General News Relating to Italians in Australia, Hatches, Matches and Dispatches Italy and Unification.* Hepburn Springs, Vic.: Studio Argento Publications, 1997.

Gervasoni, Clare. *Research Directory & Bibliography of Swiss and Italian Pioneers in Australasia: Featuring Family Names, Towns of Origin & Shipping Sections.* Ballarat, Vic: Ballarat Heritage Services, 2002.

Gjenvick-Gjonvik Archives: Social and Cultural History. *Pall Mall Gazette*, August 9, 1879, as quoted in "Steerage Class—Accommodations—Cunard Steamship Line —1879." https://www.gjenvick.com/Steerage/1879-SteerageAccommodations-Cunard. html#ixzz3gfGX3HND.

Gleeson, Brandon. "Backrooms, Wards and Backlanes: The Landscape of Disability in Nineteenth-Century Melbourne." Urban Research Program, Working Paper #64, December 1998. Research School of Social Sciences, Australian National University Series Editor: R. C. Coles Canberra. https://openresearch-repository.anu.edu.au/bitstream/1885/116291/1/ apo-nid120556-484351.pdf.

Golden Gate Speranza Lodge No. 30, F. & A.M. "History from 1852 to 2005." https:// docplayer.net/62185372-Golden-gate-speranza-lodge-no-30-f-a-m-history-from-1852- to-2005.html.

Goldstein, Leslie Friedman. *Constituting Federal Sovereignty: The European Union in Comparative Context.* Baltimore: JHU Press, 2003. https://epdf.tips/constituting-federal- sovereignty-the-european-union-in-comparative-context-the-j.html.

Grueningen, John Paul von. *The Swiss in the United States: A Compilation Prepared for the Swiss-American Historical Society as the Second Volume of Its Publications.* San Francisco: R and E Research Associates, 1970.

Guinn, James Miller. *A History of California: Extended History of Its Southern Coast Counties Containing Biographies of Well-Known Citizens of the Past and Present,* vol. II. Los Angeles: Historic Record Company, 1907. https://archive.org/details/historyofcalifor02inguin/ page/n1.

Guinn, James Miller. *History of the State of California and biographical record of Coast Counties, California.* Chicago: Chapman Pub. Co., 1904. https://archive.org/details/ historyofstateof00guin/page/n1.

Hahn, Calvet M. "Adams' Express and Independent Mail," Carriers and Locals Society, The Penny Post, 1990. https://www.pennypost.org/pdf/Adams-Express-by-Hahn-1990. pdf.

Hall, Jacqueline and Joellen Hall. *Italian-Swiss Settlement in Plumas County, 1860 to 1920.* Chico: Association for Northern California Records and Research, 1975.

Hall, Mary. "Where did the Bull and Bear Market Get their Names?" https://www. investopedia.com/ask/answers/bull-bear-market-names/.

Hamilton, Geneva. *Where the Highway Ends: A History of Cambria . . .* Cambria: Central Coast Press, 1999.

Harrison, Frederic. *My Alpine Jubilee.* London: Smith, Elder, & Co., 1908. https://catalog.

hathitrust.org/Record/006527375.

Hartley, Florence. *The Ladies' Book of Etiquette, and Manual of Politeness, A Complete Handbook for the Use of the Lady in Polite Society.* Lee & Shepherd, 1872. https://www.gutenberg.org/files/35123/35123-h/35123-h.htm.

Heig, Adair. *History of Petaluma: a California river town.* Petaluma: Scottwall Associates, 1982.

Helper, Hinton Rowan. *The Land of Gold: Reality Versus Fiction.* Gale, Sabin Americana, 1855. http://www.archive.org.

Heritage Council of Victoria. Victorian Heritage Database Report. "Former Macaroni Factory." http://vhd.heritagecouncil.vic.gov.au/places/592/download-report.

Hirsch, August. *Handbook of Geographical and Historical Pathology*, vol. 1. Translated by Charles Creighton. London: New Sydenham Society, 1883. https://archive.org/details/handbookofgeogra01hirsuoft/page/n6.\.

History of Monterey and Santa Cruz Counties, California: cradle of California's history and romance... Chicago: S. J. Clarke Pub. Co., 1925. https://www.google.com/books/edition/History_of_Monterey_Santa_Cruz_and_San_B/I53ekEweI5sC?hl=en&gbpv=0.

History of Switzerland. "Switzerland's Long Way to Women's Right to Vote." http://history-switzerland.geschichte-schweiz.ch/chronology-womens-right-vote-switzerland.html.

Hittell, John S. *A History of the City of San Francisco and Incidentally of the State of California.* San Francisco: A. L. Bancroft, 1878. https://catalog.hathitrust.org/Record/100136364.

Hittell, John S. *All About California and the inducements to settle there. California as a Home to the Immigrant.* San Francisco: California Immigrant Union, 1874. https://catalog.hathitrust.org/Record/100734647.

Hittell, John S. *The resources of California: comprising agriculture, mining, geography, climate, etc., and the past and future development of the state.* 5th ed. San Francisco: A. Roman, 1869. https://catalog.hathitrust.org/Record/009561000.

Hoffman, Abraham. *California's Deadliest Earthquakes: A History.* The History Press, 2017.

Holsworth, Carol. "Chinese Herbalists 1850s–1930s." Rural Victoria. https://chineseruralvictoria.wordpress.com/chinese-herbalists-1850s-1930s/.

Howitt, William. *Land, labour, and gold: two years in Victoria: with visits to Sydney and Van Diemen's Land.* London: Longman, Brown, Green, and Longmans, 1855. https://archive.org/details/landlabourgoldor00howirich/page/n6/mode/2up.

Hudson, Alfred. *Lectures on the study of fever.* Philadelphia: Henry C. Lea, 1869. https://www.google.com/books/edition/Lectures_on_the_Study_of_Fever/p8FjBsHQQVUC?hl=en&gbpv=0.

Humber, Sara. "Overseas Property: The Plum Location in France." *The Sunday Times.* May 15, 2005. https://www.thetimes.co.uk/article/overseas-property-the-plum-location-in-france-t50wp8vqxn3.

Hume, James B. *Wells, Fargo & Co. Stagecoach and Train Robberies, 1870–1884: The Corporate Report of 1885 with Additional Facts About the Crimes and Their Perpetrators,* revised edition. North Carolina: McFarland, 2010.

Hutchings, James Mason. "The Poison Oak" in *Hutchings' California Magazine*, No 11. San Francisco: Hutchings & Rosenfield, 1857. https://babel.hathitrust.org/cgi/pt?id=uc1. b2982597&view=1up&seq=7.

Immigration Museum. "Wine, Water & Stone: The Swiss and Italians of Hepburn." Melbourne: Immigration Museum, 2007. Intercolonial Exhibition of Australasia, Melbourne, 1866–67.

Investor Publishing Co. "West Coast Fruit and Wine Growers Association," *United States Investor,* vol. 16, Issue 26, Nov 18, 1905. Investor Publishing Co. 1905. https://books.google. com/books?id=4k3_y4_wOfQC.

Italian Historical Society (Australia). *Swiss-Italian Family History Research: A Guide to Tracing Archival Material in Switzerland: Tessin and Grisons Cantons.* Carlton, Vic: Italian Historical Society-Co.As.It, 1994. Italian Historical Society—COASIT. http://coasit.com.au/IHS/index.html.

Italy on this Day. "Domenico Ghirardelli—chocolatier." http://www.italyonthisday. com/2018/02/domenico-ghirardelli-Italian-chocolatier-San-Francisco-Ghirardelli-Square-Rapallo-Genoa.html.

Jones, Thomas R. "October in California Fifty Years Ago—Big Lottery Drawing Holds States Attention." *The Grizzly Bear,* Official Organ Native Sons and Native Daughters of the Golden West, v. 28–29. October 1920. https://babel.hathitrust.org/cgi/pt?id=uc1.$c194549& view=1up&seq=18.

Jorio, Luigi. "A Home of the Family; a Church for the Parish Priest." May 11, 2009. SWI Swissinfo.ch. https://www.swissinfo.ch/eng/a-home-for-the-family--a-church-for-the-parish-priest/6795444.

Judge, Cliff and Roma Emmerson. *Children Australia,* vol. 2, no. 1. Cambridge Univ. Press, 1977.

Kemble, John Haskell. *The Panama Route, 1848-1869.* Berkeley: University of California Press, 1943.

King, Joseph L. *History of the San Francisco Stock Exchange.* San Francisco: J. L. King, 1910. https://archive.org/details/historyofsanfran00kingrich/.

Krackher, Hans-Jurgen. "Discover the Chapter of Marketing before Coca Cola." SpiritSchweppes. https://spiritschweppes.com.

Langley, Henry G. *The San Francisco Directory.* San Francisco: Langley, 1858–1879. https:// sfpl.org/locations/main-library/magazines-newspapers-center/bay-area-city-directories-and-phone-books/san-0.

Lavizzari, Luigi. *Escursioni nel cantone Ticino.* Ticino: Valadini e comp., 1863. https://www. google.com/books/edition/Escursioni_Nel_Cantone_Ticino/LfdCAQAAMAAJ?hl..

Lawrence, Polly Ghirardelli. *The Ghirardelli family and chocolate company of San Francisco.*

Berkeley, Calif: Regional Oral History Office, Bancroft Library, University of California, 1985. http://digitalassets.lib.berkeley.edu/roho/ucb/text/lawrence_polly_ghiradelli.pdf.

Lawrence, Sidney. *The Ghirardelli Story*. UC Press: 2002. https://www.thefreelibrary.com/ The+Ghirardelli_story.-a0104669393.

Lawrence, Susan and Peter Davies. "Striking Gold in Water Management." LaTrobe University. http://www.latrobe.edu.au/our-work/water-and-land-management/striking-gold-in-water-management.

Lewis Publishing Co. *A Memorial and Biographical History of Northern California; containing a history of this important section of the Pacific Coast . . .* Chicago: Lewis Pub. Co., 1891. https:// catalog.hathitrust.org/Record/012393325.

Lewis Publishing Co. *An illustrated history of Sonoma County, California: containing a history of the county of Sonoma from the earliest period of its occupancy to the present time.* Chicago: Lewis Publishing Co., 1889. https://archive.org/details/illustratedhisto02lewi/page/n10/ mode/2up.

Library of Congress. "The Civil War in America: Biographies. William T. Sherman." http:// loc.gov/exhibits/civil-war-in-america/biographies/william-t-sherman.html.

Livermore Heritage Guild. *Early Livermore*. Charleston, SC: Arcadia Pub., 2006.

Livingston, D. S. (Dewey). *A good life: dairy farming in the Olema Valley: a history of the dairy and beef ranches of the Olema Valley and Lagunitas Canyon, Golden Gate National Recreation Area and Point Reyes National Seashore, Marin County.* San Francisco: National Park Service, Dept. of the Interior, 1995.

Livingston, Dewey, and Elaine Doss. *Nicasio: The Historic Valley at the Center of Marin.* Nicasio Historical Society, 2008.

Livingston, Dewey. *Ranching on the Point Reyes Peninsula: a history of the dairy and beef ranches within Point Reyes National Seashore, 1834–1992.* Point Reyes Station, Calif.: Point Reyes National Seashore, National Park Service, 1994.

Lloyd, Benjamin E. *Lights and Shades in San Francisco.* San Francisco: A. L. Bancroft & Co., 1876. https://archive.org/details/lightsshadesins00lloy/page/n10/mode/2up.

Lockwood-Matthews Mansion Museum. "Wedding Traditions and Fashion from the 1860s to the 1930s." https://www.lockwoodmathewsmansion.com/exhibit/wedding-traditions-fashion-1840s-1930s/.

Lodge Devotion 723. "Masonic Buildings—Daylesford Masonic Centre & its Craft Lodge." http://www.lodgedevotion.net/devotionnews/masonic-buildings---articles-editorials-and-histories/masonic-buildings/masonic-buildings---daylesford-masonic-centre-its-craft-lodge.

Long, Clarence D. "Wages and Earnings in the United States." National Bureau of Economic Research, Inc., 1960. https://www.nber.org/chapters/c2497.pdf.

Lost Museum. "Barnum's American Museum Illustrated." http://lostmuseum.cuny.edu/ archive/assets/images/archive/barnum_american_museum_illustrated.pdf.

Maddicks, Henry T. and Keith H. Butler. *100 Years of Daylesford Gold Mining History*, August

1851 to 1951. Daylesford, Vic.: Daylesford & District Historical Society, 1981.

Madley, Benjamin. *An American Genocide: The United States and the California Indian Catastrophe*. New Haven: Yale University Press, 2009.

Maguire, Roslyn. "Italians in Evidence in 19th Century Australia." https://swissitalianfesta. com/wp-content/uploads/2020/09/Italians-in-evidence-in-19th-Century-Australia.pdf.

Major, Thomas and Elizabeth Spedding Calciano. "The Majors Family and Santa Cruz County Dairying." University of California, Santa Cruz, Regional History Project. January 18, 1965. https://escholarship.org/uc/item/9qj4h9v6.

Marcacci, Marco. "Stefano Francini, 150 anni dopo." SWI Swissinfo.ch. https://www. swissinfo.ch/ita/stefano-franscini--150-anni-dopo/6010546.

Maritime Heritage Project. "Steamships at San Francisco." http://www.maritimeheritage. org/ships/Steamships_P-to-S.html.

Martin, Charles, File, Tomales Regional History Center, Tomales, CA.

Mary Aaron Museum. "About Marysville, California." https://maryaaronmuseum.com/ about-marysville-california/.

McArthur, Seonaid and David W. Fuller. *Cupertino Chronicle*. Cupertino: California History Center, De Anza College, 1975.

McGroarty, John Steven. *California of the South*, vol. II. Chicago, Los Angeles, Indianapolis: Clarke Publ., 1933. https://babel.hathitrust.org/cgi/pt?id=umn.319510019591738.

Measuring Worth. https://www.measuringworth.com/calculators/.

Medical Society of the State of California. *Registry and Directory of Physicians and Surgeons in the States of California, Oregon and Washington, 1905*. https://books.google.com/ books?id=s2EHAQAAIAAJ.

Menefee, C.A. *Historical and descriptive sketchbook of Napa, Sonoma, Lake, and Mendocino: comprising sketches of their topography, productions, history, scenery, and peculiar attractions.* Fairfield, Calif: J.D. Stevenson, 1994. http://books.google.com/books?id=U944AQAAMAAJ.

Mitchell, Bruce. "Hargraves, Edward Hammond (1816–1891)." Australian Dictionary of Biography. http://adb.anu.edu.au/biography/hargraves-edward-hammond-3719.

Mortuary Record of the City and County of San Francisco, 1871. San Francisco Public Library History Center, San Francisco Mortuary Records, 1865–1873, Reel 1.

Munro-Fraser, J. P. *History of Marin County. San Francisco.* Alley Bowen & Co., 1880. https:// archive.org/details/historyofmarinco00munr/page/n10/mode/2up.

Munro-Fraser, J. P. *History of Santa Clara County including its geography, geology, topography, climatography and description . . .* San Francisco: Alley, Bowen & Co., 1881. https://archive. org/details/historyofsantacl00munr/page/n6/mode/2up.

Museum of Australian Democracy. "Chinese Immigration Act 1855." Documenting a Democracy. https://www.foundingdocs.gov.au/item-sdid-18.html.

National Bureau of Economic Research. "Wages and Earnings in the United States, 1860–

Bibliography

1890: Wages by Occupational and Individual Characteristics." Outrun Change. http://outrunchange.com/2012/06/14/typical-wages-in-1860-through-1890/.

National Park Service's National Register of Historic Places, the City of Santa Clara, the California Office of Historic Preservation, and the National Conference of State Historic Preservation. "Economic History." Santa Clara County: California's Historic Silicon Valley. https://www.nps.gov/articles/economic-history.htm.

Nelson, H.N. "Parker, Edward Stone (1802–1865)." Australian Dictionary of Biography. National Centre of Biography, Australian National University. http://adb.anu.edu.au/biography/parker-edward-stone-4363.

New South Wales State Archives and Records. "Italian Migration Stories." https://www.records.nsw.gov.au/archives/collections-and-research/guides-and-indexes/stories/italian-migration-stories.

NoeHill in San Francisco. San Francisco Landmarks. "Feusier Octagon House." https://noehill.com/sf/landmarks/sf036.asp.

Nosetti, Pietro. "La Banca Svizzera Americana (1896–1920): une Immigrant Bank multinationale active entre le Tessin et la Californie" in *Rivista storica svizzera*. Bern: The Swiss History Society, 2014. https://www.e-periodica.ch/cntmng?var=true&pid=szg-006:2014:64::394.

Notre Dame des Victoires. "History." https://www.ndvsf.org/about/history.html.

Pagliaro, Tony. "Letters from Swiss-Italian Immigrants to Victoria in the 19th Century." Newsletter of the Italian Historical Society, Jan–Feb–Mar 1991, vol. 2, no. 1. Melbourne: Italian Historical Society—COASIT.

Panama Railroad. http://www.panamarailroad.org.

Parks, Recreation and Cultural Affairs Administration, Landmarks Preservation Commission, City of New York, SOHO Cast Iron Historic District Designation Report, 1973. http://sohobroadway.org/wp-content/uploads/2018/08/LPC-SoHo-CastIron-Historic-District-Designation-Report_1973.pdf.

Pedrazzini, Clay. *Biographical information about Swiss-Italians in California*. 1930.

Penrose, Beris. "The State and Gold Miners' Health in Victoria, 1870–1910." Labour History, no. 101, Nov. 2011. doi:10.5263/labourhistory.101.0035. https://www.jstor.org/stable/10.5263/labourhistory.101.0035?seq=1.

Perret, Maurice Edmund. *Les Colonies Tessinoises En Californie*. Lausanne: F. Rouge et Cie., 1950.

Pitt, Les. *Mud, Blood and Gold: Daylesford The Early Years*. Victoria: Paradise Books, 2016.

Prospecting Australia. "A history of mining in the Daylesford area." https://www.prospectingaustralia.com.au/forum/doc/member-docs/655/1403087334_daylesfordhistory.pdf.

Queensland Government Statistician's Office. http://www.qgso.qld.gov.au/products/tables/life-expectancy-birth-years-sex-qld/index.php.

Quinn, T. Anthony. *On Wings of Gold: The Journey to America of the Salmina, Morosoli and Dodini Families of Switzerland*, Camonica Club of North America. http://camonica-club. blogspot.com/2008/12/on-wings-of-gold.html.

Radcliffe, J. Netten. "Report On Cholera in 1867." *Reports of the Medical Officer of the Privy Council and Local Government Board with Regard to the year 1874*. London: Privy Council, 1875. https://babel.hathitrust.org/cgi/pt?id=hvd.hx3udu&view=1up&seq=8.

Raup H. F. "The Italian-Swiss in California." *California Historical Society Quarterly*, vol. 30, December 1951.

Regione Lombardia, Direzione Generale Istruzione Formazione e Cultura, Archivio di Etnografia e Storia Sociale (AESS), Intangible Search, Inventario del Patrimonio Immateriale delle Regioni Alpine. http://arm.mi.imati.cnr.it/aess/intangible_wrk/show_ich_detail. php?db_name=intangible_ich&lingua=inglese&idk=ICH-MBS01-0000000617.

Repubblica e Cantone Ticino. OltreconfinTI. "Edifii e tracce sul territorio." https://www4. ti.ch/can/oltreconfiniti/dalle-origini-al-1900/edifici-e-tracce-sul-territorio/.

Rolle, Andrew. *The Immigrant Upraised: Italian adventures and colonists in an expanding America*. Norman: University of Oklahoma Press, 1968.

Rollfing, Louisa Christina. *Autobiography* as quoted in "The Trip to Texas." Piwetz Family. http://freepages.rootsweb.com/~piwetz/genealogy/.

Ruiz Sr., Bruce C. "The Isthmian Crossing-The Argonauts." Panama History. http://www. bruceruiz.net/PanamaHistory/isthmus_crossing.htm.

San Diego Parks and Recreation Department. "Santa Isabel Preserve Draft Resource Management Plan, San Diego County, California," 2018. http://www.sdparks.org/content/ dam/sdparks/en/pdf/Resource-Management/Draft%20Santa%20Ysabel%20Preserve%20 Resource%20Management%20Plan%20May%202018.pdf.

San Francisco Mercantile Association. Constitution of the San Francisco Mercantile Library, in the Catalogue of the San Francisco Mercantile Library. San Francisco: Mercantile Association, 1854. https://archive.org/details/cataloguesanfra00davigoog/page/n5/ mode/2up.

San Francisco Municipal Government. San Francisco Municipal Reports for the fiscal year 1869-70, ending June 30, 1870. https://archive.org/details/sanfranciscomuni69sanfrich/ page/n8/mode/2up.

San Jose City Directory including Santa Clara County. San Jose, Calif: Mrs. F.M. Husted, 1901.

San Luis Obispo County Genealogical Society. Morning Tribune, San Luis Obispo County, California, 1896, http://www.slocgs.org/Tog.100/Tog-1896.html.

Scazighini, Pietro. Letter dated May 20, 1864 in "Emigranti Ticinesi in Australia". http:// www.scuoladecs.ti.ch/emigrazione/materiali-didattici/Lettere_per_attivita_didattica. pdf.

Shea, Michael A. "Nineteenth Century Medicine in the Santa Clara Valley." San Jose: California Pioneers of Santa Clara County, 2012. California Room of the Martin Luther

King/San Jose State Library, San Jose, CA.

Sheppy, Paul P.J. *Death Liturgy and Ritual: Volume II: A Commentary on Liturgical Texts.* Ashgate Pub Ltd, 2003. https://books.google.com/books?isbn=0754639002.

Shumard, Ann. "Domingo Ghirardelli: Chocolate in the Golden State." Facetoface, National Portrait Gallery. http://npg.si.edu/blog/domingo-ghirardelli-chocolate-golden-state.

Simpson, Lee M.A. *Selling the City, Gender, Class, and the California Growth Machine 1880-1940.* Stanford University Press, 2004.

Sizes. https://sizes.com/units/sluice_head.htm.

Slow Food Foundation for Biodiversity. "Bull boar Sausage." https://www.fondazioneslowfood.com/en/ark-of-taste-slow-food/bull-boar-sausage/.

Smilax, Linnæus. *Sarsaparilla, and Sarsaparilla so-called: a popular analysis of a popular medicine; its nature, properties, and uses.* London: Aylott, 1854. https://books.google.com/books?id=ZOJZAAAAcAAJ.

Smithsonian National Postal Museum. "Making Way: Steamship Mail in the 19th Century." https://postalmuseum.si.edu/research-articles/making-way.

Società genealogica della svizzera italiana. "20 anni di Genealogica nella Svizzera Italiana" Biblioteca Cantonale, Bellinzona. June 2017.

Stafford, Justin. SBS—Special Broadcasting Service. http://www.sbs.com.au/firstaustralians/. https://player.slideplayer.com/20/6048001/#.

State Library of Victoria. "Aborigines & the Gold Rush." http://ergo.slv.vic.gov.au/explore-history/golden-victoria/life-fields/aborigines-gold-rush.

State Library of Victoria Online Archive. *Victoria Government Gazette.* Melbourne: Government Printer, 1836–1997. http://gazette.slv.vic.gov.au.

Stow, Marietta. *Probate Confiscation: Unjust Laws which Govern Woman.* Place of publication not identified: Published and sold by the author, 1877. https://catalog.hathitrust.org/Record/008678622.

Strahan, Derek. "Lost New England Goes West: Dupont Street, San Francisco." Lost New England. http://lostnewengland.com/2016/06/lost-new-england-goes-west-dupont-street-san-francisco/.

Strozzi, Giuseppe, and Oliveto Rodoni. *Diario d'Australia: quando si andava per oro.* Locarno: A. Dadò, 1992.

Summermatter, Stefania. "Women were the 'Stationary Engine' of Migration," Jan. 23, 2009. SWI Swissinfo.ch. http://www.swissinfo.ch/eng/women-were--stationary-engine--of-migration/6782948.

Sutherland, Alexander. *Victoria and its Metropolis, Past and Present.* McCarron, Bird & Company. Victoria, 1888. https://www.google.com/books/edition/Victoria_and_Its_Metropolis_Past_and_Pre/WUU7AQAAIAAJ?hl=en.

Swenson, Timothy. "The Great Earthquake of 1868." Museum of Local History. http://museumoflocalhistory.org/wordpress2/wp-content/uploads/2014/10/Hayward1868.pdf.

Swiss National Library. "The Gotthard in Newspapers and Periodicals." https://www.nb.admin.ch/snl/en/home/publications-research/dossiers/gotthard-periodicals.html.

Teiser, Ruth. *An account of Domingo Ghirardelli and the early years of the D. Ghirardelli Company.* San Francisco: D. Ghirardelli Co., 1945.

The ShipsList. "Days of the Old Packet." http://www.theshipslist.com/accounts/packets.shtml.

Thornber, Craig. "Glossary of Medical Terms Used in the 18th and 19th Centuries." History of Medicine. https://www.thornber.net/medicine/html/medgloss.html.

Tilston, John. *Bull Market: The rise and eclipse of Australian stock exchanges.* Lulu, 2016. https://books.google.com/books?isbn=1326568825.

Toth, I. Michael, director. *Inside the Freemasons: The Grand Lodge Uncovered.* Reality Films, 2010.

Trow's New York City Directory. New York: John F. Trow. 1861. New York City Public Library Digital Collections. https://digitalcollections.nypl.org.

Trust for Public Land. "Coast Dairies." https://www.tpl.org/our-work/coast-dairies#sm.0006rp86t11yzdx2t7n2ej21u6gn2.

Trust for Public Land. "The Coast Dairies Long-Term Resource Protection and Use Plan." http://cloud.tpl.org/pubs/local_ca_coastdairies2003_allchapters_merged.pdf, 2001.

Twain, Mark. *Roughing and the Innocents at Home.* George Routledge & Sons: New York, 1882. https://books.google.com/.

Twain, Mark. *The Works of Mark Twain; Early Tales & Sketches*, vol. 1, 1851-1864. Univ. of California Press, 1979. http://www.twainquotes.com.

U.S. Census Bureau. "Agriculture of the United States in 1860." Washington D.C.: U.S. Government Printing Office, 1864. https://www2.census.gov/library/publications/decennial/1860/agriculture/1860b-05.pdf#.

U.S. Census Bureau. Agricultural Schedules. Compendium of the Ninth Census. https://www2.census.gov/library/publications/decennial/1870/compendium/1870e-35.pdf?#.

U.S. Census Bureau, Decennial Census, 1860–1930. https://www.census.gov/programs-surveys/decennial-census/.

Valentine, David Thomas. *Manual of the Corporation for the City of New York*, part 2. New York: Common Council, 1859. https://babel.hathitrust.org/cgi/pt?id=nyp.33433066342696&view=1up&seq=13.

Vanoni, Giovanni Antonio. Ex-Voto of Emigrants to Australia, dated Apr. 5, 1868. Chiesa di Santa Maria delle Grazie, Maggia, Ticino.

Vaucher, Jean G. "Emigration from Switzerland," https://www.iro.umontreal.ca/~vaucher/Genealogy/Documents/Emigration1.html.

Victoria Dept. of Mines, A. B. Ainsworth, A. Alderdice, G. Allen, M. Amos, A. Armstrong . . . P. Wright. *Reports of the Mining Surveyors and Registrars quarter ended 31st March 1873.* Melbourne: John Ferres, Government Printer, 1873. https://www.parliament.vic.gov.au/

papers/govpub/VPARL1873No22.pdf.

Victorian Cultural Collaboration. Gold! SBS, Special Broadcasting Services, Melbourne. https://www.sbs.com.au/gold/.

Victorian Places. Monash University and the University of Queensland. http://www.victorianplaces.com.au.

Vincent, John Martin. *State and Federal Government in Switzerland*. John Hopkins Press, 1891. https://catalog.hathitrust.org/Record/001752721.

Virtual Museum of the City of San Francisco. http://www.sfmuseum.org/hist1/1868eq.html.

Von Grueningen, John Paul, ed. *The Swiss in the United States: A Compilation Prepared for the Swiss-American Historical Society*. Madison, Wisconsin: Swiss-American Historical Society, 1940.

Voss, Carol. "Some Giacobbi History," 2009.

Wait, Frona E. *Wines & Vines of California: Or, a Treatise on the Ethics of WineDrinking*. Berkeley: Howell-North Books, 1973. https://www.google.com/books/edition/Wines_and_Vines_of_California/vnVNAAAAYAAJ?hl=en.

Ward, Andrew. *Daylesford and Hepburn Springs Conservation Study*. Victoria: Shire of Daylesford and Glenlyon, 1985.

Wegmann, Susanne. *The Swiss in Australia*. Grüsch, Switzerland: Verlag Rüegger, 1989.

Weir, Robert E. *Knights Down Under: The Knights of Labour in New Zealand*. Newcastle upon Tyne: Cambridge Scholars Pub., 2018. https://catalog.hathitrust.org/Record/010615474.

*West Coast Reporter . . . Containing All the Decisions . . .*Vol. 9, Feb–Mar 1886. San Francisco: A. L. Bancroft & Co., 1886. https://books.google.com/books?id=8slGAQAAIAAJ.

Whatford, J. Charles. "Fuel for the Fire: Charcoal making in Sonoma County: An Overview of the Archaeology and History of a Local Industry." Sacramento, CA: Society for California Archaeology. California Office of Historic Preservation, 1994. https://www.scahome.org/publications/proceedings/Proceedings.13Whatford.pdf.

Wishart, Edward and Maura Wishart. *Spa Country: Victoria's Mineral Springs*. Melbourne: Dept. of Sustainability and Environment in conjunction with Victorian Mineral Water Committee, 2010.

Young, Edward. "Report of Consul Byers in 1873" in *Labor in Europe and America: a special report on the rates of wages, the cost of subsistence, and the condition of the working classes, in Great Britain, France, Belgium, Germany and other Countries of Europe and the United States and British America*. Philadelphia: S.A. George & Co., 1875. https://books.google.com/books?id=syIpAAAAYAAJ.

Young, Edward. *Special report on immigration; accompanying information for immigrants relative to the prices and rentals of land, the staple products, etc., in the year 1869–'70*. Annual Report of California Labor Exchange. Department of the Treasury, Bureau of Statistics. Washington: U.S. Government Printing Office, 1872. https://catalog.hathitrust.org/Record/011537584.

Young, W. "Report on the condition of the Chinese population in Victoria." Melbourne: John Ferres, Government Printer, 1868. https://www.parliament.vic.gov.au/papers/govpub/VPARL1868No56.pdf.

NEWSPAPERS AND PERIODICALS

Advocate (Melbourne)
Argus (Melbourne)
Blade-Tribune (Oceanside)
Corriere del Ticino
Daily Alta California
Daylesford Advocate and Hepburn Courier
Daily Morning Chronicle
Empire (Sydney)
Geelong Advertiser
Harper's Weekly
Kyneton Observer
La Nuova Elvezia
Leader (Melbourne)
Los Angeles Times
Marin Journal
Mount Alexander Mail
New York Herald
Observer (Adelaide)
Pacific Rural Press
Petaluma Argus
Petaluma Argus-Courier
Press Democrat (Santa Rosa)
Riverine Herald
Sacramento Bee
San Francisco Bulletin
San Francisco Examiner
San Francisco Morning Call
Santa Maria Times
Socialist (Australia)
Sonoma Democrat
Southern Australian Register
The Straits Times
Sydney Morning Herald
West Coast Times

Age (Melbourne)
Australia Gazette
California Farmer and Journal of Useful Sciences
Daylesford Express
Daylesford Mercury
Democrat (Sonoma)
Fresno Bee
Gazetta Ticenese
The Guardian
Herald (Melbourne)
La Democrazia
La Voce del Popolo
Livermore Herald
L'Unione Nazionale
Marysville Daily Appeal
New York Times
Oakland Tribune
Pacific Oil Reporter
Pall Mall Gazette
Petaluma Journal and Argus
Petroleum Review
Richmond Dispatch
Russian River Flag
Sacramento Daily Union
San Francisco Chronicle
San Francisco Merchant
San Luis Obispo Morning Tribune
Sausalito News
Solicitors' Journal and Reporter
South of Market Journal
Star (Ballarat)
The Sunday Times
West Coast Reporter

FIGURES

4–5. *Pacific Mail Steamship Company's through line to California, touching at Mexican Ports, and carrying the U.S. Mail.* The Huntington Library, San Marino, California.

4–6. *Broadway Wharf, San Francisco.* Sonoma County Library Digital Collections.

4–7. Stillwell, B.F. *Directory of the township and city of Oakland for the year 1869.*

5–1. Gifford, C.B. *San Francisco. Bird's-eye view.* 1864. Library of Congress, LC-DIG-ppmsca-08305.

5–2. *L'Unione Nazionale,* Nov. 10, 1870.

5-3. *Bull and Bear Fight* in *Century Illustrated Monthly Magazine,* Dec. 1890.

5-4. *Oakland Ferry and Steamer Washoe, San Francisco.* 1866. Library of Congress, LC-USZ62-27493.

6–1. *Bedolla's Spring Creek Hotel.* c.1870s. Ballarat Heritage Services.

6–2. Hawley, Graham and Bridget Carlson. *Map Spring Creek* in *Immigrant Placemaking in Colonial Australia: the Italian-speaking Settlers of Daylesford.*

6–3. Geary, Marilyn L. *Lucini Macaroni Factory.* 2016. Author's Collection.

6–4. Geary, Marilyn L. *Ceiling of Macaroni Factory painted by Giacomo Lucini.* 2016. Author's Collection.

6–5. *Township* [Daylesford]. c.1873–1882. State Library Victoria.

6–6. *Chinese on Cobb and Co. Coach on Way to Diggings.* c.1860–71. Picture Collection, State Library Victoria.

6–7. Cooper, T.B., *The Fossicker.* 1898. National Library of Australia.

6–8. *Mining Scene* [Daylesford]. c.1873–1882. State Library Victoria.

7–1. *Locarno Market.* La Società Genealogica della Svizzera Italiana.

7–2. Geary, Marilyn L. *Cascade and Chapel, Vallemaggia.* 2015. Author's Collection.

8–1. *Immigrants at Castle Garden, New York City.* 1866. Library of Congress. https://www.loc.gov/pictures/item/2001697361/.

8–2. *Pacific Mail Steamship Company's steamer Golden Age, Saturday July 26th, 1863, bill of fare.* Honeyman (Robert B., Jr.)—Collection of Early Californian and Western American Pictorial Material. BANC PIC 1963.002:1552—Courtesy of The Bancroft Library, University of California, Berkeley.

8–3. *Pacific Mail Steamship.* The Huntington Library, San Marino, California.

9–1. *Envelope from San Francisco to Maggia, 1861.* Seigel Auctions. Siegelauctions.com/exhibits/Pony_Express.pdf.

9–2. Kuchel & Dresel, *Marysille.* California State Library, Sacramento, California.

9-3. *Envelope from Cevio-Locarno to Jim Crow Gold Fields* in SWITZERLAND 1854 – 1863 "CONFOEDERATIO HELVETICA." https://honegger-philatelie.ch/images/pdf/STRUBEL-OVERSEAS-DESTINATIONS.pdf. Collection of Walter Haemmerli.

9–4. *View of D Street, Marysille* in *Hutchings Illustrated Magazine,* February 1859.

10–1. *Doyle Prune Orchard and Vineyard.* Arnold Photograph Album of San Jose. 1890. History San José.

10–2. Sarsaparilla ad, *Marin Journal,* December 1888.

10–3. Gray (W. Vallance) & C.B. Gifford. *Bird's eye view of the city of San José, Cal.* 1869. Library of Congress. https://www.loc.gov/item/75693107/.

11–1. *San José, Santa Clara County* in *Hutchings' Illustrated California Magazine,* Dec. 1859.

12–1. *Swiss and Italian Association.* c.1870. Daylesford Historical Museum.

12–2. Daintree, Richard. *Deserted Diggings at Spring Creek, Victoria [picture],* 1859. State Library Victoria.

12–3. *The Age,* Melbourne, May 7, 1875.

12–4. Tensfeld, J. *Vincent Street, Daylesford,*1862. State Library Victoria.

13–1. Geary, Marilyn L. *Ceiling, Church of S. Maria Assunta and S. Giovanni and Ossuary, Cevio.* Author's Collection.

14–1. *Petaluma.* Sonoma County Library Digital Collections.

14–2. Letter to Francesco. June 5, 1868. Collection of Claudio Rotanzi.

15–1. *Charles Martin.* Collection of Sally Gale.

15–2. *Charles Martin Home in Chileno Valley.* Collection of Sally Gale.

15–3. H. Austin, excerpt of *Map of Marin County*, 1873, Chileno Valley. Anne T. Kent California Room, Marin County Free Library.

15–4. Goddard, G. H, Rey Britton & Co, and Snow & May. *Birdseye view of San Francisco and surrounding country.* Library of Congress, https://www.loc.gov/item/75693103/.

16–1. *Daily Alta California*, June 19, 1868.

16–2. *Daily Alta California*, January 6, 1869.

16–3. *L'Unione Nazionale*, November 1870.

16–4. *DuPont Street.* 1865. San Francisco History Center, San Francisco Public Library.

16–5. *Daily Alta California*, April 19, 1870.

16–6. Lawrence & Houseworth. *San Francisco from Russian Hill, looking down Vallejo Street.* Library of Congress. https://www.loc.gov/pictures/item/2002719070/.

17–1. Geary, Marilyn L. *Exterior of a Rotanzi House, Peccia.* 2015.Author's Collection.

18–1. *Railroad House, Clay St.* California History Room, California State Library, Sacramento, California.

18–2. Geary, Marilyn L. *Bust of Luigi Filippini.* 2015. Author's Collection.

18–3. Geary, Marilyn L. *Plaque in Church of S. Maria Assunta e S. Giovanni*, Cevio. 2015. Author's Collection.

18–4. Geary, Marilyn L, *Emigrant houses in Brontallo.* 2015. Author's Collection.

19–1. *Mt. Alexander Mail*, December 13, 1880.

19–2. *La Pirocorvetta Magenta ormeggiata a Napoli.* July 1870. Wikipedia.

19–3. *Shire of Mount Franklin, Victoria Government Gazette*, 1876.

20–1. Letter from Virgilio to Luigi Rotanzi, June 16, 1870. Collection of Sally Gale.

20–2. Lawrence & Houseworth. *Chinese Market, Sacramento Street, San Francisco, 1866.* Library of Congress.   https://www.loc.gov/pictures/item/2002724195/.

21–1. *Notre Dame des Victoires.* 1956. San Francisco History Center, San Francisco Public Library.

21–2. Thomas, Henry Atwell. *Camille Urso.* National Portrait Gallery, Smithsonian Institution.

21–3. *Buena Vista Park Headstone.* Wikimedia.

22–1. *Francois Giacobbi.* Collection of Carolyn Voss.

22–2. *Martin, Feusier & Steffani ad* in Fugazi, J. F. *Almannaco Italosvizzero Americano*, 1881.

22–3. *Portrait of Mrs. Marietta L. Stow, showing her "Equal Rights Costume."* c. mid 1880s. Oakland Museum of California.

22–4. *Ballot for Presidential Election.* 1884. Oakland Museum of California.

23–1. George, Hugh for Wilson and MacKinnon. *The Daylesford Hospital fete.* March 17, 1877. National Library of Australia.

23–2. *Member, Swiss and Italian Association.* Collection of Joan McEwen.

23–3. Daintree, Richard and Antoine Fauchery. *Group of Diggers*, 1858. State Library Victoria.

23–4. *Daylesford Hospital.* 1872. State Library Victoria.

24–1. *Francesco Rotanzi insurance ad. Daylesford Advocate*, March 15, 1879.

25–1. *Women Gathering Hay.* Museum of the Vallemaggia.

25–2. Geary, Marilyn L. *Pigna.* Author's Collection.

26–1. *Francis Rotanzi Will and Codicil.* Public Record Office, Victoria.

27–1. *Newspaper Announcement.* Daylesford Museum and Historical Society.

27–2. *Probate Paper, Francis Rotanzi Will and Codicil.* Public Record Office, Victoria.

27–3. Geary, Marilyn L. *Graves of Francesco Rotanzi and Nellie Borsa.* 2016. Author's Collection

28–1. Geary, Marilyn L. *Cherub painted on ceiling of Ossuary, Coglio,* Author's Collection.

E–1. *Map, Livermore Valley.* 1889. Livermore Heritage Guild.

E–2. *Francois Giacobbi Family.* c.1875. Collection of Carol Voss.

E–3. *Letterhead.* Collection of Carol Voss.

E–4. *The Fresno Bee,* May 29, 1948.

E–5. *Dairymen's Union Notice. Sausalito News,* Dec. 26, 1892.

E–6. *Charles Martin Jr.* in Cheda, *L'emigrazione ticinese in California, vol 1.*

E–7. *Portrait of Charles Martin.* Collection of Sally Gale.

E–8. *Church of the Assumption.* Tomales Regional History Center.

E–9. *Church of the Assumption after the 1906 Earthquake.* Tomales Regional History Center.

E–10. *Carlo and Caterina Martinoia.* Collection of Sally Gale.

E–11. *Pietro and Anita Dolcini.* Collection of Virginia Mossi.

E–12. *San Francisco Alms House.* c.1890. San Francisco Western Neighborhoods Project.

E–13. *James Bloom* in *History of State of California and Biographical Record of the Coast Counties.*

E–14. *Swiss-Italian Celebration, Bloom Ranch, 1890.* Sonoma County Library.

E–15. *Baldwin Dairy Trademark.* California State Archives.

E–16. *Swiss Hotel. 1895.* California Room, San Jose Public Library.

E–17. *Cartoon spoofing SF Supervisor T.A. Rottanzi. San Francisco Call,* Nov. 12, 1897.

E–18. *Santa Ysabel Dairy.* c.1900. San Diego History Center.

E–19. Geary, Marilyn L. *American Cemetery, Someo.* 2015. Author's Collection.

E–20. *Moretti and Respini.* Collection of Sally Gale.

E–21. Geary, Marilyn L. *Museo di Valmaggia, Cevio,* 2015. Author's Collection.

E–22. *Coast Dairies State Park,* Bureau of Land Management.

E–23. *Bellinzona Guest House.* 1915. State Library Victoria.

E–24. Daniels, Mark. *Hepburn & Hepburn Springs.* 1903. State Library Victoria.

E–25. *Pozzi Brothers Store.* Italian Historical Society, Melbourne.

E–26. *Leonardo Pozzi. The Herald* (Melbourne), Nov. 24, 1914.

INDEX

V

W

Y

Z

ACKNOWLEDGEMENTS

A big thank you to Laurie Thompson, librarian of the Anne T. Kent California Room of the Marin County Free Library, for including in the library's collection Professor Giorgio Cheda's compilation of letters written in Italian by nineteenth century immigrants to California. Finding this book on the library's shelves set me on an enriching and deeply satisfying journey of discovery. Throughout the sixteen years it took me to complete this book, many people helped me discover the history of the Rotanzi family and their fellow Swiss-Italians.

In Ticino: Professor Giorgio Cheda, without whose comprehensive work on Swiss-Italian emigration this book could never have been written; Mr. Claudio Rotanzi, Ivonne Rotanzi, Katie Rotanzi, Gabriele and Patrizia Maccarinelli, Natalia DeBernardi, Dale Bechtel of SwissInfo.ch, Stefano Aniello at the Archivio di Stato del Cantone Ticino, the librarians at the Biblioteca Cantonale in Locarno, and the curators at the Museum di Vallemaggia in Cevio.

In Australia: Clare Gervasoni, Bridget Carlson, Graham Hawley, Dr. Paolo Baracchi of the Italian Historical Society in Melbourne, Barbara Mullin, Joan McEwen, librarians at the Victoria State Library and volunteers at the Daylesford & District Historical Society.

In California: Sally Gale, Carol Voss, Jay Grossi, Troy Goss, Tony Quinn, Dennis Morelli, Susan Luccini, Patty McDonough of the Belvedere Tiburon Library, Kurt Boldt, Virginia Mossi and Lisa Christiansen, Librarian of the California History Center at De Anza College.

Many thanks are due to West Marin Historian Dewey Livingston; my Marin County writers group members, Vicky Sievers, Karen van Kriedt and Sandy White, who critiqued and encouraged; and members of the Institute for Historical Study writers group who helped me hone the story. Finally, editor Marty Levine's frequent reminders to stay on the Rotanzis' path kept me from veering off into boundless bordering territories. Thank you all.

THE AUTHOR

A native of California's Santa Clara Valley, Marilyn L. (Longinotti) Geary has seen vast stretches of fruit orchards uprooted to make way for Silicon Valley sprawl. This enormous change fostered in her a deep awareness of transience and a passion for exploring and preserving the past.

As owner of Circle of Life Stories, Marilyn provided history recording and preservation services for individuals, families, organizations and communities. After graduating Phi Beta Kappa from the University of California, Berkeley with a degree in English and history, she worked for five years in San Francisco for ENIT–Ente Nazionale Italiano Turismo, the Italian Government Tourist Office. There she grew to know and love the country of her heritage, eventually becoming an Italian citizen.

Marilyn conducted her first oral histories with Sicilian fishermen on San Francisco's Fisherman's Wharf. As a Local Legacy project of the Library of Congress, she documented the annual festival of The Madonna del Lume/ the Blessing of the San Francisco Fishing Fleet. She serves as oral historian for the Anne T. Kent California Room of the Marin County Free Library, and with Laurie Thompson, she created the film *Marin Mind/Scapes: Stories of Art, Nature and Healing*, based on oral histories of Marin landscape artists.

Marilyn is author of *Marin City Memories,* which presents the voices of Blacks who migrated from the South to work in the Sausalito shipyards during World War II. She is co-author with Jacqueline Janssen of *LeaveLight: a Motivational Guide to End-of-Life Planning.* Her writings have appeared in *Turning Memories into Memoirs: A Handbook for Writing Lifestories*, the *Oral History Review*, and the *West Marin Review*, among other publications.

From her home in rural San Geronimo Valley, California, surrounded by the golden hills of West Marin, Marilyn writes, creates fiber art and travels when possible to more remote regions of the world to explore her interests in textiles and tribal cultures.

Visit her website: www.marilynlgeary.com

Email: MarilynGeary@comcast.net

Made in United States
Troutdale, OR
11/18/2023

14706398R00199